European Jewry in the Age of Mercantilism 1550–1750

JONATHAN I. ISRAEL

CLARENDON PRESS · OXFORD

1985

Oxford University Press, Walton Street, Oxford OX2 6DP
Oxford New York Toronto
Delhi Bombay Calcutta Madras Karachi
Kuala Lumpur Singapore Hong Kong Tokyo
Nairobi Dar es Salaam Cape Town
Melbourne Auckland
and associated companies in
Beirut Berlin Ibadan Mexico City Nicosia

Oxford is a trade mark of Oxford University Press

Published in the United States
by Oxford University Press, New York

British Library Cataloguing in Publication Data
Israel, Jonathan I.
European Jewry in the age of mercantilism,
1550–1750.
1. Jews—Europe—History—70–1789
I. Title
940'.04924 DS135.E8
ISBN 0-19-821928-8

Library of Congress Cataloging in Publication Data
Israel, Jonathan Irvine.
European Jewry in the Age of Mercantilism, 1550–1750.
Bibliography: p.
Includes index.
1. Jews—Europe—History. 2. Jews—History—70–1789.
3. Europe—Ethnic relations. I. Title.
DS135.E8T87 1985 940'.04924 85-13755
ISBN 0-19-821928-8

Set by Wyvern Typesetting Ltd
Printed in Great Britain
at the University Press, Oxford
by David Stanford
Printer to the University

Preface

IN recent decades a most impressive and steadily mounting corpus of scholarly monographs and articles have vastly enriched our understanding of the history and culture of European Jewry in early modern times. But as more and more material and data have become available, so seemingly it has become ever harder to weld it all together into any sort of general synthesis which can be used by the general reader looking for a coherent overall view or the non-specialist scholar interested in widening his grasp of early modern European history as a whole. There is undoubtedly a crying need for new general interpretations of the role of Jewry within Europe in this period. Indeed, it is no exaggeration to say that the number of such general surveys which have tried to recapitulate and re-interpret what the last sixty or seventy years of research have unearthed, even counting those which are now many decades old and are basically obsolete, is easily to be counted on the fingers of one hand. The present study is then an attempt to add to our meagre stock of such surveys. It is based mainly on the existing secondary literature but it incorporates the results of some new archival work mostly relating to the political and economic activities of western Sephardi Jewry. While I have endeavoured to be comprehensive, as a specialist in western European political and economic history, I have not attempted to say anything new, or impart any substantially new emphases, on the religious history of the period. Where there is an element of re-interpretation in the sphere of intellectual history it mainly concerns the cultural interaction between Jews and non-Jews. But essentially this is a secular history which focuses on the changing patterns of political and economic interaction between Europe's Jews and the states and societies amongst which they dwelt.

The rendering of place-names in a work such as this presents a number of peculiar problems. Indeed, I seriously doubt the possibility of finding a satisfactory set of rules which is at the same time fully consistent. For towns and provinces for which there exists a familiar anglicized form I have of course used it. Thus the reader will encounter Cologne, Hanover, Danzig, and Cracow rather than their

German or Polish equivalents and similarly with provinces such as Bohemia, Silesia, Lithuania, and (less familiarly perhaps) Volynia and Podolia. On the other hand, where there is an English form which, arguably, sounds antiquated or artificial, I have employed the local name instead so that the reader will find Livorno for Leghorn and Frankfurt for Frankfort. For less well-known place-names I have used the local form in the case of Iberian, French, German, Dutch, and Italian places. I have also followed this rule in the case of most Polish towns and localities still within the confines of Poland today. In the case of other East European place-names, however, it hardly seems satisfactory to employ the local name in an English work as the Lithuanian, Ukrainian, and Byelorussian versions are generally less familiar to the English reader than other forms of the names, especially transliterated renderings of the Russian equivalents. What I have done, therefore, is to use these anglicized versions where they have been fairly extensively used in recent scholarly literature in English. Thus the reader will encounter Lvov (not Lwów), Pinsk (not Pińsk), Mogilev, Vitebsk, and so forth. In the same way for the city known in Polish as Wilno, in Lithuanian as Vilnius, and in German as Wilna, I have opted for the now quite frequently employed anglicization 'Vilna'. However, there is a further category of central and East European place-names, attaching to places which had unusually large Jewish populations but which were not otherwise very notable which became (and remain) so familiar to Jews everywhere, including the English-speaking world, under the Yiddish or German forms of their names that it would seem altogether artificial in a work dealing with Jewish history to use the present-day Slavonic versions of their names. And so, without intending the least offence to non-Jews who inhabit those places today, I have opted for Nikolsburg (not Mikulov), Prossnitz (not Prostejov), Lissa (not Leszno), Gross-Glogau (not Głogo), Dubno, Brody, and so on. As regards the personal names of princes and rulers, I have used English equivalents on the whole except in cases such as Gustavus Adolphus and Louis XIV where the foreign form is thoroughly familiar.

Finally, there is the pleasant task of thanking all those family, friends, and colleagues who have assisted in one way or another with the writing of this book. In the first place I would like to thank my wife, Jenny, for her constant and unfailing help and support throughout. Secondly, I gladly acknowledge having accumulated scholarly debts to quite a spectrum of historians both in Britain and abroad, especially Israel, The Netherlands, and the United States. Above all, for his close interest in the project and his helpful criticism at all stages, I wish to thank Edgar Samuel, director of the Jewish Historical Museum in London. I am also particularly indebted to Richard H. Popkin, Roberto Bonfil, Daniel Swetschinski, Benjamin Ravid, Yosef Kaplan, Bernard Cooperman, David Jacoby, Chimen Abramsky, Raphael Loewe, and Maurice Woolf. Finally, I should like to express my gratitude to the British Academy for providing me with a research grant with which to pursue a number of key themes in the archives of Amsterdam and Venice.

Contents

Abbreviations   xi

Introduction   1

I Exodus from the West   5

II Turning-point (1570–1600)   35

III Consolidation (1600–1620)   53

IV Jewish Culture (1550–1650)   70

V The Thirty Years War   87

VI The High Point (I): The 'Court Jews' (1650–1713)   123

VII The High Point (II): Jewish Society (1650–1713)   145

VIII The High Point (III): 'A Republic Apart'   184

IX The High Point (IV): Spiritual Crisis (1650–1713)   207

X Decline (1713–1750)   237

XI Conclusion   252

Works Cited
1. *Primary Printed Sources*   260
2. *Secondary Works*   263

Index   281

Abbreviations

Archival Abbreviations

AGR SEG Archives Générales du Royaume, Brussels, Secrétairerie d'État et de Guerre

AGS Estado Archivo General de Simancas (Valladolid), Council of State papers

AGS Hacienda AGS Papers of the former Council of Finance

AGS La Haya AGS Papers of the former Spanish Embassy in The Hague

ANTT Inqu. Arquivo Nacional da Torre do Tombo, Lisbon, Inquisition Papers

ANTT Misc. da Graça ANTT Section known as *Miscelânea da Graça*

ARH SG Algemeen Rijksarchief, The Hague, archive of the former States General

ARH WIC ARH Archive of the former Dutch West India Company

ASV CSM Archivio di Stato, Venice. Papers of the former Venetian Board of Trade (Cinque Savii alla Mercanzia)

BL MS British Library, London, Department of Manuscripts

GAA NA Amsterdam City Archive. Papers of the city notaries

GAA PJG GAA Archives of the Portuguese Jewish Community of Amsterdam

PRO SP Public Record Office, London, State Papers

SAH JG Hamburg City Archive. Archives of the German and Portuguese Jewish Communities

Other Abbreviations

CSP Calendar of State Papers, Domestic

CTB Calendar of Treasury Books Preserved in the Public Record Office

BGJW *Bijdragen en Mededeelingen van het Genootschap voor Joodsche Wetenschap in Nederland*

BMGN *Bijdragen en Mededeelingen betreffende de Geschiedenis der Nederlanden*

BMHG *Bijdragen en Mededeelingen van het Historisch Genootschap*

BZIH *Biuletyn* of the *Zydowski Instytut Historyczny*, Warsaw

GEV 'Gli Ebrei e Venezia' (XIV–XVIIIth Centuries). Conference Papers delivered in Venice in June 1983 to be published by Fondazione Giogio Cini, Venice

Abbreviations

GJN	H. Brugmans and A. Frank (eds.), *Geschiedenis der Joden in Nederland* (Amsterdam, 1940)
JJLG	*Jahrbuch der jüdisch-literarischen Gesellschaft* (Frankfurt am Main)
JJS	*Journal of Jewish Studies*
JJV	*Jahrbuch für jüdische Volkskunde*
JQR	*Jewish Quarterly Review*
MGWJ	*Monatschrift für Geschichte und Wissenschaft des Judenthums*
MJV	*Mitteilungen zur jüdischen Volkskunde*
MWJ	*Magazin für die Wissenschaft des Judenthums*
PAAJR	*Proceedings of the American Academy for Jewish Research*
REJ	*Revue des études juives*
RMI	*La rassegna mensile di Israel*
SHDJ	*Studies in the History of Dutch Jewry* (Hebrew), ed. J. Michman, 3 vols. thus far (Jerusalem, 1975–)
SR	*Studia Rosenthaliana. Journal for Jewish Literature and History in the Netherlands*
TJHSE	*Transactions of the Jewish Historical Society of England*
VSW	*Vierteljahrsschrift für Sozial- und Wirtschaftsgeschichte*
ZGJD	*Zeitschrift für Geschichte der Juden in Deutschland*
ZGJT	*Zeitschrift für die Geschichte der Juden in der Tschechoslowakei*

Introduction

In the past most authors have treated the early modern period in Jewish history as basically just an extension of the Jewish Middle Ages. Certainly it has not often been depicted as an essentially new phase intervening between the medieval and later modern eras. And yet there is much to commend the drawing of a firm dividing-line between the medieval and early modern epochs in the historical experience and consciousness of western Jewry. Following the virtual elimination of this oppressed and battered people from western and central Europe in the fifteenth and first two-thirds of the sixteenth century, an altogether different trend, towards reintegration, set in from around 1570 in much of the continent west of Poland. During the next few decades, the standing and functions of the Jews in western civilization were totally transformed. Amid a flurry of new charters, privileges, and concessions, Jews were all at once released from many, though admittedly by no means all, of the old, stifling restrictions on their economic and cultural activity and lifestyle. As a consequence, they now exerted, especially in the period 1650–1713, the most profound and pervasive impact on the west which they were ever to exert whilst still retaining a large measure of social and cultural cohesion, that is to say, whilst still displaying a recognizably national character. No doubt the contributions of Jews to modern western culture, since 1750, are a good deal more diverse and better known. But it is only (at any rate in the view of this writer) in the preceding period, down to the mid-eighteenth century, that there is, permeating the west in ways that are both novel and important, a widely ramified Jewish influence which can be seen to derive from a still largely traditional framework of Jewish activity and thought, a framework immediately distinguishable from that of the non-Jewish majority.

The key factor behind the reversal of pre-1570 trends, and thus the transformation of Jewish life in the west, it is here argued, was the political and spiritual upheaval which engulfed European culture as a whole at the end of the sixteenth century. Above all, the Catholic–Protestant deadlock, or rather realization that the only outcome of the relentless struggle between the western churches was deadlock, generated, from around 1570, a radically changed political and intellectual context. The last third of the sixteenth century witnessed the rise of *politique* philosophies and attitudes to government which cut free not just from the conflicting demands of the churches for exclusive control but, more comprehensively, from the claims of tradition, privilege, and established jurisdiction. The sudden flowering of *raison d'État* thought at this time was part and parcel of a wider shift towards a freer, more flexible society and cultural system. Inevitably, so momentous a change could not come about without plunging the west into a prolonged theological and intellectual crisis. And at the heart of this spiritual crisis was the upsurge of radical scepticism which now pervaded the thought and writings of key figures such as Montaigne, Bodin, Lipsius, and Bacon. The shock waves emanating from the new philosophies of religion and politics profoundly jolted the European mind, and mark the beginning of modern thought. But this general upset and disruption of western religious, political, and intellectual norms did not merely coincide with the beginnings of Jewish re-entry into the mainstream of western civilization. Rather, the reintegration of the Jews has to be grasped as an integral part of the wider process of release from the doctrinal and legal shackles of the past.

In the course of this book, the term 'mercantilism' will be repeatedly encountered. Mercantilism was, indeed, one of the major currents of the epoch from the late sixteenth down to the middle of the eighteenth century. As employed here, the concept does not denote any specific package of economic policies. Rather it signifies the new political approach to socio-economic questions which became widespread at the end of the sixteenth century, hand in hand with the *politique* approach to government of which, in fact, it formed part. Mercantilism as used here signifies the deliberate pursuit of the economic interest of the state, irrespective of the claims of existing law, privilege, and tradition, as well as of religion. This is perhaps the one use of the term which remains generally acceptable in the light of recent debate among historians as to the usefulness or otherwise of deploying the term to denote an economic system. Most scholars now agree that mercantilism was never a coherent set of economic principles, though it tended to stress certain attitudes toward economic management and regulation. What, in essence, it was, from the time of Bodin and Laffemas onwards, was a political impulse involving the systematic intervention of the state in the economic sphere in order to buttress the state. 'Most interpretations', it has been aptly said, 'emphasize the conscious quest for the economic welfare of the state by the state.'[1] And this, assuredly, was no small shift. Indeed, implicit in it is virtually the whole of the revolution which occurred in western civilization at the end of the sixteenth century. As a pre-eminent historian of mercantilism expressed it, mercantilism represented an 'emancipation', a 'secularization and an amoralization', and nothing said on the inconsistencies of mercantilist theorists on one or another aspect of economics detracts in any way from the force of this perception.[2] Mercantilism, and the *raison d'État* politics of which it was part, triggered what might be termed Europe's first great emancipation, a process of release from the restrictions of the past, arising two whole centuries before the better-known, but not necessarily more fundamental, emancipation which swept Europe in the nineteenth century, with the partial triumphs of liberalism. And just as the latter set in motion a crucial shift in Jewish history, finally releasing the Jews to enter the mainstream of European life unimpeded in any formal sense, so, at least as far as many of the more oppressive restrictions were concerned, did the former, the chief difference being that the emancipation of the seventeenth century ushered the Jews into the western world as a tightly cohesive group, not as uprooted individuals stripped of their former political and social autonomy and culture.

A word of explanation as to one or two other key terms would also seem in order. In recent years, there has been a mounting controversy among historians whether or not a genuine crypto-Judaism, with authentic links with pre-1492 Spain, really existed in the Iberian Peninsula after around 1550. My own view is that the evidence for such crypto-Judaism throughout the Peninsula, and especially in Portugal and Mallorca, is overwhelming, but that one must also recognize that many, and possibly most, descendants of medieval Spanish Jewry who stayed in the Peninsula after 1492 were completely Christianized and absorbed into the majority culture. For this reason I have differentiated between the term 'New Christian' on the one hand, meaning any supposedly Christian descendant of medieval Iberian Jews whether his or her real allegiance was Catholic, Jewish, or ambivalent, and on the other hand the term 'Marrano', which here

[1] Coleman, *Revisions in Mercantilism*, pp. 2–4.
[2] Ibid., pp. 31–2.

designates an ostensible Christian who is a crypto-Jew. There are, admittedly, some objections to this use of the terminology. In Italy, where there were frequent references to *Marrani* in sixteenth-century political and ecclesiastical correspondence, the term normally referred to such former Iberian Christians who had gone the whole way and reverted to normative Judaism in Italy. But in a work dealing with Europe as a whole, it seems best to use the term to encompass ostensible Christians who were living in Spain, Portugal, and the Iberian colonies, and practising a secret Judaism, as well as those growing colonies of Portuguese crypto-Jews in France and at Antwerp who retained a thin veil of perfunctory Christianity to cover a private Judaism which, at least from the 1630s onwards, they took less and less trouble to conceal.

I

Exodus from the West

THE first near-elimination of Jewish life from western and central Europe occurred at the end of the Middle Ages and at the dawn of the modern era. Despite the brutal massacres of Jews perpetrated by the Crusaders in the Rhineland and Bohemia, in 1096, and the sporadic persecution which followed during the next two centuries, western and central Europe remained the heartland of the Jewish world throughout the later medieval era. Indeed, the ascendancy of the west in Jewish life was reinforced by the steady decline of the Jewries of Egypt and elsewhere in the Near East in the period after 1300. By the late thirteenth century when the famous 'Altneu' Synagogue—the oldest Jewish building still standing north of the Alps—was completed in Prague, a substantial if scattered Jewish population had arisen in eastern Europe, especially Poland; but the Jews of the west were still incomparably more numerous and possessed a far more developed religious and general culture. It was also the western Jews, especially of Italy, Spain, and Provence, who enjoyed the closest contact with the ancient and numerous but now inexorably dwindling communities of the Islamic world and of the Holy Land. While the expulsions of the Jews from England and France, in 1290 and 1394 respectively, were notable setbacks, in the early fifteenth century the Jewries of Spain, Italy, Germany, and Provence still greatly eclipsed in numbers and importance the Jews dwelling in the Slavonic lands. In the late fifteenth century, the Jewish population of Poland and Lithuania—the main centres of east European Jewry, for there were at that time only a negligible number living to the east of Polish territory—totalled, as near as historians can tell, around 25,000, small indeed compared with the roughly 200,000 Jews still in Spain, or the 50,000 or so surmised to have been then living in Italy.

Following the horrific Black Death massacres of 1348–9, in Germany, when the Jews were accused of having poisoned the wells, the pressure on the Jews in the west gradually increased. Despite the catastrophic loss of population and contraction of economic activity which characterized most of Europe in the century 1350–1450, the persecution of the Jews intensified virtually everywhere except in Italy. In Spain, where the Jews had previously enjoyed exceptionally favourable conditions, there was a sharp deterioration in the late fourteenth century, culminating in a massive outbreak in 1391, when dozens of large Jewish communities, including those of Toledo, Burgos, Seville, and Valencia, were brutally pillaged, thousands being slaughtered and tens of thousands being dragged forcibly to the baptismal font.

And yet, remarkably, despite the twin catastrophes of the Black Death massacres in central Europe and the 1391 pogroms in Spain, the Jews in the west were mostly able to regroup and stabilize their society once more. In Germany, the survivors, encouraged by the princes, rapidly rebuilt much of the fabric of pre-1348 German Jewish life. Vibrant communities formed again in Augsburg, Nuremberg, Ulm, Mainz, Worms, and many other cities where the Jews had temporarily been all but destroyed. It was only from 1421, with the massacre of the Jews of Vienna, and their being banned from that city, and the ensuing expulsions from Linz (1421), Cologne (1424), Augsburg (1439), Bavaria (1442 and 1450), and the so-called 'crown cities' of Moravia (1454), that a powerful impulse toward expulsion and exclusion developed. Even so, in Spain there were only sporadic, local incidents during the century after 1391. Despite the conversion to Christianity of over 100,000 Jews in the years 1391–1415, the process of disintegration was temporarily halted when the worst frenzy of persecution was over and between half and two-thirds of the original Spanish Jewish community, numbering around 200,000, managed to reconstitute a large part of Spanish Jewish life. In Italy, meanwhile, in contrast to Spain and Germany, the position of the Jews improved throughout the post-Black Death century.

Thus the real mass exodus of Jews from western and central Europe which finally shifted the focus of European Jewish life to Poland, Lithuania, and the Ottoman Balkans began only in the later fifteenth century. It was the outcome of a rising tide of anti-Jewish agitation which swept the whole of Europe from Portugal to Brandenburg and from the Netherlands to Sicily. This new and vast process continued relentlessly down to the 1570s by when the exodus was almost complete. Thus this new phase, a sequence of expulsions which drastically restricted Jewish life west of Poland, was essentially a

product of the dawning modern era—of the age of the Renaissance—
rather than of the Middle Ages. Paradoxical though it may seem, this
new and more thorough-going rejection of Jews and Judaism
coincided with what in other respects represented a dramatic broadening in culture and attitudes, including a deeper Christian involvement in Hebrew and Hebrew literature than had ever been seen
previously.

It is therefore evident that the installing of the Inquisition in Spain
in 1481 and the general expulsion from Spain of all Jews who refused
baptism in 1492, as well as the expulsion from Navarre in 1498 and
the mass forced baptism of the 70,000 or so Jews (mostly Spanish
émigrés) who were in Portugal in 1497,[1] by no means represent a
solely, or specifically, Iberian phenomenon. While it is doubtless true
that the expulsions from Spain and Portugal lingered more
poignantly than the other calamities in the collective memory of the
Jewish people, these events really need to be seen in a wider European
context. The 100,000 or so who refused baptism and departed Iberian
shores for North Africa, Italy, and particularly the Levant were
joined in their trek eastwards by thousands more expelled by
Ferdinand from Sicily and Sardinia, in 1492, expelled by the French
crown from Provence in 1498, and from many parts of the German
lands at this time.

At the same time, in Italy, a new popular anti-Semitism, whipped
up by itinerant Franciscan and Dominican preachers—it was also the
Dominicans who led the anti-Semitic campaign in Spain and Germany—spread across the country. The most notable agitator was
Bernardino da Feltre who, like Savonarola and other popular religious leaders of the time, was a fierce critic of the lax and permissive
manners and morals of the Italian courts. Bernardino, it is true, railed
furiously against devotees of luxury, promiscuity, and sodomy, as
well as Jews, but the Jews were always his prime target and wherever
he went on his pious travels he stirred up feeling against them. The
ultimate objective in Italy, as elsewhere, of the campaign, was to
expel the Jews; but, in Italy, it seemed necessary, as a preliminary
step, to replace the Jewish loan-banks with civic institutions known as
monti di pietà, for, in many areas, the Jews were the only source of credit

---

[1] Though the standard accounts report that 150,000 Spanish Jewish émigrés
entered Portugal, in 1492, this figure is certainly a gross exaggeration, and even
70,000 may well be too high: Lúcio de Azevedo, *História*, p. 43; Ferro Tavares, *Os judeus*,
i. 74.

for the poor.[2] The clamour, and setting-up of *monti di pietà*, was accompanied by sporadic rioting. At Ravenna, in 1491, the synagogue was destroyed and the Jewish quarter ruthlessly sacked. Some expulsions were put into effect. Driven from Perugia in 1485, the Jews were expelled from Vicenza in 1486, Parma in 1488, Milan and Lucca in 1489, and, following the downfall of the Medici in 1494, from Florence and other Tuscan towns.[3] A few years later, in 1510, King Ferdinand, having beaten the French out of Naples and secured what was the largest principality in Italy, drove out the bulk of the Jews living south of Rome.

In the German lands, the anti-Semitic fervour of this period was also mainly urban and popular in character, an explosive fusion of economic grievance and religious passion. Linking the agitation in Italy with the ferment in Germany, Austria, and Switzerland was Bernardino's inflammatory preaching at Trent, in 1475, which further aroused feeling against the Jews either side of the Alps. Bernardino's demagoguery led to a terrible sequel following the disappearance of a Christian boy, Simon and the old medieval accusation that the Jews had murdered him to use his blood for ritual purposes. A group of Trent Jews were seized, tortured, and burned at the stake; the rest were expelled. A widely disseminated woodcut of the torment and burning of Trent Jews further excited passions north and south. Such was the fury this episode aroused that the Papacy, despite its reluctance, felt impelled to beatify Simon and sanction the entire proceeding.

The expulsions from Switzerland and the German lands reached their peak in precisely the same decade, the 1490s, as the Jews were driven from the Iberian Peninsula, Provence, and Sicily.[4] Sent out of Geneva in 1490, and from the duchies of Mecklenburg and Pomerania in 1492, they were driven from Halle and Magdeburg in 1493, from Lower Austria, Styria, and Carinthia in 1496, from Württemberg and the archbishopric of Salzburg in 1498, and from two of the most important Imperial Free Cities—Nuremberg and Ulm—in 1499. There were riots against the Jews in Berlin in 1500, and a general expulsion of the Jews from the electorate of Brandenburg in 1510. Having been ejected from most of Alsace during the second half of the fifteenth century, the Jews were driven

[2] Pullan, *Rich and Poor*, pp. 456–60.
[3] Ibid.; Cassuto, *Ebrei a Firenze*, pp. 55–63; Carpi, 'Alcune notizie', p. 20.
[4] Nordmann, 'Histoire des Juifs à Genève', p. 35.

from Colmar, Mulhouse, and Obernai in 1512; by 1520, there were scarcely 120 Jewish families left in the whole of Alsace.[5]

A key feature of this first phase of the early modern expulsions, from the mid-fifteenth century down to the expulsion from Regensburg in 1519, the expulsions of the pre-Reformation, is that the momentum emanated chiefly from the towns and the lower clergy, especially the friars. By and large, the senior clergy, including the prince-bishops of Germany and, indeed, the Papacy as well as Europe's secular authorities held aloof from the agitation. The Papacy not only dissociated itself from what occurred but took steps to protect the Jewish communities of the Papal States. If the Venetian authorities failed to prevent the expulsion from Treviso, in 1509, they intervened to stop the Jews being expelled from Conegliano in 1511, and again in 1522, as well as from other places in the Veneto.[6] In Tuscany, where the Medici had a long tradition of protecting the Jews, their fate was closely bound up with that of the ruling house. The Jews were turned out of Florence along with the Medici but returned on their restoration, in 1513; ejected again with the Medici, in 1527, they returned once more in their wake, in 1531.[7] At Mantua, the ruling Gonzaga refused to yield to the demands of the guilds and lesser clergy for the expulsion of the Jews, despite repeated bouts of anti-Semitic violence in the 1480s and 1490s. At Ferrara, the House of Este not only protected the Jews already dwelling in the duchy but welcomed new arrivals fleeing from Spain.[8] While the Jews were forced out of Austrian Alsace in 1474, and the Emperor Maximilian I acquiesced in their expulsion from Styria and Carinthia in 1496, he insisted on financial compensation (for himself) and allowed the exiles to settle elsewhere in his domains. Though the Jews had been driven out of the cities of Cologne and Mainz, the prince-archbishops of these two electorates permitted the exiles to remain in the villages and small towns around. Thus, in 1513, the Archbishop-Elector of Mainz confirmed the privileges of the Jews of his territory, designating the village of Weisenau as the seat of its rabbinate. Meanwhile, in Brandenburg, Elector Joachim II, having found that the thirty-eight Jews tortured and burned alive at the stake in Berlin in 1510 had been falsely charged with desecrating the host, invited the exiles to return.[9]

[5] Weill, 'Recherches', pp. 53–4.
[6] Luzzatto, *Comunità ebraica di Conegliano*, pp. 7–8.
[7] Cassuto, *Ebrei a Firenze*, pp. 80, 83–90; Cassuto, 'Famille des Medicis', pp. 132–45.
[8] Balletti, *Gli ebrei e gli Estensi*, pp. 206–9, 219; Milano, *Storia*, pp. 264–9.
[9] Davidsohn, *Beiträge*, pp. 15–19, 62.

Several dozen Jewish families percolated back to Berlin, Frankfurt an der Oder, and Stendal, though not to all the Brandenburg towns from which they had been ejected.

The second—and last—phase of the exodus from the west was integral to the Reformation and Counter-Reformation. This later stage differed from that of the 1470–1520 period in that the driving force was now princely and ecclesiastical as much as popular. This final push towards the liquidation of Jewry from the life of western and central Europe was fitfully sustained for about half a century. As regards actual numbers of Jews driven out, this last drive was less virulent than that of the late fifteenth century. But as regards the curtailing of Jewish participation in Europe's economy and culture, the post-1530 campaign was in fact a more systematic, total, and ideological assault than any which preceded it.

Initially, Luther, Bucer, and other Reformation leaders were by no means overtly hostile to the Jews. Indeed, they hoped that now, at last, the renewed and purified Christianity they were offering would win over Jewish hearts and that those who had been obstinate for so long would now accept baptism. In his pamphlet *Das Jesus Christus ein geborener Jude sei*, of 1523, Luther held that the Jews had been right to reject the claims of Papist Christianity and that he himself would have done so had he been one of them. What was expected was that they would now embrace Christ. For their part, the Jews at first reacted to the split in Christendom with scarcely disguised satisfaction.[10] Luther, after all, rejected papal supremacy and insisted on the primacy of Scripture, a major shift which seemed momentarily to indicate a mitigation of the age-old antagonism of Christianity and Judaism. But, in reality, Luther's appeal to Scripture, far from softening, further aggravated the clash of Christian and Jewish teaching. For the Reformers staked their position on their construing of the Bible. But the Jews not only insisted that their Hebrew Bible was the only authentic version of God's word but that they alone were equipped, with their commentaries and Talmud, to construe it correctly. This was not just an affront, but a challenge to the new basis for religious authority. It was more than unsettling, it was totally unacceptable. By 1526, Luther was already vehemently complaining of the Jews' stubbornness.[11] From that point on his bitter frustration

[10] Ben-Sasson, 'Reformation', pp. 286–9.
[11] Feilchenfeld, *Rabbi Josel*, pp. 120–1; Poliakov, *Histoire*, pp. 242–44; Oberman, *Wurzeln*, pp. 160–2.

at what he called the 'impossibility' of arguing with Jews, such was
their obduracy, steadily intensified, culminating in his tract *Von den
Juden und iren Luegen* of 1543. In this tract Luther treated the Jews to
the full blast of his invective, assailing them as 'disgusting vermin'
and their synagogues as 'devils' nests of insolence and lies'.[12] It was
owing to his realization that the Jews were impervious to his arguments that Luther switched to a policy of driving them out. Luther
specifically urges Christians, as Christians, to be foes of the Jews,
politically and in a physical sense as well as doctrinally. Thus he
instigated the decision to expel the Jews from Saxony in 1537, and
wrote to Joachim II of Brandenburg in 1545, expressing anger and
disapproval at the Elector's having readmitted the Jews to his
territory.[13]

   In spite of their increasingly precarious position, the Jews of the
Holy Roman Empire were not mere silent onlookers of the Reformation debate. Indeed, Josel of Rosheim, the then 'gemeiner Judischait
Bevelhaber in Teutschland', the Alsatian rabbi who was acknowledged by princes, prelates, and Jewish communities alike as the chief
spokesman of German Jewry, played a remarkable role in the
proceedings. It was Josel who obtained from the young Emperor
Charles V in 1520 renewal of the privileges and letters of protection
conceded to German Jewry by his predecessors. In 1530, Josel
presided over a meeting of the delegates of the German Jewish
communities, at Augsburg, which was held simultaneously with the
Imperial Diet then and there in progress. This was a routine synod of
German Jewry and it was partly concerned with internal matters, as
well as new restrictions on Jewish money-lending then before the
Diet, but as it was being put about in princely and ecclesiastical
circles that it was the Jews who had inspired Luther to challenge the
Papacy, it was inevitable that the Jewish leadership should be drawn
into the religious controversies of the time.[14] Charles personally
ordered Josel to engage in disputation with Antonius Margarita, son
of a former rabbi of Regensburg who had converted to Catholicism
and just published, at Augsburg, an inflammatory attack on the Jews
entitled *Der Gantz Jüdisch Glaub*. Josel succeeded in persuading the
Emperor that Margarita was a scoundrel whose charges that rabbinic
literature flagrantly reviles Christ and Christianity were spurious.

---

[12] Luther, *Von den Juden*, Aiii–iv, Fi, Ji, Lii–iii.
[13] Ibid., Oiii; Davidsohn, *Beiträge*, p. 15.
[14] Feilchenfeld, *Rabbi Josel*, p. 183; Zimmer, *Jewish Synods*, pp. 62–5.

Margarita was imprisoned on the Emperor's orders and later banished from Augsburg. He subsequently became a Lutheran, his book being cited by Luther in his anti-Jewish tirades.

While Josel's encounter with Margarita did not directly touch on Luther, the Augsburg Jewish synod of 1530, meeting under the eye of the Emperor, could not help distancing itself from the Lutherans and their readings of Scripture. Gradually, Josel's rejection of Protestant claims became more emphatic as the Reformers themselves increasingly espoused the anti-Semitism of the populace. When the Elector of Saxony, prompted by Luther, prepared to expel the Jews from his territory in 1536, Josel travelled to Saxony armed with texts refuting Luther's charges against the Jews.[15] Luther refused to see Josel. Finding that the elector was at Frankfurt, Josel followed him there and obtained a hearing before several princes in which he strove to combat Luther's teaching. The elector nevertheless went ahead with the expulsion from Saxony. Having failed to see Luther, Josel did obtain an interview with Martin Bucer, at Strasbourg, which, however, degenerated into indignant abuse on Bucer's part, the latter threatening Josel with the imminent destruction of the Jewish people. In a hearing before the Strasbourg city council in 1543, Josel offered to engage in a public disputation with Martin Luther so that 'with the help of God and the words of the Prophets, with uprightness and sincerity, in the presence of leading scholars' he could show that Luther's construings of Scripture were false.[16]

Ejected from electoral Saxony in 1537, the Jews were driven from Zwickau, Mühlhausen, and other Thuringian towns in the 1540s. There was also a wave of riots against the Jews in Brunswick in 1543, followed by general expulsion from the duchies of Brunswick, Hanover, and Lüneburg in 1553. As a result of this anti-Semitic upsurge in Protestant Germany, Luther acquired a more evil reputation in Jewish literature than almost any other figure in the history of the Christian churches. One of the exiles from Brunswick who later made his way to Safed, in the Holy Land, where there was then a community of German, as well as larger groups of Spanish, Portuguese, and Italian Jewish, exiles, wrote of the expulsion from Brunswick 'on the advice of this foul priest Martin Luther and the other scoundrels who derive from the stock of the arch-heretic'.[17] The

---

[15] 'Journal de Joselmann', p. 92; Feilchenfeld, *Rabbi Josel*, p. 121; Stern, *Josel von Rosheim*, pp. 125–9.

[16] 'Journal de Joselmann', p. 92.   [17] Ben-Sasson, 'Reformation', p. 289.

anti-Semitic ferment in the Lutheran states continued through the 1560s, culminating in new riots and the sacking of the synagogue in Berlin in 1572, followed by the re-expulsion of the Jews from the whole of Brandenburg the following year. There was also much agitation in Silesia which led to the expulsion of the Jews from that territory except for three communities—Gross-Glogau, Zulz, and Hotzenplotz—in 1582.

But not all the Reformers were as hostile to the Jews as Luther and Bucer. Others, notably Wolfgang Capito and later Calvin, were markedly more conciliatory.[18] Calvin probably met Jewish leaders during his sojourns at Frankfurt and Strasbourg, possibly including Josel himself. The great French theologian ran up against the same basic contradiction over Scripture as Luther, but overall his teaching tended to mitigate rather than inflame Christian–Jewish antagonism. He avoided the anti-Semitic invective of the Lutherans and considerably modified the traditional Christian stance on usury in his tract *De Usuris*. In his late treatise, *Ad Quaestiones et Obiecta Judaei cuiusdam Respondio*, Calvin is remarkably objective in reporting the arguments of the Jew.[19] Of course, Calvin joined in the stock Reformation practice of denouncing opponents as 'Judaizers', condemning Michael Servetus, for instance, for his 'Jewish interpretations', meaning his rejection of the doctrine of the Trinity. Even so, Calvin's relative lack of animosity toward the Jews, as well as his abiding preoccupation with the Old Testament, lent a certain weight to the repeated Lutheran charges that he was a 'Judaizer'.

Yet Calvin's moderation did not prevent the Calvinist Reformation from lending added momentum to the drive to exclude the Jews from western and central Europe. The Jews had been driven from Geneva and Lausanne in the 1490s, but their request for readmission in 1582, after the Calvinist Reformation, was rejected overwhelmingly by city council, clergy, and populace alike.[20] In Germany, the principal Calvinist state was the Palatinate, where in 1550 there were 155 Jewish families resident.[21] These were driven out 'for all time' by the Elector Frederick III in 1575, though as it turned out this expulsion was only temporary.

While it may seem that the spreading campaign against the Jews, whether popular or Lutheran, ran counter to the humanist ideals of

---

[18] Stern, *Josel von Rosheim*, pp. 125–7.

[19] See Salo W. Baron's observations on Calvin and the Jews in his *Social and Religious History of the Jews*, xiii, 281–90.

[20] Nordmann, 'Histoire des Juifs à Genève', pp. 35–9.

[21] Arnold, *Juden in der Pfalz*, p. 9.

the period, this is in fact hardly so, except perhaps in Italy, where the distancing from Christian tradition in the work of certain humanists went furthest. The rise of Hebrew learning among Christian scholars had begun in Italy in the later fifteenth century with the work of Manetti and Pico della Mirandola. Hebrew studies became an important strand in German humanism from the second decade of the sixteenth century. Yet immersed though Pico was in Hebrew—and in his case in cabbala, the writings of Jewish mysticism, especially the *Zohar*—he saw cabbala as essentially a means of demonstrating 'Christian truth' and overcoming 'Jewish obstinacy'. Johannes Reuchlin (1455–1522), the chief figure among the German Hebraists of the period, had little or no sympathy for Jews and Judaism as such. The same is true of Sebastian Münster, another outstanding Hebraist, who became Professor of Hebrew at Basel University in 1528.[22] Philip Melanchthon (1497–1560), one of Luther's principal lieutenants, was another accomplished Hebraist who was nevertheless deeply imbued with Luther's anti-Semitic attitude, though he did denounce the blood libel and other crudities of medieval popular anti-Semitism. All these scholars acknowledged that the Jews had preserved crucially important ancient texts but deemed the entire body of post-biblical non-cabbalistic Hebrew commentary and interpretation to be generally obdurate, wicked, and worthless.

But the towering exponent of Christian humanist anti-Semitism was Erasmus himself. Indeed, Erasmus may be regarded as having preceded both Luther and the Papacy in enunciating the new, more ideological anti-Semitism of the sixteenth century. In his letters to Wolfgang Capito, a Reformer with Hebraist leanings, Erasmus expressed his disapproval of the new Hebraism, fearing that, whatever the intentions of its practitioners, Christian Hebraism would in some way lead to a Jewish revival. He felt in his bones that study of the Talmud, cabbala, and rabbinic books, even too much interest in the Old Testament, could only deflect the Christian scholar from Christ, not draw him nearer. Greatly though he detested the medieval schoolmen, Erasmus felt closer to them on this issue than to his Hebraist colleagues. He saw Jewish learning and Jewish interpretations as more dangerous to Christian truth than any medieval obscurantism. 'Nothing more adverse and nothing more inimical to Christ', he wrote, 'can be found than this plague.'[23] The

22 Burmeister, *Sebastian Münster*, pp. 82–6.
23 Gundersheimer, 'Erasmus', pp. 40–7.

bitter controversy over Hebrew books which raged in Germany in the years 1518–19, in which Reuchlin argued the usefulness of Jewish literature to the Christian scholar against an assortment of unscrupulous converts, monastic obscurantists, and Inquisitors, proved a painful embarrassment to Erasmus. He could not be seen to side with Inquisitors against fellow humanists but neither could he agree with Reuchlin that the study of Hebrew was desirable from the Christian point of view, an assessment which may have been more astute than Reuchlin's. Amid this predicament, Erasmus took the extraordinary step of writing to the Cologne Inquisitor, Hochstraten, urging him to damp down the furore and assuring him that in private he largely agreed with his stance. 'Who is there among us that does not sufficiently hate that race of men?' 'If it is Christian to hate the Jews' he assured the Inquisitor, 'here we are all Christian in profusion.'[24]

The collapse of Jewish life in western and central Europe in the century 1470–1570 would have been virtually complete, outside Italy, were it not for the policy of the Emperor. At the Imperial diets of Augsburg (1530) and Speyer (1544), Charles confirmed his protection of German Jewry. At the Regensburg diet of 1546, Josel obtained wording more favourable than any conceded previously.[25] Meanwhile the Catholic prince-bishops, caught by the rising tide of Lutheranism in their towns, were also forced to rely more heavily than before on the Emperor and tended to see their Jews as a kind of counterweight, however limited in scope, to the Protestant bourgeoisie. Charles's success in preventing a total Protestant triumph in Germany was therefore a major factor in the survival of the Jews in the Holy Roman Empire. Of particular importance was the provision of the 1555 Augsburg religious settlement which specifically excluded the ecclesiastical states (roughly one-quarter of Germany) from the otherwise generally agreed rule that henceforward each individual prince should be sole arbiter of religion in his territory. This precluded the likelihood of prince-bishops turning Protestant in the expectation of converting their states into conventional dynastic principalities with the support of the other secular princes, most of whom were Lutheran. Thus the ecclesiastical states stayed Catholic under the Emperor's eye and the Jews remained in

---

[24] 'Journal de Joselmann', pp. 95, 101; Kracauer, *Juden in Frankfurt*, i. 292–5.
[25] Ibid., p. 48; Oberman, *Wurzeln*, 50, 75: 'Si Christianum est odisse Iudeos, hic abunde Christiani sumus omnes.'

the archbishoprics of Cologne (outside the city), Mainz, and Trier, in the prince-bishoprics of Münster, Minden, Halberstadt, Paderborn, Würzburg, Bamberg, and Speyer, and in the abbey-principality of Fulda.

The Jews for their part followed a definite policy. Josel considered Luther a lout and a scoundrel, but the Emperor he deemed an 'Angel of the Lord'. During the War of the Schmalkaldic League (1546–7), prayers were recited morning and evening in the synagogues for the triumph of the Emperor's arms, remarkably enough even in the Imperial Free City of Frankfurt, even though this city participated in the Protestant coalition against the Emperor. Nor did the Jews rally to Charles with prayers alone.[26] They actively joined in his war effort with subsidies and loans and contributed 'over fifty wagons' full of 'bread and wine' to his baggage-train. Doubtless this is why Charles went out of his way to be courteous to the Jews at Regensburg in 1546. It is also recorded that when some of the Emperor's Spanish troops began pillaging Jewish homes, Charles exerted himself with vigour to ensure the Jews' protection. When Frankfurt eventually submitted to the Emperor, the city's Jews were specifically exempted from having troops billeted on them, in contrast to the rest of the citizenry.

Charles's Jewish policy within the Holy Roman Empire stands out all the more in that he generally emulated the intolerance of his Spanish grandparents Ferdinand and Isabella in his territories outside the Empire.[27] Thus he went ahead with the final expulsion of the Jews from the viceroyalty of Naples, in 1541, despite contrary advice from local officials. After adding Gelderland to his Netherlands inheritance, he confirmed the exclusion of the Jews from the province, and ordered the partial expulsion of the Portuguese Marranos from Antwerp in 1549–50. It was also he who finally persuaded a reluctant Papacy to authorize the setting up of an Inquisition on the Spanish model in Portugal in 1543.[28] Charles V's Jewish policy in the Empire was thus exclusively a matter of political expediency though none the less significant for that.

The Reformers' attack on Jewry was soon followed by the anti-Semitic onslaught of the Counter-Reformation. By the 1550s, the

---

[26] Kracauer, *Juden in Frankfurt*, i. 296–300; Stern, *Josel von Rosheim*, pp. 160–70.

[27] Schmidt, *Histoire*, pp. 14, 23–6; Poliakov, *Banquiers juifs*, pp. 194–5; van Agt, 'Joodse gemeente van Nijmegen', p. 173.

[28] Lúcio de Azevedo, *História*, pp. 106–9.

hapless Jews were getting it in the teeth from both sides in Europe's theological war. Down to the 1550s, the Papacy had been, next to the Emperor, the foremost protector of Jewish life in the west. Not only did Renaissance popes express strong doubts as to the justifiability of forced baptism, and the mass forced baptism of 1497 in Portugal in particular, as well as dissociating themselves from popular agitation against Jews, but they permitted a sizeable influx of Jewish refugees from Spain and Portugal, as well as from Sicily and Provence, showing the immigrants many tokens of their favour. In the early sixteenth century, about half of Rome's large Jewish population was of Iberian or Sicilian origin; the separate 'Catalan' and 'Castilian' synagogues became enduring features of Roman Jewish life.[29] In 1541, Paul III invited those whom Charles drove out of Naples to settle in his port of Ancona and, in 1547, issued a strikingly liberal bull inviting both Spanish-speaking 'Levantine' Jews and Marranos from Portugal who had reverted to Judaism to settle there in order to help stimulate trade with the Balkans. By 1552, there were over 100 Portuguese Jewish families in the papal port of Ancona, besides 'Levantine' Jews and a flourishing 'Italian' Jewish community.[30]

The dramatic volte-face in the Papacy's Jewish policy began in 1553, at the instigation of Cardinal Caraffa, shortly to become Pope Paul IV, who was as virulently anti-Jewish as he was anti-Protestant. But the change was by no means merely a matter of personalities. Rather it was inherent in the Counter-Reformation, the great reorganization and reform of the Church in response to the Protestant challenge, which began in the 1550s. This campaign against the Jews, like other features of the Counter-Reformation, was not really a reversion to pre-Renaissance papal attitudes, but rather something basically new. Before 1450, whatever the humiliations heaped on the Jews, the spiritual gulf between them and Christian society had been so vast that no one spoke of the necessity of driving the Jews out, or squeezing them into walled ghettos. There was an uneasy coexistence which seemingly posed no threat to Christian culture and modes of thought, medieval Christian scholars knowing nothing about, and taking no interest in, the Hebrew language and Jewish literature. There were set-piece, ritual disputations, in which Jewish spokesmen were subjected to the crudest psychological intimidation, but there

---

[29] Morosini, *Via della Fede*, p. 227; Cara Baroja, *Judíos*, i. 259–63; Shulvass, 'Jewish Population', p. 142.

[30] Toaff, 'Nuova luce', pp. 263–4.

was no genuine dialogue or critical examination of texts. After 1450, however, there was a profound change of the cultural scene, at any rate in Italy. The upsurge of interest in pagan Roman and Greek culture generated, in many minds, an initial distancing, however tentative, from traditional Christian attitudes. This created a Christian–Jewish dialogue which made it possible for such Italian Jewish scholars as Judah Abrabanel, commonly known in Italy as Leone Ebreo, Elijah Levita (1469–1549), and Azariah de' Rossi (*c*.1511–*c*.1578) to participate if not fully, then extensively, in the learned debates of their time. Whilst, in the minds of Manetti and others of the first generation of Italian Christian Hebraists, the point of the Christian scholar's immersing himself in Hebrew was to convert Jews, this polemical purpose was to some extent lost sight of and Hebrew became an integral part of the culture of the High Renaissance. Several popes and cardinals took an interest in Hebrew literature, especially cabbala. The volte-face of the 1550s was thus a reaction, specifically a rejection, of a previous spiritual *rapprochement* of however tentative a kind. Paul IV's Jewish policy had two specific purposes: to accelerate the process of Jewish conversion, by piling heavier pressure on the Jews, and no less important, to insulate the Catholic world against Hebrew influences.[31] At bottom, the anti-Judaism of the Counter-Reformation derived from the perception, shared by Erasmus, that Jewish learning was not a valid adjunct to Christian faith, or a supplement to other scholarship, but a living force capable of 'seducing' minds, as it was put, from Christ and, in particular, of deflecting baptized Marranos from allegiance to the Church.

Papal hostility to Jews and Judaism in the late sixteenth century was thus a symbol of the new age, and was to remain integral to papal attitudes throughout the seventeenth and eighteenth centuries as well. The repression began with an event which said much of its general purpose: the burning alive on the Campo dei Fiori in Rome of a Franciscan friar found guilty of having been persuaded by Jewish arguments, having denied Christ, and espoused Judaism. Word of his martyrdom spread among all the Jewish communities of Europe. In August 1553, the Pope condemned the Talmud, the basis of post-biblical Jewish tradition and law, as sacrilegious and blasphemous, banning its possession and use. The condemnation applied also to Talmudic summaries and commentaries. Italy erupted in an orgy of

---

[31] Stow, *Catholic Thought*, pp. 5–13.

pious vandalism, great heaps of Hebrew books and manuscripts
being burned in Rome, Bologna, Florence, in the Piazza San Marco in
Venice, and in numerous other places, including the Venetian
colonies of Crete and Corfu.[32] The oppression intensified in 1555
when Paul IV issued his bull *Cum Nimis Absurdum*, enforcing a rigid
segregation into ghettos on all the Jews of the Papal States. Modelled
on the already well-established ghetto of Venice, the first ghetto in
Italy, the ghettos in the Papal States henceforth confined the Jews to
heavily overcrowded, walled-off precincts, which were bound to be
insanitary traps in times of epidemic, governed by a host of petty
regulations intended to minimize Christian–Jewish contact. Paul IV
also reversed previous papal policy condoning the reversion of forced
converts, and their children, from Christianity to Judaism, decreeing
that the Portuguese mass baptism of 1497 should henceforward be
valid and irreversible. A legate was dispatched to Ancona to root out
Marranos who had reverted to Judaism. Many Portuguese lapsed
Catholics living in the port escaped in time to the duchies of Urbino
and Ferrara, but fifty-one were caught, interrogated, and tortured,
some being sentenced to the galleys, twenty-five being burned alive
by the Pope's Inquisitors, at Ancona, in April and June 1555.

The burning of the Ancona martyrs aroused Jewish feeling
everywhere. An attempt at retaliation against the Papacy was
instigated by the powerful Nasi or Mendes family who, after many
years living as ostensible Christians in Lisbon, Antwerp, and Venice,
had reverted to open Judaism in Turkey and risen high in the Sultan's
favour. As the Ancona Jews were chiefly involved in trade with
Constantinople and Salonika, moves were made in the Balkans to
impose a commercial boycott on Ancona, re-routeing Jewish trade
between the Balkans and Italy through the nearby port of Pesaro, in
the duchy of Urbino. The Sultan also lodged a diplomatic protest in
Rome. The boycott had some initial effect but ultimately failed, partly
because Ancona was better situated than Pesaro on the route between
the Balkans and Florence, which at that time was still one of the main
suppliers of cloth to the Near East, and partly because the boycott hit
not only papal interests, and the city of Ancona, but also the non-
Portuguese Jews who were still there.[33] Jewish reaction within Italy

[32] Kaufmann, 'Verbrennung der talmudischen Litteratur', pp. 533–8; in 1558, the
Jews of Corfu, a fairly recent community composed chiefly of Spanish, Sicilian, and
Neapolitan exiles, numbered around 2,000, those of Crete, an ancient community
reaching back to Roman times, around 1,000.

[33] Kaufmann, 'Marranes de Pesaro', pp. 61–5; Toaff, 'Nuova luce', pp. 274, 278.

was more muted. Italy's Jewish communities, like those of Germany, had convened occasional general synods to frame policy on matters of common concern since at least the early fifteenth century. Delegates now gathered from all over central and northern Italy at Ferrara, in 1554, to confer on the various aspects of the papal campaign and deliberate the banning of the Talmud. The Jews' leaders agreed to try to appease the Papacy by offering to delete offending passages, a delegation being later sent to petition the council of prelates meeting at Trent to hold back from a total prohibition of the Talmud. Helped by Paul IV's early decease, and the less rigid attitude of his successor, the Jews and the episcopal committee drawing up the papal Index of forbidden books reached a compromise whereby the Index of 1564 prohibited the 'Talmud', but stipulated that, if the title 'Talmud' and specified passages were removed, the text could be used. And the next printed edition of the Talmud, published at Basel in 1578–80, was expurgated accordingly so that it could be used in Italy.

The campaign against the Marranos, to ghettoize Jewish life and to expurgate Jewish literature, soon led to papal pressure on the north Italian states to follow suit. Venice at this stage was regarded as something of a model, having been the first of all to squeeze the Jews into a walled-off ghetto, under night curfew, and having expelled its Marranos in 1550. Notably more tolerant toward the Jews in this period were the dukes of Urbino, Tuscany, Mantua, and Ferrara. Ferrara, which then had one of the largest Jewish communities in Christian Europe, exceeding 1,000, had taken in a particularly large number of Iberian exiles and was now the most liberal of all the Italian states toward the reversion of Marranos to Judaism, ironically enough under a safe-conduct to the 'nazione hebraica lusitana et spagnola' issued by Duke Ercole II in 1550, modelled on the clauses of the papal charter of 1547.[34] Pius IV indignantly demanded that the Este Duke expel the 'perfidious and abominable race of Marranos', but Ercole refused, citing previous papal practice. The Papacy had more immediate success, however, with the duchy of Urbino, which expelled its Marranos in 1558 and, eventually, with Cosimo I of Tuscany who, in return for papal favours, embarked on a series of anti-Jewish measures in the 1560s.

One prime papal object was to stop the printing of Jewish books in European vernacular languages, a new phenomenon which arose at Ferrara and Venice in the early 1550s. Before 1550, all printed Jewish

[34] Balletti, *Gli ebrei e gli Estensi*, pp. 220–1.

books in Christian lands were in Hebrew, knowledge of which was restricted to professing Jews and a handful of Christians. But there was now a growing demand for Jewish material in vernacular languages, mainly among Marranos resident in Italy and France who had little Hebrew but who wished to revive their links with Judaism. In 1552, there were almost simultaneous, though not identical publications of Jewish prayer-books in Spanish, at Ferrara and Venice, and in 1553, the Marrano printer Abraham Usque published the famous Ferrara Bible, a literal Spanish rendering from the Hebrew which diverged markedly from, and was an outright challenge to, the Catholic Vulgate.[35] In the same year, Usque also published in Portuguese the *Consolation for the Tribulations of Israel*, a long mystical and historical work by his relative Samuel Usque, which was the first Jewish apologetic publication to appear in a European tongue. All this amounted to an undisguised appeal to the Marranos of Spain and Portugal to defect from Christianity and an insufferable affront to the newly militant Papacy. The 1552 Spanish renderings of Jewish prayers percolated into the Peninsula and had a considerable impact on the formulation of the crypto-Jews' prayers in Portugal in subsequent decades.[36] Doubtless they also had some effect on non-Marrano Christians with a tendency toward crypto-Judaism. On this issue, Duke Ercole did comply with the Pope's wishes, and, in 1555, the printing of Jewish books in European languages ceased for over a quarter of a century.

The papal offensive against the Jews culminated in the pontificate of Pius V (1566–72), who abhorred them with a passion exceeding even that of Paul IV. Under his bull *Hebraeorum Gens* (1569), he expelled the Jews from all the localities where they lived in the Papal States except for the port of Ancona, the main commercial entrepôt of the Papal States, and the city of Rome itself. At a stroke, dozens of Jewish communities, some of which had survived in unbroken continuity since ancient times, were liquidated. In all, 108 synagogues were sequestrated by the Pope's officials and closed. Many thousands of refugees streamed out of their forcibly abandoned homes in Orvieto, Viterbo, Forlì, Tivoli, Ravenna, Rimini, and a good many other localities. The heaviest blow was the expulsion of the 800 Jews of Bologna, previously one of the most flourishing communities in Italy. Pius's relentless policy applied also to the Jews of the Papal

[35] Verd, 'Biblias romanzadas', pp. 344–51; Morreale, 'Sidur ladinado', pp. 332–8.
[36] Salomon, 'Portuguese Background', pp. 116–21.

States in France—Avignon and the Comtat Venaissin; the Jews of those regions likewise packed their bags and prepared to leave. Many did leave but there were repeated delays in enforcing the decree of expulsion in France and eventually, with some hundreds still remaining, the decree was suspended.[37] In this way, reduced Jewish communities survived at Avignon, Carpentras, and two or three neighbouring places.

At the same time, the campaign against the Jews was intensified in Tuscany. All the contracts for Jewish loan-banks in the small towns of Tuscany were ended in 1570–1, leading to expulsion from Prato, Arezzo, Cortona, and other localities. As in the case of the Papal States, some of the refugees migrated to Ferrara, Mantua, and beyond, others crammed into the one or two places where ghettos were authorized. In Tuscany, Jewish settlement was restricted to Florence and Siena where ghettos were now formed.[38] Meanwhile, more restrictive measures were introduced in Urbino and in the duchy of Parma, where the number of places where Jews were allowed to live was reduced from sixteen to eight. In 1579, Duke Ercole's more amenable successor as ruler of Ferrara, Alfonso II, effectively expelled the Marranos from his territory, allowing some of them to be dragged off to Rome in chains. There was a pause in the campaign during the pontificate of Sixtus V (1585–90), who relaxed some of the draconian restrictions on Jewish economic activity introduced by his predecessors and allowed the refugees from the Papal States to return to the places from which they had been forced out.[39] And communities were briefly reconstituted at Bologna, Ravenna, and some other places. But there was to be no lasting reintegration in the Papal States outside Rome. In 1593, Pope Clement VIII reverted to the policy of Pius, ordering the Jews out again from all his domains except the cities of Rome, Ancona, and Avignon, hoping that by thus restricting the Jews to so few places, they could be so pressured and tightly regulated as to make them accept Christ. The last of the Italian expulsions was that from the Spanish Milanese (outside the city of Milan, from where the Jews had been expelled in 1489). Philip II had provisionally decided to expel the Jews from the rest of the Milanese, in 1565, but the decision was temporarily suspended on the advice of his governor Requesens, who believed that the presence of the Jews

[37] Moulinas, *Juifs du Pape*, pp. 37–9.
[38] Cassuto, *Ebrei a Firenze*, pp. 112–14; Poliakov, *Banquiers juifs*, p. 206.
[39] Milano, 'Ricerche', pp. 456–8; Stow, *Catholic Thought*, pp. 24–6.

was useful to the state and, in particular, to the support of the military garrison.[40] Christian merchants of those towns where Jews were permitted to reside, particularly those of Cremona, now mounted a strident campaign, alleging every sort of ill of the Jews, to overcome official doubts and hesitation. Finally, when the King was on his deathbed, in 1597, he ruled that expediency must submit to the dictates of faith and the 500 or so Jews remaining in the duchy were ordered out. There was one curious exception, however, in that the Vitale family were permitted to continue living and operating their loan-bank at Alessandria, an exemption which provided the basis for a small community which grew to 120 individuals by the mid-seventeenth century and to 231 Jews by 1684.

2

The century 1470–1570 thus witnessed the near-destruction of Jewish religion, learning, and life in western and central Europe. Open allegiance to Judaism was now entirely extinguished in Spain, Portugal, Italy south of Rome, the Netherlands, and Provence outside the Papal territories of Avignon and the Comtat Venaissin. And in Germany and Italy, where the last remnants persisted, Jewish life had suffered a drastic contraction. By 1570, the Jews had been cleared from every major German secular territory except Hesse, and from every Imperial Free City of any importance except Frankfurt. What was left was a much reduced remnant largely confined to the ecclesiastical states of the Empire and some, though not all, of the principalities of northern Italy. Economically, the role of the Jews had been reduced to an extremely narrow span of functions. As money-lenders they still had a certain significance here and there. William of Orange was one of Europe's great men who turned to Jews in this period to help assuage his need for cash, even before he embarked on his fateful struggle against Spain: in September 1563 he borrowed 20,000 Frankfurt gulden for six years at 5 per cent interest from the Jewish money-dealer Wendel of Deutz, who lived in the village of that name outside Cologne.[41] But, beyond money-lending, the Jewish role in western and central Europe had become altogether marginal practically everywhere.

[40] Segre, *Ebrei Lombardi*, pp. 56–8, 80–1, 112–13; Simonsohn, *Jews in the Duchy of Milan*, iii. 1702, 1725, 1756.
[41] Zuiden, 'Over de relaties van Prins Willem van Oranje', pp. 214–15.

All told, the disruption and loss to Jewish society were incalculable. Yet this vast catastrophe had many paradoxical aspects. Indeed, this immense process of uprooting culminated not just in the most fundamental restructuring of Jewish life in Europe down to the twentieth century but in a remarkable expansion and strengthening both of Jewish culture internally and, what is most striking, of its role in Europe's economic life and politics. Communities which, collectively, had long been the core of the Jewish world were now entirely erased or savagely diminished. By 1497, the year of the mass baptism in Portugal, a majority of what had been Spanish and Portuguese Jewry, totalling over 200,000 men, women, and children, had been forcibly baptized in the Iberian Peninsula. Even so, a sizeable minority, possibly up to 100,000, had already departed Iberian shores and successfully re-established their communities and way of life principally on Ottoman territory, in the eastern Mediterranean. Outside the Peninsula, there had been numerous conversions to Christianity, in Sicily, Naples, and the Papal States, but further north such conversion had been relatively rare. The vast majority of the Jews formerly living in Provence and central Europe, and a high proportion of those forced out of southern and central Italy, remained Jews and trekked to eastern Europe and the Levant. Furthermore, there now began a steady stream of Marranos, or secret Jews, who had been compulsorily converted in Portugal, to the Near East, where they reverted to Judaism. For the 70,000 or so 'New Christians', subjected to compulsory baptism in Portugal, consisted in their majority of former Spanish Jews who had been prepared to uproot themselves (and in many cases undergo great suffering and financial despoliation) to avoid baptism in 1492 and were scarcely likely to submit tamely to forced Christianization in Portugal.

Portugal, indeed, was a central factor in the subsequent evolution of European Jewry, owing to the continued vitality of crypto-Jewish tradition there, which survived in places even down to the twentieth century and which supplied a ceaseless flow of Judaizing emigrants over the next two and a half centuries. There were three major reasons why an enduring, resilient crypto-Judaism took root in Portugal but not in Spain. Firstly, in Portugal, in contrast to Spain, there was no Inquisition until the 1540s and even then it was not a very effective force until around 1580; this meant that little danger attached to the cultivation of private Judaism at any rate throughout the first half of the sixteenth century. Secondly, the Portuguese converts, consisting

largely of those who had uprooted themselves to avoid baptism in
Spain in 1492, were, as a group, much more loyal to their past than
those who had preferred to remain in Spain.[42] Added to this was a
factor which the great philosopher Spinoza thought more important
than anything else in consolidating crypto-Judaism in Portugal,
namely, that in Portugal, in contrast to Spain, New Christians were
effectively excluded from all honours and offices. This ensured the
perpetuation of a rigid caste system which was bound to generate
feelings of resentment and separate identity.[43] Meanwhile, in Spain,
except for Mallorca and Ibiza, where a clearly identifiable New
Christian (and crypto-Jewish) caste did evolve, the Inquisition made
rapid inroads into the remaining vestiges of Jewish belief, assisted by
the migration of many of the more hardened Spanish crypto-Jews in
the period 1497–1540 to Portugal where, as yet, the Inquisition did
not exist. Judging from the large numbers of Inquisition trials in
many parts of Spain, crypto-Judaism remained fairly widespread in
both Castile and the realms of Aragon down to around 1540, but with
the gradual disappearance of the generation which had been educated in Judaism before 1492, intermarriage and absorption of New
Christians into civic, military, and ecclesiastical positions led to a
process of rapid assimilation. Discrimination on grounds of racial
descent received official sanction in Spain from the 1550s but, by that
stage, the process had gone too far for this to affect anyone other than
those who had had relatives punished for Judaism or else Portuguese
New Christians who later moved back into Spain. By the 1570s it is
correct to speak of a mass crypto-Jewish sub-culture in Portugal,
which had dwindled to around 50,000 owing to heavy emigration
since 1497, contrasting with an effectively Christianized and mostly
no longer identifiable convert element in Spain.

The migration of Iberian Jews to the Balkans and the Levant is
thus characterized by a large wave of Spanish émigrés (up to 100,000)
who left by sea in 1492, together with a sizeable number (possibly
20,000) of Jews from Sicily, followed by approximately 20,000 Portuguese who departed surreptitiously in waves, particularly in 1497–
1500, in the 1530s, and again in the 1580s when the Portuguese
Inquisition began to bite hard. Though never as large as the original

[42] Lúcio de Azevedo, *História*, pp. 109, 120; Revah, 'Les Marranes', pp. 45–53;
Paulo, *Os criptojudeus*, pp. 33–40; Yerushalmi, *From Spanish Court*, pp. 31–47.

[43] Spinoza, *Tractatus Theologico-Politicus*, p. 56; exactly the same point was made by
Vieira; see Vieira, *Obras escolhidas* iv. 44, 50–1.

Spanish exodus, the subsequent Portuguese migration was of considerable importance as it remained culturally and linguistically
distinct from the Spaniards throughout the Near East. Separate
Portuguese synagogues arose not only in Salonika and Constantinople but throughout the Near East including Syria, Lebanon, and
the Holy Land.[44] From Turkish tax records we know that at Safed, in
Galilee, which increasingly emerged as the devotional and intellectual centre of the Jewish world in the mid-sixteenth century, there
were in 1567 143 Portuguese families compared with around 300
families of Spanish Jews, some 80 families of Italian exiles and under
50 families of German and Hungarian Jews. Similarly in Jerusalem,
Hebron, Gaza, and Tiberias there were considerable numbers of
Portuguese as well as Spaniards and to a lesser extent Italians and
Germans. The Portuguese friar Pantaleão d'Aveiro, who toured the
Holy Land in the 1580s, found that the Portuguese Jews, whom he
considers very numerous, having formerly been Christians themselves, were the most vehement critics of and —to his horror—scoffers
at Christianity in the Levant.[45]

The refugees from Italy settled all over eastern Europe and the
Levant, being especially numerous on the Dalmatian coast and in
Salonika, Morea, and Constantinople.[46] The great bulk of the German exiles migrated to Poland-Lithuania, which, together with the
Ottoman Balkans, now emerged as one of the twin centres of the
newly reconstituted Jewish world. The Polish King and the great
landed magnates of Poland, though Christian, proved just as receptive as the Sultan to large numbers of Jewish immigrants. For the vast
expanses of Poland-Lithuania, like those of the Ottoman empire,
were not just underpopulated but conspicuously backward economically and technically compared with western Europe, the Jews being
wanted essentially for their crafts, skills, and wealth. Thus the greater
tolerance of eastern and south-eastern Europe to the Jews in the
sixteenth century is directly tied to a willingness to allow them to
perform a far greater range of activities and functions than had been
the case in western and central Europe. Well before their actual
expulsion, the Jews of Provence, Germany, and Italy had been
effectively squeezed out economically by the general development of

---

[44] Galanté, 'Hommes et choses', pp. 5–7; Cohen and Lewis, *Population and Revenue*,
pp. 156, 158, 160; in Safed, there was an entire quarter known as 'Purtughal'.

[45] Aveiro, *Itinerário da Terra Sancta*, pp. 226, 302, 307^v, 309, 326^v.

[46] Milano, *Storia*, pp. 234–5.

Christian trade, industry, and banking. Christian merchants and craftsmen wanted no Jewish competitors and, as and when they became sufficiently powerful, the aim of their guilds was to eradicate Jewry from the crafts and trade. In Italy, by 1450, the Jews had virtually no important commercial functions other than pawnbroking and providing petty loans to the poor. In large-scale banking the role of the Jews was of some significance in Rome, but was dwindling.[47] Only in Spain and Portugal had the Jews continued to fill a much wider range of occupations, being active in the woollen-cloth, silk, and leather industries, as well as in general commerce. But in Spain, by 1492, total expulsion of the Jews, without excessive economic damage, was feasible owing to mass conversion from Judaism as well as substantial immigration of Italian and Flemish merchants. It was thus the mass forced baptism of 1391–1415 in Spain which prepared the ground economically and socially for 1492, shielding the essential interests of crown, nobles, and towns.

The sixteenth-century expansion of Jewish life in Poland-Lithuania fuelled by immigration from central Europe and Italy, is really astounding.[48] In 1500, Polish Jewry is thought to have amounted to around 30,000, a total then less than the Jewish population of Italy. In a total Polish population of around five million, the Jews at that time constituted a mere tiny minority. By 1575, whilst the population as a whole had risen to around seven million, the Jews had multiplied by four or five times to between 100,000 and 150,000, a figure only slightly less than that of Spanish Jewry on the eve of its expulsion. After 1575, Polish Jewry continued to increase rapidly both as a percentage of the whole and in absolute terms.

This growing Polish-Jewish population was by no means evenly distributed across the lands of the Polish monarchy, its distribution revealing a good deal about the place of the Jew in eastern European life. The most developed part of the country, the Baltic seaboard around Danzig and Elbing, was dominated, as were Courland and Livonia, by an entrenched German Lutheran bourgeoisie who were vehemently opposed to the Jews and for the most part did their best to exclude them from any role. In Danzig itself, there was a complicated residence system which allowed a small, partly transient, Jewish community to form, though there are signs that this too became larger

---

[47] Poliakov, *Banquiers juifs*, pp. 80–4, 147–56; but this too had sharply declined by 1570.

[48] Baron, *A Social and Religious History*, xvi. 207, 414.

and more settled from the late sixteenth century onwards. In the central and western parts of Poland where the towns were also fairly strong, the Jews were far more numerous than along the Baltic seaboard. Nevertheless, they were either excluded altogether from such towns as Warsaw, Toruń, and Kielce, which enjoyed the privilege *de non tolerandis Judaeis*, or else, as at Poznań and Cracow, encountered a favoured Christian merchant and artisan class which were at constant pains to restrict Jewish involvement in trade and the crafts.[49] In some parts of south-central Poland, around Nowy Sącz and Sanok, Jewish settlement remained rather sparse until well into the seventeenth century, even though at Nowy Sącz the privilege *de non tolerandis Judaeis* was cancelled at the demand of local magnates at the end of the sixteenth century.[50] It was only further east, where the country was more open as well as less developed, and where the great landed magnates wielded undisputed control, that the Jews were in a position to participate in a wide range of crafts and to dominate trade. By the 1570s, the Jews had become the preponderant bourgeoisie in the newly colonized regions, to the east of Lublin and Lvov, to almost as great an extent as were the Lutheran Germans along the Baltic seaboard.[51] The vast eastern fringe of the Polish monarchy, though much the most thinly populated part of the kingdom, was at that time of rapidly growing importance owing to the burgeoning of exports of grain and timber down the big rivers, via Danzig, Königsberg, and Elbing, to Holland and the west. Western Europe's mounting appetite for cheap Polish grain—wheat and rye sold at Danzig for a mere fraction of its cost in Amsterdam, Seville, or Venice—made the Polish landowning class rich and further galvanized the settlement of Poland's eastern territories.

To develop their immense domains in the east, what the great Polish and Lithuanian landed dynasties chiefly needed was not so much capital or modes of transportation, for those regions were marvellously well served by eastern Poland's river network, as manpower, skills, and general business expertise. Ability to manage estates and tolls and handle long-distance trade was especially in demand. Thus all the great families, the Radziwiłł, Lubormirski,

---

[49] Perles, *Juden in Posen*, pp. 15, 32–3; Bałaban, *Historja*, i. 230–7.

[50] Mahler, 'Zdziejów żydow w Nowym Sączu', pp. 3–5; Leszczyński, 'Zydzi w Choroszczy', pp. 5–9.

[51] Hence Carew's assertion 'allmost all trade is in their handes, the Poles esteeming it sordide', Carew, *Relation*, p. 68; Baron, *A Social and Religious History*, xvi. 270–8.

Ostrogski, Sobieski, Zamojski, and others adopted markedly pro-Jewish policies, the motive for which was purely and simply to stimulate the economic growth of entire regions comparable in size to many of the principalities of Germany and Italy. The Ostrogski owned dozens of small towns and hundreds of villages in the western part of the Ukraine and allocated to the Jews the role of inter-mediaries between themselves and the toiling peasantry, ignoring the objections of their Christian townsmen.[52] Much the same is true of the other leading dynasties. Jan Zamojski, Polish Chancellor in the 1580s, besides settling local Jews on his domains, arranged, through his connections at the Turkish court, for a group of Spanish and Portuguese Jews to settle in his chief town, Zamość. For, besides developing production and sales on his lands, he hoped to focus on Zamość Poland's then flourishing Levant trade, via Lvov and the Black Sea, and overland across Romania.[53]

It was this diffusion of large sections of Poland's Jewish population in small towns and villages belonging to the great magnates which opened up the possibility of major new Jewish population growth. For in those crown cities further west where Jews were permitted to live, the presence of a sizeable Christian bourgeoisie and artisan class, backed by an elaborate network of restrictions on Jewish settlement and activity, placed a tight ceiling on Jewish demographic growth. Nowhere in Poland-Lithuania was it possible, in the sixteenth or seventeenth century, for a really large concentration of Jews to accumulate, such as was then to be found in Constantinople or in Salonika, both of which by 1550 had Jewish populations exceeding 20,000 individuals.[54] Indeed, even Safed, in the Holy Land, where, in the 1560s, around half of the town's population of 10,000 was Jewish, far outstripped in the size of its Jewish community, any existing community in Poland-Lithuania. By 1570, only Poznań, Cracow, Lublin, and Lvov had Jewish populations which exceeded the 1,000 mark and none of them by very much. But in Poland-Lithuania, the proliferation of thousands of small communities on the lands of the magnates created a new framework which, during the course of the

---

[52] Kardaszewicz, *Dzieje dawniejsze miasta Ostroga*, pp. 117–19; Horn, 'Żydzi przeworscy', pp. 5–6, 10.

[53] Horn, 'Skład zawodowy', pp. 12–13.

[54] However, these two were the only communities in the Balkans of real size. Sofia, the next largest, had only some 800 Jewish families. Other substantial communities with more than 300 families were Kavalla, Trikkala, Plovdiv, Monastir (Bitola), and Adrianople; see Panova, 'On the Social Differentiation', pp. 135–36.

next century, was destined to transform the demographic balance of the Jewish world.

The key institution fixing the economic nexus between Polish Jewry and the great landowners of Poland's eastern territories was the so-called *arenda* or lease. However eager to profit from the growing demand for Poland's produce in the west, Polish nobles showed little inclination to manage their properties and business affairs themselves and from the middle of the sixteenth century onwards the leasing of their estates and properties to Jews became increasingly frequent. Jewish managers and leaseholders ran estates, mills, and distilleries and arranged the sale of produce and its transportation down river, ultimately to Danzig and other Baltic ports. Jews were thus the main agents at the eastern terminus of a vast traffic encompassing the whole of Europe, the intermediate stages of which were handled by the Lutheran burghers of the Baltic ports—and the Dutch, who supplied some 70 per cent of the shipping which transported Polish grain and timber to the west. At all stages the Jews' management of noble estates in Poland's eastern territories was closely tied to the rhythms of international trade; for just as they sold the produce of the land for shipment to Holland and beyond, it was they who distributed the western cloth, salt, wine, and luxuries, such as spices and jewellery, shipped from Amsterdam and Hamburg via Danzig and Königsberg.[55] And the Polish nobility, or at least its wealthy elite, could afford to spend lavishly on a wide variety of foreign imports.[56] While most leases were small, a few wealthy Jews were able to take on colossal packages of leases. Thus Israel of Złoczew, in 1598, took on the management of an entire region together with all its tolls, taverns, and mills from a consortium of nobles for 4,500 złoty yearly. The big lessees tended to sub-let the mills and taverns to relatives and adherents. The management of distilleries and the selling of spirits to the peasantry on noble *latifundia*, on behalf of the nobility, became one of the most typical strands of Jewish activity in Poland's eastern territories. From the time they first became numerous in the regions of Lvov, Chełm, and Sambor, to the east of Lublin, there was also a widespread Jewish involvement in crafts such as soapmaking, tanning, glaziery, and fur-processing, with relatively little resistance from Christian townsmen.[57]

[55] Morgensztern, 'Udział Zydów', pp. 18–22, 24–9; Horn, 'Zydzi przeworscy', pp. 21–2. [56] Maczak, 'Money and Society', pp. 74–7.
[57] Horn, 'Działalność gospodarcza', pp. 22–4.

The Jewish migrations of the sixteenth century, plainly, did not merely effect a transfer of population from west to east but shifted an entire people from a rigid, narrowly confined, economic framework to a much broader-based economy, encompassing a wide spectrum of crafts, trade, and management.[58] Thus in some ways the great trek to the east was a form of economic emancipation. Not only was the range of Jewish activity vastly expanded but the Jews, by bringing western techniques and knowledge to Poland and the Levant, were at once in a far more advantageous position within society than had been the case previously. Despite many tokens of submission and inferiority heaped on the Jewish communities by both the Sultan and the Polish crown, the fact is that the Jews were now a dynamic and crucially important force in the east whereas in the west they had been squeezed into the tightest and obscurest margins of economic life.

This revolution in Jewish life was accompanied by a corresponding transformation in Jewish culture. The catastrophes of the century 1470–1570, and above all the expulsion from Spain in 1492, the greatest single disaster to descend on the Jews between the destruction of the Second Temple and Hitler's holocaust, transmitted shock waves to the furthest reaches of the Jewish world. For a time uprootedness, disruption, and despair prevailed. But very soon the expulsion began to have an unforeseen creative impact which, from spreading turmoil and disintegration, generated an unprecedented extension and maturing of Jewish activity and culture. Economically, this transformation of the mid-sixteenth century meant a wider Jewish role and a much more intensive interaction with Gentile society than had been known before, at any rate outside the Iberian Peninsula. And yet, and this is the central paradox of the Jewish revolution of the sixteenth century, psychologically and culturally it meant that the Jews now turned in on themselves and became more distant from non-Jewish society. They were foreigners in Poland and Turkey in a way that they had not been in western Europe. In place of cultural fragmentation and roots in a variety of western languages, the migrations created a more unified and integrated Jewish culture but one which was increasingly remote from that of the peoples among whom Jews lived.

The immigrants into Polish and Turkish lands were westerners bringing western techniques and languages, and these they now adhered to in their changed milieu. Furthermore, such was their

[58] Nehama, *Histoire*, ii. 125; Panova, 'On the Social Differentiation', pp. 136–38.

ascendancy over the indigenous Jews of eastern Europe and the
Levant that they rapidly imposed their culture and their two
principal languages—Spanish and German—on the Greek, Arabic,
Hungarian, and Slavonic-speaking synagogues which they
encountered where they settled. In Salonika, there were by 1532
thirteen Jewish congregations in all, organized by region of origin,
including Greek-speaking, Italian and Sicilian synagogues as well as
three Portuguese. But by the late sixteenth century all the Greek and
Italian, and to some extent the Portuguese Jews, had been absorbed
into the dominant Spanish Jewish culture. Much the same was true of
Constantinople and a host of other Levantine communities,[59] including those of Bulgaria, Bosnia, and Albania. By the end of the sixteenth
century, all the 500 Jews of Rhodes, though some belonged to families
which had lived in the Near East for centuries, had adopted the
'Ladino', or Spanish, speech of the newcomers. At Jerusalem, Safed,
and the other communities of the Holy Land a parallel process,
whereby Italian, Provençal and other immigrants were absorbed into
speaking Spanish or German, was under way.

   In western Europe, the Jews had in the past spoken Italian,
Spanish, German, or French according to which country they resided
in. The same had been true of the Greek, Arabic, and Slavonic-
speaking Jews. By the late sixteenth century, however, Spanish and
Portuguese had emerged not merely as the common tongues but as
the principal spoken languages, of all the Jews of the Balkans south of
Belgrade, and of the Levant, even though no non-Jews in those
regions spoke those languages. A parallel process took place
simultaneously in eastern Europe north of Belgrade and Bucharest. It
is true that most Polish Jews spoke Yiddish (or Jewish German) even
in the fifteenth century. But there were also significant groups of old-
established Jews who spoke Slavonic languages or Crimean Tartar
while, after 1500, there was also a trickle of immigration from Italy,
Provence, and Spain. Yet, during the sixteenth century, virtually all
these elements became German-speaking even though most of the
Lutheran German population in the Polish Monarchy was concentrated in regions from which Jews were effectively excluded. The
one notable exception was the Karaites, a heretical Jewish sect which
had come into being in the eighth century and whose adherents in
Poland-Lithuania continued to speak Tartar. Apart from the use of
Hebrew terms for religious concepts and procedures, the language of

59 Nehama, *Histoire*, ii. 28–9, 39; Angel, *Jews of Rhodes*, pp. 22–3.

the Polish Jewish communities, as we encounter it in the communal records and correspondence of the time, is basically pure High German.[60] Sixteenth-century Polish Jews themselves called their language 'German'.

This dual process of Hispanicization of Levantine, and Germanization of east European Jewry, in a milieu where few others spoke Spanish or German, created a Jewish world in which the sort of intellectual interaction between Christians and Jews characteristic of Renaissance Italy, and pre-1492 Spain, became much more difficult. But, in a unique fashion, it also imparted a remarkable degree of cultural cohesion to a people scattered in small groups over vast distances in a score of lands. What is more, the two spheres, the Hispanic and the Germanic, were now brought into a high degree of interaction, the whole responding to intellectual and cultural stimuli emanating from Safed, Salonika, and Constantinople, on the one hand, and Prague, Cracow, and Lublin on the other.

Constant social, cultural, and economic contact between the Hispanic and Germanic spheres was evident during the early modern period throughout the zone of Jewish settlement from Jerusalem to Lithuania. On one level, the linguistic divide, and the small but significant differences in ritual as between Sephardic and Ashkenazic usage, assured the perpetuation of two distinct Jewish cultures. Where both groups lived side by side, as in many places in the Balkans and Near East, separate congregations and avoidance of intermarriage were the rule. Yet at a deeper level the two spheres developed intellectually and spiritually largely as one, at any rate in the period 1550 to 1750, the age of maximum cohesion in the history of Jewish culture.

In the long run, the transplanting of Sephardi and Ashkenazi Jewish life from the west to eastern Europe and the Levant undoubtedly strengthened the position of the Jews in Europe as a whole, despite the apparent collapse of Jewish life west of Poland. And, in the long run, it was the demographic implications of Jewish settlement in the eastern territories of Poland which mattered most. But, regarding the reversal of the trend towards exclusion and collapse in the west— and this reversal definitely took place in the period 1570–1600—what mattered most was the swift rise of the Spanish exiles to commercial preponderance in the Balkans. Before 1492, non-Jews, particularly Greeks, Ragusans, and Armenians, had dominated exchange

[60] Bałaban, 'Krakauer Judengemeinde-Ordnung', pp. 300–2.

between Constantinople and the Dalmatian coast whilst most trade between the Balkans and Italy had passed in Venetian ships. But, during the first half of the sixteenth century, Iberian Jews fanning out from Salonika and Constantinople rapidly took over all the internal trade routes within the Balkans.[61] By 1550, the buying up of wool, silk, and cotton in Greece, Bulgaria, Serbia, and Bosnia was mainly a Jewish activity, as was the distribution of cloth irrespective of whether it was Venetian or locally produced by the flourishing Sephardi woollen-cloth industry of Salonika. By the 1540s, Spanish Jews had largely ejected the Ragusans from the trade centres of Belgrade and Sarajevo and, working with Ashkenazi immigrants to Czernowitz and Jassy, dominated the overland route between the eastern Balkans and Poland across Romania. These changes, in turn, placed Balkan Sephardi Jewry in a strong position to control trade on the Dalmatian coast and to influence the flow of traffic between the Balkans and Italy. As a prelude to the imminent reversal of policy toward the Jews in Italy, the Dalmatian Republic of Ragusa (Dubrovnik), beaten out of its inland markets, dropped its traditional policy of debarring Jews from settling in the town as from 1538. From this point on, a large part of Ragusa's own trade was handled by Spanish Jews. In 1546, the city authorities organized the Spanish and Portuguese immigrants into an autonomous ghetto which was later enlarged, in 1571.

[61] Emmanuel, *Hist. Israélites de Salonique*, pp. 254–61; Gold, *Gesch. Juden in der Bukowina*, i. 3–4, 7; Paci, '*Scala' di Spalato*, pp. 33–5.

II

Turning-Point (1570–1600)

THE tentative readmission of Jewry into western and central Europe from the 1570s onwards signalled a reversal of trends which had previously prevailed everywhere west of Poland. And this post-1570 shift is, without doubt, a historical phenomenon of the first significance. In several ways it marks the real beginning of modern Jewish history. For, in a matter of a few years, the whole hitherto fixed pattern of restricted interaction between western Christendom and the Jews was transformed in a way which continued to shape subsequent development for some two centuries. The transformation in European Jewry's status was rapid, dramatic, and profound, affecting and affected by much else that was then in flux, for at bottom Jewish readmission was merely a symptom of the more general revolution which convulsed and renewed western life and thought at the close of the sixteenth century. Nor did this change in Jewish status occur first in any one place and then spread. On the contrary, it is remarkable that the change of policy toward the Jews is discernible at pretty much the same moment in the Czech lands, Italy, Germany, France, and the Netherlands.

Not infrequently intellectual historians date the first stirrings of modern attitudes and modes of thought, of the 'philosophic spirit' as the seventeenth century called it, to the years around, or just before, 1600—and with good reason. Of course, in their way, the Reformation and Counter-Reformation had already sent vast, unsettling waves and counterwaves rampaging in all directions. The whole sixteenth century was an age of turmoil. But, through the period down to 1570, western culture, whatever the theological rift and ensuing disputes, always remained securely rooted in its Christian allegiance and outlook. Pre-1570 western Europe was a Christian world. All its more articulate minds were filled with a total and sufficient sense of possessing truth and the true explanation of things. Compared with this underlying certainty, the implacable quarrel between Catholic, Lutheran, and Calvinist was but a surface froth which contemporaries confidently imagined would soon cease with the overwhelming and definitive triumph of one side or another. This does not mean that earlier giants of the intellect such as Pico, Erasmus, and Reuchlin did not contribute substantially to the break-up of traditional modes of thought, or were not profoundly innovative in their rejection of scholasticism, and in immersing themselves in Classical and Hebrew studies. But, to all appearances, their researches did not weaken but, on the contrary, reinforced western Europe's adherence to Christianity. If Erasmus was apprehensive that research into Hebrew literature could undermine this conscious unity of outlook, none of the great Christian Hebraists of the age ever doubted that Jewish interpretations were fundamentally perverse and misconceived.

During the final third of the sixteenth century, though, both Reformation and Counter-Reformation lost their former momentum and the hitherto universal Christian foundations of western culture began to crack and contract. It was now that Christianity embarked on that age-long retreat which has since become its familiar role in western culture—no longer the all-embracing, universal whole but what, to all appearances, has been a shrinking force compelled to compete with a host of rival outlooks and attitudes and, in particular, a rising tide of doubt, deism, and atheism. But what lay behind so basic a shift and why should it have come so suddenly rather than imperceptibly over a much longer span? Intellectually, this most fundamental of all modern revolutions stemmed from the erosion of confidence in Christian teaching, that upsurge of radical scepticism which began to permeate western thought in the age of Montaigne, Bodin, Lipsius, and Bacon. Suddenly, in the 1570s, Europe's fore-most thinkers were enveloped in the seemingly infinite difficulty of accepting received 'truths' handed down from the past and of ascertaining truth with the aid of existing scholarship and learning. Thinkers began to wrestle feverishly with the question of how one is to attain what Bacon termed 'good and sound knowledge' as distinct from what society had hitherto accepted as being knowledge. Montaigne's great philosophical essay, the *Apologie de Raimond Sebond*, written in 1575–6, mirrors the collapse of Europe's intellectual world into a chaos of doubt infused with the sense of what he called the 'faiblesse de notre jugement'.[1] A lesser figure, but symptomatic of his time, was Francisco Sanches (1552–1623), a Portuguese New Christian who became a philosophy lecturer at the University of

[1] Popkin, *History of Scepticism*, pp. 38–41, 44–57.

Toulouse, and who, in 1576, compiled his *Quod nihil scitur*, rejecting all previous systems and theories of knowledge. Most far-reaching and radical of all, Jean Bodin set out on a spiritual quest which eventually led to total divorce from Christian belief and his adherence to what has been termed a 'non-ritual Judaism'. Bodin's intellectual odyssey culminated in 1593 when he wrote his *Colloquium Heptaplomeres*, a powerful dialogue about religion which is perhaps the first outright rejection of Christianity composed in the early modern west.[2]

But the upsurge of radical scepticism was an intellectual process, and such processes, history teaches, tend to derive from deep-seated shifts in life and experience. What shook confidence in past belief so severely, as the literature of the time abundantly documents, was the unbreakable deadlock into which the Wars of Religion in France and the Low Countries, indeed on the whole continent, had now lapsed. There was no clear decision anywhere. In France, the Huguenots did not triumph but they did force a far-reaching compromise, the Edict of Nantes, which ensured the public practice of Calvinism in large parts of the country. In the Netherlands, Protestant and Catholic had fought each other to a standstill which left the one entrenched in the north and the other in the south. And just as France and the Low Countries were now irretrievably sunk in an exhausting and exhausted stalemate, so equally were Germany, Switzerland, Bohemia-Moravia, and Poland. Indeed, by the 1570s, religious deadlock was the rule practically everywhere north of the Alps and Pyrenees. And it was precisely this lack of a decision and the resulting proliferation of new sects and theologies which, as Bacon put it, 'move derision in worldlings and depraved politics who are apt to contemn holy things'. The profound sense of shook caused by this totally new and unsettling predicament also inspired revulsion, fear, and, in some, such as Giordano Bruno and not a few other esoteric intellects of the late sixteenth century, a plunge from Christianity into visions of a purer, 'hermetic' religious tradition which would somehow supersede, even eventually conjure away the wretchedness, misery, and inhumanity associated with Christian strife.[3] But Bruno, like Bodin and Lipsius, was a critic of his times, not just a dreamer of some unrealizable 'Egyptian' religion, and he knew that, in part, the solution he so earnestly hoped for could come about only with the aid

[2] Bodin, *Colloque*, pp. 101–39; Baxter, 'Jean Bodin's Daemon', pp. 7–17; Roellenbleck, *Offenbarung*, pp. 146–8, 152–3.
[3] Yates, *Giordano Bruno*, pp. 211–12, 225, 286.

of such *politique* practitioners of statecraft as Henri IV of France
(whom he much admired) and radically new political solutions.

Confronted by the unprecedented and shocking dilemma of
irresolvable religious deadlock, momentous and far-reaching intellectual adjustments were inevitable. In France and the Netherlands
especially, key thinkers, most notably Bodin and Lipsius, now developed an entirely new vision of politics directed at achieving the
restored wholeness, stability, and good of society, through the power
of the state, rather than the fulfilment of the aspirations of churchmen.[4] They preached a new message, a philosophy of worldly action
orientated to the here and now. And just as these scholars built their
thought on an essentially non-Christian basis, so also key political
leaders and princes chose, or were forced, to adopt policies which cut
clear across the claims of church and faith. These *politique* leaders,
such as Henri IV, William of Orange, and Maximilian II of Austria,
created a statecraft which was the political counterpart of the new
radical scepticism of the philosophers. Politicians and thinkers alike
were seeking an escape from the relentless antagonism of rival
theologies, dissociating themselves in the process from the demands
of the churches. Thus, the political turmoil, and the strong undercurrents of scepticism, deism, and atheism which arose at this time, fed
on and nourished each other. And in this radically changed milieu, it
was no longer possible, as Bodin's ideas so strikingly illustrate, to
assume as a matter of course that Jewish interpretations were
groundless.

The first signs of a general trend towards the readmission of
the Jews came just before 1570 under the aegis of the Emperor
Maximilian II (1564–76). The middle years of the sixteenth century,
disastrous for the Jews of the Empire as a whole, had brought
particular disruption to Jewish life in Bohemia. Indeed, Maximilian's
father Ferdinand I, in contrast to Charles V, had pursued an actively
anti-Jewish policy in the Czech lands, where, as elsewhere, a surge of
anti-Semitic feeling accompanied the spread of Protestantism. In
1541, a wave of anti-Jewish agitation culminated in major pogroms in
Raudnitz, Saaz, and elsewhere, and in the expulsion of the Jews from
all the crown cities of Bohemia except for Prague.[5] Subsequently, in
1557, on a request from the Prague city council for the expulsion of the
Jews from that city too, Ferdinand determined on a final eviction of

---

[4] Skinner, *Foundations*, i. 253–4; Oestreich, *Neostoicism*, pp. 43–56.
[5] Bondy and Dworsky, *Gesch. Juden in Böhmen*, i. 337–8.

the Jews from Bohemia altogether, though not from Moravia, where there was stronger pressure from the nobles to retain them and where the voice of the towns was weaker. Ferninand duly published his decree of expulsion and most of the Jews departed, but the measure was not fully enforced and a remnant in Prague solicited and obtained repeated extensions of permission to delay their departure, to settle debts and other matters. So it was that when Maximilian became Emperor, in 1564, Jewish life in Bohemia was at a nadir but not wholly extinguished. Radically diverging, as he did in most things, from his father's policy the new Emperor cancelled the expulsion from Bohemia and granted permission for the few Jews still in Prague to stay indefinitely.[6] Their position was now more secure. But, as late as 1570, there were still only around 413 families, some 2,000 Jews, in the entire realm of Bohemia.

Maximilian II, outwardly a Catholic ruler, is known to have nurtured strong Protestant leanings during his youth and, the indications are, was throughout his life torn within by the relentless religious conflicts and doubts of his time.[7] Evidently, he also evinced a certain sympathy for, and interest in, the Jews, which contrasted as sharply with the attitudes of his father and his Spanish uncle, Philip II, as did his lack of religious militancy. The Prague Jewish chronicler David Gans (1541–1613) wrote of the 'love' that Maximilian showed the Jews and describes a famous occasion, in 1571, when the Emperor visisted the Prague Jewish quarter (*Judenstadt*) as a mark of favour, accompanied by the Empress and his whole court.[8] However, it was Maximilian's successor Rudolph II (1576–1612) who, in the 1570s, created the political and legal framework which made possible the rapid expansion of Jewish life and activity in Bohemia. In February 1577, Rudolph issued a charter to Bohemian Jewry, assigning major new privileges and promising that they would never again be expelled from Prague or from the realm as a whole—though they remained excluded from the other crown cities.[9] Under the 1577 charter, there ensued a rapid growth in Bohemian Jewry, both in Prague and in the villages and small towns outside the lesser crown cities. It was also during Rudolph's reign that Jewish communities were reconstituted in Vienna and at Innsbruck. These remained small, however,

---

[6] Ibid. i. 418–22, 428–9, 438–9.
[7] Evans, *Making of the Habsburg Monarchy*, pp. 19–20.
[8] Gans, *Zemach David*, p. 118; Neher, *David Gans*, pp. 37, 87.
[9] Bondy and Dworsky, *Gesch. Juden in Böhmen*, ii. 554–5.

compared with the community in Prague, which grew from a few dozen, in 1564, to over 3,000 Jews by 1600. This represents the first important build-up of Jewish population west of Poland since the thirteenth century and there can be no doubt that it marks the beginning of the reversal of the Jewish migration from west to east, for many of the immigrants to Prague came from Poland or were German exiles who came there via Poland.

Rudolph's court at Prague was a key cultural manifestation of the late sixteenth century. Its flavour differed markedly from the Catholic and Protestant militancy which reigned officially elsewhere. And this could hardly have been otherwise given the ostensible Catholicism of the court surrounded by a then dominant Protestantism, not only in Bohemia and Moravia but in the towns of Austria. The tolerant, cosmopolitan atmosphere, strongly influenced intellectually by the Neostoicism of the Netherlands scholar Lipsius, arose from an inescapable need to transcend the Catholic–Protestant conflict. Yet, beyond this, Rudolph, like Maximilian, showed an unmistakable partiality for the Jews and their culture. This Emperor, who so immeasurably strengthened the position of the Jews in Czech lands, on a famous occasion requested an interview with the pre-eminent intellectual figure of Prague Jewry, Rabbi Judah Loew, a personage shrouded in legend and known in Jewish tradition as the Maharal. This interview took place at the Hradschin palace, in Prague, on 16 February 1592, where these two remarkable personalities doubtless indulged their common preoccupation with mystical prophecy and matters esoteric.[10]

Rudolph's concessions to the Jews of Prague included the right, previously denied them, to engage in a range of crafts, including the working of jewellery, gold, and silver. It is this curtailing of the monopoly of the Christian guilds, this partial economic emancipation, which made possible the astounding growth of Prague Jewry, within three or four decades, to become the largest urban Jewry in Christendom—that is, outside Ottoman territory—after Rome. In addition to the old-style money-lenders, pawnbrokers, and pedlars, there now arose in Prague groups of Jewish artisans and shopkeepers as well as numerous merchants. This sudden expansion in activity in turn made possible the emergence of the 'Court Jew', the large-scale Jewish merchant-financier with court connections, a type which was to become a key feature of central European life in the century 1650–

[10] Sherwin, *Mystical Theology*, pp. 15–16.

1750. The first of these personages in the Habsburg lands was Markus
Meysl of Prague (1528–1601) who, in 1593, in recognition of his
financial services to the crown, received unprecedented privileges
placing him directly under the Emperor's protection. Meysl in fact
enjoyed the legal status, if not the title, of a noble. At his death, he
bequeathed over 500,000 florins, without counting numerous bene-
factions made during his life.[11] In Prague, he supported Jewish
scholars, repaved the *Judenstadt* at his own expense, and built a
hospital for the Jewish sick. With the Emperor's permission he also
built a handsome new synagogue, known as the 'Meysl shul' which
survives to this day. He is also known to have donated money, Torah-
scrolls, and other religious items to the Jews of Jerusalem and various
Polish communities with which he had links.

In Germany, the revival of Jewish life begins at the same time as in
Bohemia and Austria, in the 1570s. In this period, Frankfurt Jewry
outstripped any single community in Poland-Lithuania, and this fact
is particularly striking when we observe that in 1500 there were a
mere 130 Jews in the city.[12] During the period of expulsions from
other parts of Germany, the Frankfurt city council would allow only a
very modest increase in the size of Frankfurt's Jewish population. In
1542, there was still a total of only 419 souls in the Frankfurt ghetto. It
was, in fact, only in the 1570s that this community began to grow
rapidly out of all proportion to the overall expansion of the city.[13] As
in Prague, this acceleration was caused by a sudden relaxation of
previous restrictions leading to a dramatic broadening in the scope of
Jewish economic activity, particularly in general commerce. By 1613,
Frankfurt Jewry numbered nearly 3,000 out of the city's total population of 20,000, the number of Jews being some six times the figure for
1550. Historians of Frankfurt traditionally link this spurt in Jewish
activity with the setback to the rest of the city's economy which arose
from feuding between the Lutheran majority and the large groups of
Dutch and Flemish Calvinists who arrived in the 1560s and 1570s.
The friction between Lutherans and Calvinists in Frankfurt erupted
in crisis in the years 1593–1607 when numerous Netherlanders were
forced out of the city. The Jews then supposedly stepped into the gap.
Yet the fact is that the expansion of Jewish activity in Frankfurt must

[11] Stein, *Juden in Böhmen*, pp. 62–8; Bondy and Dworsky, *Gesch. Juden in Böhmen*, ii.
657, 670–1, 757.
[12] Kracauer, *Juden in Frankfurt*, i. 311.
[13] Ibid., i. 312, 320–3; Bothe, *Beiträge*, pp. 60–73; Dietz, *Stammbuch*, p. 433.

have begun in the 1570s, when the rise in the city's Jewish population began to accelerate, and that is precisely when the influx of Calvinists bringing new wealth and trade was at its height. It would seem, therefore, that it was the arrival of the Netherlanders which gave the Jews their chance, by breaking up the traditional guild-structure, enabling Jews, for instance, to participate in the distribution of imports from the Low Countries through South Germany.

Meanwhile, in the German ecclesiastical states, there ensued an equally radical change. Down to around 1570, the often vociferously Lutheran towns of the ecclesiastical principalities had generally succeeded in throwing their prelate-princes onto the defensive. Once Protestant momentum began to flag, though, the prince-bishops slowly regained the initiative and began to assert themselves once more. Consequently, the position of the Jews in such bishoprics as Mainz, Speyer, Minden, Paderborn, and Strasbourg suddenly improved markedly.[14] Here and there, where Jews had been expelled altogether during (or before) the Reformation, they were now readmitted, on the initiative of ecclesiastical princes and invariably over strong objections from the local citizenry. Thus, the Jews were recalled to the bishopric of Hildesheim in 1577, to the abbey-principality of Essen in 1578, and slightly later, to the bishopric of Halberstadt. The tussle between the prince-bishop and town of Hildesheim over the readmission of the Jews dragged on for years, the case ultimately coming before the Emperor who, predictably, found in favour of the bishop and the Jews.[15] By 1600, when there were thirty Jewish families living in the town, and a dozen more in the surrounding countryside, Hildesheim was already one of the principal Jewish communities of North Germany. The same princely prelate, Ernst, who brought back the Jews to Hildesheim, later became Archbishop-Elector of Cologne, where he again combined an uncompromising anti-Lutheranism with notable favours to the Jews, enabling them to resettle, in the 1580s, in the towns of Hallenberg, Geseke, Werl and Rüthen.[16]

Among the most important of the new Jewish communities in Germany was that of Fürth, a small town close to Nuremberg. Nuremberg, a solidly Lutheran city, was one of the principal

[14] Salfeld, *Bilder*, pp. 35–6; Arnold, *Juden in der Pfalz*, p. 23; Krieg, 'Juden in der Stadt Minden', p. 116.
[15] Rexhausen, *Rechtliche und wirtschaftliche Lage*, pp. 50–5.
[16] Holthausen, 'Juden im kurkölnischen Herzogtum', pp. 55–6, 66.

manufacturing, trading, and banking cities of central Europe, lying
astride the main overland routes between North Germany and
Venice. There were several small Jewish communities scattered
around the city outside its jurisdiction. Fürth came under the joint
jurisdiction of the Bishop of Bamberg and Margrave of Ansbach, both
of whom now took to encouraging Jewish settlement as a method of
diverting part of Nuremberg's business onto their own territory. By
1582 there were 200 Jews in Fürth and the number grew rapidly in
subsequent decades. Before 1600 Fürth had emerged as the pre-
eminent Jewish community located on the main routes linking
Frankfurt with Prague and with Vienna.

Meanwhile, along the North German coast, there had never been a
Jewish presence of any significance during the Middle Ages, owing
largely to the exclusionist attitude of the Hansa which controlled
trade in the region; what communities had existed, as in East
Friesland, had disappeared—like medieval Netherlands Jewry—
during the course of the fifteenth century. But now, in the 1570s and
1580s, a remarkable change set in. The Count of East Friesland took
to encouraging Jewish settlement at Emden and Aurich.[17] Very likely
his initiative was linked to the departure from the region at that time
of Dutch refugees who had fled there during Alva's regime in the
Netherlands and who now drifted back, as the revolt against Spain
was consolidated, taking capital and trade with them. Apparently,
most of the Jewish immigrants into late sixteenth century East
Friesland came from ecclesiastical states in Westphalia. At the same
moment, other groups of Jews, likewise chiefly from Westphalia,
began percolating into the environs of Hamburg, though definitely
not into the city itself. Most notably, Count Adolf XII of Holstein-
Schauenburg allowed a group to settle in his port of Altona, outside
Hamburg, in 1584.[18] He also granted them land for a cemetery at
nearby Ottensen. The city of Hamburg had never before admitted
Jews but, in the 1590s, while still excluding German Jews, allowed a
dozen Portuguese refugee families, whom the city council knew to be
crypto-Jews, to settle within the city limits and engage in trade.[19] This
was the origin of what, before long, was to develop into the second
most important Sephardi community in northern Europe (until

---

[17] Gans, *Zemach David*, p. 125; Anklam, *Judengemeinde in Aurich*, p. 5.
[18] Grunwald, *Hamburgs deutsche Juden*, pp. 6–7; Marwedel, *Privilegien der Juden in
Altona*, pp. 69, 71, 90.
[19] Feilchenfeld, 'Portugiesengemeinde in Hamburg', pp. 200–1.

London overtook it in the eighteenth century) after that of Amsterdam. Meanwhile the Count of Wandsbek invited a group of Jews to settle in his township of that name, on the east side of Hamburg, around 1600. To some extent, notably at Altona, the admission of the Jews would seem to be part and parcel of a general liberalization in the sphere of religion, designed to attract a variety of immigrants and thereby to boost the local economy. Thus religious freedom was granted to Catholics in Altona, in 1591, and to Calvinists and Mennonites in 1601. On the other hand, at Stade, in the archbishopric of Bremen, the town council began to negotiate first, in 1611, with a group of Portuguese Jews, and then, in 1613, with a group of German Jews, agreeing to Jewish admission only after a group of Walloon Calvinists and the English Merchant Adventurers had damaged the local economy by departing.[20]

The general revival of German Jewish life at the end of the sixteenth century is clearly reflected in the resolutions of the general synod of German Jewry convened in 1582. This assembly renewed several forms and procedures which had lapsed since the fourteenth century, restoring a comprehensive judicial and fiscal machinery encompassing all the Jews of Germany. This convention stipulated five principal rabbinic courts, namely those of Frankfurt, Worms, Fulda, Friedberg and Günzburg, of which only one, that of Frankfurt, was located in a major city, two—those of Worms and Fulda—being under ecclesiastical jurisdiction, one—Günzburg, a small town near Ulm—being territory of the Emperor and the fifth—Friedberg—coming under a lesser secular lord. Additionally, a handful of other major German Jewish communities, or at any rate major by the standards of the time in Germany from which so many Jewish communities had been eliminated over the previous century, were recognized as tax-collecting centres subordinate to the five leading communities. These included Wallerstein, a village outside Nördlingen, and Schnaittach, outside Nuremberg, a largely Jewish village which at that date still retained precedence over Fürth. Friedberg was acknowledged as head of the Jewish communities of Hesse. Frankfurt enjoyed much the widest jurisdiction, being made responsible for Jewries as far afield as those of Münster, Paderborn, and East Friesland.

In Italy, as in Germany, Bohemia, and the Netherlands, the decisive turning-point comes in the 1570s. But in Italy unmistakable

[20] Asaria, *Juden in Niedersachsen*, pp. 180–1.

signs of a dawning mercantilist attitude toward the Jews had appeared sporadically in the earlier sixteenth century even before the Counter-Reformation took hold. From 1553 for roughly twenty years, the Counter-Reformation, then at its height, effectively interrupted, indeed largely nullified the effects of the earlier trend. But then the process resumed, tentatively at first, in the early 1570s. What is more this Italian mercantilist policy toward the Jews resumed along much the same lines as it had proceeded on in the quarter of a century before 1553. In the years around 1530, it was the increasing ascendancy of Sephardi Jews in Balkan commerce which had first induced Italian princes to disregard local vested interests and privileges and grant generous concessions to such Jews who had connections with the Ottoman empire, that is in the main to Spanish and Portuguese exiles drifting into Italy from the Ottoman empire. It was these 'Levantines' whom the Duke of Ferrara principally had in mind when issuing his charter of 1538. And it was this Ferrarese charter, seemingly, which finally persuaded the Venetian Senate which, in the past, had always been resolutely opposed to Jewish participation in Venice's trade, to grant 'Levantine' Jews, that is Jews who were Turkish subjects (albeit usually Spanish-speaking), permission to sojourn for periods as transients, supposedly without their families, alongside the small 'German' Jewish community already inhabiting the ghetto. After prolonged debate the Venetian government took this momentous step, in 1541, expressly because the 'commerce of Upper and Lower Romania [i.e. the whole Balkans] was being diverted from this city, being now principally in the hands of Levantine Jews'.[21] A few years later in 1547, and again in 1553, just before the decision was taken to switch over to militantly anti-Jewish policies, the Papacy offered liberal terms to Balkan Jews prepared to settle in the papal Adriatic port of Ancona. Again, it was transparently obvious that the measure was taken in response to the recent initiatives of Ferrara and Venice. Indeed, so it seemed, no Italian ruler with an eye on the Levant traffic could afford to hold back from the scramble to attract Levantine Jews and, in 1551, the Grand Duke of Tuscany followed suit, issuing fulsome charters which attracted groups of Sephardi merchants from the Balkans to Pisa from where they traded with the Dalmatian emporia using the overland routes to Ancona and Pesaro.[22] This is why in the late sixteenth and early seventeenth century, the main

[21] ASV CSM, 1st ser., cxxxvii, fos. 135ᵛ–36 and cxliii, fos. 20ᵛ–21.
[22] Cassuto, *Ebrei a Firenze*, pp. 89–90, 179.

synagogue in Pisa was known as the *sinagoga levantina* and the Jews who tended it the *nazione ebrea levantina di Pisa*. The Duke of Urbino also invited in Balkan Jews. The ruling groups at Genoa, by contrast, concentrating increasingly in this period on their growing trade with Spain and the west, and having largely discarded their old ambitions in the Levant, expelled all Jews first from the city, in 1550, and then, in 1567, from the rest of their territory.

But considerable though the appeal of Balkan Jewry and its Levant trade was, it could not and did not withstand the impact of the Counter-Reformation once the Papacy embarked in earnest on its anti-Jewish drive. A good many Levantine Jews as well as Marranos departed Ancona in 1554–5 and the city's trade slumped.[23] Once the Papacy was geared to answer the challenge of Protestantism it was clear that local commercial interests would have to be sacrificed to the wider requirements of Church and doctrine. And this reaction in the Papal States was soon reflected elsewhere, first in Urbino, then Tuscany, and then Venice. In March 1570, on the verge of war with the Sultan, the Venetian government resolved to detain all 'Turks, Levantine Jews, and other Turkish subjects and their goods' anywhere on Venetian territory and many Jews fled.[24] At Venice, the wave of anti-Jewish feeling culminated amid the euphoria following the victory of Lepanto over the Turks in the Senate's decision of 18 December 1571 to expel all Jews, Sephardi, and Ashkenazi, from the city of Venice and her Adriatic islands.[25] And while this drastic measure was not actually enforced it is probable that some more Jews did leave.

It was only when the Turkish war ended that the Italian states, despite papal pressure to the contrary, resumed the courting of Levantine Jewry and this time with more widespread and permanent results. On this occasion, the initiative was taken by Duke Emmanuel Philibert of Savoy, the first Italian prince to adopt a generally, if not altogether consistently pro-Jewish policy. Earlier, in 1560–1, this prince had decided to follow the example of his Genoese neighbours and expel the Jews entirely from his territory. A large part of Piedmontese Jewry did in fact leave. In 1565, however, the Duke changed his mind and invited them back. More controversially, in 1569–70, he invited some of the refugees from the Papal States,

---

[23] Nehama, *Histoire*, iii. 57–8.
[24] Ravid, 'Socioeconomic Background', pp. 41–2, 47.
[25] Ibid., Kaufmann, 'Contributions', pp. 228–30.

including émigrés from Avignon, to settle on his lands. Then, in 1572, after negotiations with Jewish leaders, the Duke issued a sensational charter inviting both Levantine Jews and former Marranos to come to his port at Nice, both to develop Levant trade and to set up textile factories, under guaranteed protection against the papal Inquisition.[26] This was an open challenge to the Papacy and Spain, both of which now applied pressure on Turin to retract. Under protest, and with repeated appeals to the Pope to stop Venice playing host to Marranos and assigning privileges to Levantine Jews, the Duke gave way. In 1574, his recent guarantees to the Jews were withdrawn. However, he did take in many of the 900 Jews expelled from the Milanese in 1597, and the main communities in the Savoyard state— Turin, Vercelli, Asti, Acqui, Moncalvo, Nice, and later Saluzzo— expanded appreciably during the last third of the sixteenth century.

Venice meanwhile had not only allowed the 1571 expulsion to lapse but began to reverse its stance on the Jews even before peace was signed with the Sultan in 1574. It seems that Levantine Jews were being encouraged to resettle in the city as from 1573. Moreover, this time, unlike before, Marranos were also welcome and were, it would seem, entering Venice unimpeded from 1573-4 onwards. When, in 1581, the new duke of Ferrara yielded to papal pressure and permitted the arrest of Portuguese suspected of having defected from Christianity to Judaism, the bulk of the Ferrarese Marranos migrated to Venice, having probably ascertained beforehand that they would be afforded protection.[27] Venice, unlike Ferrara and Savoy, was now openly defying papal Jewry policy, a point underlined by the resumption, after a gap of nearly thirty years, of the printing of Jewish books in Spanish, at Venice, in the early 1580s. Then, in 1589, the Senate went a step further, issuing a new charter granting full rights of residence to both 'Levantine' and 'Ponentine' (western) Jews, the latter term being a euphemism for 'Marranos'. The 1589 charter was an act of defiant *raison d'État* decided on in the economic interest of the Republic as a whole. It provided the basis for the subsequent rapid increase in the Jewish population of Venice, signifying the final abandonment of Venice's age-old hostility toward the Jews.

As in Savoy, Jewish spokesmen played a prominent part in the reversal of policy at Venice. The key figure was an enterprising

---

[26] Foa, *Politica economica*, pp. 15-18; Beinart, 'Venuta degli ebrei', pp. 110-19; Pullan, *Jews of Europe*, pp. 182-3.

[27] Roth, 'Marranes à Venise', p. 205; Zorattini, *Processi*, pp. 32-5.

Dalmatian Spaniard named Daniel Rodriguez who, it seems, first visited Venice in 1563 on a mission to buy cloth for the Bosnian market. His connections with the Turkish governor of Bosnia, and experience of the traffic in Venetian wares in the Balkans, enabled him to address the Venetian Senate with some authority. Beginning in 1573, he submitted a series of petitions, arguing that Venice could restore, indeed tighten, her grip over Balkan trade, by linking the internal land-routes of the Balkans (dominated by Jews) with Venice by developing an entrepôt on the Dalmatian coast close to Venice. Though, as yet, there was little traffic there in the 1570s, he recommended the port of Split.[28] One need only recall for how long, and how completely, fleets of Venetian vessels had dominated the sea lanes to Constantinople and the Black Sea, as well as to Cyprus, Crete, and Egypt, to realize how revolutionary a departure for Venice such a scheme implied. In the past, Venice's Balkan trade, chiefly in the hands of her ruling oligarchy, had passed by sea around the Peloponnese, in her ships. To re-route her trade with Constantinople and Salonika via Split and Sarajevo, as Rodriguez was proposing, was to turn the Serenissima's age-old commercial strategy upside down, and we can well imagine how long and agonizing were the deliberations devoted to Rodriguez's proposals.[29] But in the end it was felt that the Republic had no choice. By this date foreign, and especially English, shipping was rapidly displacing Venetian vessels from the sea lanes of the eastern Mediterranean. Increasingly, Venice's ruling oligarchy were pulling their capital out of trade. If Venice did not accommodate Balkan Jewry, then other Italian states would—and at her expense.

The 1589 charter, and the adoption of Rodriguez's schemes for an entrepôt at Split, did indeed bring about the change in the structure of Venice's Balkan trade that he advocated, except that Valona, on the Albanian coast, far to the south of Split, on the overland route to Salonika, developed into a scarcely less important Dalmatian depot for Venice's re-routed Balkan trade. As early as the 1590s, most Venetian exports to the Balkans and Black Sea passed via Split and Valona, being transported overland and distributed mainly by Jews.[30] Much of the shipping of goods to and from the Dalmatian

[28] ASV CSM 1st ser., cxxxvii, fos. 73ᵛ, 96ᵛ–97, 105–6, 188ᵛ–19.

[29] Luzzatto, *Discorso*, pp. 31–41; Novak, *Židovi u Splitu*, pp. 13–18; Ravid, *Economics and Toleration*, pp. 30–2.

[30] Tenenti, *Naufrages*, pp. 15, 88, 199, 243; Blumenkranz, 'Commerce maritime', pp. 144–51; Paci, *'Scala' di Spalato*, pp. 103–10.

depots from Venice remained in Christian hands, though the
Sephardi Jews who now settled in Venice itself did capture a sizeable
share, amounting perhaps to twenty or thirty per cent. At the same
time, Jews now dominated Venice's trade with her island colonies of
Corfu and Zante. In contrast, Venice's sea-borne commerce with
Egypt and Syria remained almost entirely in Christian hands. Swol-
len by the influx of 'Levantines' and 'Ponentines', the number of Jews
in the Venetian ghetto rose from 900 in 1552, to 1,694 in 1586, and at
least 2,500 by 1600. By 1590, Marrano emigrants from Portugal had
virtually ceased migrating to Salonika and other Ottoman ports.[31]
Most now settled in Venice or Tuscany. Rodriguez, who played a
prominent role in the Venetian–Turkish negotiations and agreement
over the Dalmatian depots, and who also negotiated the release of
some Venetian prisoners from the Uskoks, was publicly proclaimed
'inventor' of the Split entrepôt and appointed head of the Jewish
community which now took root there. Many of the Jewish merchants
who settled in Split and Valona around 1590 moved from Ragusa,
where traffic passing between Florence and the Balkans, via Ancona
and Pesaro, now slumped.

Outdone by Venice in the matter of the Dalmatian depots, the
Grand Duke of Tuscany answered with a dramatic liberalization of
his own Jewish policy. Already, in the 1580s, the Grand Duke had
abandoned his former subservience to Rome in the matter of the
Marranos and had began to encourage refugees from Portugal to
settle in Pisa, condoning their defection from Christianity to Judaism.
Then, in response to the Venetian charter of 1589, Ferdinand I issued
a charter for his new port at Livorno, the so-called 'Livornina' of
1593, a document guaranteeing both 'Levantine' and 'Ponentine'
Jews who settled there unprecedented freedoms and privileges
besides full protection from pursuit by papal Inquisitors.[32] Thus, in
contrast to the Jews of Venice and Florence, those of Pisa and Livorno
were not obliged to live in ghettos and evaded most of the irksome
restrictions which the Counter-Reformation had imposed on the
majority of Italian Jewry.

Nor was the re-expansion of Jewish life in Italy at the end of the
sixteenth century by any means confined to Savoy, Venice, and
Tuscany. There was, almost certainly, some growth in Jewish numbers at Padua, Verona, and other centres in the Veneto and in Friuli,

[31] Nehama, *Histoire*, iii. 57–8.
[32] Laras, 'Delatore', pp. 66–7; Toaff, 'Cenni storici', pp. 356–9.

and probably also at Ferrara. In the case of the duchy of Mantua there was a particularly dramatic increase in Jewish numbers. Back in 1500, Mantuan Jewry had still been very small, numbering a mere 200 souls. But like the dukes of Ferrara and Savoy (and unlike those of Tuscany and Urbino), the duke of Mantua had permitted the Jewish exiles from papal territory to settle in his domain and later also received refugees from Milan. By 1587, Mantuan Jewry had increased to 960 souls. But the most emphatic increase came during the next two decades, the number of Jews in Mantua rising to a high point of 2,325 by 1610, which means that Mantua at that time had one of the four or five largest Jewries in the Christian West.[33] There were also another 700 Jews in the Montovano, outside the city, making a grand total of over 3,000. Thus we see that the period of fastest increase in the numbers of Mantuan Jewry, which must have been largely due to immigration, coincided with an acceleration of Jewish immigration into Venice, Savoy, and Tuscany.

The Netherlands, in contrast to Italy, had been effectively cleared of Jews by 1549 except for a rump of Marranos who were allowed to remain in Antwerp. But, once again, readmission and reintegration were essentially a phenomenon of the closing decades of the century. A key factor here was the collapse of stable government, following the revolution of 1572, and the general turmoil which now engulfed much of the country. This served both to disrupt old-established rules and privileges and to create a situation in which elements of the rebel leadership believed it politic to turn to the Jews for material assistance in their struggle against Spain. William of Orange also hoped, through the Jews, to pull more weight at the court of that other arch-enemy of Spain, the Turkish Sultan. It is true that the sack of Antwerp, in 1576, caused most of the Antwerp Portuguese to disperse, some settling temporarily in Cologne, but many of these drifted back within a year or two or settled elsewhere in the Netherlands, notably at Middelburg and Rotterdam.[34] In 1577, the rebel States General, through the Antwerp city council, opened negotiations with the leaders of Frankfurt Jewry, inviting them to establish a Jewish community in Antwerp in return for financial assistance against Spain.[35] Nothing came of this, presumably owing to the insecurity then prevailing at Antwerp. Even so, groups of German Jews, mainly

---

[33] Simonsohn, *History*, pp. 191–3.
[34] Pohl, *Portugiesen in Antwerpen*, pp. 65–7.
[35] Prins, 'Orange and the Jews', pp. 96–101.

from East Friesland, did now enter the north-eastern parts of the Netherlands, especially the province of Groningen, where, as recent research on Jewish tombstones has shown, a network of village communities arose in the 1570s and 1580s.

Despite the recapture of Antwerp by the Spaniards in 1585, most of the Marranos in the Low Countries continued to congregate in Antwerp, traditionally the chief business centre, until, in 1595, the Dutch decided to extend their blockade of Antwerp by preventing ships entering and leaving the Flemish sea-ports, from where Antwerp merchants were transporting their imports of Portuguese colonial products via the inland waterways. This wider blockade meant that the New Christian exporters of Lisbon and Oporto could no longer use Antwerp as a depot from which to distribute Portuguese colonial products in northern Europe. For this reason they now switched to other entrepôts and this is why the Portuguese crypto-Jewish community in Amsterdam was established in 1595, and not ten years earlier, and why the Marrano colonies in Hamburg, Emden, and Rouen arose more or less simultaneously with that of Amsterdam.[36] By 1600, the Portuguese crypto-Jewish community in Amsterdam was probably already quite substantial though still smaller than the community in Antwerp, which then numbered around 400 souls.

In France, the disruptive impact of the civil wars and the succession to the throne, in 1574 and 1589 respectively, of the *politique* kings Henri III and Henri IV, tended to the subordination of the churches, vested interests, and ancient privileges to the requirements of *raison d'État* and national unity. It is true that even before the outbreak of civil war in 1562, some Portuguese New Christians had settled in Bordeaux and Bayonne and that in 1550 Henri II issued *lettres patentes* granting them protection so as to promote 'trade and industry'. But at that stage the numbers involved were minute. The subsequent turmoil seems to have encouraged not only increased immigration but also increasingly dissident behaviour in point of religion. In November 1574, Henri III issued new *lettres patentes* not only reaffirming royal protection but pointedly, even cynically, dismissing protests about their religious conduct as 'groundless'.[37] With the intensification of Inquisition pressure in Portugal from 1579, what previously had been a trickle of Marrano immigration into France

[36] Israel, 'Economic Contribution', p. 508.
[37] Léon, *Histoire*, p. 19.

became a broad stream. Several thousand Portuguese settled, at first mainly at Bayonne, St. Jean de Luz, and Bordeaux but, from the 1590s, also at Nantes, Rouen, and Paris.[38] Henri IV, like his predecessor, took little or no notice of the mounting mercantile, ecclesiastical, and popular protests against this 'Jewish' penetration. The King did seemingly yield to the pressure in the case of Bayonne, in 1602, when a local decree of expulsion received royal assent. But nothing was done to enforce this expulsion or prevent those Portuguese who did leave the city from settling wherever else they wished in the realm. Nor was Henri IV's liberal attitude reserved only for the Portuguese, with one of whom, Manoel de Pimentel, a man who later became a professing Jew in Venice, he is known to have personally played cards and whom he reportedly called the 'king of gamblers'.[39] On France's eastern border, the King took the step of sanctioning the seepage of German Jews into the garrison town of Metz, a trend in progress since shortly after the outbreak of the civil wars. But not only did Henri tolerate the Jewish community in Metz but, in 1595, he issued privileges guaranteeing the public practice of Judaism in the city. This laid the basis for the emergence of Metz during the course of the seventeenth century as one of the principal Jewish communities in western Europe.

[38] Brunschvigg, *Juifs de Nantes*, pp. 13–14; Revah, 'Autobiographie', p. 54.
[39] *Mémoires du Maréchal de Bassompierre*, i. 206–8; Franco Mendes, *Memórias*, pp. 13, 21.

III

Consolidation (1600–1620)

RADICAL scepticism was a negating force which brought in its wake
the impulse to construct models of state and society divorced from
traditional theology. Bodin, the first major western intellect to
envisage society outside the framework of Christian doctrine was, at
the same time, the discoverer of sovereignty as a political reality
divorced from religious sanction and, as part of such sovereignty,
economic policy based on the material and social interest of the state.
It might be tempting to dismiss Bodin as an exception whose more
radical ideas, as expressed in the *Colloquium Heptoplomeres*, were little
known about at the time. But this would in several ways be an error.
For Bodin's impulse to distance himself from the doctrine of the
churches and mould an encompassing world-view on a non-Christian
basis is, in many ways, profoundly typical of his age. Montaigne was
not just a sceptic but sought a new morality, new criteria for life.
Justus Lipsius, probably the most influential scholar of his time, spent
part of his career at Calvinist Leiden and part at Catholic Louvain;
yet, what he wrote was equally acceptable to both. For decades,
Lipsius's influence was preponderant in central Europe and
pervasive in Spain and Italy as well as the Low Countries. Acknowledged as the most accomplished Latinist and Classicist of his time,
Lipsius, like Erasmus earlier, constructed a monumental synthesis of
classical and early modern ideas. But there was a crucial difference.
Where Erasmus was steeped in Christianity and Christ was the centre
of his world, in Lipsius Christian allegiance is reduced to occasional
lip-service. His values and attitudes he derives from Seneca, Tacitus,
and other Roman writers, of whom he is a tireless advocate.

Inherent in the revolutionary outlook of the post-Wars-of-Religion
era was the increasing separation of natural law from the teaching of
the churches. This dichotomy already manifest in Bodin, who postu-
lates the Mosaic Law as the best basis for defining and perceiving the
natural rights of peoples and individuals, attained its definitive
expression in the works of the Dutch jurist Hugo Grotius (1583–
1645). Assuredly, Grotius did not share Bodin's propensity to

'promote the Old Testament to the position of Natural Law'.[1] But his great legal works presented a fully developed philosophy of natural law which is essentially independent of Christian doctrine. As a prop to *politique* attitudes, the work of men such as Bodin, Lipsius, and Grotius had much practical as well as theoretical significance. For, at the outset of the sixteenth century, Machiavelli had postulated a rudimentary *raison d'État* stripped not just of Christian but of all moral and legal restraint. After Machiavelli, such theorizing had been submerged for decades by the Reformation and Counter-Reformation only to surface again after 1570. But in the rebirth of *raison d'État* concepts at the close of the sixteenth century, the west absorbed not a revamped Machiavellianism but a political philosophy which dwelt on the duties and responsibilities of the state to society, an outlook rooted at once in *raison d'État* and natural law. Thus, whatever his own religious beliefs, Grotius redeemed the rights of all individuals, groups, and states, accounting all mankind a unity possessed of dignity and worth irrespective of the claims of the churches.

No less inherent in the intellectual revolution of the late sixteenth century was the sudden, explosive rise of modern science and speculative philosophy. For amid the theological deadlock, the question what truth is and how it is to be ascertained took on immense urgency. The propositions of Bacon and Descartes were the quest of an age absorbing the implications of doubt, loss of confidence, and rampant *raison d'État*. Moreover, it was inevitable that the spiritual crisis should revolutionize all studies. Scholars devoted to the pursuit of truth were now impelled to embark on a voyage of discovery. Just as some immersed themselves in the new astronomy, others began to ransack languages and literatures which had never been studied or taken seriously before. Especially in France and the Netherlands, there was now a marked resurgence in Hebrew and Aramaic studies, a systematic exploration of Talmud and rabbinic literature and the beginnings of Arabic, Turkish, and Koranic studies. And the new search through oriental languages and texts was quite different from the blinkered preoccupations of Reformation Hebraists. The mood had changed from confident self-assertion to an attitude hesitant, searching, and perplexed.

Perhaps the greatest western orientalist of the age was Joseph Justus Scaliger (1540–1609), the son of an Italian humanist father

[1] Grotius, *De Jure Belli ac Pacis*, prolegomena; Ettinger, 'The Beginnings of the Change', p. 198.

who became caught up in the turmoil in France, discarded his early
Catholicism and eventually, in 1593, took up Lipsius's former chair at
the Calvinist University of Leiden. The immensely erudite and
critical Scaliger became convinced that all western renderings of
Scripture, Beza's New Testament and the Vulgate alike, were
seriously corrupt and divergent from the originals on which they were
based. As he saw it, Scripture could only be rescued by means of study
in fields previous scholars had known little or nothing about. His
private jottings about the Jews are as remarkable as his doubts about
the texts of the New Testament. Much to their astonishment, he
debated with learned Jews in Hebrew at Avignon and in Rome. 'On
ne saurait croire', he noted, 'combien les Juifs sont savants et subtils.'[2]
It was typical of Scaliger that he was in favour of allowing the Jews to
resettle in the west not just because 'they bring wealth' but because
'we need to learn from them'. He was quite ready to acknowledge that
generally speaking, Jews took care of their poor more conscientiously
than did Christians. He even went so far as to acknowledge that most
Jewish converts to Christianity were worthy only of contempt.
'Rarement', he averred, 'un juif converti au Christianisme est homme
de bien; les convertis sont généralement mauvaises gens'. Most
radical of all, Scaliger believed that, until his own time, Christians
had totally failed to grasp the significance of post-biblical Jewish
literature and therefore had been, and still were, unable to confront
Judaism intellectually: 'il faut les convaincre à l'aide du Talmud', he
wrote, 'non du Nouveau Testament qui les fait rire'.

Few matched Scaliger's learning, but many emulated, or shared,
his profoundly critical approach to traditional scholarship and
attitudes. In Holland, there were the Hebraists Drusius, Coddaeus,
and Rhaphelengius, as well as Ferdinandus, a converted Polish Jew
who, in 1599, became first Professor of Arabic at Leiden. Grotius was
one of those who imbibed the new critical scholarship and, although
his own Hebrew was limited, his excursions into the field of biblical
commentary, culminating in his *Annotationes* on the Old and New
Testament, treat traditional Christian interpretations with such
scant regard that one irate divine denounced him as 'deterior
Judaeis'. Similar trends were evident in France and England and
even in Spain, the great Hebraist Benito Arias Montano (1527–98)
not infrequently giving preference to rabbinic over Church construings of Scriptural passages, a habit which eventually led to his trial by

[2] Reinach, 'Joseph Scaliger', pp. 173–5.

the Inquisition. Even those Hebraists who remained basically anti-Jewish in the old mould, such as the famous Johannes Buxtorf (1564–1629), Professor of Hebrew at Basel, shared the new approach in so far as he emphasized Talmud and post-Talmudic Hebrew literature and the need for genuine study of Jewish tradition, dismissing the blood libel and other crudities of popular anti-Semitism.

Philosemitic scholarship was thus born at the same moment, and in the same context, as philosemitic mercantilism, both mercantilism and the 'philosophic spirit' of the seventeenth century being fruits of the distancing from Christian tradition. Mercantilist attitudes, like radical scepticism, may have existed before 1570 and even, at least in Italy before the Counter-Reformation, been sporadically fashionable; but it took the shock of religious stalemate, ensuing from the deadlocked Wars of Religion, to render the pursuit of the economic interest of the state, irrespective of religion, tradition, and privilege, a prevalent social ideal. Intellectually, mercantilist thought was an offshoot of late sixteenth-century *raison d'État* political philosophy, and it is no mere chance that Bodin was at the centre of both initiatives. And, like Bodin, many other early mercantilists—Laffemas, Montchrétien, Gomes Solís, Lopes Pereira, Thomas Shirley—were *politiques*, doubters, or Judaizers, or all three at once. But, of themselves, neither the new Hebraism, nor *raison d'État* philosophy, nor mercantilism, necessarily implied the adoption of philosemitic attitudes. If some Hebraists combined old prejudice with new techniques, there were different ways of arguing the economic interest of the state. While, at the beginning of the seventeenth century, in Italy, there was a tendency for rulers to invite Jews in so as to stimulate commerce, there were numerous commentators on trade who insisted that the commercial activity of Jews harmed the state.[3] Outside Italy, mercantilist anti-Semitism was still more prevalent. Certainly, the French mercantilist Montchrétien, in his *Traicté de l'œconomie politique* of 1615, maintained that the Marranos in France were undesirable not just because they denied Christ and spread Jewish ideas, but because they were sucking wealth out of the country rather than bringing it in.[4] And similar sentiments continued to permeate some mercantilist writings throughout the seventeenth century.

Yet mercantilism, along with *raison d'État* politics and the new learning, did powerfully contribute to the fundamental shift in ideas

---

[3] Ravid, *Economics and Toleration*, pp. 42–6.
[4] Montchrétien, *Traicté*, pp. 191–2; Cole, *French Mercantilist Doctrines*, pp. 139–40.

about the Jews then in progress. By and large, the anti-Semitic strand in mercantilism was a minority stance. The senators who staffed the Venetian board of trade repeatedly reiterated, from the 1570s onwards, that they regarded the Jews as an indispensable prop of the Venetian economy.[5] The Spanish *arbitrista* Martín González de Cellorigo urged the Spanish crown, in 1619, to curb Inqusition persecution of Portuguese Marrano immigrants in Spain, arguing that this group should be tolerated and encouraged out of reasons of '*razón de Estado*', to improve Spain's finances and trade. In his tract there is at least the implication, bold enough in Spain, that such considerations ought to take precedence over any suspicions that might arise as to the sincerity of their Christianity.[6] The Portuguese mercantilist Duarte Gomes Solís, himself a New Christian, urged Philip III not just to restrain persecution of New Christians but to allow professing Jews to settle in the Portuguese colonies in Asia, and have ghettos there 'as they do in Rome and other parts of Italy' as a means of defeating Dutch and English commercial rivalry in the east.[7] Thomas Shirley, assuring the English monarch that the 'Duke of Savoy were not able to maintain his state without their help and the benefit he reaps from them', urged James I to invite the Jews back into England 'by privilege of trade only, without a synagogue'. Should that be too much, James being 'most zealous' in his Christianity, then the Jews should at least be invited to settle in Ireland—a neat reconciling of anti-Semitism and mercantilist philosemitism which was taken up again later by the mid-seventeenth century political writer, Harrington.[8] Another Spanish mercantilist, Francisco Rétama, combined anti-Semitism with acknowledging that economic benefits to the state accrued from Jewish activity, advising Philip III that he could sap the economic strength of Spain's enemy, the Dutch Republic, by employing agents in Holland to incite feeling against the Jews and provoke their expulsion to Germany or Poland.[9]

And the changed intellectual and political climate did make an immense difference. For European Jewry, the opening decades of the new century were a time of rapid and mostly successful consolidation. Where readmission had already been secured, in the previous period, there was now a further increase in Jewish population, notably in

[5] ASV CSM 1st ser., cxl, fos. 8^v–11, 34^v, cxli, fos. 168^v–69, and cxliii, fos. 19^v–21.
[6] González de Cellorigo, *Alegación*, preface and fo. 22^v.
[7] Gomes Solís, *Memoires*, pp. 12, 16.
[8] Samuel, 'Sir Thomas Shirley's "Project" ' p. 195.
[9] AGS Estado 634, expediente no. 322, fos. 13–14.

Prague, Frankfurt, Mantua, Venice, Amsterdam, Hamburg, and Livorno. At the same time, many more principalities—though rarely any free cities—invited the Jews to return, mostly after prolonged negotiation and on the basis of elaborate charters. This increasing stream of Jewish population and resources into western and central Europe flowed from three main external sources, though in Germany the major factor was internal migration, with Jews from the old-established communities in the ecclesiastical states fanning out to the north and south. The immigration from outside derived, firstly, from the Marrano population of Portugal: where during the middle decades of the sixteenth century, Portuguese New Christians reverting to Judaism had migrated mainly to Ottoman territory, by 1590 most of those leaving Portugal settled in Spain, France, Italy, the Low Countries, and Hamburg.[10] A second source of immigration was the Balkans from where Spanish-speaking Jews settled mainly in Venice, Livorno, and other parts of Italy, though a few moved on to Holland. Finally, there was also a steady trickle of immigration from Poland into Bohemia and Moravia and, to a lesser extent, Germany.

The influx of Portuguese into Spain had begun in the 1580s, following the annexation of Portugal to the Spanish Crown in 1580. Qualitatively, this post-1580 immigration into Spain probably differed from earlier waves of Portuguese Marrano migration to Ottoman territory in being less specifically crypto-Jewish in character. Around 1580, the Portuguese Inquisition, its powers recently strengthened, began to arrest far more suspects and confiscate more New Christian property than previously, and it is likely that the new wave into Spain consisted as much (or more) of families fleeing their increasing vulnerability in Portugal, or seeking the economic opportunities now available in Spain, as of families concerned to preserve their Judaism, though, of course, all these motives frequently coalesced. But, whether or not those Portuguese Marranos who chose Spain rather than northern Europe or Ottoman territory were more Catholic than others, there can be no doubt that they formed a distinct sub-group in Castilian society, rarely intermarrying or assimilating socially with other Spaniards. Though the Portuguese Inquisition was now more virulent than the Spanish, cases of Judaizing crop up with increasing frequency in Spanish Inquisition files from the 1580s onwards, the prisoners being almost always 'Portuguese' immigrants or their children.[11] Thus, while many of the

[10]   Nehama, *Histoire*, iii. 57–8.   [11]   Caro Baroja, *Judíos*, i. 474–81.

immigrants into Spain were content to live as good Catholics,
Spaniards tended to view the whole group with a prejudiced eye, and
there certainly were numerous crypto-Jews among them.

Despite meeting a habitual disdain—the anti-Semitic outbursts of
Lope de Vega and Quevedo are all too characteristic—the Portuguese New Christian influx into Castile met with suprisingly little
resistance. Within the space of half a century, several thousands of
them settled in the Castilian cities, especially Madrid, Seville, and
Málaga, and quickly invaded Spanish commerce, particularly the
wool trade, the import of cloth, and the traffic with the Indies.
Sizeable groups also settled in the Spanish viceroyalties of Peru and
Mexico, where they frequently acted as commercial agents of their
relatives in Spain.[12] Yet the backlash remained largely psychological
and literary. Inquisition persecution, down to the 1640s, continued to
be rather muted compared with the situation in Portugal. Nor were
there calls for the expulsion of the newcomers such as were voiced in
this period by the city councils of France's Atlantic seaboard.

No doubt one reason for the ease of Portuguese Marrano entry into
Spain was the lack of any vigorous native entrepreneurial class. In
1580, most of Spanish commerce was in the hands of immigrant
Genoese, Flemings, and others who lacked the standing in the
Castilian cities to prevent the incursion of fresh competition. Indeed,
there are signs that the Genoese may have been even more unpopular
than the Portuguese New Christians. Moreover, as from 1599, when a
virulent epidemic swept the country, there was a sharp fall in the
population of most Castilian cities, and this too eased matters for
Marrano immigrants. And then account must be taken of the change
in the attitude of the Spanish crown. Philip II (1556–98), the
archetypal Counter-Reformation monarch, had been vehemently
hostile to Jews and Portuguese New Christians alike. But the succession of Philip III in 1598 changed matters appreciably. The Duke
of Lerma, the new favourite, was as close to being a *politique* as was
then possible in Spain and softened his predecessor's policies in a
variety of ways, including the granting of immunity, on Spanish soil,
to English and Dutch Protestant seamen and merchants. Lerma also
entered into negotiations with leaders of the Lisbon New Christian
community, being eager to barter concessions for money. Despite
vehement opposition from the Portuguese clergy and towns, he both
eased the restrictions on New Christian emigration from Portugal and

[12] García de Proodian, *Judíos en América*, pp. 27–31, 66–80.

in 1605 arranged a papal general pardon for past religious offences which led to a temporary emptying of Portugal's Inquisition gaols.[13] As part of this policy, Lerma took no steps to block the increasing Marrano percolation into Castile and pointedly began signing government contracts, for instance for naval supplies, with recently arrived Portuguese New Christian financiers.

The rapid progress of the 'Portuguese' in Castile during the Lerma period was debated several times by Philip III's councillors of state and finance. By 1620 most ministers acknowledged, were indeed prone to exaggerate, the success of the newcomers from Portugal in Castile's finance and trade. While most accepted that this had some advantages, others believed that the economic activity of the 'Portuguese' in Spain was damaging.[14] This emerges especially from deliberations about contraband dealings and the problem of evasion of the Spanish crown's intricate system of commercial regulations. For the 'Portuguese' were notoriously active in the illegal export of Spanish silver to northern Europe and in evading the crown's numerous restrictions on trade with the Spanish Indies.[15] There is also evidence that it was mainly the Portuguese New Christians in Spain who were responsible for the damaging influx of counterfeit copper coinage, manufactured in Holland and imported surreptitiously, which greatly aggravated the monetary chaos experienced in Spain in the years 1615–21. Thus, it is not surprising that ministers disagreed over the wisdom of allowing 'Portuguese' financiers to take over the farming of customs duties and other royal revenues which in the past had been allocated to Genoese or other tax-farmers. One such debate concerned João Nunes da Veiga who, in 1620, applied for the farm of the customs imposts on overland trade between Castile and Aragon.[16] Despite strong misgivings, his bid was accepted and this merchant joined the growing band of Portuguese New Christians who held contracts with the Spanish government in the 1620s.

The debate about the Portuguese in Spain echoed the wider debate about Jews then in progress throughout western Europe. By 1600, Jewish activity was basic to the economy of Venice, but it was

[13] Gomes Solís, *Discursos*, pp. 12–13; Lúcio de Azevedo, *História*, pp. 155–68; Yerushalmi, *From Spanish Court*, pp. 66–7.

[14] AGS Hacienda 592, *consultas* 26 July 1620, 25 Feb. 1621, 24 July 1622; Cantera Burgos, 'Dos escritos', pp. 40, 45–7; Domínguez Ortiz, *Política y hacienda*, p. 128.

[15] AGS Estado 2308, expedientes 113 and 114.

[16] AGS Hacienda 592, *consulta* 26 July 1620.

noticeable that it was spreading beyond the confines of Balkan and Adriatic trade. During the 1600–20 period, Portuguese Jews in Venice became active in Iberian trade, not only importing sugar and other colonial goods from Lisbon and Seville but also a sizeable share of the Spanish wool and Spanish American dyestuffs which were vital to Venice's principal industry, the manufacture of fine woollen cloth. Most of the ruling oligarchy accepted this expanding Jewish role, but not all. One such was Alvise Sanuto, a member of the Venetian board of trade who strongly dissented from the decision to renew the privileges of Venetian Jewry taken on the recommendation of most of his colleagues, in 1604.[17] Sanuto claimed that there were now more 'perfidious' Jews doing business on the Rialto than Christians and that the policy of the state since the 1570s had, in effect, favoured Jews at the expense of Christians, which he regarded as intolerable in a Christian Republic. Nor were Venice's Jews performing any indispensable function. As he saw it, there were Christians enough who could handle the merchandise the Jews dealt in.

Yet in Venice, as in Tuscany, there was, in general, remarkably little opposition to the shift in the balance of commercial power now underway. In Tuscany, indeed, that shift was more marked than at Venice. In the early sixteenth century, Florentine merchants had still been one of the leading mercantile groups in the Mediterranean. On the wane since the 1520s, when Florentines disappeared from the markets of the Balkans, they had steadily weakened in the late sixteenth century with the decline in Florence's cloth exports. Finally, in the decades 1600–20, they effectively ceased to be an active trading group, the bulk of Tuscany's overseas trade now falling into the hands of the Portuguese Jews living in Pisa and Livorno. It was the Jewish merchants who acted as the main distributors of the English and Dutch products which were increasingly capturing the Italian market. But then Tuscany was an absolutist principality and both Ferdinando and his successor Cosimo II deemed it in the best interests of their state to favour the progress of the 'Portuguese'. As Shirley put it, the 'politique Duke of Florence will not leave his Jews for all other merchants whatsoever'.[18] Such a mercantile strategy inevitably provoked hostile comment yet would scarcely have been practicable had there been any really determined opposition.

In the Dutch provinces, the debate was as localized as were the

---

[17] Ravid, *Economics and Toleration*, pp. 42–5.
[18] Samuel, 'Sir Thomas Shirley's "Project" ', p. 195.

country's politics generally. As usual in early seventeenth-century Europe, lip-service was paid to religious considerations, but it was the economic arguments and counter-arguments which counted. In practice, each city made its own decision, though at times, notably in the years 1614–15, there was some attempt to forge a Jewish policy for the province of Holland as a whole. At Amsterdam, (and Hamburg) in contrast to Venice and Florence, the local bourgeoisie was burgeoning at this time, and yet there was the same lack of resistance to the rapid Jewish penetration, essentially because the Jews who settled there—mainly Marranos who came direct from Portugal—were bringing new trade which the city had previously lacked. As the freight-contracts drawn up before Amsterdam notaries reveal, in the period 1595–1620 nearly all Dutch Jewish commerce was with Portugal and the Portuguese colonies: their importing of sugar, Brazil-wood, and Indian diamonds, via Oporto and Lisbon, added to Amsterdam's stock of trade without competing with any pre-existing interests. The diamonds and other Asian products which they shipped in the early stages, notably cinnamon from Ceylon, came from Portuguese colonies where the Dutch East India Company had as yet failed to penetrate.[19] It is true that, at first, they also imported pepper; but this soon lapsed as the Company began shipping larger quantities of pepper to Europe than the merchants of Lisbon. However, the Christian guilds, in Amsterdam and Hamburg, successfully intervened with the city councils to block Jewish entry into shopkeeping and most of the crafts. Despite this, at any rate at Amsterdam, the Portuguese did gradually develop a flourishing, if somewhat narrow, craft sector based chiefly on the processing of colonial products imported from the Indies. This was already noticeable by 1620, though Amsterdam Jewish crafts then still consisted mainly of diamond-processing.[20] Jewish entry into the field was assisted by the prominence of Portuguese Jewish merchants in the importing of diamonds, most of which came via Goa and Lisbon. However, the techniques of diamond-cutting and polishing were learned from Christian craftsmen who had themselves recently migrated to Amsterdam, from Antwerp. Amsterdam had no previous flourishing jewel trade or industry and it is this which opened the way for the Jews, for there was no established guild to block their path.

Other Dutch towns were caught between a desire to emulate

---

[19] Israel, 'Economic Contribution', pp. 508, 511.
[20] Fabião, 'Subsidios', pp. 476–80.

Amsterdam and fear of prejudicing the interests of their existing populations. And certainly Amsterdam was not the only attraction for the Jews themselves. Amsterdam treated its Jewish immigrants liberally in point of trade but not only refused to allow them into retailing and the crafts but for a long time would not allow public practice of Judaism in the city, only private prayer-sessions in the Jews' homes. Doubtless many were content with that, but others were intent on building a fuller Jewish community and life. In particular, there was a group, a mixture of Portuguese and 'Levantines', who arrived in the years around 1600, from Venice, and were used to a more developed form of Judaism than those who were fresh from Portugal or who had been living as New Christians in France or Antwerp. It was these Venetian Sephardim who applied to Haarlem in 1604–5 for permission to transfer there from Amsterdam with their families and erect a public synagogue.[21] The applicants styled themselves, no doubt somewhat to the bafflement of the burgomasters, as members of the 'Portuguese and Spanish nation, both Levantine and western Hebrews by origin, formerly living and professing the Jewish religion in Italy and parts of Turkey'. They offered to bring Haarlem trade with Venice and the Levant. This sparked a good deal of controversy in Haarlem, but the city council was interested enough to draw up a charter providing for the settlement of fifty Jewish families in the city and specifically allowing the public practice of Judaism and a public synagogue. Nothing came of the scheme, probably due to hard-line Calvinist opposition rather than failure to persuade enough Jews to move from Amsterdam. Either way, the orthodox tried again in 1610, when, once more embroiled in controversy, they secured a charter conferring the right to erect a public synagogue at Rotterdam.[22] But such were the protests that the city council cancelled the contract after just two years, whereupon a group of seven Jewish families moved back from Rotterdam to Amsterdam. Then, in 1612, the more committed element went ahead with the construction of a public synagogue in Amsterdam, lacking written permission but probably with a vague verbal assent from members of the city administration.[23] Again there was a furious outcry, this time partly fomented by Spanish agents,

[21] Seeligmann, 'Het marranen-probleem', p. 112; Reinach, 'Joseph Scaliger', p. 173.
[22] Hausdorff, *Jizkor*, pp. 8–11.
[23] AGS Estado 627, consulta 7 July 1612; Zwarts, *Eerste rabbijnen*, pp. 65–71; SR, vi. 116–17.

under orders from the Spanish minister in Brussels to incite Calvinists against the Jews. The more liberal members of the Amsterdam city council were forced to back down and the projected synagogue was stopped half-built. It was to take another twenty-seven years until a public synagogue was finally inaugurated in Amsterdam in 1639.

Following the controversies in Haarlem, Rotterdam, and Amsterdam, the issue of the Jews and their religion was raised formally in the States of Holland, at The Hague, in 1614–15. Two written reports were drawn up and submitted to the States, one of which was composed by Grotius, who had already been involved in the Jewish debate in Rotterdam. Grotius's paper was liberal on some points, reactionary on others.[24] In his opening, he echoed Erasmus's dictum that nothing was more fundamentally at odds with Christianity than Judaism. And yet, he refused to regard the Jews as enemies or advocate their exclusion from the country, which in any case was no longer practicable as several town councils had already decided to admit them. He justified Jewish settlement in Holland on the grounds that opinion in some Dutch towns was receptive to them, by which he meant that their economic usefulness was widely perceived, and because it was the duty of every Christian to strive for the conversion of the Jews, which was hardly to be expected if the only Christianity they knew was the idolatrous cult of the Catholics. In any case, he averred, Christians needed to learn Hebrew and this was best done from Jews. Grotius, echoing the then policy of his own city, came out strongly against allowing public synagogues anywhere in the province. He also advocated that Christians be forbidden to attend Jewish worship, that conversion from Christianity to Judaism be outlawed, that Jews be rigorously excluded from public office, and that Jewish shops be made to close on Sundays and Christian holidays. Conventionally, he also wanted sexual contact between Christians and Jews forbidden. This may sound harsh, but such were the attitudes of the age that what is remarkable about all this is its relative generosity towards the Jews. For Grotius did not advocate segregation of Jews into sealed-off ghettos and, most noteworthy of all, did not demand their exclusion from shopkeeping and the crafts—as was then the policy of Amsterdam. Both this debate, and another States of Holland discussion on the Jews in 1619, proved inconclusive. No policy for the province, or the Dutch Republic as a whole, was ever formulated.

Meanwhile, in Germany, Jewish life continued to expand along the

[24] Grotius, *Remonstrantie*, pp. 112–16.

same lines as in the period 1570–1600, that is, principally in the ecclesiastical states and at Frankfurt and Hamburg. At Halberstadt, where Jews reappeared at the close of the sixteenth century, their resettlement in the town was formally confirmed by the bishop in 1606, and, with the latter's permission, a public synagogue was erected in 1621.[25] In the bishopric of Strasbourg, Jews now resettled in several localities from which they had previously been excluded.[26] And in the same way there are clear signs of expanding Jewish communities in the archbishoprics of Cologne and Mainz and in bishoprics such as Speyer, Paderborn, Bamberg, and Münster. Nevertheless, Jews continued to be shut out of episcopal capitals such as Münster and Würzburg and restricted to a handful of families in the cities of Mainz, Minden and others. The Imperial Free Cities by and large continued to debar Jews altogether. The Hamburg Senate placed its protection of the Portuguese community and its right to practise Judaism on a formal footing under a charter drawn up in 1612.[27] But German Jews continued to be excluded from Hamburg, as they were from Lübeck, Nuremberg, Augsburg, and the city of Cologne. Moreover, the Hamburg Portuguese were debarred from all crafts and shopkeeping and obliged to practise Judaism, like their relatives in Holland, only in the privacy of their homes.

Like Hamburg, and in contrast to Lübeck, a number of small towns along the north German coast, and also the Danish crown in its territory in Schleswig-Holstein, showed interest in attracting Portuguese if not German Jews. Emden acquired a small, if mostly transitory Portuguese community in the years around 1600. Stade, to the west of Hamburg, negotiated a contract with a group of Amsterdam Jews in 1611, inviting them to set up a sugar-refinery, the Jews providing the capital, equipment, and skilled personnel.[28] A small, probably short-lived community does seem to have taken root. More significant was the initiative taken by Christian IV of Denmark, a keen mercantilist, in 1619. This Danish king had recently founded a new town in Holstein, some forty miles down river from Hamburg towards the sea, which he called Glückstadt, and which he hoped would one day rival Hamburg in trade, though the Jews joked that it neither was a *Stadt* nor enjoyed much *Glück*. Needing merchants and

[25] Frankl, 'Politische Lage', p. 322; Saville, *Juif de cour*, p. 17.

[26] Weiss, *Juden im Fürstbistum Straßburg*, pp. 21–3.

[27] Cassuto, 'Neue Funde', pp. 58–63.

[28] SR, vi. 116–17; Asaria, *Juden in Niedersachsen*, p. 180.

capital, which were both in short supply in the Danish lands, the king sought to attract Dutch Arminians and Portuguese Jews. In 1619, he drew up terms with a group of Hamburg Portuguese, following this up, in 1622, with a royal letter offering generous terms, sent to the Portuguese Community in Amsterdam.[29] Christian offered greater religious and economic freedom than was currently on offer from either Hamburg or Amsterdam. It is noticeable that several of the Portuguese who did move to Glückstadt around 1620 proceeded to set up sugar, soap, and olive-oil refineries. By 1623, there were twenty-nine families of Portuguese Jews in Glückstadt, representing 8 per cent of the town's population. Friedrich III, Duke of Holstein-Gottorf, who purchased jewels from, and had other dealings with, Sephardim in Hamburg, emulated Christian's example and sought to attract both Dutch Remonstrants and Portuguese Jews to his ports of Friedrichstadt and Tönning in the 1620s, though it is not clear with how much, if any, success as regards the Jews.[30]

Given the appeal of the Portuguese in North Germany, it is curious to find that Frankfurt, which tolerated the largest Ashkenazi community in the empire after that of Prague, refused to admit a group of Venetian Portuguese Jews who applied to settle there in 1609. It may be that, whereas the Portuguese in North Germany were bringing in new products and types of trade at a time when commerce with the Iberian Peninsula was being increasingly dominated by Holland, so that admitting Jews meant gaining ground commercially without damaging vested local interests, in the case of Frankfurt the transit trade overland, from the Low Countries to Italy, was shrinking (owing to the success of Dutch shipping) but well-established, so that admitting Venetian Portuguese would have harmed local merchants. But, whatever the reason, no Portuguese community seems to have taken root anywhere in central or southern Germany, though the group turned away from Frankfurt did negotiate also with the Count of Hanau. The Ashkenazi community of Frankfurt continued to increase after 1600 but much more slowly than in the period 1570–1600 when it multiplied by at least three times. The ghetto's inhabitants increased from around 2,500 in 1600, to still under 3,000 by 1620. An even more marked arrestation of growth is noticeable at

---

[29] Kellenbenz, *Sephardim*, pp. 61–3; Köhn, 'Ostfriesen', pp. 81–3; meanwhile at Altona the Jewish population grew from four families, in 1611, to thirty families by 1622, Marwedel, *Privilegien der Juden in Altona*, p. 50.

[30] Kellenbenz, *Sephardim*, pp. 70–1.

Friedberg, where the Jewish population nearly doubled, from 56 to
107 families, in less than three decades, from 1585 to 1609, before
falling back to 99 families in 1620.

The probable reason for the slowing down in growth in the
established Jewish centres of central Germany was the increasing
tendency of secular states which had previously debarred Jews to
change their policy. Jews returned to several localities in the Palatinate at this time, including the town of Landau from which they had
been expelled in 1545.[31] The Margrave of Ansbach allowed Jewish
resettlement in his principality, from which they had been expelled in
1561, under a charter drawn up in 1603; Jews were not, as yet,
allowed back into the town of Ansbach itself but were permitted to
form communities at Crailsheim, Creglingen, and neighbouring
places.[32] In the county of Hanau, Jews were allowed to resettle
following a famous three-sided theological disputation between
Lutherans, Calvinists, and Jews, one of the participants being the
English Puritan controversialist Hugh Broughton. In 1603, the
Count designated a 'Jewish Street' in Hanau and settled the first ten
Ashkenazi families there.[33] By 1607, there were already 159 Jews in
Hanau, a number which rose rapidly thereafter. The Count also
permitted the building of a public synagogue which was inaugurated
in 1608.

In Germany, as in Italy, the change of policy toward the Jews owed
something to a handful of urban patricians but was chiefly the work of
princes. The increasing reintegration of Jewry into the mainstream of
European life was thus inseparable from the growing trend towards
princely absolutism. Wherever princely power continued to be
restrained by representative assemblies and diets, as in the electorates
of Brandenburg and Saxony or in the Lower Rhine duchies, Jewish
re-entry rarely, or never, occurred. In France, similarly, it was the
crown which protected the Marranos and which had allowed Jewish
settlement at Metz, and the Papacy which permitted Jewish life in
Avignon. The towns and clergy were altogether more hostile, and the
last meeting of the French States-General, in 1614, led to an eruption
of renewed anti-Jewish feeling. It was in response to this that the
regency government reissued the fourteenth-century decree expelling

---

[31] Arnold, *Juden in der Pfalz*, pp. 20–2.
[32] Cohen, 'The "Small Council" ', pp. 371–2; Sauer, *Die jüdischen Gemeinden*, pp. 59,
63.
[33] Rosenthal, *Juden im Gebiet der ehemaligen Grafschaft Hanau*, pp. 50–2.

the Jews from France, though nothing of a practical nature was done to enforce it. But neither did the ill-feeling against the Portuguese in the Atlantic ports desist. The worst incident occurred at St. Jean de Luz, in 1619, when a certain Catherine Rodrigues, newly arrived from Portugal, was burned at the stake for having emerged from church and spat out the holy wafer. Her execution sparked fierce popular riots against the Marranos followed by their expulsion from the town. Most moved only a short distance, however, to Bayonne and neighbouring places, notably Labastide-Clairence and Peyrehorade.

Nor was there any sign of change in popular attitudes in Italy. There were riots against the Jews in Verona in 1599. At Mantua, in 1602, there was a particularly vicious upsurge of popular fury incited by a Franciscan friar. Such was the uproar that the duke deemed it politic to hang seven Jews for blasphemy and introduce additional measures to limit contact between Jews and Christians. But the most widespread agitation was in central Germany in the lands of the margrave of Bayreuth and especially on the Middle Rhine in and around Frankfurt.[34] The departure of the Dutch Calvinist community from Frankfurt, in the early years of the century, pushed the city into sharp decline at a time when the Jewish population and its activity continued to expand. In particular, the Lutheran cloth guilds were feeling the pinch and local textile production was in full decay. The invasion of German markets by Dutch and English cloth at this time was in any case inevitable, but Jews were active in the importing of foreign cloth and for those who suffered they were the only available scape-goat. Once the Calvinists had been ejected there was no one else on whom the guilds could vent their deepening sense of economic grievance. Thus the Fettmilch rising of 1614–15, the biggest in Frankfurt's history, was essentially economic in character, though it made use of Luther's abusive rhetoric and also evinced hostility towards the ruling patricians. But, in form, the revolt was an attack on the Jews.[35]

The ferment in central Germany began around 1610. In 1612, guild-leaders in Frankfurt, headed by Vincent Fettmilch, began to submit a series of vehement complaints against the Jews to the city

---

[34] Eckstein, *Juden im Markgrafentum Bayreuth*, pp. 25–30; Kracauer, *Juden in Frankfurt*, i. 358–70.

[35] Wagenseil, *Belehrung*, pp. 112–17; Schaab, *Diplomatische Geschichte*, pp. 202–7; Kracauer, *Juden in Frankfurt*, i. 370–92.

council. The working people's leaders reprinted Luther's tract *On the Jews and their Lies* and adroitly manipulated the economic and religious sentiments of the artisan masses. Tension became so acute that the Emperor Mathias intervened, trying to mediate between the guilds and the city council. Finally, on 22 August 1614, Fettmilch triggered a full-scale insurrection against the patriciate and seized the city hall. Having taken control, the insurgents then turned their attention on the barricaded ghetto. After some hours of tumult, the mob broke in and pillaged the homes of the Jews. It is remarkable, though, that there was no mass slaughter. In that respect times had indeed changed since the massacres of the fourteenth and fifteenth centuries. Apparently only two Jews were murdered. The rest of the community, beaten and humiliated, were herded into their cemetery from where they were summarily expelled from the city. The news of events at Frankfurt spread rapidly along the Rhine valley. At Worms, the guilds took to the streets, ransacked the city's ancient synagogue, and expelled the 1,400 Jews who lived there. Further south, with the assent of the margrave, the Jews were expelled from the territory of Baden.

The riots, and especially the risings in Frankfurt and Worms, were regarded as a challenge to their authority by both the ecclesiastical princes and the Emperor. And it was the princes who had their way. Troops were raised by the Emperor and the Elector of Mainz to restore order. Frankfurt was taken and Fettmilch and his fellow ringleaders caught and hanged. The former city council was restored to power and the order expelling the Jews rescinded. The exiles were escorted back into the city by soldiery under the Emperor's banner.[36] Edicts were proclaimed ordering the restitution of property stolen from the Jews. The city council even agreed to pay towards the cost of repairing the synagogue and Jewish houses damaged in the riots. In January 1616, the Jews were escorted back into Worms, again under armed guard and the Imperial banner. To conclude the proceedings, Mathias conferred new privileges on the Jews of Frankfurt and Worms, taking them under his special protection and curtailing the rights of the city councils over the Jewish communities in their own cities.

[36] Schudt, *Jüdischer Merkwürdigkeiten*, ii. 61–2.

IV

Jewish Culture (1550–1650)

In his *Consolation for the Tribulations of Israel*, a difficult, somewhat rambling work in Portuguese, published at Ferrara in 1553 and later reprinted at Amsterdam in 1599, Samuel Usque, a western Jew thoroughly versed in Latin, Christian theology, and the vernacular literatures of Italy, Spain, and Portugal, agonized over the tragedy of the expulsions from the west, probing for hidden meanings and striving to relate such suffering and turmoil to his certainty of the uniqueness of Israel and its mission among mankind. The book is profoundly western and European. And yet, it derives from no specific regional milieu. Rather it expresses a distinctively Jewish outlook and mentality. It diverges radically from the prevailing attitudes of western culture while yet being profoundly European itself. Its content is a coherent but rather startling mix which in several ways exemplifies the new Jewish culture which began to form and take root during the middle decades of the sixteenth century. Usque's book is at once realistic and enquiring, preoccupied with general history and politics and yet also mystical and poetic, permeated with longings for what is felt to be an imminent redemption and ingathering of the Jews to Jerusalem.[1] Expressions of resentment against Spain and the Papacy, and of appreciation of Ottoman Turkey, alternate with mystical effusions proclaiming the pending revival and triumph of the House of Israel.

The radical transformation of Jewish culture which occurred during the middle decades of the sixteenth century was, assuredly, one of the most fundamental and remarkable phenomena distinguishing post-Temple Jewish history. Whereas medieval and Renaissance-Italian Jewish intellectual life was essentially Talmudic, confined in the main to ritual and legal matters which left European Jewry either impoverished culturally (as in Germany and France) or else closely attuned to the philosophical, literary, and artistic pursuits of their Muslim and Christian neighbours (as in Spain and Italy), the changes of the mid sixteenth century produced an altogether more

[1] Usque, *Consolaçam*, iii. 53ᵛ, 62–75.

rounded, complete, and coherent Jewish culture. Jewish society, indeed Jewish nationhood, as something distinct from Jewish religion, now emerged as much more definite realities than before. As late as the early sixteenth century, some Italian Jewish scholars, perhaps including, in a certain sense, the great Azariah de' Rossi, had adhered to traditional Judaism rather than inhabited a specifically Jewish cultural world.[2] Intellectually, they had immersed themselves in the learning of their non-Jewish contemporaries. From around 1550, by contrast, Jewish scholars, in Italy and all parts of Europe, lived and worked in a cultural atmosphere increasingly removed from that of their neighbours, even though, and here is the central paradox, in close touch and constantly interacting with it. Allegiance to traditional Judaism now fused with a whole package of new elements: a much intensified political and historical awareness, a new involvement in poetry, music, and drama, an urgent, if somewhat rambling, quest to incorporate fragments of western philosophy and science into the emerging corpus of Jewish culture, all welded by a far more potent current of mysticism than had ever pervaded the Jewish world previously.

A radical reorientation was, in any case, inevitable given the immensity of the changes in the material and social context of Jewish life, resulting from the transfer of the bulk of the Jewish population of western and central Europe, during the century 1470–1570, to Polish and Ottoman territory. And certainly the vastly changed social and economic environment had a good deal to do with the reshaping of European Jewry's outlook and mentality during the mid sixteenth century. But it would be a mistake to infer from this that the new culture was something forged in the east and then, over a period of two or three decades, transferred to the reviving communities in the west. Rather, the mid-sixteenth-century flowering of Jewish civilization, with its distinctive mix of political and mystical, secular and religious themes, seems to have arisen simultaneously in the east and west and with only a slight time-lag as between the Sephardi and Ashkenazi zones. Indeed, it would scarcely be an exaggeration to say that post-Temple Jewish culture attained its highest degree of cohesion, as well as autonomy from Christendom and Islam, precisely in the centuries 1550–1750. There was, of course, much in it that was anti-rationalist and resistant to intellectual trends in the non-Jewish

---

[2] Barzilay, *Between Reason and Faith*, pp. 183–91; but see Bonfil, 'Some Reflections', pp. 32–3, 37.

west, but there can be no mistaking its novel and, in some ways, rather modern character.

The great influx into Poland and the Levant moulded a preponderant central mass of the Jewish people which was German- or Spanish-speaking in lands where non-Jews spoke neither German nor Spanish. This was one factor lending unity and cohesion of outlook while, at the same time, interposing distance between Jewish culture and that of the surrounding populace. Among the spiritual centres of mid sixteenth century Jewry, the most important was not Cracow, Salonika, or Jerusalem but Safed, in Galilee, which, owing to its flourishing textile industry, at this time had more than twice the Jewish population of Jerusalem. The quickening of spiritual activity in the Holy Land communities, and the recently arisen ascendancy there of Spanish, Portuguese, Italian, and German immigrants, helped tighten the links between the Sephardi and Ashkenazi zones and reinforced the overall cohesion of Jewish culture. As conditions changed in western and central Europe, from around 1570, these Galilean influences spread westwards, fusing with local trends which display a clear affinity with those in the Levant, at any rate in Italy, by as early as 1550.

In Italy, the radical reorientation of the mid sixteenth century was caused less by the influx of immigration from Spain, Portugal, and the Balkans (though this was a factor) than by the programme of ghettoization and the upsurge of conversionist zeal and propaganda emanating from the Catholic Counter-Reformation. Before 1555, Italian Jews did not dwell in ghettos and had participated if not fully, then extensively, in the intellectual pursuits of the Renaissance, including philosophical debate. Now this was impossible not only due to the much intensified ideological assault which denounced Judaism, as one scholar has put it, as 'theologically inconsistent, idolatrous, irrational and immoral',[3] but also because of the ghetto itself. The ghetto, as an instrument of the Counter-Reformation, was specifically designed to segregate Jews from Christian life—to reduce contact at every level—and this it certainly did. But while the ghetto was a mark of humiliation, intended to remove Jewish influences from Italian life, this powerful cultural device enhanced Jewish political and educa- tional autonomy and powerfully boosted the vitality and comprehen- siveness of Jewish culture.

Following the Papacy's imposition of ghettos at Rome and Ancona

[3] Bonfil, 'Some Reflections', p. 36.

in 1555, and Cosimo I's forming of ghettos at Florence and Siena in
1571, the programme of ghettoization spread steadily down to the
1630s.[4] The 400 Jews of Verona were forced into a ghetto at the time of
the troubles there, in 1599, and the 900 Jews of Padua, soon
afterwards, in 1601–3. At Mantua, the ghetto was imposed in 1612, at
Rovigo, after three years of deliberations, in 1615, at Ferrara in 1624–
6, in the duchy of Urbino (three ghettos) in 1634 and at Modena in
1638. It is true that, at Turin and the other communities of Savoy, the
Jews were not made to live in ghettos until much later, and that in
Livorno they were never subjected to it. But Livorno, for all its
centrality in commerce during the seventeenth century, was a
medium-sized, rather isolated town, many of whose Christian
residents were in fact foreign Protestants. In any case, the main
Jewish language in Livorno was Portuguese not Italian. Culturally,
Livorno can in some respects be said to have been the ghetto of
Tuscany.

Many of the ghettos, including that of Venice, were surrounded by
high walls and possessed only two or three gateways. The strategy
pursued by Church and State was to isolate Jews from Christians not
just at night but also during the evening. The gates were closed from
sunset to dawn and during these hours it was forbidden for any Jew to
be outside, except where special exemptions applied, and these were
infrequent. The inevitable effect was to compress Jewish social and
intellectual life, largely, if not entirely, within the ghetto. This meant
that Jewish literary, musical, and artistic activity had no choice but to
become much more inward-looking than previously. It was natural,
in these circumstances, that inspiration should tend to derive from
other Jewish communities, however distant, rather than from the
local environment. For these reasons there occurred in the 1570s and
1580s a sudden tremendous proliferation of local Jewish societies and
fraternities. Many were charitable, concerned with helping the poor
or the sick, but others were study groups, or concerned with mystical
piety, or furthering education, and all contributed to the burgeoning
social life of the ghetto.[5]

In Germany, there was no exact parallel to the ghettoization
programme in Italy, for the Jews were anyway mostly excluded from

---

[4] Ciscato, *Ebrei in Padova*, pp. 79–83; Luzzatto, 'Comunità ebraica di Rovigo',
pp. 513–14; Milano, *Storia*, p. 264.
[5] Simonsohn, *History*, pp. 549–53; Shulvass, *Jews in the World of the Renaissance*,
pp. 80–2.

the towns and cities. At Frankfurt, the community had been transferred to a ghetto as early as 1462. Like the ghettos of Rome and
Venice, that of Frankfurt suffered by 1600 far worse overcrowding
than applied even in the most disadvantaged Christian neighbour-
hoods. But, by and large, Jewish segregation in pre-1620 Germany
took the form of confining Jews to villages and small towns close
enough to the main centres for purposes of commerce but too remote
for participation in cultural and social life. Schnaitach was somewhat
exceptional in being largely a Jewish village but, apart from Frankfurt
and Worms, nearly all the synagogues and study centres were tucked
away in such locations as Deutz, Warendorf, Friedberg, Günzburg,
and Weisenau.

The growing historical consciousness of early modern Jewry
manifested itself in the large number of chronicles of various kinds
composed during the sixteenth century.[6] Especially notable, and
most novel, was Selomoh ibn Verga's *Shebet Yehudah*, compiled in the
1520s, an account of the persecutions of the Jews from the devastation
of the Second Temple to the early sixteenth century. Ibn Verga, a
Spanish exile who lived for a time as a forced Christian in Portugal,
before reverting to Judaism in Italy, poignantly grapples with the
problem of hatred of the Jews and the question of his people's destiny.
He is notable for his disdainful attitude towards medieval culture,
Jewish and non-Jewish, his entwining of Hebrew and non-Hebrew
sources, a generally critical attitude mixed with a certain poetic
fervour. The work was first published in 1554 possibly in Adrianople.
In the same year, there appeared Joseph HaCohen's remarkable
history of the kings of France and the Turkish sultans. Shortly after,
Benjamin Nehemiah of Civitanova treated the problem of papal
hostility in his chronicle of Pope Paul IV. Gedaliah ibn Yahya (1515–
78), born into an eminent Portuguese Jewish family, after it had
transferred to the Papal States, wrote the famous history *Shalshelet ha-
Cabbalah* (Chain of Tradition) which was published at Venice in 1587
and on many occasions subsequently. On the expulsion from the
Papal States, in 1569, Ibn Yahya moved first to Ferrara and later to
Egypt where he died. Another noteworthy chronicler was David Gans
(1541–1613), a Westphalian Jew who migrated to Bohemia and spent
most of his life in Prague. Gans was much interested in astronomy as
well as history and knew both Kepler and Tycho Brahe personally.
But, for all his eagerness for a broader, more secular Jewish culture,

---

[6] Shulvass, *Jews in the World of the Renaissance*, pp. 299–303.

he showed little true scientific inclination. His chronicle, published at Prague in 1592, concentrates on general history but selects events meaningful from the Jewish point of view, such as the burning of the Franciscan friar Cornelio at Rome in 1553, for adopting Jewish ideas, and the burning of Servetus at Geneva in 1554, for denying the divinity of Jesus.[7]

One of Gans's main preoccupations is with the rising tide of theological strife and political dissension within the Christian world surrounding European Jewry.[8] The unmistakable strain of optimism which permeates Gans's chronicle assuredly derives from his perception that it was the split in western Christendom which had revolutionized his world and, at long last, eased the terrible burden of oppression from the shoulders of his people. He is not just deeply fascinated by the spectacle of Christian dissension but, understandably enough, comforted and heartened by it. Gans's political attitudes and psychology are highly evocative of the changing outlook of European Jews of his time. He extols the ideal of the wise and upright ruler, able and willing to curb the violence and fanaticism of the masses, safeguarding the well-being of dissenting minorities. He fears the people and the churches, placing his confidence in the growing strength of rulers. What we have here is that clear leaning toward absolutism which permeated the outlook of European Jewry generally in the early modern period.

The rise of a Jewish secular culture and set of attitudes was a key manifestation of the dawning new age. Amid the proliferation of ghetto fraternities and societies began to flow a stream of new communal music and poetry, needed to alleviate and uplift the teeming congestion of the potentially demoralizing ghetto milieu. The poetry was mainly composed in Spanish, Italian, and Hebrew and, as a rule, focused on historical or Old Testament themes. To some extent, the Jewish music of this period emulated conventional western techniques and styles, but it also incorporated Levantine elements and was adopted to a specifically Jewish milieu, being usually much less ornate than contemporary courtly music. From this point on, the presence of substantial numbers of musicians, especially string players, was a typical feature of virtually all Jewish communities, even very small ones, in Italy, Germany, and Poland alike. At least in Italy, the cultivation of choral music was also very popular. Among

[7] Gans, *Zemach David*, p. 109; Neher, *David Gans*, p. 87.
[8] Breuer, 'Modernism and Traditionalism', pp. 71–4, 78.

the most notable of the poets was Selomoh Usque (*c.*1530–*c.*1596), who published both Spanish and Italian verse, including his much-admired rendering, into Spanish, of Petrarch's sonnets which was published at Venice in 1567. Another was the accomplished Venetian poetess, Sarah Coppio Sullam (*c.*1592–1641), who was acclaimed for her beauty, wit, and imperviousness to the attempts of Catholic priests to convert her, as well as her sonnets. Another was Paulo de Pina (Reuel Jesurun; *c.*1575–1634), a Portuguese Marrano who originally intended to become a friar, in Italy, until persuaded to reject Christianity by the polemicist Eliau Montalto. De Pina reverted to open Judaism at Amsterdam, in 1604, and there composed a dramatic poem in justification of Judaism entitled *Dialogo dos Montes* which was recited in the *Bet Ya'acov* synagogue in Amsterdam, in 1624, interspersed with musical interludes.[9] But the most impressive of the poets was a Portuguese crypto-Jew of Rouen, João Pinto Delgado (*c.*1585–1653), whose poems reflect many of the Jewish cultural preoccupations of the time. His moving *Lamentations of the Prophet Jeremiah* scans the tragedies of Jewish history in search of consolation and salvation.[10] Pinto Delgado's Jewish poems, all in Spanish, were published at Rouen in 1627.

The Spanish migrants to the Levant of 1492 had brought with them a tradition of Hebrew chant for the synagogue and a rich collection of Spanish folk song and ballad (as well as guitar and vihuela playing) which survived down to the twentieth century. In the new milieu, however, their non-synagogal music became largely divorced from any non-Jewish context and developed into a distinctive mix of Spanish, Hebrew, and Turkish melodies. Several song-books, such as that printed by Selomoh ben Mazal Tov, in 1545, helped give form to this new musical culture which received added impulse from the mystical Neoplatonic currents emanating from Safed, which placed much emphasis on music. Then, from the 1570s, as Levantine Spaniards began to return westwards to Italy, and later Holland, their musical heritage began to mix with the native Italian tradition which was also grappling with the problem of integrating secular music into a Jewish milieu. In Italy, the trend was influenced by the courtly styles then prevalent, a number of late sixteenth-century and early seventeenth-century Italian Jews being active as court musicians. Of these, the most notable was Salomone de' Rossi, at Mantua.

⁹ Adler, *Musical Life*, p. 15.
¹⁰ Oelman, *Marrano Poets*, pp. 99–119.

Most of de' Rossi's secular music was not composed for Jews and is typical of the courtly works of the time, but he also compiled a corpus of less ornate music for the synagogue and the Jewish community. Encouraged by members of the Sullam family and by Leone da Modena, as great an enthusiast for music as for poetry and the theatre, he published his settings of Hebrew hymns and psalms, for groups of three to eight voices, at Venice in 1622.

The invasion of a broader musical culture into the tight framework of Jewish community life raised new controversies among the rabbis as to whether, and when, instruments and choirs could be used in synagogue. The introduction of choirs into Italian synagogues in the years around 1600 provoked much argument and moved Leone da Modena, one of the chief promoters of the practice, who instituted a choir to accompany services in his synagogue at Ferrara in 1603, to issue a judgement berating those who disapproved of the innovations.[11] The Amsterdam and Hamburg Sephardi communities followed Venice in the use of choirs and musical renderings. While all rabbis agreed that musical instruments were debarred from synagogue on sabbath and most festivals, there was disagreement as to whether their use was permitted on *Simchat Torah*, the most joyous festival in the Jewish calendar. Despite opposition, the use of instruments, or, at any rate, of harpsichord accompaniments to choirs, on *Simchat Torah* as well as on ordinary days did spread from Venice to Amsterdam, Hamburg, and other Sephardi centres.[12]

Just as music was adapted and incorporated into the emerging pattern of early modern European Jewish life, so had Jewish culture to absorb at least some elements of western philosophy and science. The rabbis argued intermittently over how much of such learning could be permitted, but the general trend, in the formative period 1550–1650, was to allow a tentative synthesis of traditional Talmudic and the new western learning, though the new, doubting, 'philosophic spirit' itself was definitely rejected, as it had to be. Nor was secular learning to have any independence from Talmudic pursuits: what was allowed was the fusing, or rather subordination, of certain ingredients, notably mathematics and astronomical speculation, into the rabbinic system. This was the hallmark of the cultural efflorescence of Prague at the end of the sixteenth century. It is also true of the great rabbinical scholars of Poland, though the latter were

[11] Rivkin, *Leon da Modena*, p. 56; Adler, *La Pratique musicale*, pp. 52–3.
[12] Adler, *Musical Life*, p. 20.

somewhat more conservative than their counterparts at Prague. Moses Isserles (*c*.1530–72), the chief luminary of Jewish Cracow, strove above all to order and systematize the vast mass of traditional learning while at the same time reconciling it with the new mysticism and with some ingredients of philosophy and science. The foremost scholar of the eastern territories, Solomon Luria (*c*.1510–74), was similarly occupied, though he was hostile to philosophy.

One of the most remarkable of the great synthesizers was Yoseph Shlomo Delmedigo (1591–1655), a mind obsessed with the problems of reconciling Talmudic erudition with cabbala, and both of these with western philosophy and science.[13] Born in Crete, Delmedigo became a medical student at Padua (then the only European university to accept Jewish students) where he also studied astronomy under Galileo. From Italy, Delmedigo passed to Egypt and Constantinople before moving on to Poland, and then Vilna, where he was appointed physician to Prince Radziwiłł around 1620. Subsequently, he spent periods in Hamburg and Amsterdam before moving on to Frankfurt and finally Prague, where he died. Delmedigo was neither profound nor an innovator, but he does stand out for the vast range of his interests and tireless efforts to reconcile and weld the components of his thought into a coherent whole. Restlessness, a vast range of interests, and periodic confusion pervade his life and writing, but his intellectual and spiritual quest, inconclusive as it was, epitomized that of his whole people in its new stage of cultural development.

But undeniably the most powerful factor shaping early modern Jewish culture was the new cabbalism emanating from Safed.[14] It is, of course, true that the tradition of cabbala reached back over the ages to its founding work, the *Zohar*, compiled in Spain in the late thirteenth century. Yet in the later Middle Ages and through the first half of the sixteenth century, cabbalistic mysticism remained a marginal phenomenon in Jewish life, the partially hidden preserve of small coteries of initiates. The main stream went largely unaffected. But, in the Holy Land during the sixteenth century, Jewish life was dominated by the community at Safed; and Safed now came heavily under the sway of cabbalistic cliques and schools. The principal figures in this upsurge of mystical endeavour and speculation in Galilee were a Spanish Jew, Moses Cordovero (1522–70), and Isaac

[13] Barzilay, *Yoseph Shlomo Delmedigo*, pp. 169, 175–6, 292–3.
[14] Scholem, *Jewish Mysticism*, pp. 244–6; Barzilay, *Yoseph Shlomo Delmedigo*, pp. 223–38.

Luria (1534–72), a holy man of Ashkenazi descent who spent most of his life in Egypt before settling in Safed towards the end of his life. During the third quarter of the sixteenth century the ferment in Galilee was at its height. Cordovero completed his chief work, the *Pardes Rimmonim*, around 1550, and, from this point on, cabbalistic influence emanating from Safed spread rapidly through the Jewish communities of the Balkans and Italy fusing with local trends toward a more mystical Judaism. Although the *Pardes Rimmonim* was not printed until it appeared at Salonika, in 1584, one of the chief promoters of the new cabbalism in Italy, Menahem Azariah da Fano (1548–1620), was propagating Cordovero's system as an integral part of *yeshivah* studies in Venice as early as the 1570s. Subsequently, he and his disciples also transmitted the system of Luria, though without wholly displacing Cordovero.[15] Apart from Venice, the cities of Modena, Reggio, and Mantua all emerged as key centres for the propagation of cabbala in this period.

Gradually, Cordovero's cabbala also percolated further north, the *Pardes Rimmonim* being reprinted at Cracow, the main publishing centre of Polish Jewry, in 1592. But the spiritual transformation that came about after 1550 was not merely a broadening and popularization of cabbala. Isaac Luria, whose life, visions, and teaching made a unique impact on his following in the Holy Land, eventually came to exert a pervasive influence over the innermost workings of the Jewish soul.[16] Though Luria himself never set down his teaching in written form, his sayings and concepts were collected by his disciples, most notably by Haim Vital, in a key compilation known as the *Ets Haim* (Tree of Life) assembled in the 1570s. In Luria, the deeds of man are invested with deep significance, everyday acts of piety being linked to a vast cosmological drama which is enacted to set right the defects of the world and ultimately restore all to its proper place. According to Luria, the Almighty, though infinite and perfect, does not fully manifest His perfection in the world until a certain point. The role of the Messiah, in Luria, was not to bring about redemption: rather the task of redeeming humanity and the world is imposed on the whole Jewish people in mystical communion with God through prayer, observance, and deeds of piety. Only when this process of spiritual preparation and building is accomplished is the world ripe for the coming of the Messiah. Thus, Luria arrived at an original

---

[15] Tishby, 'Confrontation', pp. 8–20.
[16] Scholem, *Sabbatai Sevi*, introduction.

explanation of evil, and the way man surmounts evil, a vision which came to exert an immense fascination on a people reeling from heavy setbacks yet buoyed by a formidable inner vitality and capacity for growth. Luria activated their underlying and intensifying messianic expectations, linking these to the doings of every individual.

Little by little, mainly through the medium of sermons and study groups, the Lurianic system percolated into the Balkans and Italy where it was first propagated in the 1590s by Israel Sarug. After 1600, it began to reach into Poland, Germany, and Holland. One of its principal exponents in the early seventeenth century, a key figure in western European Jewry's intellectual history, was Abraham Cohen Herrera (*c.*1570–1635). In early life, Herrera dwelt by turns as a New Christian and a Jew in Lisbon, Tuscany, Venice, and Morroco before passing to Cadiz, with a special licence from the Spanish crown, on the business of the Moroccan Sultan. In 1595, he was captured by the English, in their raid on Cadiz, and taken to London where he was imprisoned for a time before being released on the intercession of the Sultan. Around 1600, he settled in Ragusa where he studied the Lurianic system under Israel Sarug. After this, he joined the trickle of other former Marranos who had acquired their Judaism in Venice and the Levant and who moved to Holland soon after 1600. He spent the rest of his life at Amsterdam. Writing in Spanish, Herrera compiled a philosophic-cabbalistic work, the *Puerta del Cielo*, which set out to express Luria's system in terms of western Neoplatonic vocabulary.[17] His thought became a prime influence on the intellectual formation of Amsterdam Jewry, much as other Levantine and Venetian Jews shaped Amsterdam Sephardi Jewry's early organization and music.

Meanwhile, the pre-eminent figure in central European Jewish culture was Rabbi Judah Loew, the Maharal of Prague (*c.*1525–1609). The Maharal, like Luria, was deeply involved in the problem of Jewish exile and suffering and their meaning for the redemption of mankind. He reflected many of the cultural impulses of his time, preoccupying himself with mathematics and sanctioning scientific study which did not infringe Jewish practice and belief. Like his Polish contemporaries, he incorporated various cabbalistic ideas into his concept of higher study. It was also typical of him to impart radically new interpretations to traditional rabbinic texts and issues. The Maharal's various writings span a vast range of topics. One

17 Scholem, *Jewish Mysticism*, pp. 257–8, 410.

work, *Nesah Israel* (Eternity of Israel) (1600), is entirely devoted to the problem of redemption.[18] Here, a radical twist is given to traditional Jewish messianism, imparting an active role to the Jewish people in a way rather different, and more specifically historical, than, that envisaged by Luria. Loew sees the relationship between Israel and the other nations of the world—he takes nationhood to be the primary unit of mankind—as a perennial dialectic, the fundamental confrontation underlying history. The election of Israel he interprets as a divine burden, a continuing partnership between the Almighty and Jewry designed to lift the nations step by step from idolatry, superstition, and impurity.

The Maharal's vision of Israel interacting with the peoples surrounding it, while preserving its national and cultural separateness, corresponds in some senses to what became the actuality in late sixteenth-century Europe. The Jews of the west, though culturally now more removed from their neighbours than previously, yet began to impinge on them more actively than had their medieval forebears. One sign of this is the shift that now took place in the sphere of dispute with, and polemicizing against, Christianity.

Of course, there had been, throughout the Middle Ages, a long history of theological confrontation and dispute. But, if the quarrel between Christians and Jews is an old one, reaching back to the first century, it had passed through several stages. From 1240 onwards, starting in Paris, a series of grand disputations took place in the presence of rulers, lords, and bishops. On occasion, Jewish participants in these disputations had expressed themselves with surprising boldness, as in the case of Nahmanides' role in the Barcelona disputation of 1263. Yet these disputations had been more in the nature of trials than debates, and overwhelming intimidation was the rule. Nor could Jews ever proselytize, for this was punishable by death. It is true that there was never a time when some Christians were not convinced by Jewish objections to their faith, but, before the sixteenth-century, conversion to Judaism in Christian Europe was rare and involved the convert in migrating to distant parts or facing certain death.

Several changes came about during the sixteenth century. In the first place, the theological rifts within western Christendom caused an upsurge of perplexity and questioning which significantly increased the pull of Old Testament notions and, occasionally, of Judaism on

[18] Gross, *Messianisme juif*, pp. 85–99, 115, 126; Scholem, *Sabbatai Sevi*, pp. 65–6.

some Christians. Luther several times expressed anxiety over sporadic 'Judaizing' tendencies among Germans. In Poland, a report of 1539 tells us that the Reformation disputes had *inter alia* led to a wave of Christian conversions to Judaism, the converts fleeing to Ottoman territory to escape torture and death.[19] Above all, in France, the mood of scepticism which began to pervade French culture in the 1570s was clearly more conducive to the spread of a Jewish polemic against Christianity than the situation prevailing before the civil wars. We see this from the writings of Bodin and from many other references in the French literature of the period. Most notable, perhaps, was the spiritual quest of Jean Fontanier, a Montpellier lawyer who adopted Calvinism, and then reverted to Catholicism, before rejecting Christianity altogether, propagating Jewish notions in his book *Trésor inestimable* and finally being burnt at the stake in Paris in 1621. Another such quest was that of Nicholas Antoine, a Lorraine Catholic who became a Calvinist pastor and then a Jew 'in his heart'. He tried unsuccessfully to gain admittance to one of the Jewish communities in Italy before being burned at the stake for Judaizing at Geneva, in 1632.[20]

The push to dislodge belief in Christ was intensified by the curious situation which arose in the 1570s and 1580s when, for the first time, there was a sizeable emigration from Portugal of New Christians who were either sincere Catholics or (more often) religiously indifferent alongside those who were crypto-Jews. Most of these more Christianized 'New Christians' settled in France or Italy, showing little inclination toward Judaism. They had fled the Peninsula for one reason only—to escape suspicion and to secure their property from the threat of confiscation by the Inquisition. Thus, whereas the pre-1579 emigration from Portugal was mainly directed towards Ottoman territory and was overwhelmingly crypto-Jewish in character, the growing stream of New Christian refugees, stampeded by the increased powers of a ruthless and none too fastidious Inquisition, was more mixed in allegiance. Furious divisions arose among the *émigrés* in France, Italy, and at Antwerp, sometimes even within one family. The outcome was that, for the first time since the early Middle Ages, a Jewish proselytizing movement, albeit clandestine, aimed at winning over whole groups from Christianity, took root in western Europe. And this movement was quite a potent one. According to the

[19] Zivier, 'Jüdische Bekehrungsversuche', p. 98.
[20] Weill, 'Nicolas Antoine', pp. 165–72.

great Portuguese Jesuit António Vieira, who was in a position to
know, the pressure brought to bear by the Jewish proselytizers, even
in France (where in theory Judaism was forbidden), was so intense
that only the most committed Catholics among the émigrés were able
to withstand being sucked into Judaism and a Jewish milieu.[21] There
was also considerable smuggling of Jewish material into Spain.[22]

The new apologetic literature of the Jews assumed two guises, the
printed and a much more forthright body of work circulating in
manuscript. After the short burst in 1552–5, and the subsequent
pause, the printing of Jewish books in vernacular languages resumed
in the 1580s at Venice, and later elsewhere, so that there was now an
uninterrupted stream of such literature. Much of this output consisted of prayer-books in Spanish which, besides being used in Italy,
France, and the Netherlands, were evidently smuggled into Spain
and Portugal in sufficient quantity to influence decisively the language and prayers used in crypto-Jewish prayer-meetings in the
Peninsula.[23] Added to this was a corpus of apologetic literature,
mostly couched in guarded and cautious terms, though Usque's
Consolaçam is often surprisingly bold. Among this category of works
were Immanuel Aboab's *Nomologia*, published at Amsterdam in 1629,
Pinto Delgado's Spanish Jewish poems printed at Rouen in 1631,
and, least offensive of all, Leone da Modena's *Historia de riti ebraici*,
written in Italian at the request of the English ambassador in Venice
for presentation to James I and later printed at Paris in 1637.

But what chiefly mattered, as regards both Jewish proselytizing
and the impact of this campaign on European culture as a whole, was
the much more vehement body of writings circulating in manuscript.
For this literature, even if mainly intended to dissuade Marranos
from Christianity, or, as in the case of Modena's *Magen ve-Herev*, to
combat the papal offensive to convert Italian Jewry, did gradually
percolate more widely. While, to be sure, this batch of polemics was a
secondary factor in the broad forum of European intellectual life,
neither was it a negligible strand in the burgeoning complex of
scepticism and rejection of the dominant faith. It is obvious that the
tracts of writers such as Immanuel Aboab (*c.*1555–1628) and Eliau
Montalto (d. 1616), written in Portuguese and Spanish, were acces-
sible to others besides Marranos. But even the Hebrew polemics

---

[21] Vieira, *Obras escolhidas*, iv. 30.   [22] Lemos, *Zacuto Lusitano*, pp. 360–1.
[23] Morreale, 'Sidur ladinado', pp. 332–3; Salomon, 'Portuguese Background',
pp. 116–23.

circulated much more widely than might be supposed. One of the most systematic (and among Christian clergy notorious) attacks on Christianity of this period, the *Hizuk Emunah* by the Lithuanian Karaite Isaac of Troki (*c.*1533–*c.*1594), was composed in Hebrew, in the 1590s, on the farthest fringes of Europe. Yet, this scathing attack on the basic texts dealing with Christ's divinity and messiahship apparently became known everywhere, circulating in Latin, Spanish, and German, a whole century before it caught the eye of Voltaire and was taken up by the *philosophes*. The Lutheran pastor Johann Müller of Hamburg, who vented his fury against the Jews in his compilation *Judaismus oder Judenthumb* of 1644, was in part motivated, as he explains in his preface, by revulsion at how Troki's arguments against Christianity were spreading clandestinely in Hamburg without ever being systematically rebutted.[24] The irony was that by denouncing Troki in the most outraged terms, Müller simply lent added currency to his arguments in Germany. Meanwhile, in Holland, Jews could speak more or less openly against Christianity.[25]

Perhaps the most interesting of the new Jewish polemicists was Montalto. A medical graduate of the University of Salamanca, and a successful physician in Lisbon until his flight through France to Italy, Montalto was known in Portugal as Felipe Rodrigues. It emerges from Inquisition evidence that he stood out among Marrano circles for the fervour of his anti-Christianity even before leaving Portugal, which is of some significance in light of the fact that not only during his first stay in France but even whilst living for some years in Italy, in Florence and Pisa, he continued to dissimulate as a New Christian rather than openly proclaim his Judaism.[26] No doubt he remained an ostensible Christian in the interests of his highly successful medical career, for in the space of a few years he gained renown at the University of Pisa for his lectures and, more widely, for his medical writings which he published in Latin. Eventually, though, he joined

[24] Müller, *Judaismus*, preface; Müller, 'Christlich-jüdisches Religionsgespräch', pp. 520–3; Dietrich, 'Jüdisch-christliche Religionsgespräch', pp. 2, 10–11.

[25] Broughton, *Ovr Lordes Familie*, preface; Broughton held a series of controversies with Jews at Worms, Basle, Hanau, Frankfurt, and Offenburg, as well as in Holland but seems to have been particularly shocked by the anti-Christian utterances of the Sephardi parnas, David Farar of Amsterdam, a former New Christian; see Schudt, *Jüdischer Merkwurdigkeiten*, iv. 272–73.

[26] There are several statements in the Lisbon Inquisition files to the effect that even when Montalto was living in Portugal 'hera grande letrado nas cossas da Ley de Moyses e sabia muito dellas', see, for instance, ANTT Inqu. de Lisboa vol. 7192, 'Proceso de Duarte Nunes da Costa', fos. 9, 12ᵛ.

the 'Ponentine' Jewish community in Venice, where he wrote a series of furious tracts and letters, some of which he dispatched to Marranos in France, burning with a resentment which, no doubt, derives in part from his own experiences and those of his family, in Portugal. In Marrano Judaizers such as Montalto one encounters an anti-Christianity which is quite different in tone, being altogether more passionate and personal, than anything known to medieval Jewish literature. Montalto is not simply arguing that Christians misinterpret Scripture. Rather he is responding in kind to the growing virulence of Counter-Reformation attacks on Judaism as obdurate, irrational, inconsistent, and immoral, denouncing Christianity, with all the force of his being, as superstitious, idolatrous, hypocritical and, above all, 'cruel'.

In 1612, Montalto was invited to return to France by the Queen Regent, Marie de Médicis no less, who desired him to attend her as court physician. Since Montalto would not go unless he were permitted to conduct himself as a professing Jew, the Queen Regent obtained a papal dispensation allowing Montalto and his attendants to observe Judaism in France. Montalto and his young disciple Saul Levi Morteira, who later became a renowned and (in private) vehemently anti-Christian rabbi in Amsterdam, were thus placed in the unprecedented position of embodying Judaism at the French court and, indeed, in France. Nor need we suppose that, whilst in Paris, they confined their anti-Christian propaganda to fellow Marranos. Montalto was close to Leonora Galigai, wife of Concini, favourite of the Queen Regent, and Galigai's circle, which included a number of Portuguese New Christians one of whom, by the name of Manoel Mendes, was her *parfumier*, was widely suspected of highly unorthodox opinions. Had Montalto not died in 1616, at Tours, he might well have been entangled in the trial of Galigai which followed her husband's downfall in 1617. She was hauled before the Parlement of Paris charged among other things with unbelief and 'Judaism'. Morteira, meanwhile, conveyed Montalto's body to Amsterdam for a Jewish burial.

The intensifying counter-polemic against Christianity, like Lurianic cabbala and the general urge to consolidate, systematize, and iron out inconsistencies from traditional rabbinic and Talmudic learning, were, in large measure, aimed at restoring the confidence, lifting the morale, and soothing the doubts of a people reeling from immense mishaps and disasters in the recent past and now, in the face of a stepped-up bombardment of Lutheran and Counter-Reformation conversionist zeal, striving to achieve a new stability and equilibrium. All Jews needed reassurance that catastrophe, suffering, and humiliation were at, or were coming to, an end, that Jewish suffering at Christian hands had a deep meaning, and was soon to be followed by redemption and release, including the restoring to the Jews of an honoured, indeed the most honoured, place among the nations. Thus nothing was more typical of Jewish culture in the century 1550–1650 than the tendency to invest Jewish suffering with some special, albeit hidden significance pregnant with promise for the future. In this respect, Menasseh ben Israel reflects much that is typical of the cultural world of early modern European Jewry when he both promises, in his *Esperança de Israel* (Hope of Israel) of 1650, imminent release from humiliation and oppression and sees signs of pending redemption in the very persecution of his people.[27] In particular, he glorifies recent martyrs who, in Spain, Portugal, and Spanish America, had been burned alive at the stake by the Inquisition for their Jewish beliefs. 'And seeing our perseverance amid such great hardships', concluded Menasseh, 'we judge that the Almighty has preserved us for great rewards to come.'

[27] 'Although we cannot specify the exact moment of our redemption,' wrote Menasseh, in a well-known passage, 'we consider that it is now very close'; see Menasseh ben Israel, *Esperança de Israel* pp. 95–6, 99–100, 101–2.

V

The Thirty Years War

THE Thirty Years War (1618–48) marked a new phase in the interaction between Jews and European society in several respects. Especially in central Europe, the long and terrible conflict accelerated the reintegration of Jewry in progress since the 1570s, preparing the way for the 'Court Jews' of the later seventeenth century. For while, as we have seen, significant changes had already taken place in the period from 1570 down to the commencement of the Thirty Years War, care must be taken not to exaggerate the extent of central European Jewry's gains by 1618. The expansion of Jewish activity and communities was then still at a comparatively early stage. The Jews were still excluded from nearly all the larger territories of the Empire except for the lands of the Bohemian crown and Hesse. They were shut out of all the major Imperial Free Cities except Frankfurt and (in respect of the 'Portuguese' only) Hamburg. Furthermore, they were excluded from the great majority of the lesser Imperial Free Cities. Even where Jewish life was most strongly entrenched, in the ecclesiastical states of western and central Germany, they had only very limited rights of residence in such ecclesiastical capitals as Mainz and Speyer and were completely excluded from the cities of Würzburg and Münster, being confined to the villages and small towns around.

The first point to take into account in explaining the proliferation of Jewish communities in Germany, the Czech lands, and Alsace during the Thirty Years War is the special relationship between German Jewry and the Emperor. Of course, it had long been a fact that the chief protector of the Jews of the Holy Roman Empire was the Emperor. But, in the sixteenth century, even the most sympathetic emperors, such as Maximilian II and Rudolph II, had always been obliged to balance concessions, or favours, to Jews against their constant need to placate regional assemblies and towns which, down to the 1620s, were permeated with Lutheranism and a vigorous particularism. And, virtually everywhere, the hostility of the towns to the Jews remained implacable.

The further shift in favour of the Jews, from 1618, is all the more remarkable in that Ferdinand II (1619–37), in contrast to his predecessors, was personally inspired by the militant Catholicism of the Counter-Reformation which in Italy (as later in Austria) had led to an intensification in anti-Jewish policies rather than the reverse. But, from the outset of his reign onwards, Ferdinand was chronically short of the cash and supplies he needed to maintain forces strong enough to confront his Protestant rebels and foreign foes. Without massive Spanish aid, his cause would probably have been wrecked in any case for in the years 1618–19 Bohemia, Moravia, Silesia, and even parts of Austria itself were overrun by insurgents and the towns and assemblies of the rest were decidedly unenthusiastic about helping him out of his predicament. In the midst of this great crisis of the Austrian Habsburg Monarchy, the Jews were one of very few local assets which the Emperor could readily mobilize. Jewish victuallers had already shown their usefulness in supplying Austrian troops in the south during the recent confrontation with Venice.[1] And this capacity to provide cash, munitions, and food to the soldiery was now again to play a substantial part. Though most of the Jews of Bohemia and Moravia were in areas controlled by the rebels, Ferdinand raised sizeable subsidies from the Jews of his territories through the elders of the community in Vienna.[2] Very likely some of the money came from Frankfurt and elsewhere in southern Germany. Nor is it hard to see why Jews were more willing than others to advance cash to the Emperor at this critical juncture: Catholics or Protestants had no reason to offer cash except for repayment at interest, of which, especially in the years 1618–20, there was scant prospect. Jews, on the other hand, could be repaid in a different form, in concessions and privileges of which they alone had need and which were within the Emperor's power to grant.

The rewards for this co-operation began to accrue almost directly following the crushing of the Bohemian Protestants at the battle of the White Mountain, in November 1620. With the rebel forces dispersed, the city of Prague was ruthlessly pillaged, all, that is, except for the *Judenstadt*. The Emperor's soldiery were under strict instructions, which they obeyed, not to enter the Jewish quarter.[3] To commemo-

---

[1] Wolf, *Ferdinand II*, pp. 22–4.

[2] Grunwald, *Samuel Oppenheimer*, pp. 16, 20; Markbreiter, *Beiträge*, pp. 18–19; Hodik, *Beiträge*, p. 13.

[3] Spiegel, 'Prager Juden', pp. 117–18.

rate the imperial victory, and their own escape from peril, Prague Jewry instituted a special *Purim* celebration which survived as a distinctive feature of Prague Jewish life down to the days of Maria Theresa. The privileged treatment continued under the new governor of Bohemia, Karl von Liechtenstein, a nobleman with close links with Jacob Bassevi, the financier who was at the centre of the efforts to raise Jewish subsidies for the Emperor. A large number of confiscated Protestant houses adjoining the ghetto were allocated for purchase by the Jews. The Emperor, apparently, transferred two of the best houses to Bassevi as a present. In this way the Prague *Judenstadt* was substantially enlarged during the 1620s. More far-reachingly, in January 1623, an imperial edict lifted or curtailed the stringent restrictions on Jewish dealings in grain, wine, and cloth previously in force throughout Bohemia.[4]

In the same way, the Jews obtained favours in Vienna and elsewhere in the Austrian lands. In December 1624, disregarding local protests, Ferdinand allocated the Leopoldstadt district, on the outskirts of Vienna, as a precinct of the Jews where they might congregate and erect a public synagogue, something forbidden previously since 1421.[5] The concession of a *Judenstadt*, free of control by the Vienna city council—the Jewish community was placed directly under the Imperial Chancery—was deemed a major privilege and cause for celebration by the Jews. Numbering around fifty families in 1625, Viennese Jewry grew rapidly thereafter to reach approximately 2,000 by 1650. In 1627, in return for a further loan of 40,000 gulden, the Emperor granted the Jews of his territories access on equal terms with Christians to all the trade fairs of Bohemia and Silesia, a very radical change in economic policy which greatly stimulated Jewish activity throughout the Habsburg lands in central Europe.[6]

Bassevi's role as a Thirty Years War financier is well known. He specialized in handling the output of Bohemia's silver mines and, generally, in the buying and selling of silver. In 1622, he entered the notorious consortium licensed by the Emperor to supervise Bohemia's supplies of silver and 'mint' (in reality debase) the coinage. The four main members of the consortium were Liechtenstein and Wallenstein, who provided the political clout, and Hans de Witte

---

[4] Ibid., pp. 128, 130; Gindely, *Geschichte*, pp. 339–40.
[5] Wolf, *Juden in der Leopoldstadt*, pp. 3, 9; Přibram, *Urkunden*, pp. 84–8.
[6] Brilling, *Juden in Breslau*, pp. 18–23.

and Bassevi, who organized the financial side. De Witte, a Calvinist Netherlander, and then one of the principal bankers of Europe, put 402,652 silver marks into the operation, nearly three times as much as Bassevi and his associates who invested 146,353. Even so, Bassevi ranked as the second financier of the Austrian lands. In its first year, the clique manufactured 42 million debased gulden, registering a huge profit which was shared between the participants and the Imperial Treasury. In the 1620s, Bassevi, who had been ennobled— the first Jew to receive such an honour from a Holy Roman Emperor—by Matthias in 1614, dominated the politics of the Prague *Judenstadt* and its board of elders. But at length his domineering personality and questionable methods aroused some determined Jewish opposition. In the early 1630s, he slipped from influence and was forced to take refuge with Wallenstein who protected him until his own assassination. Bassevi died in 1634, a broken man but nevertheless something of a symbol of Jewish access to the Emperor.

After the reconquest of Bohemia came the subjugation of the Rhenish and upper Palatinate, the lands of the Elector Frederick, the Winter King, who had sought to dispossess Ferdinand of the crown of Bohemia. In 1622, both Protestant and Catholic armies manoeuvred close to Frankfurt, both sides vociferously demanding cash and supplies from the Jews, threatening reprisals should they fail to comply. The Frankfurt Jewish council did in fact promise 10,000 gulden to the Protestant commander Mansfeldt, but this subsidy was never paid.[7] A combination of Catholic success and sheer luck enabled Fankfurt Jewry both to remain loyal to the Emperor and escape Protestant retribution. During the years 1623–5, the Habsburgs and their allies swept northwards across Germany pursuing the remnants of the opposition. Numerous towns and localities with Jewish populations were overrun, including Halberstadt where, shortly before, in 1621, the local Lutheran populace had rioted against the Jews and destroyed the recently constructed synagogue.[8] In all known cases, Ferdinand's instruction that the Jews be protected was observed. This imperial protection also extended to other localities which remained unoccupied by Habsburg or Catholic League troops but which were now firmly under Habsburg dominance. In July 1627, for instance, the Emperor intervened, at the request of the elders of the Vienna *Judenstadt*, on behalf of the Jews of Hanau, a now substantial community, terrorized by a wave of popular anti-Semitic

---

[7] Kracauer, *Juden in Frankfurt*, ii. 2–5.   [8] Frankl, 'Politische Lage', p. 322.

agitation incited by local clergy who blamed the Jews for the war and the misfortunes befalling the German people.[9]

Meanwhile, further north, notable gains were made during the opening years of the war by the fledgeling Jewish communities on the Lower Elbe. The key factor here was the benefit which accrued to the Portuguese Jews of Hamburg and Glückstadt from the economic embargoes imposed by the Spanish crown, in April 1621, against Dutch ships and cargoes.[10] From 1621 down to 1641, in the case of Portugal, and down to 1647, in that of Spain, the Dutch were officially excluded from trade with the Iberian Peninsula and colonies. Though not entirely effective, these measures had an appreciable impact on patterns of trade generally and especially on the North German maritime zone. For with or without the Dutch, Spain and Portugal required naval stores and other munitions from the Baltic as well as supplies of Baltic grain and Swedish copper. Hamburg became the chief entrepôt for this diverted north–south carrying trade avoiding Holland. This, in turn, meant that the Lower Elbe region now began to rival Amsterdam as a distribution centre for colonial merchandise, especially Brazil sugar, diamonds, indigo, cochineal, and, of course, silver. Each year, throughout the rest of the Thirty Years War, large convoys sailed from Hamburg and Lübeck, circumventing Scotland and Ireland so as to avoid the Dutch navy, which was under orders to stop the flow of munitions to the Peninsula. From the records of the Hamburg *Admiralitätskollegium*, it is possible to extrapolate a reasonably detailed picture of this wartime convoy trade[11] Between 1621 and 1648, Iberian trade accounted for at least 20 per cent of Hamburg's business in terms of bulk and a much higher proportion in terms of value. Much of this new Iberian business was with Portugal, and something like half of this was handled by Hamburg's Portuguese Jewish merchants. The Jewish share of Hamburg's temporarily burgeoning commerce with Spain was much smaller but nevertheless appreciable.

Since most of Dutch Jewry's pre-1621 trade had been with Portugal and its colonies, the shift in the centre of gravity in Iberian commerce from Amsterdam to Hamburg was fraught with implications for the Portuguese Jewish diaspora in northern Europe as a whole. In the

---

[9] Wolf, *Juden in der Leopoldstadt*, p. 20.

[10] Israel, *Dutch Republic*, pp. 93–5, 134–43.

[11] For lists of which Hamburg merchants were sending what cargoes to Spain and Portugal during the Thirty Years War, see SAH Admiralität series F4/1–15.

years 1620–5, there was in fact a substantial migration of Portuguese Jews from Holland to the Lower Elbe region.[12] It is quite possible that as much as a quarter of the then Sephardi community of Amsterdam moved to North Germany. Moreover, the *émigrés* included some of the most eminent Jewish merchants of Amsterdam such as Duarte Nunes da Costa (Jacob Curiel), who settled first in Glückstadt and then, in 1627, in Hamburg where he was the wealthiest member of the Hamburg Portuguese Jewish community down to the arrival of the Teixeira family in 1646.[13] The Hamburg Jewish community now swelled to several hundred persons. Thus North German Portuguese Jewry was substantially reinforced by the effects of the Thirty Years War both in numbers and wealth. The number of Portuguese Jewish accounts with the Amsterdam Exchange Bank fell from 114 to only 76, or by more than a quarter, between 1620 and 1625: the corresponding figure for Sephardi accounts with the Hamburg Bank rose from 28 in 1619, to 43 by 1623 and, doubtless, a considerably higher figure subsequently.[14]

Admittedly, though, these developments had only very limited ramifications for the immigrant German Jews of the maritime region, or 'Hochdeutsche Juden' as they were known on the Lower Elbe. The imports from Spain and Portugal were mainly luxuries and included few items needed by the marauding armies further south. There was, clearly, a vast upsurge in imports of foodstuffs and materials, especially from Holland through Hamburg, during the Thirty Years War. But this traffic in supplies for the soldiery was largely controlled by Hamburg's Christian merchants. There was some rise in the numbers of Ashkenazi Jews in and around Altona and Wandsbek at this time, but only a slight one.[15] The policy of excluding German Jews from Hamburg proper continued at any rate down to the early 1640s when a number were allowed in on a temporary basis. In general, there was in the northernmost regions of Germany little or none of that fanning out, that proliferation of new communities, which was so striking a feature of developments further south.

The Danish defeats of 1626–7 involved something of a setback for the Jews on the Lower Elbe, but only a temporary one. Glückstadt, the chief Danish base on the Elbe, was tightly blockaded and traffic

[12] Israel, 'Economic Contribution', p. 516.
[13] Kellenbenz, *Sephardim*, pp. 40, 47, 167–9.
[14] Israel, 'Economic Contribution', p. 510; Kellenbenz, *Sephardim*, pp. 257–9.
[15] Feilchenfeld, 'Älteste Geschichte', pp. 274–5.

along the river heavily disrupted. The entire region along with Mecklenburg, East Friesland, and the Lower Weser valley swarmed with victorious Habsburg and Catholic League soldiery. The slump at Hamburg generated a short-lived counterflow of recent Portuguese Jewish immigrants back to Holland.[16] But commercial expansion soon resumed along the same lines as before.[17] The diplomatic volte-face of May 1629, whereby the Danish king came to terms with the Emperor, switching to a non-belligerent but unmistakably pro-Habsburg stance, heralded a resumption in the migration of Portuguese Jews from Holland to North Germany. In October 1630, Christian IV also signed a treaty with Spain which, among other things, assured Glückstadt an appreciable role in the revived commerce with the Peninsula. In this connection, the Danish monarch simultaneously issued fresh privileges to the Portuguese Jews of Glückstadt, this charter of 1630 being notably more generous than that of 1619, allowing, for instance, a public synagogue to be erected for the first time on Danish territory.[18] As an extension of his Jewish policy, the king subsequently, during the 1640s, extended his protection and issued new privileges to the Ashkenazi communities of Altona, Wandsbek, and also Moisling, situated on Danish territory outside Lübeck.

The Austrian and Spanish preponderance in Germany of the 1620s ended abruptly with the Swedish invasion of July 1630. With a series of crushing hammer blows, Gustavus Adolphus, the new champion of the Protestant cause, pulverized his Habsburg foes and their allies at Breitenfeld (September 1631), Rain (April 1632), and Lützen (November 1632). The Swedes swept all before them, most of German Jewry soon passing under their control. Gustavus's troops entered Frankfurt, Hanau, and Friedberg, the centre of Hessian Jewry, all in November 1631. At once, the Jews of these and many neighbouring places, including those of Mainz, Worms, Würzburg, and Wertheim were subjected to heavy exactions by the Swedish commanders.[19] These forced loans of 1631–3 coincided with a sudden sharp deterioration in the economic circumstances of central and southern Germany. In the 1620s, the Jewish population of Frankfurt

---

[16] Kellenbenz, *Sephardim*, p. 90.
[17] Israel, 'Central European Jewry', p. 15.
[18] Balslev, *Danske jøders historie*, pp. 4–5; Hartvig, *Jøderne i Danmark*, p. 52.
[19] Schaab, *Diplomatische Geschichte*, pp. 209–10; Kracauer, *Juden in Frankfurt*, ii. 15; Rosenthal, *Heimatgeschichte der badischen Juden*, pp. 85–6.

had continued to increase both in absolute numbers and in proportion to the overall population of the city, rising from 2,200 in 1620 to around 2,400, or slightly more, by 1630. By contrast, during the ensuing decade 1631–40, Frankfurt Jewry contracted in line with the overall population of the city, by about one-third, down to 1,600.[20] This decline was due to a mixture of migration and epidemic, particularly the outbreak of 1635 which killed 222 people in the ghetto, mostly children. The fall in numbers was accompanied by an even more marked drop in the financial power of Frankfurt Jewry. The number of Frankfurt Jews assessed for tax purposes as possessing 15,000 gulden or more fell from nineteen, in 1624, to only five by 1645.[21] While there is no hard evidence, there are also grounds for supposing that the other main communities in the central area, Hanau, Fulda, Worms, and Friedberg, likewise diminished in numbers and wealth as from 1630.[22]

In view of the clear preference for the Emperor's cause displayed by German Jewry from the outset of the Thirty Years War, it is pertinent to ask why there was no major reaction against the Jews among the Lutheran German populace, following the tremendous Swedish victories of 1630–2. The staunchly Lutheran Swedish crown had always rigorously excluded Jews from Sweden's Baltic territories adjoining Poland as well as from Sweden proper. Furthermore, with the exception of the Lower Elbe region, the economy and conditions of life were now worsening rapidly throughout Germany. Yet it was precisely under the Swedes, from 1630 onward, and during the period of relentless economic decline, that the Jews achieved, or were allowed to achieve, their real breakthrough to an altogether new level of involvement in German life, politics, and trade. For the Swedes and their allies were in urgent need of cash and supplies for their armies and garrisons, and the logistics of the war presented commanders with chronic and increasing difficulties. It is this which explains the pathbreaking Jewish policy which evolved, more or less haphazardly, under Gustavus Adolphus and, after his death, under his generals. It was an attitude tough, pragmatic, and calculating, a policy born of necessity. To the outraged objections voiced by burgomasters, merchants, and clergy against the rapid Jewish economic penetration

---

[20] Kracauer, *Juden in Frankfurt*, ii. 31–3; Dietz, *Stammbuch*, p. 433.
[21] Ibid.; Dietz, *Frankfurter Handelsgeschichte*, iv. 8–9, 20–2.
[22] Kober, 'Documents', p. 23; Rosenthal, *Juden im Gebiet der ehemaligen Grafschaft Hanau*, 58.

which now ensued, Swedish garrison commanders turned a deaf ear. Frequently, there evolved a regular collaboration between Swedish paymasters, quartermasters, and provisioners and Jewish financiers, victuallers, and horse-dealers (trade in horses being one of the main specialities of the Jews of central Germany). Why were Jews so prominent in the purveying of provisions to the garrisons? Aside from the fact that most German Jews lived in villages and small towns and were used to acting as intermediaries between town and country, cash was so scarce that the Swedes were compelled to seek ways of obtaining supplies without paying for them in money. The simple fact was that it was both easy and convenient to procure much of what they needed from the Jews in return for favours, concessions, and protection. It is true that the Swedes levied some heavy forced loans on the Jews, especially at first, but they also took care not to pillage, disrupt, or otherwise endanger what to them was a useful captive asset. No Jewish community of any size is known to have been attacked or looted by the Swedes or the Lutheran populace under their control. Some sporadic despoliation of Jews and debauching of their women by Swedes and their allies went on in south and central Germany but only in the case of a few small and isolated rural communities.[23] What is really remarkable is that wholly unprotected communities in towns such as Fulda and Friedberg which were constantly being occupied and reoccupied by the soldiery of either side escaped totally or largely unscathed. Friedberg was a notorious 'whore of war', repeatedly changing sides, and yet its Jewish community remained largely intact.

That the Swedes, like the Imperialists, generally treated the Jews better than the rest of the population emerges from a good deal of contemporary evidence.[24] It is equally clear that this fact, even a hint at it, was in the past deeply disturbing to German Jewish historians who habitually swept it under the carpet with profuse assurances that the Jews were treated during the Thirty Years War 'no better and no worse than their Christian neighbours'.[25] Thus, the assimilationist instincts of nineteenth- and early twentieth-century German Jewry were projected back to pervade the historiography of the 'Great War' as it was once known. And, indeed, from their standpoint this instinct

[23] Eckstein, *Juden im ehemaligen Fürstbistum Bamberg*, pp. 17–18; Arnold, *Juden in der Pfalz*, p. 23.

[24] Schaab, *Diplomatische Geschichte*, pp. 209–10; Kracauer, *Juden in Frankfurt*, ii. 1–2.

[25] Rosenthal, *Juden im Gebiet der ehemaligen Grafschaft Hanau*, p. 58; Carlebach, *Juden in Lübeck und Moisling*, p. 11; Salfeld, *Bilder*, pp. 37–8.

was sound enough, for the realization that during the Thirty Years War Jews were not just exempt from recruiting drives but were specially 'favoured' by both sides was acutely offensive to the conservative, anti-Semitic element in German historical scholarship and was later seized on by historians during the Nazi period.[26] Yet, for all the twisted sense of outrage, the Nazi contention on this point was actually more accurate than the assumptions and wishful thinking of pre-1939 German Jewish historians.

It is frequently assumed that, owing to the chronic insecurity prevailing in the countryside, large numbers of rural Jews drifted to walled towns in search of security.[27] To some extent this did indeed happen. We even have a record of a rabbi from a village near Hanau who migrated from town to town in the 1630s and 1640s looking for a secure haven.[28] But it is quite wrong to infer from this that the Thirty Years War marked a reversal of previous trends, away from the countryside to the towns, and the beginnings of the re-urbanization of German Jewry.[29] It is also erroneous to argue that, because some rural Jews moved to walled towns while some urban Jewish communities such as those of Frankfurt, Hanau, Worms, and Hildesheim did, or may have, declined, 'total Jewish demographic losses may not have been much smaller than those estimated for the entire German population'.[30] For both assumptions entirely ignore the unquestionable fact that many new Jewish communities, urban and rural, arose during the Thirty Years War as well as the equally unchallengeable fact that some previously existing urban communities, notably those of Prague, Vienna, Speyer, and Hamburg–Altona–Wandsbek, actually increased in size or remained stable during the war. Urban communities in such fortress towns as Gross-Glogau, Breisach, and Philippsburg, not to mention Glückstadt, often grew vigorously, despite being repeatedly occupied and reoccupied, and became more strongly rooted than before.[31] The truth is that there is not a scrap of evidence to show that central European Jewry declined at all in size during the Thirty Years War, much less that it declined only slightly less than the population as a whole.

What the evidence does show is that there was now a fanning out in all directions from the localities where Jews were living in 1618, not

[26] Sander, 'Juden und das deutsche Heerwesen', p. 339.
[27] Arnold, *Juden in der Pfalz*, p. 23; Baron, *Social and Religious History*, xiv. 269.
[28] Bloch, 'Vielbegehrter Rabbiner', pp. 116–17.
[29] Baron, *Social and Religious History*, xiv. 269.　　　　　　　[30] Ibid.
[31] Ibid., xiv. 269, 403; Brilling, *Jüdischen Gemeinden Mittelschlesiens*, p. 4.

only geographically but also in the sense of penetration of economic sectors from which they had previously been wholly or largely excluded. This happened practically everywhere except in north-eastern Germany, beyond Halberstadt and Dessau. From Brandenburg, Pomerania, Mecklenburg, and electoral Saxony, the Jews continued to be rigorously debarred. This expansion of Jewish life in central Europe in the Thirty Years War occurred both in areas occupied by one side for prolonged periods and in districts which constantly changed hands. In north-west Germany, the rise of new Jewish communities and growth of older ones took place within a context of largely undisturbed Swedish and other foreign Protestant predominance. At Minden, the city council had permitted the existence of a small Jewish community since the 1590s but one officially restricted to five families. By the end of the war, the Minden Jewish community had increased by four or five times, specifically because the Swedish garrison commander took no notice of the burgomasters' objections.[32] In the neighbouring principality of Schaumburg-Lippe, there was a marked increase in the number of Jewish inhabitants of the towns of Bückeburg and Stadthagen, again due to the fixed proximity of Swedish troops.[33] At the same time, other Jewish immigrants (mostly from nearby ecclesiastical states) resettled in Herford, the other side of Minden, a town from which Jews had previously been completely excluded.[34] In and around Hanover, Jewish resettlement dates from slightly before 1618 but clearly gathered momentum during the 'Great War'.[35] And yet, while there is evidence to suggest some decline in the Jewish population of the bishopric of Hildesheim, in the other ecclesiastical states of the region—Münster, Paderborn, Halberstadt, and Cologne—the Jewish population continued to increase.[36] This is particularly clear in the case of the towns of the duchy of Westphalia and in Warburg and Paderborn.

Further south, Swedish control was more sporadic, the impact of the great conflict generally more disruptive. But, as far as the Jews were concerned, the situation was again one of general expansion. In 1630, before the entry of the Swedes, the Elector of Mainz granted the

[32] Krieg, 'Juden in der Stadt Minden', pp. 116–19.
[33] Hasselmeier, *Stellung der Juden in Schaumburg-Lippe*, pp. 4–5.
[34] Stern, *Preußische Staat*, ii. 68, 72.
[35] Löb, *Rechtsverhältnisse*, pp. 5–6; Wilhelm, *Jüdische Gemeinde . . . Göttingen*, p. 60.
[36] Holthausen, 'Juden im kurkölnischen Herzogtum', pp. 103–4; Schnee, *Hoffinanz*, iv. 178; Evers, *Juden in der Stadt Warburg*, pp. 19, 24, 58–9.

Jews of his territory the right to establish a rabbinate and communal institutions in his capital city from which they had been debarred in the sixteenth century and to which they had had only tentative access since around 1600.[37] But the Swedish occupation of 1631–6 occasioned a further expansion in the Jewish role in the city. The size of the community increased and, in 1639, acknowledging the changed situation, the Elector granted new and more generous privileges, including the right to erect a public synagogue. In the bishopric of Speyer there was a notable growth in the Jewish communities both in the town of Speyer itself and in Bruchsal and Grombach as well as in the key fortress-town of Philippsburg, on the Rhine opposite Heidelberg.[38] There was a parallel expansion in the Jewish role in the county of Wertheim where Jewish merchants now obtained the contract to supply the mint with silver and other financial concessions.[39] In the extensive region around Mergentheim, Weikersheim, Dörzbach, and Crailsheim, it is possible to speak of systematic Jewish colonization during the Thirty Years War with a whole network of new communities arising in the 1620s and 1630s.[40] It may be that some of the Jewish immigrants to these small country towns were coming from larger centres such as Frankfurt and Worms; in any case, in this area there was a marked strengthening of the Jewish presence in rural society. In Weikersheim, Hohebach, Hollenbach, and neighbouring places, permanent Jewish settlement arose directly from the Emperor's temporary confiscation of the district from the counts of Hohenlohe, in 1637.

In the east-central zone of Germany, the position was very similar. At Fürth, a few Jewish houses were destroyed and the newly-completed main synagogue (1617) damaged by Mansfeld's soldiery, at the beginning of the war, but subsequently Fürth Jewry suffered remarkably few mishaps, aside from a Croat cavalry contingent using the damaged synagogue as a stables, in 1634.[41] Once again, the Jewish communities in and around Fürth, Bamberg, Bayreuth, and Ansbach were respected by Imperialists and Swedes alike.[42]

---

[37] Stadtarchiv Mainz MS 6155: Belegbuch 1614, p. 311; Schaab, *Diplomatische Geschichte*, pp. 207–10.

[38] Rosenthal, *Heimatgeschichte*, pp. 133–4; Arnold, *Juden in der Pfalz*, p. 23.

[39] Rosenthal, *Heimatgeschichte*, pp. 59–61.

[40] Sauer, *Die jüdischen Gemeinden*, pp. 40, 49, 59, 63, 68, 70, 107, 188–9.

[41] Haenle, *Juden im ehemaligen Fürstenthum Ansbach*, pp. 5, 180–1.

[42] Ibid., p. 63; Eckstein, *Juden im ehemaligen Fürstbistum Bamberg*, p. 267–9; Eckstein, *Juden in Markgrafentum Bayreuth*, pp. 24–30.

Gustavus Adolphus himself issued guarantees to the Fürth community which was now the largest in Franconia. In the lands of the Margrave of Ansbach, some Jews had returned, as we have seen, since around 1609; but this did not apply to the town of Ansbach itself or to several other towns in the principality. In the towns, the Jews first regained a foothold under Swedish occupation in the 1630s. Of course, the Swedes soon left, but the Jews stayed. The town council of Ansbach acknowledged the permanent right of a limited number of Jews to reside there in 1643.[43] A year later, recognizing the increased and increasing importance of the Jews in his territory, the prince-bishop of Bamberg lifted previous restrictions on their dealing in textiles and wine. But whilst there was a clear strengthening of the Jewish position in the towns, there are also definite signs of Jews percolating into ruined and half-ruined villages, including villages where they had not lived before.[44] In some cases, it is by no means impossible that they were the first to recolonize devastated villages. In any case, around Bamberg and Ansbach, as in the region further west, a strengthening of Jewish life in the towns went hand in hand with expansion of their activity in the countryside.

Further east, in Bohemia and Silesia, the picture is by no means dissimilar. The Swedish victories of the early 1630s did precipitate a vast upheaval in these regions with Gustavus Adolphus's Saxon allies advancing on several fronts. As they approached, several thousand Bohemian *Landjuden* fled into Prague so that the *Judenstadt* there was filled to bursting point. Yet, under the terms of Prague's surrender to the Protestant commander in 1632, the safety of the roughly 7,000 Jews then in the city was expressly guaranteed and this clause was fully respected.[45] Before long, the rural Jews seeped back to their villages. At the same time, the chaotic conditions prevalent since the 1620s had enabled appreciable numbers of Jews to settle in the many Bohemian and Moravian towns which, before 1620, had strictly excluded them. The now half-ruined town of Kaaden (Czech Kadaň), for example, close to the Saxon border, had had no Jews at all before 1620, in the century since their expulsion from the town in 1520, but contained a quite sizeable community in the 1630s.[46] In the same way, the re-emergence or strengthening of the Jewish communities of

[43] Haenle, *Juden im ehemaligen Fürstenthum Ansbach*, p. 140.
[44] Pfeifer, *Kulturgeschichtliche Bilder*, pp. 2–3.
[45] Spiegel, 'Prager Juden', p. 120.
[46] Hoffmann, 'Juden in Kaaden', pp. 110–17.

Stampfen, Feldsburg, Jamnitz, and many other towns of the Czech lands dates specifically from the 1620 and 1630s.[47] At Kolin, the only Bohemian royal town other than Prague which officially admitted Jews, the community, which had occupied thirty-two houses in 1615, comprised forty-five houses by 1630.[48] In Silesia, the Jewish presence remained much less significant than in Bohemia or Moravia, and was still confined to just three or four communities, but here, too, there was very definitely a steady expansion in the Jewish role stimulated by the presence of Swedish and Saxon occupation forces.[49]

In the southernmost regions of Germany, Jewish life on the eve of the Thirty Years War was of an extremely fragmented and marginal nature. After the expulsion from Baden-Baden, in 1614, the Jews were debarred from all the larger principalities of the region and from all the important cities, being confined to a few small towns and some small scattered territories belonging either to lesser lords or else to the Emperor. The most important of these southern Jewries were those of the Burgau, a small Austrian enclave situated between Ulm and Augsburg, of the Breisgau, another Austrian jurisdiction around Breisach on the Rhine, and of the duchies of Öttingen-Spielberg and Öttingen-Wallerstein, encircling the Imperial Free City of Nördlingen.[50] There was also an assortment of tiny communities further south around Saulgau, Stühlingen, and along the northern shore of Lake Constance. Even though local efforts to expel the Jews from the Burgau in the years 1617–19 were blocked by the Emperor (despite his then weakness), there was a noticeable fanning out of Jews from the territory during the 1620s and 1630s. Burgau Jews took the lead in founding the new community at Hohenems on the south-eastern corner of Lake Constance, in part of the Vorarlberg which was then not yet under Austrian rule. Other Burgau Jews moved westward and were among the small groups which percolated back into Baden-Baden during the 1630s, taking advantage of the mounting turmoil to evade the recent decree of expulsion from that territory.[51] Jews from the Burgau also figured prominently in the resettlement of Jews in the Palatine county of Neuburg (Pfalz-

[47] Marmorstein, 'Juden in Jamnitz', pp. 30–4; Schwenger, 'Zweite Ansiedlung', pp. 37–40; Herzog, 'Juden in Stupava (Stampfen)', p. 124.
[48] Grunwald, 'Contribution', p. 444.
[49] Brilling, *Juden in Breslau*, pp. 120–23, 152, 169–70; Brilling, *Jüdischen Gemeinden Mittelschlesiens*, pp. 148–9.
[50] Tänzer, *Juden in Tirol*, pp. 12, 16, 18–21; Sauer, *Die jüdischen Gemeinden*, p. 31.
[51] Rosenthal, *Heimatgeschichte*, pp. 77, 189, 196.

Neuburg), a sizeable jurisdiction lying between the duchies of Würt-temberg and Bavaria from which the Jews had been expelled in 1553. Jewish re-entry into this district preceded the arrival of the Swedes, the Duke of Neuburg having allowed Jews to settle at Weiden in the 1620s and negotiated a contract with the financier Abraham of Goldkronach for the supply of silver and copper to the ducal mints. But the brief Swedish occupation of 1632–4 does seem to have accelerated the process of Jewish reintegration.[52] A Jewish com-munity formed in the garrison town of Lauingen, in 1632, precisely when the Swedes arrived, and, as happened elsewhere, stayed after they left. In 1636, there were fifty-eight Jews living in Lauingen, virtually all migrants from neighbouring parts of South Germany. Inevitably, the resistance to this process of Jewish penetration was most intense in the Imperial Free Cities; but a small group of Jews did manage to settle for some years even in Augsburg.[53]

The favourable consequences of the Swedish occupation for the Jews were paralleled by the effects of other foreign occupations around the fringes of Germany. This can be seen, for instance, in the resettlement of Jews in the territory under Dutch occupation on the Lower Rhine. By 1618, Dutch forces already garrisoned several border towns on the German side and, after capturing Wesel from the Spaniards in 1629, held the entire duchy of Cleves.[54] Even so, there were repeated Spanish and Imperialist incursions into this area during the 1630s, so that much of the countryside was devastated. This combination of circumstances, the dislocation of the local economy and the presence of Dutch garrisons in the walled towns, gave rise to a network of new Jewish communities, albeit very small ones, where previously Jews had been completely shut out. It is instructive that in the town of Cleves itself, where there was no fixed garrison, the Jews were less successful in establishing themselves than in Emmerich, Rees, and Wesel where there were permanent garrisons and Dutch military governors.[55] At Wesel, the community seems to have formed before 1629 under Spanish occupation. Emmerich became the base of the Gomperz family, destined to become one of the principal dynasties of 'Court Jews' of the later seventeenth century. The founder of the family's fortunes, Gumpert Salomon, amassed his

[52] Vokert, 'Juden in Fürstentum Pfalz-Neuburg, pp. 582–5.
[53] Grünfeld, *Juden in Augsburg*, p. 46.
[54] Israel, *Dutch Republic*, pp. 97–9, 178–9.
[55] Baer, *Protokollbuch*, pp. 13–17.

initial capital in the 1620s and 1630s selling foodstuffs and tobacco to the Dutch soldiery.[56]

The Jews who settled in Cleves and Mark at this time mostly originated from the nearby ecclesiastical principalities of Cologne and Münster or from East Friesland. Gumpert Salomon became the acknowledged leader as well as rabbi of Cleves Jewry. His great rival was the still more prominent figure of Berend Levi, originally from Bonn, who had settled in the village of Warendorf, the centre of Münster Jewry. Like Gumpert Salomon, Berend Levi made his initial fortune by supplying the soldiery but by the 1640s had already graduated to handling fiscal operations in the territories of Mark and Ravensburg on behalf of the Elector of Brandenburg. Levi succeeded in extending his financial influence all over Westphalia and the Lower Rhine, his brother, Salomon Levi, being for a time the leading figure among Paderborn Jewry. By the mid-1640s, Berend's financial status was such that the Great Elector, Frederick William, entrusted him with the handling of the finances of the Brandenburg delegations to the Münster and Osnabrück peace congresses.[57]

As for the impact of the French invasions, from 1635, this undeniably expanded further the Jewish role throughout the south-west and middle Rhine areas. The Jewish community which had formed at Metz in the sixteenth century had long been closely involved with the French garrisons in the area, so that even before France's entry into the Thirty Years War French commanders on the borders of the empire were accustomed to purchasing horses and provisions from the Jews.[58] Indeed, in 1632, whilst on a visit to Metz, Louis XIII himself praised the Jewish community there for its contribution to the upkeep of the border garrisons. From 1638, when the French overran large parts of Alsace and captured the Austrian fortress of Breisach, much the same collaboration developed between French commanders and the Jews of Alsace in the upper Rhine valley. Despite continuous heavy fighting in Alsace, it is evident that the revival of Alsatian Jewry, which had declined steadily during the two centuries from 1400 to 1600, owing to local expulsions, and which had reached a low point of only a few dozen families in the entire region by the end of the sixteenth century, really begins during the Thirty Years War.[59]

[56] Baer, *Protokollbuch*, pp. 57, 64, 68–9, 72.
[57] Ibid., pp. 19–21; Schnee, *Hoffinanz*, i. 97–101.
[58] Baron, *Social and Religious History*, xiv. 286.
[59] Weill, 'Recherches', pp. 53–5.

By 1650, there were a number of new Jewish communities in Alsace and the total Jewish population of the territory had increased to around 2,000. Similarly, the French garrisons in Breisach and Philippsburg attracted a good deal of Jewish commercial activity while the emergence of new Jewish communities east of the Rhine in towns such as Heilbronn, from which Jews had previously been rigorously excluded, is once again directly attributable to the disinclination of French generals to pay any attention to the vociferous protests of the local Christian burghers.[60] However, at Heilbronn, an Imperial Free City, Jewish resettlement was a temporary phenomenon which ended with the withdrawal of the French at the close of the war. In the electorate of Mainz which they occupied in the years 1644–8, the French proved as protective of the Jews as had been the Swedes in the 1630s.

The initially favourable attitude shown by the Emperor toward the Jews continued subsequently after the crushing defeat inflicted on the Swedes at Nördlingen, in 1634. The Imperialists were now once again in the ascendant, at least in southern Germany. The numerous and intricate links between Jewish communities and Protestant armies do not seem to have produced any change in the Jewish policy of either Ferdinand II or of his successor, Ferdinand III (1637–57). On the contrary, eager to rebuild their shattered authority in Germany, the Habsburgs continued to emphasize their role as protectors of the Jews. In 1636, as was to be indignantly recorded centuries later by at least one Nazi historian, Ferdinand II issued instructions to his commanders that the Jews of Worms were not to be subjected to billeting, forced loans, or any interference whatsoever.[61] These orders were issued after Worms Jewry had lodged complaints with the elders of the Vienna *Judenstadt*. The Worms city council subsequently tried to increase its control over the Jews in the city and impose special financial exactions on them. Again the Jews appealed to Vienna and not without effect. In November 1641, Ferdinand III drew up new privileges for Worms Jewry, restating his protective claims over them in unprecedently emphatic terms.[62]

In the final stages of the Thirty Years War, the Swedes regained something of their former momentum at any rate in the eastern

---

[60] Rosenthal, *Heimatgeschichte*, pp. 87, 133–4; Franke, *Juden in Heilbronn*, pp. 39–40.
[61] Wolf, *Ferdinand II und die Juden*, pp. 62–3; Sander, 'Juden und das deutsche Heerwesen', p. 339.
[62] Wolf, *Juden in Worms*, pp. 22–3.

regions of the Empire. Following their victory of Jankov, in 1645, Swedish forces ranged right across Bohemia and parts of Austria and, in 1648, the last year of the war, laid siege to Prague. This was one of the most renowned episodes in the history of the city. The Jews participated energetically, not only in supplying and financing the defence, but manning a section of the walls at the cost of twenty-two men killed. Eventually, the Swedes raised the siege and pulled back. In recognition of their contribution to the defence of Prague, Ferdinand III further amplified the privileges of Prague Jewry, allowing them, among other concessions, to adopt an emblem—a Swedish helmet within a star of David—which was now affixed to all the communal buildings of the *Judenstadt*. The siege of Prague may have been brief, but Bohemia and Moravia suffered severely from the ravages of war in the 1640s, as they had in the previous two decades, and on top of this there was a major epidemic in 1639 and several lesser ones. Nevertheless, there is no sign of any serious decline in the Jewish population of either realm in general or of Prague in particular.[63] On the contrary, it is established that the city's Jewish population continued to increase down to 1638, and while it may have fallen back somewhat during the last decade of the war, there is little doubt that this community was larger at the end of the conflict, when it numbered between four and five thousand, than it had been at the beginning.

But if many new communities arose in central Europe, and some older ones expanded, how is one to account for the undoubted emigration of some German Jews during the Thirty Years War? Networks of German Jewish communities formed in the 1620s and 1630s in the Dutch Republic and Switzerland while at least some German Jews migrated to Poland. It is important, though, not to jump to the conclusion, as some historians have done, that such migration was essentially flight from the ravages of war.[64] In fact, the seepage of Ashkenazi Jews into Holland was remarkably sparse in the period before 1648. It was not until 1635 that the Ashkenazi community in Amsterdam was sufficiently numerous to form their own congregation and, as late as 1650, there were at most a few hundred of them in the city.[65] It is true that some poor German Jews requiring

[63] Spiegel, 'Prager Juden', pp. 121, 174, 182.

[64] As is frequently done, see, for instance, Fuks, 'De Amsterdamse Opperrabbijn David Lida', p. 166.

[65] Gans, *Memorboek*, pp. 54–5; Meijer, '*Moeder in Israël*', p. 16.

charity from the Sephardi community in Amsterdam were shipped
off, with their fares paid by the Sephardi elders, to Poland, but the
numbers were not enough substantially to alter the picture.[66] The real
influx of German Jews (as well as, to a lesser extent, of Polish Jews)
into Holland began only after 1648.[67] In Rotterdam, organized
Ashkenazi communal life began only around 1660, not before.
Similarly at Leeuwarden, Workum, and several other places in
Friesland where Jews settled in the seventeenth century, the formation of organized communities took place in the 1660s and 1670s but
not earlier.[68] And precisely the same is true of Amersfoort which, in
the late seventeenth century, evolved into one of the principal Dutch
Jewish communities.

In Switzerland, by contrast, the sudden proliferation of scattered
Jewish groups in the 1620s and 1630s did mark the high point of
Jewish penetration into the country, at least as far as the early modern
period is concerned. After 1648, most of these newly formed Swiss
Ashkenazi communities disintegrated, mostly disappearing altogether, as the bulk of the migrants moved back into Germany.[69] But it
seems that their activity in Switzerland was, all along, chiefly confined to the border areas and was mainly concerned with procuring
cattle, forage, and other supplies for nearby military garrisons in
Germany rather than with the Swiss interior as such. Thus, the Jews
were expelled from the environs of Basel, in 1637, expressly for having
cornered so much grain and other local produce for transportation
into Baden and Alsace that they were distorting food prices in Basel.
It would therefore seem that the string of mostly minute communities
which took shape at this time, at Rheineck, Mammeren, Klingnau,
Lengnau, and neighbouring places, was essentially an extension of
the expanding activity of Jews in Germany itself. Only two of these
new Swiss communities took root permanently, those at Lengnau and
Endingen, both in the Aargau. In any case, the extent of the
Ashkenazi migration into Switzerland, comprising at most a few
hundred individuals, is scarcely plausible evidence of a major disruption of Jewish life in Germany. In all likelihood, the relatively small
number of German Jewish migrants to Switzerland and the Dutch

[66] Vaz Dias, 'Nieuwe bijdragen', pp. 153–4, 162.

[67] Zwarts, 'Joodse gemeenten', pp. 413–14; Rijnders, *'Joodsche Natien' tot joodse Nederlanders*, pp. 132, 140.

[68] Beem, *Joden van Leeuwarden*, pp. 1–3.

[69] Ulrich, *Sammlung jüdischer Geschichten*, 252–3, 259–60; Haller, *Rechtliche Stellung der Juden im Kanton Aargau*, pp. 413–14; Weldler-Steinberg, *Juden in der Schweiz*, pp. 19–22.

provinces during the years 1618–48 was more than counterbalanced by the simultaneous immigration into the Empire of several hundred Portuguese Jews settling on the Lower Elbe, and North Italian and Polish Jewish newcomers settling in and around Vienna and doubtless also other localities. For while it is true that there was a large exodus of Bohemian and Moravian Jews to Poland in the years 1618–20, especially to the Cracow region, it is no less true that most of them seem to have returned to Bohemia in the later 1620s and that they were joined in this westwards trek by a number of Polish Jews who moved to various parts of the Empire, penetrating, in some cases, as far west as Alsace.[70]

But if the seepage of German Jews into the Dutch provinces during the 1618–48 period was nothing like the large-scale influx it is sometimes imagined to have been, it remains true that the Thirty Years War exerted a profound influence on Dutch Jewry. Due essentially to the Spanish measures cutting the Dutch out of direct trade between northern Europe and the Iberian Peninsula, the period was one of acute difficulty and temporary decline for Dutch Sephardi Jewry.[71] As we have seen, a sizeable proportion of the Portuguese Jews in Holland migrated to North Germany. But it was not just a period of setbacks. It was also a time of fundamental restructuring which helped pave the way for the golden age of Dutch Jewry which can be said to have begun with the end of the Thirty Years War in 1648. Among the changes of the period 1618–48, perhaps the most important was the temporary Dutch conquest of north-east Brazil (1630–54) which made possible the founding of the first organized Jewish community in the New World—at Recife, the main Dutch base. By 1644, the Jews of Dutch Brazil numbered 1,450, which amounted to approximately one-third of the white civilian population of the colony, though it is true that a few of the Jews were mulatto half-castes. The Jews played only a marginal role in the running of the colony's sugar plantations and in actual production of sugar, but they handled a large part of the colony's trade with Holland and stood high in the favour of the West India Company, the directors of which regarded them, their skills, and their resources, as indispensable to Dutch colonial expansion in the Americas. And, indeed, the rise of the Sephardi community in Brazil made Dutch Jewry for the first time

---

[70] Bałaban, *Historja*, i. 290–2; Halpern, 'Jewish Refugees', p. 200–3; Shulvass, *From East to West*, p. 21, 23, 34, 46.

[71] Israel, 'Economic Contribution', pp. 516–17.

into a truly trans-Atlantic social and commercial network. Despite the collapse of Dutch Brazil, in 1654, and the dissolution of the Jewish community at Recife, Dutch Jewry retained a large part of its newly forged link with the Americas, many of the *émigrés* from Brazil settling in the Caribbean, where they laid the basis for Amsterdam Sephardi Jewry's flourishing post-1650 trade with the Dutch and (eventually) the Spanish colonies as well as with Barbados and Martinique.[72]

Lack of alternatives ensured that Iberian trade remained the basis of post-1621 Sephardi activity, as it had been before, despite the formidable obstacles now obstructing their activity. Putting up with astronomical insurance and freight charges, and using false papers and seals, Dutch Sephardi merchants continued sending cargoes to the Peninsula, often for re-export to India, Africa, or the Americas, in most cases using Hamburg or other Hanseatic ships, and receiving their returns via Hamburg, London, or some other neutral port. Of course, the volume of this contraband trade was much less than the traffic which they had carried on legally (except in so far as Dutch Jews had had to conceal their Jewish names and identities from the Spanish authorities) before 1621. Moreover, even the cleverest subterfuge constantly risked detection by the *Almirantazgo*, Olivares's new inspectorate for commerce, and there were some spectacular losses. In 1626, three Hamburg ships loaded with textiles and other merchandise by Francisco Lopes d'Azevedo and other Amsterdam Sephardim were seized in Lisbon, their cargoes, worth thousands of gulden, being condemned and confiscated by the *Almirantazgo* court in Madrid.[73]

Yet, paradoxically, the harsh pressures of the Thirty Years War also tended to reinforce the Jewish role in what was left of Dutch trade with the Peninsula. And this increased role in the remaining traffic was pregnant with implications for the future. Working hand in hand with local Portuguese New Christian factors who were often relatives, rather than expatriate Flemings or Hanseatics resident in the Peninsula, Sephardi traders were less exposed than other Dutch merchants to Spanish scrutiny, and their activity harder for the *Almirantazgo* to eradicate. And where the Jews had already, before 1621, been handling a large part of Dutch trade with Portugal and the Portuguese colonies, it would seem to have been precisely the Thirty Years War which first gave Dutch Sephardi, as distinct from other Dutch merchants, an important role in trade with Spain. Thus, from

[72] Wolff, *A Odisséia*, pp. 84–5 ff.   [73] Van Dillen, 'Vreemdelingen', p. 32.

1621, with Dutch ships excluded from Spanish ports, there arose a thriving contraband trade between Amsterdam and Madrid, chiefly textiles in exchange for silver and wool; the goods were carried overland to and from Bayonne across Navarre and the Pyrenean passes, Bayonne being the closest port to which Dutch ships had access. There survive several Spanish reports on this overland contraband traffic in the 1620s and 1630s to and from Bayonne, and they all stress that the trade was mainly carried on by Amsterdam Jews working hand in hand with the Portuguese New Christians of Bayonne and Madrid.[74] At the same time, Amsterdam Sephardim were active in collecting cargoes of Spanish American goods and silver from the Moroccan ports of Saleh and Tetuan where such wares were transferred (presumably via the Portuguese North African enclaves at Tangiers and Ceuta) by Portuguese New Christian merchants residing in Seville, San Lúcar, Cadiz, and Málaga.

In December 1640, taking advantage of the rebellion against Philip IV in Catalonia, Portugal seceded from Spain and the new king of Portugal, John IV promptly threw open his ports to Spain's enemies. There ensued a rapid resurgence of traffic between Holland and Portugal so that Dutch Sephardi Jews were now once again able to import sugar, tobacco, and other Portuguese colonial goods via Lisbon and Oporto. The Portuguese secession also greatly stimulated Dutch Sephardi involvement in the European arms and munitions trades. Before 1641, Jewish participation in such traffic had been marginal, being largely confined to occasional shipments of powder and naval stores to Morocco. But now most of the guns, ammunition, and naval stores used by Portugal in her long war of independence against Spain (1640–68) were imported from Amsterdam and Hamburg, a large part of this business being handled by Sephardi Jews. What was probably the largest of John IV's arms and munitions purchases, a contract for 100,000 *cruzados* worth of muskets, powder, shot, siege equipment, and ship's rigging, was signed in Amsterdam, in July 1641, by the newly arrived first Portuguese ambassador to the United Provinces and the Portuguese Jewish merchant Lopo Ramires (David Curiel), who had left Portugal, under threat of arrest by the Inquisition, in 1611, settling in Amsterdam three years later.[75]

Just as several German Jews, such as Gumpert Salomon and

---

[74] See, for instance, AGS Estado 2139, *consulta* 23 July 1621, AGS Hacienda 592, *consulta* 31 Oct. 1622 and AGS Hacienda 664, *consulta* 15 Sept. 1630.

[75] GAA NA 1555B, pp. 1103–4, 1563; Rau, 'A embaixada', pp. 115–16.

Berend Levi, emerged in the closing stages of the Thirty Years War as 'Court Jews', able to offer sought-after services to princes, so a number of Sephardi Jews, of whom Lopo Ramires and his older brother, Duarte Nunes da Costa (Jacob Curiel) of Hamburg, are prime examples, began in the 1640s to deal with governments on a regular basis. It was this decade which saw the beginning of that much wider involvement of Jews in statecraft, state finance, and large-scale provision of military supplies, which was to remain a central feature of Jewish activity in Europe down to the middle of the eighteenth century. For some years, Lopo Ramires acted as the Amsterdam agent of John IV's bankers in Lisbon most, or all, of whom were themselves New Christians; he also handled the finances of the Portuguese embassy in The Hague as well as remittances from Lisbon, through Amsterdam, to the various itinerant Portuguese envoys seeking help for renascent Portugal against Spain. However, in 1646, the none too reliable Ramires switched sides and became Amsterdam agent of the Conde de Peñaranda, one of Spain's chief ministers, taking responsibility, among other things, for the finances of the Spanish delegation to the Münster peace congress.[76] He also fitted out several warships and shipped at least one major consignment of gunpowder to Spain. This happened after both he and his brother, Duarte, had been ennobled by John IV and made knights (*cavaleiros fidalgos*) of the Portuguese royal household. Duarte Nunes da Costa did remain loyal to Portugal and was frequently commended for his zeal and willingness to take risks on behalf of the Portuguese cause. He was nominated 'Agent' of the Portuguese crown at Hamburg in 1644 and, in 1649, played a substantial role in the setting up of the Portuguese 'Brazil Company' for which he purchased and fitted out several warships.[77] Meanwhile, in 1645, Duarte's eldest son Jerónimo Nunes da Costa (Moseh Curiel) (1620–97) who, like his father was one of the most active of the western Sephardi élite in synagogue affairs, was appointed 'Agent' of the crown of Portugal in the United Provinces, a post which involved his acting as Portuguese *chargé d'affaires* during the prolonged periods in which there was no ambassador of Portugal at The Hague.[78]

John IV, first king of a resurgent Portugal, was more willing than

---

[76] See the correspondence of Lopo Ramires with Spanish financial officials in Antwerp in the Antwerp city archive, section IB vols. 1933 and 1934.

[77] Vieira, *Obras escolhidas*, i. 87–9.

[78] Israel, 'Jerónimo Nunes da Costa', pp. 169, 172–3, 187–8.

other princes of his time to confer honours on Jews; for, being locked
in conflict with Spain, and later also the Dutch, he could not afford to
discard any possible source of help. But Portugal's predicament, if
more acute, was not essentially different from that of Spain and many
other later seventeenth-century states in its urgent need for financial
links with Holland and North Germany and for supplies and munitions. Jewish assistance was now an asset worth seeking in a way that
it had not been before 1618 while the price for Jewish co-operation—
concessions which would ease the oppressive restrictions which
tradition and the churches imposed on Jewish life—was now easier to
contemplate, with the progress of *raison d'État* attitudes and princely
absolutism. Hence the strengthening during the Thirty Years War of
those post-1570 trends which we have ventured to call 'political
philosemitism'. The great Portuguese Jesuit missionary and political
advisor, António Vieira, had deep mystical as well as practical
reasons for wanting to ease the situation of the Jews (and New
Christians), believing that it was Portugal's mission finally to win the
Jews over to Christ, but in the meantime he ardently advocated the
forging of links between the Portuguese crown and the New
Christians (both at home and in France) and with north European
Sephardi Jewry, for reasons of state: Portugal was struggling for its
independent existence and needed Jewish help if it was to finance its
war-effort, build up its fleets, and retain its colonies.[79] Vieira,
moreover had the ear of the king. Hampered by popular bigotry and
the Inquisition, John IV could not go as far as Vieira advocated, or he
himself may well have wished, but he did take some steps to restrain
the Inquisition and, in 1649, when setting up the Brazil Company,
decreed that capital invested in the company by New Christians—
even, the king implied, if they were acting for professed Jews
abroad—was to be wholly exempt from confiscation by the Inquisition.[80] Thus Duarte Nunes da Costa, who was for many years a
leading figure in the Sephardi synagogue in Hamburg, had some
reason to believe that his services on behalf of John IV helped to ease
the position of the New Christians in Portugal with not a few of whom
he had close commercial connections.

Meanwhile, in Spain, Olivares, Philip IV's chief minister in the
years 1621–43, strove heroically to sustain a vast military effort
against the numerous enemies of the House of Habsburg, deploying

[79] Saraiva, 'António Vieira', pp. 25–6.
[80] See Hanson's sections on Vieira and the New Christians.

large forces in Italy and Germany as well as in the Low Countries, Brazil, and the Caribbean. The strain on Spain's economy and the logistical problems involved were unprecedented. Acutely aware of his need to tap new resources and enlist the aid of fresh groups able to assist, Olivares ended the former monopoly of the Genoese over the servicing of Spain's state finances, in 1626, and from then on allocated roughly half of the Spanish crown's financial contracts, or *asientos* as they were called, to Portuguese New Christian bankers, some of the wealthiest of whom now moved, at the Count-Duke's invitation, from Lisbon to Madrid. These newly arrived financiers from Portugal became especially prominent in handling the payments from Madrid to Antwerp for the upkeep of the Spanish army of Flanders.[81] Before long, there were a dozen or fifteen main Portuguese firms in Madrid in which hundreds of lesser New Christians invested capital as did also an assortment of courtiers and noblemen. The Portuguese New Christian banking network, based in Madrid and Antwerp, and created by Olivares, also drew on commercial capital lodged at Seville and Lisbon.[82] Simultaneously, Portuguese New Christians now took over the farmng of more and more of the king's customs and excise duties and most of the contracts for supplying Spain's fleets and the North African garrisons.

Of course, by no means all of these Portuguese New Christian businessmen active in Spain were crypto-Jews. Indeed, it is clear that quite a number, including Jorge de Paz de Silveira, who was probably the richest of all, were sincere Catholics who did not adhere to Jewish beliefs and were not interested in developing links with the Sephardi Jewish diaspora outside the Peninsula.[83] On the other hand, it is equally evident that some members of this financial élite, most notably the powerful families of Cortizos, Montezinos, and Passarinho, were crypto-Jews who secretly rejected Catholicism and developed strong links with Sephardi Jewish communities both in Holland and in Italy.[84] Furthermore, as we shall see, the immense financial power which these families accumulated in Spain during the years of Olivares's chief ministry was later to be of great significance for Sephardi Jewish life generally in the Holy Land and the Caribbean, as well as in Europe.

[81] Dominguez Ortiz, *Política y hacienda*, pp. 65–9, 108; Israel, 'Spain and the Dutch Sephardim', pp. 43–8.

[82] Vieira, *Obras escolhidas*, iv. 18, 49.

[83] Boyajian, 'The New Christians Reconsidered', pp. 134–40, 155.

[84] Caro Baroja, *Judíos*, ii. 115–32; Israel, 'Spain and the Dutch Sephardim', pp. 44, 49.

That Olivares consciously adopted a *politique* attitude in his policy toward the Portuguese New Christians is hardly to be doubted. The fact that he himself was partly descended from Jews and that he was notoriously tolerant of those of Jewish background—one of his underlings, Manuel López Pereira, a member of the Spanish Council of Finance in the 1630s, had brothers occupying prominent positions in the Amsterdam Sephardi community—signally contributed to the seething undercurrent of opposition to his political ascendancy. It was even rumoured among anti-Olivares circles in Spain, during the 1630s, that the Count-Duke was scheming to cancel the general expulsion of the Jews of 1492.[85] No doubt this was beyond the bounds of what was politically feasible, but Olivares did make it much easier for the Jews of Oran and Ceuta, and other Spanish and Portuguese North African enclaves, to obtain permits for temporary residence in the Peninsula. And quite a number came for a variety of purposes. Indeed, Olivares himself consorted with a leader of the Oran community, Jacob Cansino, royal interpreter in Arabic, who spent years living in Madrid as an openly professing Jew, armed with an Inquisition licence, under the Count-Duke's protection.[86] But the most dramatic manifestation of Spanish philosemitic mercantilism at this time was the project, deliberated several times in the Council of State, to secure the return of the Sephardi Jews living in Holland, France, and Hamburg on generous terms, with a full pardon for past religious offences and guarantees of immunity from the Inquisition.[87] The plan was that such 'Portuguese' as accepted the terms would only be required to conform outwardly to Catholicism, as was the practice in France, so as to veil what would have amounted to a government licence to practise Judaism in private. Such a policy, ministers calculated, might dilute the purity of the Catholic religion but it would greatly strengthen the Spanish state and damage Spain's enemy, the Dutch, both in Europe and the Americas.

In Italy, the ravages of the Thirty Years War were less fearful than in Germany or the Czech lands. Even so, several regions where there were important Jewish communities, notably Mantua, the Monferrato, and Piedmont, were severely dislocated. Yet everywhere

---

[85] Cantero Vaca, 'Relación', p. 102; Castro, *Judíos de España*, pp. 219–20; Cantera Burgos, 'Dos escritos inéditos', pp. 40–6.

[86] BL MS Add. 28442, fos. 251ᵛ–252; Yerushalmi, *From Spanish Court*, pp. 167–8.

[87] Alcalá-Zamora, *España, Flandes y el mar del Norte*, pp. 249–50; Israel, 'Jews of Spanish North Africa', pp. 74, 84; this, essentially, was also Vieira's plan for Portugal in the 1640s, Vieira, *Obras escolhidas*, iv. 11, 50, 59–60.

recovery was rapid and, in general, the long-term trend of expansion in Italian Jewish life, manifest since the 1570s, continued unabated. And nowhere was this more evident than in the Grand Duchy of Tuscany where the preponderance of the Portuguese Jewish community over the principality's foreign trade, and the commercial eclipse of the great city of Florence, were now complete. By the war's end, trade focused firmly on the Jewish quarters of Livorno and Pisa. The Jewish population of Livorno increased from only 711 in 1622 to about 1,500 by 1640; and then much more rapidly, as from 1645, to around 3,000 by 1655.[88] At around 20 per cent of the city's population, Livorno by 1655 had by far the highest proportion of Jews of any sizeable town in western Europe. By the 1640s, Livorno had outstripped Venice and Genoa and become the single most important entrepôt for Dutch and English shipping and goods in the Mediterranean, the key distribution-centre from which northern and colonial wares, and Spanish American silver, were remitted to North Africa and the Levant, and Near Eastern merchandise stockpiled for shipment to Amsterdam and London. Thus, by the war's end, the unchallengeable fact that Livorno was now the chief port of the Mediterranean, and its business community mainly Jewish, had become the second most potent argument in the repertoire of philosemitic mercantilism generally, the favourite argument being the Jewish contribution to the greatness of Amsterdam.[89]

In contrast to Livorno, Venice was indisputably in decline. Yet, as the Venetian rabbi Simone Luzzatto pointed out, in his *Discorso* of 1637,[90] the one still flourishing Venetian trade route—the overland traffic, via Split and Valona, to Constantinople and Salonika—was predominantly in Jewish hands, and this is confirmed by a range of evidence. As Venice declined, the proportion of Jews in the city's population grew perceptibly from around 1 to 3 per cent between 1600 and 1650; but the importance of the Jews to Venice's decaying economy increased more dramatically. The nadir of Venice's fortunes was reached during the war of 1645–69 between Venice and the Turks, an exhausting and ruinous struggle over Crete. It is true that what was a disaster for Venice also paralysed Venetian Jewish commerce, links with the Turkish Balkans being severed for a quarter of a century. It is clear also that one major reason for the acceleration

---

[88] Toaff, 'Cenni storici', pp. 360, 363–4.
[89] See, for instance, Menasseh ben Israel, *The Humble Addresses*, p. 2.
[90] Luzzatto, *Discorso*, fos. 17ᵛ–19.

in the increase of Livorno's Jewish population was migration from Venice, from 1645. But we know from a variety of post-1669 evidence that the setback by no means diminished the now considerable influence of the Jews over the city's economic life.[91] If the trade through Split never fully recovered its former importance, the Jews increased their role in the shipping of grain, oil, and other basic foodstuffs to the city from Puglia, Sicily, Corfu, and Zante.

The setback to Jewish activity at Venice, from 1645 was compensated for not only by the surge of new immigration to Livorno but by the revival in the fortunes of the papal Adriatic ports of Ancona, Pesaro, and Senigallia, in all of which the Jews were the predominant trading element, since most business involved the overland Balkan routes (via Dubrovnik) to Salonika and Constantinople. Goods arriving from Bosnia in these ports then passed, via Florence, to Livorno for reshipment to the west. Admittedly, the growth of the Jewish communities in these towns was to some extent counterbalanced by a narrowing of Jewish life in the region of Urbino as a whole. When the duchy was incorporated into the States of the Church in 1631, Pesaro had a Jewish population of 500, Urbino of 370, and Senigallia of about 200.[92] The papal government then decided to congregate all the Jews of the duchy into these three centres, in ghettos, and to eliminate the small rural communities at Pergola, Fossombrone, and neighbouring places. Even so, the substantial increase that now took place, at least at Pesaro and Senigallia, was also partly due to outside immigration and the increased role of these ports.

During the Thirty Years War, the ghettoization process in Italy was also extended to Ferrara and Modena. Having acquired the duchy of Ferrara in 1597, in 1624 the papal government decided to abolish the small rural communities of the duchy and congregate the Jews again in three centres—at Ferrara, Lugo, and Cento. In Lugo, there were 606 Jews in 1639, about 10 per cent of the town's population. The Jewish population of Ferrara itself, still one of the foremost Jewish communities of Italy, seems to have held steady at around 1,500 throughout the century, though this too was really expansion since the population of the city as a whole declined.[93] The Jews of Modena were subjected to ghettoization in 1638, but there too Jewish numbers increased.

[91] BL MS 10130, fo. 80-80ᵛ; Ciriacono, *Olio ed ebrei*, pp. 62–7.
[92] Milano, *Storia*, p. 298; Paci, '*Scala' di Spalato*, pp. 114–16.
[93] Angelini, *Ebrei di Ferrara*, pp. 57–8.

A most perplexing aspect of Italian Jewish life in this epoch was the disparate impact of the great plague of 1630–1 on different communities. This, the most devastating epidemic in the history of early modern Italy, inflicted heavy losses on most major cities of northern Italy. Venice is estimated to have lost some 50,000 or nearly one third of its inhabitants and, like Florence and Milan, languished at well below its pre-1630 population level for the rest of the century. In many, and possibly most cases, the Jews, despite the enforced overcrowding and insalubrity of the ghettos, came through the ordeal rather better than did their Christian neighbours.[94] Certainly at Venice and Livorno losses seem to have been slight and failed to halt the steady increase in the Jewish population. Nor did it make much impact in a good many other places. And yet, in some cases, notably at Verona and Padua, the plague struck the Jews harder than anyone. At Padua, no less than 421 out of a total of 721 Jewish inhabitants were said to have perished.

Sack and pillage arising from the war was mainly confined to Mantua, Monferrato, and Piedmont, though even here, with the partial exception of Mantua, the damage seems to have been mainly in the short term. The Duke of Savoy being allied to Spain against France, Piedmont was heavily devastated in the fighting. Yet, as in Germany, the situation tended to lead to a tightening of links between the state, mobilizing its energies for war, and the Jewish communities. To raise loans, pawn jewellery, and pay his soldiery, Duke Charles Emmanuel I made extensive use of the Jewish loan-banks scattered throughout his territory and the neighbouring marquisate of Saluzzo.[95] Thus all the principal Jewish banking houses of the region, such as those of the Lattes, Treves, Foà, Momigliano, Segre, Jona, and Avigdor, were drawn into the Mechanism of military finance and military provisioning. The Monferrato, a classic area of Jewish loan-banks, found itself in the thick of the fighting. Its chief town Casale, as well as being a Jewish centre of some significance, was one of the most crucial fortresses in all Italy, dominating the route between Genoa and Milan, and was the scene of a long and terrible siege. The town's Jewish community soon recovered, however, and grew to around 600 by the later seventeenth century.[96] The capture of Mantua by Austrian troops in 1630, on the other hand, was for the Jews a major catastrophe. In contrast to the conduct of the Austrians in Bohemia

[94] Ciscato, *Ebrei in Padova*, p. 88; Roth, *Jews of Venice*, pp. 95–7.
[95] Foa, 'Banchi e banchieri ebrei', pp. 520–5.   [96] Ibid., p. 528.

and Germany, at Mantua the Jewish quarter was brutally sacked, after which the 1,600 survivors were summarily expelled from the city. Italian Jewish leaders, through the elders of the Vienna *Judenstadt*, appealed to the Emperor who ordered that the expulsion be cancelled and the Jews recalled.[97] Thus the Jews of Mantua, or at least most of them, returned. But the community never again rose to its previous level of cultural and economic vitality.

Did the pressures of the Thirty Years War also expand the role of Jews and crypto-Jews within the French monarchy? Again the answer is an unequivocal yes. The role of Metz Jewry and of the Alsatian communities in the provisioning and supplying of horses to the French soldiery has already been referred to. But the most striking development at this time, in France, is Richelieu's decision further to extend crown protection to the Portuguese crypto-Jews in the French ports. The story is a classic instance of *raison d'État* politics and mercantilism. The Spanish embargoes against the Dutch had given rise to a flourishing contraband route, as we have seen, linking Amsterdam and Madrid, via Bayonne, the Pyrenean passes, and Pamplona. This, in turn, despite the expulsion of the 'Portuguese' from St. Jean de Luz in 1618, stimulated an increased immigration of Portuguese New Christians into the extreme south-west corner of France as well as to a lesser extent to Bordeaux, Nantes, and Rouen. A report of 1633 reveals that there were then sixty Portuguese New Christian families, or around 300 individuals, in Bayonne, eighty families, or around 400 Portuguese, at Labastide-Clairence, more than forty families at Peyrehorade, ten at Dax, around forty in Bordeaux, another twenty families at Rouen—which we know from other sources to be a slight underestimate—twelve families in Paris, and a few more at Nantes.[98] This fresh influx further aggravated the simmering feud among the opposing Portuguese New Christian factions in France, 'Catholics' versus 'Jews'. The increasingly acrimonious contest reached its climax in the early 1630s, at Rouen, when the 'Catholics' secured the condemnation of their adversaries in the courts, as 'Judaizers'. The regional high court of Normandy was mobilized against the crypto-Jews, several of whom were arrested and imprisoned. At this point, Richelieu, influenced by his (probably) Marrano confidant, Alphonse López, stepped in, stopping the proceedings and turning the tables on the 'Catholics', who were being

[97] Simonsohn, *History*, pp. 54–8.
[98] BL MS Eg. 343, fo. 259; Nahon, 'Inscriptions', i. 355–6.

spurred on by two disguised Spanish priests.[99] Louis XIII's decree of 12 July 1633 on the 'Portuguese' in France is a consummate piece of *politique* fudging on the part of Richelieu. The case against those charged with 'Judaism' was halted on the cynical grounds that their Portuguese accusers were known to be of Jewish extraction and, in some cases, to have been punished in Portugal for the 'crime of Judaism', which rendered their testimony worthless. The good people of Rouen were forbidden to insult or otherwise harass the released 'Portuguese'. It is worth adding that the leaders of the group rescued by Richelieu—the Rodrigues Lamego and De Caceres families—can be definitely shown, from other evidence, to have been active crypto-Jews, a fact of which Richelieu was doubtless perfectly aware.[100]

The implications of Richelieu's *politique* stance for the Portuguese New Christians in France were profound. For these were now crypto-Jews in a quite different sense from their counterparts in the Iberian Peninsula. Their obligation to conform outwardly to Catholic practice was from now on a mere charade which probably no one took too seriously. In their homes they practised a relatively highly-developed form of Judaism helped by Hebrew-reciting Dutch relatives who were frequent visitors to Portuguese homes in Rouen, Bordeaux, and Bayonne. In Peyrehorade, second largest of the inland communities of Portuguese in France—there were roughly 275 members of this community in 1640—it became usual to inscribe Jewish rather than Catholic names on gravestones from as early as 1641.[101] The same is true of Labastide, which, for a time, was the largest concentration after Bayonne, as from 1659. In practice, the fact that most of these Portuguese were really Jews was perfunctorily veiled rather than actively concealed. Not only did leading crypto-Jewish families in France freely intermarry with Dutch Sephardi Jews, they participated by post in Dutch Jewish societies such as that for providing marriage portions for poor Portuguese Jewish girls which, indeed, also allocated dowries to young New Christian women in France who subsequently married in synagogues abroad.[102] Thus Richelieu can be said to have knowingly condoned the shift to Jewish rather than Catholic allegiance in France, a policy subsequently continued by Colbert. It was this government stance which made possible that

[99] Revah, 'Autobiographie d'un Marrane', pp. 63–76.

[100] ANTT Inqu. 7192, 'Proceso de Duarte Nunes da Costa', fos. 14ᵛ, 15ᵛ, 40–4.

[101] Nahon, 'Inscriptions', i. 355–8 and ii. 349, 351.

[102] Revah, 'Le premier règlement', pp. 660–1.

steady transition from the 1630s down to the 1680s by when the Portuguese communities in France had cast off all remaining pretence and openly organized as Jewish congregations with rabbis and services in Hebrew.[103]

If the dictates of war often induced a mercantilist stance favourable to the expansion of Jewish life within Europe, this was not the case everywhere, as is evident from Swedish policy. In Germany, during the 1630s and 1640s, Swedish forces, as we have seen, were pivotal in the spread of Jewish communities, because there the Swedes required provisions and did not need to heed the objections of the populace. The situation was quite otherwise, however, in Sweden's newly secured Baltic provinces of Livonia and Ingria. Here Swedish strategy was to hold ground with as few troops as possible while concentrating most of Sweden's strength in Germany. And this could only be done, in the face of Poland and Muscovy, through close collaboration with the Lutheran German bourgeoisie of the eastern Baltic seaboard. This is why the Lutheran merchants of Sweden's Baltic provinces were finally successful in winning their ancient battle to prevent Jewish encroachment on their trade in grain, timber, and naval stores.[104] Poland, the main threat to Sweden's political hegemony, was likewise the chief menace to this Lutheran German ascendancy over the Baltic seaboard's commerce. When Riga was temporarily annexed to Poland, in 1581, the Polish governor, Prince Radziwiłł, had allowed Jewish merchants from Lithuania to become active in the area. But when Gustavus Adolphus captured Riga in 1621, he specifically undertook to exclude Jews from the city and its surroundings, and this became a pillar of Swedish policy in her Baltic provinces generally.

South of Riga, wedged between Swedish territory and Lithuania, were the autonomous duchy of Courland and bishopric of Pilten, principalities loosely under Polish protection. Both of these had substantial Jewish communities. Duke James (1642–82), the most famous ruler of Courland, was a tireless devotee of mercantilist projects, not just in the Baltic but throughout Europe and beyond. Keen to eclipse the nearby emporium of Riga, Duke James strove, with some success, to build up a large merchant fleet and exploit the rich resources of his underdeveloped duchy. As part of this programme, and ignoring the protests of the Christian burghers of

---

[103] Nahon, *'Nations' juives*, 3, 133, 259.
[104] Baron, *Social and Religious History*, xvi. 174–5.

Mitau, he invited in more Jews with various privileges and concessions. Besides dealings with local Lithuanian Jews, James was for many years in contact with Sephardi merchants of Hamburg, Amsterdam, and the Caribbean.[105] In 1649, through the Nunes da Costa, he became a participant in the Portuguese Brazil Company, not only supplying naval stores to Lisbon but sending whole ships and cargoes to sail in the convoys to Brazil. In 1645, the Duke purchased the West Indian island of Tobago from the Earl of Warwick—a transaction recognized by Cromwell in 1657. The duke then collaborated with a group of Dutch Caribbean Sephardi families in trying to develop sugar and tobacco production on the island.

In the 1620s, Swedish action on the Baltic seaboard, combined with the effects of the Spanish embargoes against the Dutch, caused a severe but temporary disruption of Baltic trade. But exports to the west of grain, timber, and naval stores from the hinterland picked up after 1630 and there was a final boom in the years down to 1648, powered by the heavy demand for war supplies in Holland and Germany. This period was also the final phase of Polish political and military expansion eastwards. In a series of campaigns, Polish forces pushed the Russians back beyond Smolensk, initiating a period of stable Polish rule over White Russia. In the wake of the Polish armies came a rapid spread of Jewish colonies through the regions of Minsk, Polotsk, Vitebsk, and Mogilev. There was also some Jewish settlement in and around Smolensk. Not unnaturally there was considerable resistance from the burghers and guilds to this influx, and at Vitebsk, Polotsk, and Mogilev the Jews congregated and built their synagogues in outlying communities rather than in the towns themselves. There was an outbreak of rioting against the Jews in Mogilev in 1645.

This expansion in the east went hand in hand with a continuing rapid growth in the older Jewish communities which had formerly been on the eastern fringes of Jewish life. The Jewries of Vilna, Pinsk, Slutsk, and Slonim, where a magnificent stone synagogue was erected in 1642, now developed into large and vibrant communities with a varied economic life. Vilna Jewry, still quite small in 1600, and despite an outbreak of pogroms in 1635, numbered over 2,000 by 1648. The Pinsk community, numbering 275 in 1566, had grown to over 1,000 by 1648.[106]

---

[105] Mattiesen, *Kolonial- und Überseepolitik*, pp. 37, 115, 213; Kellenbenz, *As relações*, pp. 25–6.
[106] Nadav, 'Jewish Community of Pinsk', pp. 153–64.

But if the growth in the northern parts of the Polish Monarchy was considerable the enlargement of Jewish life in the Ukraine was still more dramatic.[107] Here, in contrast to further north, there was little in the way of pre-existing towns, crafts, and agriculture, so that Christian merchants and guilds were either few or non-existent. The driving force in the colonization of the Ukraine was the Polish landlords, eager to extend their latifundia and create private towns often from scratch. Poland was their state. Its institutions were designed to further their interests; and the readiest tool available for advancing the programme of colonization was the Jews. In the footsteps of hundreds of wealthier Jews who took over the contracts for administering estates, marketing produce, operating mills and distilleries, collecting tolls and the like, came a much greater number, many thousands of poor Jewish pedlars and artisans who effectively captured petty trade and the crafts throughout the new territories in the south. In the Ukraine, the undisputed primacy of the Polish nobility, combined with the absence of any real economic rival to the Jews, created, in the zone around Brody, Belz, Lutsk, Dubno, Ostrog, and Bratslav, a uniquely broad and varied base to the Jewish role.[108] Here, in the western Ukraine, to a much greater extent than in western or central Poland, or in White Russia, it would be true to say that the Jews occupied most, as opposed to much, of the middle ground between the peasantry, on the one hand, and the nobility and clergy on the other.

Burgeoning in the east, Polish Jewry also expanded its role in the west, in part owing to the diffused impact of the Thirty Years War. The new privileges conceded to the Jews of Bohemia, Moravia, and Silesia by Emperor Ferdinand II, together with the rise of the Vienna ghetto, generated a vibrant new Polish Jewish overland traffic, based on Cracow, to Prague and Vienna. The provisioning of Gross-Glogau and other garrison towns in Silesia also stimulated a vigorous export of foodstuffs and livestock from Poland into the eastern regions of the Empire, which accounts for the growth in this period of the Jewish communities of Poznań, Kalisz, and Lissa, where the Christian bourgeoisie was now in decline.

The most terrible catastrophe suffered by the Jews of Europe during the early modern era—the Chmielnicki massacres of 1648 was

---

[107] Ettinger, 'Jewish Participation', pp. 113–18, 135–7; Horn, 'Żydzi województwa bielskiego', pp. 40–6; Kardaszewicz, *Dzieje dawniejsze miasta Ostroga*, pp. 117–19.

[108] Horn, 'Żydzi województwa bielskiego', pp. 40–6.

less a major turning-point in the history of Polish Jewry than a brutal but relatively short interruption in its steady growth and expansion. This is not to belittle a horrific episode which dwarfed every other Jewish tragedy between 1492 and the Nazi holocaust. But the widely accepted notion that this appalling episode marked the end of the long period of expansion, and a decisive turn for the worse in the fortunes of Polish Jewry, seems in the light of recent research to place this key event in a misleading light.[109]

Bogdan Chmielnicki (1595–1657), son of a minor noble, unfurled the banner of revolt against Polish rule in the Ukraine among the Cossacks of the eastern part of the territory during 1647. Drawing support from the downtrodden Ukrainian peasantry, as well as from the Crimean Tartars, Chmielnicki achieved the swift collapse of the Polish regime throughout the Ukraine. The insurgents vented their grievances in a savage slaughter of all the Polish nobles, Catholic clergy, and Jews they could lay hands on; but, as the Jews were more numerous than these other categories, they inevitably took the brunt of the losses. The worst massacres occurred during the spring and summer of 1648. Having killed virtually all the Jews who refused to convert to Christianity either side of the Dnieper, the insurgents advanced westwards. The mass of rural Jews fled into the fortified towns which is where the big massacres took place. The first of these was at Nemirov, where several thousand Jews are said to have been butchered, the synagogue destroyed, and its Hebrew scrolls strewn through the streets.[110] The fortress town of Tulchin fell at the end of June, the garrison handing the Jews over in exchange for their own lives. At Ostrog, there was a frightful slaughter in which 7,000 Jews reportedly met their end, a figure which is certainly greatly exaggerated.[111] At Tarnopol there was another mass killing, while at Dubno, the Polish soldiery refused to take the Jews into the fortress and the whole community was butchered. Lvov survived a siege by Chmielnicki's army but several thousand Jews in the surrounding region, who failed to get within its walls in time, or flee far enough westwards, were massacred in their homes, on the roads, and in the fields.

As the rebels swept west and north, the terror they inspired

[109] Traditional conceptions are partly based on Hannover's grossly inflated figures for the slaughtered; see Weinryb, *Jews of Poland*, pp. 192–9; Nadav, 'Jewish Community of Pinsk', pp. 190–6; Horn, 'Skład zawodowy', pp. 15–28.

[110] Hannover, *Yeven Mezula*, p. 19–20.

[111] Meisl, *Juden in Polen*, pp. 13–14; Kardaszewicz, *Dzieje dawniejsze*, pp. 171–4.

preceded them, causing a vast scattering of the Jews to the west. By the time Chmielnicki captured Pinsk, in October, most of the Jews of eastern Lithuania had escaped to Vilna, Grodno, or into central Poland, though assuredly many scores of old and infirm were dispatched with appalling brutality. In south-eastern Poland, the Cossacks failed to take Lublin or Zamość, though both suffered siege and the less defensible towns around were fearfully ravaged. Some Jews were massacred in Tarnogród, Bilgoray, and especially further south, at Narol, where hundreds were slain in the synagogue which was then burned down with the bodies inside.[112] Yet again, as in the cases of Volhynia, Podolia, and White Russia, the vast majority of the Jews survived by fleeing either into the walled fortresses which did not fall or sufficient distances to the west and south.

Following the provisional agreement of August 1649 between the Polish crown and Chmielnicki, the Cossacks pulled back east of the Dnieper. Almost at once the nobles began to recolonize their lands and, with their encouragement and assistance, the Jews streamed back. Fighting flared up again in the spring of 1651 but the Polish forces now offered more effective defence, and it is noticeable that the Polish commanders, especially Prince Wiśniowiecki, went to some lengths to shield the Jewish population. In some places, such as Bar, where there had been fearful massacres in 1648, hundreds of Jews were again slaughtered in 1651, But, on the whole, the losses now were much smaller. Finally, in 1654–5, the Muscovites, in alliance with Chmielnicki, poured into the eastern territories of Lithuania, sacking Mogilev, Vitebsk, and Minsk, and brutally pillaging and burning Vilna. Some thousands of Jews were massacred. But again the bulk escaped westwards and to the south.

[112] Hannover, *Yeven Mezula*, pp. 41–5.

VI

The High Point (I): The 'Court Jews' (1650–1713)

THE age of the 'Court Jew' (1650–1713) marked the zenith of Jewish influence in early modern Europe. The remarkable role of the Jews in European affairs at that time rested on the solid foundations laid during the Thirty Years War. By 1650, a scattered but socially closely intertwined élite of provisioners and financiers had emerged who, in contrast to European Jewish bankers of a later age, were simultaneously agents of states and the effective leaders of Europe's Jewish communities. Sometimes, they showed a strong sense of commitment to one particular government, but this was, in fact, both unusual and untypical. Generally, Jewish court factors, or *Hoffaktoren* as they were known in Germany, lived outside, even far away from the states which they served. Not infrequently, they acted for several governments at once. Most typical of all, the close collaboration and interdependence between them, interlocking with the correspondence between *kehillot* in different countries, made their activity more thoroughly international and specifically Jewish than the banking and contracting of later times. Assuredly, the system centred on Germany, Austria, and Holland, but it ramified far beyond these limits, exerting an appreciable influence also on affairs in Spain, Portugal, the Spanish Netherlands, Denmark, Poland, Hungary, Italy, England, and Ireland.

It was inherent in the rise of the Levi, Gomperz, Oppenheimer, and other German financial dynasties, through the supplying of garrisons during the Thirty Years War, that one chief function of the Court Jews was military purveying and, indeed, on a grander scale, army contracting. The drawing up of contracts to supply whole armies, with financiers who were professing Jews, occurs only after 1650. However, at an earlier stage, certainly from the 1630s, several Portuguese New Christians in the service of the Spanish crown branched out from handling payments for the Spanish forces into regular provisioning of entire armies. In particular, García de Yllan, a Portuguese banker at Antwerp, handled the shipments of bread, forage, and gunpowder to the Spanish army of Flanders for several years during the 1630s and 1640s.[1] Although not himself a crypto-Jew—he remained a Catholic throughout his life and later became a baron in the Spanish Netherlands—he had Jewish relatives in Amsterdam and many of his sub-contractors were professing Jews. In the years 1639–41, for instance, the gunpowder which he delivered to the Spanish troops in Flanders was supplied, from the Baltic, by a group of Portuguese Jews at Hamburg, headed by Duarte Nunes da Costa, the same who later switched his allegiance to Portugal.[2] To avoid interception by the Dutch and French, the gunpowder was shipped through Danish territory, via Glückstadt and Dover, and into the Spanish base at Dunkirk on English ships. At the same time, one of the principal Portuguese contractors in Spain, Manuel Cortizos of Madrid, chief supplier of horses, forage, and other necessities to the Spanish forces on the Catalan front during the 1640s, is definitely known to have been a secret Jew who sent much of his capital to Holland.[3] But, as a fully-fledged system, Jewish army contracting matured only in the 1670s, its heyday continuing down to the end of the War of the Spanish Succession, in 1713.

The most important of the Jewish army contractors was Samuel Oppenheimer of Heidelberg (1630–1703), who first emerged in the 1660s as a main supplier to the garrisons of the Elector of the Palatinate. During the 1673–9 war between Austria and France, he was entrusted by the Emperor Leopold I with provisioning the entire Austrian army on the Rhine. Oppenheimer sent his factors all over South Germany to procure grain and fodder, and obtained clothing for the troops, as well as their horses, gunpowder, and ammunition, mainly from Jewish dealers at Frankfurt, though some items he purchased much further afield, notably at Hamburg and at Amsterdam, where his agent was Moses Gomperz.[4] It is true that Oppenheimer never relied exclusively on fellow Jews, but the lists of his suppliers show that he did depend overwhelmingly on relatives and other Jews. As his influence increased so did the opposition to him at court, in Vienna. When Austria made peace with France, in 1679, his position temporarily collapsed. It soon revived, though,

[1] On Yllan, see Salomon, 'The "De Pinto Manuscript" ', p. 30.

[2] AGR SEG 558, fo. 92: Christian IV of Denmark to the Cardinal-Infante in Brussels, Glückstadt, 3 July 1639; Kellenbenz, *Sephardim*, pp. 131, 163, 167, 275.

[3] Caro Baroja, *Judíos*, ii. 115–19.

[4] Grunwald, *Samuel Oppenheimer*, pp. 39–41, 55; Kober, 'Reichsstadt Köln', pp. 415–17.

with the outbreak of war between Austria and Turkey, in 1682. During the Turkish siege of Vienna, in 1683, it was Oppenheimer who organized the defenders' logistics. When the siege was lifted, he took up permanent residence in Vienna and was entrusted with supplying the rapidly advancing Austrian forces in Hungary. His most celebrated device was the fleets of river barges he built to victual the Emperor's soldiery besieging Budapest in 1686, and, again, using the river system crossing Hungary, the forces confronting Belgrade in 1688–9.[5] While Oppenheimer himself remained in Vienna, his son, Emmanuel, who became well known throughout central Europe in his own right, took charge of provisioning Philippsburg and other Austrian garrisons on the Rhine.

The power of the Austrian counter-offensive of the 1680s, which brought Hungary, Croatia, and Belgrade under Habsburg sway, was one of the great dramas of late seventeenth-century Europe. For the Jews, the fighting involved the utter disruption of the Hungarian communities, the Jewish quarters of Budapest, Belgrade, and many other places being brutally sacked by the Austrian soldiery. But the war also meant a rapid extension of the central European Jewish financial and communal network right across Hungary. Besides the sheltering of thousands of refugees, especially in Moravia, a vast financial operation was initiated by the surrounding Jewish communities, with Oppenheimer at its head, to ransom and rehabilitate the Jewish captives. At the same time, Oppenheimer's factors in Hungary organized an elaborate garrison supply network which did much to create the basis for a remodelled and revived Hungarian Jewry supplied with fresh settlers from Poland, Bohemia, and Moravia. Oppenheimer's principal agents in Hungary were Lazarus Hirschel, who supervised the victualling of the Austrian forces at Budapest and Belgrade, and Simon Michael, an ancestor of the poet Heinrich Heine, who moved from place to place, eventually securing permission, the first Jew to do so, to settle in Pressburg (Bratislava). Michael's speciality was the gathering up of Turkish coin from all over Hungary which he then delivered for melting down at the Imperial Mint, in Vienna.[6]

Oppenheimer's career reached its culmination during the Nine Years War (1689–98) when he simultaneously organized the supplies both of the Austrian armies in Germany, fighting the French, and the

---

[5] Grunwald, *Samuel Oppenheimer*, pp. 58–61, 70–1.
[6] Ibid., pp. 266–73; Kaufmann, *Samson Wertheimer*, pp. 4–7.

forces in Hungary. Nor did he handle just the basic necessities. He supplied the officers with their wine and the troops with their tobacco while at the same time supplying the court, in Vienna, with its wine, spices, jewels, confectionery, and the costumes of its coachmen and lackeys.[7] To distinguish him from lesser *Hofjuden* such as Hirschel and Michael, Oppenheimer bore the official titles of *Oberhoffaktor* and *Oberkriegsfaktor*. Cardinal Kollonitsch, the doyen of anti-Semitism in Vienna, concerted two attempts to dislodge Oppenheimer, in 1692 and 1697, and replace him with 'loyal, patriotic, Catholic factors' but without success. Nevertheless, in the interval between the end of the war, in 1698, and the start of the War of the Spanish Succession, in 1702, Oppenheimer's standing again collapsed. The Emperor no longer needed him. In July 1700, a raving mob ransacked his Vienna mansion, destroying his papers. Oppenheimer's death in 1703, with large sums still owed him by the Imperial Treasury, brought on a financial crisis not only in Austria but throughout central Europe.[8] There was a flood of claims from different parts of Germany. At the instigation of their own Court Jews, and that of Emmanuel Oppenheimer, several princes put pressure on the Emperor to repay Emmanuel's far-flung creditors. The Dutch States General, anxious for the sums raised for Oppenheimer in Amsterdam, also intervened. Finally, matters were patched up with the aid of Samson Wertheimer, who now emerged as the senior Jewish *Hoffaktor* in Austria. Emmanuel Oppenheimer and his organization resumed the provisioning of Austria's armies, throughout the War of the Spanish Succession (and subsequently), though he never enjoyed quite the power or prestige of his father.

Other German Jewish army contractors operated on an altogether smaller scale than the Oppenheimers. The Great Elector, and his son King Frederick I of Prussia, employed the Gomperz on a regular basis for provisioning their garrisons on the Rhine and, on a more occasional basis, did use the services of one or two Jewish suppliers in the east, notably Aaron Israel of Gross-Glogau, founder of the revived Berlin Jewish community in the 1660s. Reuben Elias Gomperz (1655–1705) of Emmerich and Cleves, the most pre-eminent of his family, also supplied munitions to the Elector of Cologne.[9] But if

---

[7] Grunwald, *Samuel Oppenheimer*, pp. 78–9.

[8] Ibid., pp. 150–7; *The Life of Glückel*, pp. 135, 146–7; *Weensche Gezantschapsberichten*, ii. 260–1, 275, 281.

[9] Schnee, *Hoffinanz*, i, 79–80, 84.

Prussia, like Denmark, never permitted Jewish contractors the overall control of logistics that the Emperor assigned to the Oppenheimers, several lesser states did. Nor were these simply insignificant
armies such as that of the margrave of Ansbach, equipped by Marx
Model. Lemle Moses of Mannheim, *Obermilizfaktor* of the Palatinate
from the 1680s, was a key figure in German military provisioning in
the late seventeenth and early eighteenth century, working closely
with the Oppenheimers in victualling garrisons on the Rhine which
played a pivotal part in the efforts to prevent Louis XIV dominating
Germany.[10]

The closest parallel to the Oppenheimers in the scale of their
operations, however, were the group of Dutch Sephardi army
contractors provisioning the armies of William III (1672–1702),
Stadhouder of the United Provinces and later King of England.
Indeed, for a time, it was The Hague as much as Vienna which was
the centre of the Jewish army provisioning network in Europe. The
French invasion of the United Provinces, in 1672, was one of the great
turning-points in Dutch and all European history, precipitating a
tremendous conflict which engulfed much of the world for over four
decades. This immense struggle between Louis XIV and adherents
on one side, ranged against the Dutch, Austria, Spain, several
German states and, later, also England, unfolded in stages, punctuated by short intervals of peace, down to the peace settlement of
Utrecht in 1713. For most of this period, The Hague was effectively
the nerve-centre of the anti-French coalition. The Dutch military
leader, down to his death in 1702, was their Stadhouder William III,
a prince who, probably from as early as 1672, was in frequent contact
with Jewish leaders. From early on in the 1672–8 war, two Dutch
Sephardi contractors, Antonio (Moseh) Álvarez Machado and Jacob
Pereira, son of the Abraham Pereira who had once participated in the
Spanish military payments system, emerged as the chief suppliers of
bread, wagons, horses, and fodder to the Republic's fixed garrisons
and army in the field.[11] They, in turn, employed other Portuguese
Jews as their commissaries to arrange their grain-ships and river
barges, procure horses and wagons, and handle deliveries. Year in,
year out, from 1674 down to the early eighteenth century, the Dutch
States-General signed contracts with the firm of Machado and
Pereira for the provisioning of the Republic's land forces.

[10] Grunwald, *Samuel Oppenheimer*, pp. 211–12.
[11] Ten Raa, *Staatsche Leger*, vi. 28, 42, 53; Meijer, *Zij lieten hun sporen*, pp. 83–4.

When, as in 1689, Dutch troops spread into north-west Germany, towns such as Cologne which debarred Jews from living, staying, or trading within their limits were forced by the government in The Hague to allow Machado and Pereira's Jewish factors who, in that year, were named as Abraham Pereira, David Pereira, Pedro de Palma, Manuel Pimentel, Jacob Bravusa and four or five Ashkenazi assistants, to take up temporary residence.[12] At Cologne they stockpiled munitions and supplies and transported them to the army. Soon, the Emperor followed the Dutch example and compelled the Cologne authorities to permit Samuel Oppenheimer's agents to enter and purchase munitions in the city. In the next few years, the electors of the Palatinate and Brandenburg followed suit and aranged for the factors of their Court Jews to stay and conduct their affairs in Cologne.

The business of army contracting required the use of very large sums and Machado and Pereira, officially designated 'Providiteurs Generaal', operated using a combination of advances by the state and capital invested by themselves and fellow Dutch Sephardi Jews. They also drew on their links with New Christians in Antwerp and Spain, an important factor once Spain threw in its forces in the South Netherlands to fight alongside the Dutch against Louis XIV. The Spanish crown was beset with chronic financial problems and was only able to mobilize and supply significant forces with financial and logistical aid from Holland. The Amsterdam Sephardi élite, headed by Antonio Lopes Suasso, himself a former New Christian from Antwerp who had migrated to Holland in 1652, supplied cash advances, gunpowder, and other munitions to the Spanish army of Flanders, in concert with Machado and Pereira.[13] According to the English ambassador in The Hague, Sir William Temple, this Dutch logistical aid to Spain in Flanders was one of the key factors which eventually enabled William to turn the military tide against the French. The Sephardi *providiteurs* also figured prominently in equipping the Dutch expeditionary force which William landed in England in 1688. William's bid for the English throne was a uniquely bold adventure on the part of the Dutch and one which incurred considerable risks, as James II was effectively in alliance with France. Despite the dangers, it proved possible to mobilize resources with great speed. Besides Machado, Pereira, and the second Baron Lopes Suasso,

---

[12] Kober, 'Reichsstadt Köln', pp. 514, 425.
[13] Swetschinski, 'Portuguese Jewish Merchants', i. 257, 261.

another Dutch Sephardi Court Jew involved in the venture was Jeronimo Nunes da Costa who handled the transit costs of the contingent sent to participate in the expedition by the Duke of Württemburg. In concert with the English opposition, William's bid succeeded and James II was deposed. The Dutch leader's triumph in securing the English throne for his Stuart wife Mary and himself, as joint sovereigns, effectively captured England for the anti-Louis XIV coalition. Immediately, the operations of William's Sephardi *providiteurs* spread across the Channel. In particular, Isaac Pereira, a younger son of Jacob, moved from Holland to London and became 'commissary general', handling the bread, wagons, and fodder of the army William took with him to Ireland. The sums involved in Isaac Pereira's Irish operations were vast: in the year from September 1690 to August 1691 he was paid £95,000 for the supplies and shipping services he provided.[14]

William also soon coaxed the London Jewish community to contribute to the state's advances to Isaac Pereira, using methods with English Jewry which were somewhat cruder than he was wont to employ in Holland, English Jewry being both much weaker and less secure than its Dutch counterpart. In February 1690, the Earl of Shrewsbury wrote to the Lord Mayor of London that

Taking into consideration that the Jews residing in London carry on, under favour of the Government, so advantageous a trade, it was thought that they ought to be called upon to shew their readiness to support that Government by advancing such sums of money under the late Acts of Parliament as they are agreeable to lend. They have been asked what they are willing to furnish towards supplying one of their brethren, Mons. Pereyra, in part of the contract made with him for providing bread for the army and have made an offer only of £12,000 which is below what his Majesty expected from them, and he directs you to send for their elders and principal merchants and let them understand the obligations they are under to his Majesty for the liberty and privileges they enjoy, and how much it is to their advantage to make suitable returns of affection and gratitude for the kindness they have received and may expect. And since the money demanded carries with it more than the ordinary interest allowed, it was supposed they would, without difficulty, raise among them £30,000, or if not that amount, that they could not propose less than £20,000; and his Majesty believes that, upon second thoughts aided by such representations as your Lordship may make to them, they will come to new resolutions and such as may be accepted by his Majesty.[15]

[14] CTB ix. 1318–19.
[15] CSP 13 Feb. 1689–Apr. 1690, p. 453; also quoted in Swetschinski, 'Portuguese Jewish Merchants', i. 283–4.

Meanwhile Machado and Pereira took over the contracts for supplying the English as well as the Dutch forces in Flanders. Their agent in London who signed contracts with the English crown on the firm's behalf, remitted the English payments to the firm, and handled those of the firm's grain purchases as were made in England, was Solomon de Medina (*c.*1650–1730), a Dutch Jew who also now moved to London.[16] Medina, together with other leading London business houses, notably the Mendes da Costa, who were bankers and diamond and bullion merchants, also handled the English payments to Machado and Pereira for the pay and supply of the German contingents sent to Flanders in support of the Dutch and English by the rulers of Brandenburg, Hanover, Hesse, and Münster. As a token of regard for Medina, the King himself dined on a November evening, in 1699, at his home on Richmond Hill. The following year, in a ceremony at Hampton Court, Medina became the first professing Jew to be knighted in England. After William's death, in 1702, he continued as the regular supplier of bread and wagons to the English forces both on the continent and in Ireland, in concert with Machado down to the latter's death. He thus handled the logistics for all Marlborough's campaigns, though towards the end of the War of the Spanish Succession he seems to have badly miscalculated and ended up virtually bankrupt.[17]

Another pre-eminent Jewish contractor of the Spanish War of Succession was Joseph Cortizos (1656–1742), a former Antwerp Marrano who became a Jew in Holland and probably began as a factor of Machado and Pereira. He was a descendant of the Manuel Cortizos who was prominent in Spanish army contracting in the 1640s. In 1705, he was appointed principal supplier to all the allied armies fighting in Spain on behalf of the Austrian Archduke Charles against the French candidate for the Spanish throne, Philip V. With occupied Catalonia as his base of operations, Cortizos built a complicated supply network linking eastern Spain with Lisbon, English-occupied Gibraltar, and Morocco, from where he transported much of his grain.[18] The British government undertook to pay him for the provisions of both the British and Portuguese forces fighting the Bourbons in the Peninsula. But, like Medina, he overreached himself. When he finally settled in London, in 1711, he was owed some

[16] CSP 1691–2, p. 50; CTB x. 1065, 1361 and xi. 1696–7.
[17] Rabinowicz, *Sir Solomon de Medina*, pp. 48–54.
[18] Rubens, 'Joseph Cortissos', pp. 123–7.

£100,000 by the English crown but seemingly only ever recovered about half that amount. Eventually bankrupted, by the time of his death, in 1742, he had sunk into utter destitution.

The spectacle of Jews provisioning the armies of the coalition ranged against Louis XIV excited comment and not infrequent disapproval almost everywhere in central and western Europe. Vienna constantly echoed with talk of the alleged unscrupulousness of the Oppenheimers. The fact that the Duke of Marlborough took bribes from Solomon de Medina was ruthlessly exploited during the campaign to discredit the famous general in the years 1711–12. If bribery and corruption were integral to the functioning of the military (and much other) finance in the Europe of the time, it was hardly to be avoided, given the prejudices of society, that Jewish involvement in such corruption should be singled out for special blame. In 1711, Medina admitted that he had paid over around 66,000 gulden, some £6,000, yearly to Marlborough in the years 1707–11 for the 'contracts for supplying bread and bread-wagons to the forces in the Low-Countries in the Queen of Great Britain's pay' and that Antonio Alvarez Machado before him had paid Marlborough a like sum for the contracts for bread for the forces 'in the English pay' during the years 1702–6.[19] But whoever aspired to secure and keep such contracts had to sweeten the generals with such sums, not to mention frequent gifts of wine and other wares. The chief reason that Jewish contractors predominated was not that they had greater effrontery, or means, in the matter of enveloping generals in bribes, but that on the whole they proved efficient and reliable, having the necessary organization, in supplying the required provisions. There can be no other reason why William III stuck to Jewish provisioners throughout his wars against France and in Ireland. And if Marlborough spoke approvingly of Machado and (until 1711) of Medina, and princes Eugene of Savoy and Louis of Baden of the Oppenheimers, these renowned commanders were certainly motivated by military as much as any other consideration. The standards of financial morality of the Jewish contractors have to be measured against the standards of those with whom they dealt. The Earl of Peterborough, who commanded the allied troops in Spain, remarked of Joseph Cortizos, another target for smear and innuendo,

---

[19] *The Report of the Commissioners . . . with the Depositions at Large of Sir Solomon Medina . . .*, pp. 3–5.

that in fact he 'dealt better with other people than they did with him', an allusion to Cortizos's treatment at the hands of British ministers.[20]

No less important than army contracting, and perhaps more so, was the increasing role of Jews in state finance and international payments generally. This rested essentially on Amsterdam's role as Europe's chief bullion and money market combined with Jewish dominance of the gold, silver, and other metal trades in central Europe. It arose also from the Jews' particular need of government favours and concessions as well as from their exceptional vulnerability to government pressure. But most crucial of all was the wide, not to say pervasive, reach of the closely knit Sephardi–Ashkenazi financial network and its ability to raise large sums with great speed, often on mere trust, and to remit the money swiftly from one part of Europe to another. In a Europe of empty treasuries and armies operating on overstrained credit, all this amounted to a unique and formidable factor in international affairs. In Germany, Austria, and Hungary, Jewish involvement in state finance would seem to have been as closely linked with the precious and non-precious metal trades as with army contracting. The entire system resembled a pyramid, the middle strata of which consisted of the metal dealers of Frankfurt, Hamburg, and Prague and the base of which was composed of thousands of poor Jewish pedlars who scoured the villages and towns of central Europe buying up old metal and coin which they fed into the major ghettos. It is true that even before 1600 there had been Jewish mint-masters and suppliers to mints in Germany. But during the Thirty Years War this had become more frequent and after 1650 still more prevalent. In 1629, Jews had supplied twenty-nine per cent of the silver delivered to the Austrian Imperial Mint in Breslau; by 1656, when Zacharias Lazarus was appointed official supplier to the Breslau mint, this figure had risen to around 50 per cent; by 1704, when Lazarus Hirschel was appointed *Hoffaktor* in Breslau, the proportion of silver supplied to the mint by Jews had risen to 80 per cent.[21]

The pre-eminent German Jewish court financier was Samson Wertheimer (1658–1728) whose sensational career was built on his ability to assemble packages of loans raised, with the help of fellow Jews, in a dozen different places at once. While Wertheimer was not an army contractor, and was never directly involved in the provision-

[20] Rubens, 'Joseph Cortissos', p. 127.
[21] Brilling, *Juden in Breslau*, pp. 69–70.

ing of armies, his financial operations were inexorably geared to the demands of war. At crucial points in his career, speed was the prime ingredient of his success. His prompt provision of cash, when nothing else was immediately available, during the Austrian siege of Landau in 1702, earned him the lasting gratitude of the Austrian Crown Prince Joseph, who was commanding his father's troops.[22] As we have seen, it was Wertheimer who rescued the Austrian Treasury from the fracas of the collapse of the Oppenheimers. From then until the end of the War of the Spanish Succession, he advanced millions of gulden each year to the Emperor, being repaid out of the revenues (when they came in) of Bohemia, Moravia, and Hungary. Without Wertheimer's advances, or some equivalent, the Emperor could not have waged war on France and on his Hungarian rebels simultaneously. But neither could Wertheimer have assembled his packages of loans without his wide-ranging network of associates, prominent among whom were Aaron Beer and the Kann family of Frankfurt. Nor was it only for Austria's own armies that Wertheimer had to procure funds. Subsidies were needed for the Emperor's allies in Germany and one of Wertheimer's main tasks was to remit cash, on behalf of the Emperor, to the Palatinate, Mainz, Trier, and elsewhere.[23] For his incalculable services, Wertheimer was the recipient of honours and privileges unique among German Jews of his day. He and his son Wolf were present at the coronation of the Emperor Charles VI at Frankfurt, in 1711, an occasion at which he was presented with a golden chain.

The capacity to summon up large sums swiftly and transfer them secretly was crucial to the execution of sudden, bold initiatives of state. And for this the Court Jews of the late seventeenth and early eighteenth century proved peculiarly well suited. Many or most of their more dramatic interventions reveal a definite leaning on their part towards The Hague and Vienna and against Louis XIV. If Samson Wertheimer was the most important of the Ashkenazi financiers, pre-eminent among the Sephardim were Antonio (Isaac), 1st Baron Lopes Suasso (d. 1685) and his son Francisco (Abraham), 2nd Baron Lopes Suasso. In 1674, Antonio Lopes Suasso, who had financial connections everywhere from Vienna and Venice to the Spanish Caribbean, smuggled funds into southern France for the use of malcontent Huguenots whom William III was attempting to stir into revolt against the French king. In 1675, Spain came close to

[22] Kaufmann, *Samson Wertheimer*, pp. 23, 35.
[23] Ibid., pp. 20, 28.

losing Sicily to the French who were forestalled chiefly by the timely intervention of a Dutch fleet under De Ruyter: this Dutch intervention, largely negotiated by Spain's Jewish agent in Amsterdam, Manuel de Belmonte, was much facilitated by Lopes Suasso who advanced cash to the Dutch admiralty authorities on behalf of Spain on the sole security of promises of honours and repayment from the Spanish ambassador in The Hague.[24] It was for these and like services that Charles II of Spain conferred on Lopes Suasso, a practising Jew, the unheard of honour of making him a baron of the Spanish Netherlands. And the contributions of the second Baron were even more spectacular. A well-known story has it that he advanced William III two million gulden which the Stadhouder needed to make ready his expedition to England in 1688, without requiring any security whatever, remarking merely 'Si vous êtes heureux, je sais que vous me les rendrez; si vous êtes malheureux, je consens de les perdre'.[25] True or not, it is known for certain that in the same year the second Baron did advance 600,000 urgently needed thaler to clinch the election of the pro-Dutch candidate to the strategically vital bishopric of Münster: and again Louis XIV was thwarted, the Dutch candidate, Bishop Friedrich Christian von Plettenburg (1688–1706) winning and then committing Münster's forces to the anti-French coalition. At stages during the Nine Years War (1689–98), Lopes Suasso played the most important role of any financier in handling the payments from Spain for the Spanish army of Flanders. In the summer of 1696, for instance, after the great effort of the previous year in which the forces of the coalition had pushed the French back from Brussels and retaken Namur, it was Lopes Suasso's *galantería*, as Spanish ministers called it, in taking the risk (which no other Dutch financier was willing to do) of advancing large sums months ahead of the agreed schedules which staved off a disastrous breakdown of the Spanish finances.[26] Max Emmanuel of Bavaria, the then governor of the Spanish Netherlands, who had, in his own words, 'many experiences of the zeal with which Baron Suasso serves his Majesty', was nevertheless awed by this latest display of financial *sang-froid*.

Admittedly, Louis XIV had allies in Germany and some Court Jews did collaborate intermittently with the French. But instances of

---

[24] Swetschinski, 'Portuguese Jewish Merchants', i. 263.

[25] Silva Rosa, *Geschiedenis*, p. 101; Meijer, *Zij lieten hun sporen*, p. 85.

[26] AGS Estado 3890, Max Emmanuel of Bavaria to Charles II, Noirmont, 13 July 1696; and *consulta* of the *Consejo de Estado* on Baron Lopes Suasso, Madrid, 2 July 1696.

this are relatively rare. When Ernst Augustus of Hanover deserted the Emperor and the Dutch, in 1691–2, in return for a French subsidy, Leffman Behrends (1634–1714), his court factor and one of the principal Court Jews of North Germany, smuggled the French cash from Metz to Hanover concealed in wine barrels. But Behrends's most renowned feat concerned Hanover's subsequent defection from the French side and *rapprochment* with the Emperor which, indeed, had possibly been the intention all along, in exchange for the conferment of the much-coveted title of 'Elector' on Hanover's ruler. Behrends was entrusted with the negotiation with Vienna and raised the 500,000 gulden, demanded as the price of his prince's elevation, chiefly from Hamburg. Subsequently, he handled the Dutch subsidies paid to a string of North German princes, including the payments to Bishop von Plettenburg of Münster. During the War of the Spanish Succession, he collaborated closely with Samson Wertheimer in the packaging of loans for the Austrian treasury.[27] Behrends's last major intervention was his raising of the 700,000 thaler which George, Elector of Hanover (later George I of England), lent to Denmark, in 1711, on the security of the districts of Oldenburg and Delmenhorst, near Bremen.[28] This was an intricate manœuvre intended to further the Elector's designs on the two localities and which paved the way to a subsequent alliance between Denmark and Hanover against Sweden, Denmark's perennial enemy. Behrends raised and tranferred the cash through his usual consortium of Hamburg Ashkenazi bankers, negotiating in Hamburg, and with Danish ministers, through two delegates, his book-keeper and right-hand man, Michael David, originally from Halberstadt, and Isaac, son of Jost and Esther Liebmann of Berlin, who, though primarily court jeweller to Prussia's first king, had recently visited Copenhagen and had close financial links with both Hanover and Denmark as well as Gotha and Weimar. Behrends died shortly before the Elector became George I of England and so it was left to his successor as court factor at Hanover, Michael David, to style himself 'königlich Gross-Brittanischer Hof- und Kammeragent'. In December 1715, David was presented to King Frederick IV of Denmark, at Stralsund, and entrusted with 39,000 thaler of Danish public funds with which to bribe Hanoverian officials to adhere to the Danish alliance.

One of the best-known exploits of Jewish financiers at the expense

---

[27] Schnee, *Hoffinanz*, ii. 22–30.
[28] Arnheim, 'German Court Jews and Denmark', pp. 126–9.

of Louis XIV was the operation mounted in 1696 by the Court Jew
Behrend Lehmann of Halberstadt (1661–1730) on behalf of Elector
Augustus II of Saxony. The demise of King John Sobieski precipitated a furious clash between the pro- and anti-French factions in
Poland over who was to succeed to the Polish throne. William III and
the Emperor decided to back Augustus against the French candidate
and it fell to Lehmann to find the funds for his publicity campaign and
to sweeten enough Polish nobles to clinch his election.[29] This was
politics of the sort apt to be settled by a swift deployment of ready
cash. Lehmann raised funds on all sides, from the Sephardi families
de Pinto and Teixeira of Amsterdam and Hamburg, as well as from
numerous North and South German agents and relatives. Samson
Wertheimer travelled personally from Vienna to Breslau with
300,000 thaler in cash to lend a hand. The French could not compete
with this. Their effort faltered and Augustus won Poland's crown. As
his reward, Lehmann received concessions and privileges in both
Saxony and Poland and, while continuing to live in Halberstadt, was
appointed 'Polish resident in Brandenburg', a post which gave him a
regular role in diplomatic interchanges between the Polish and
Brandenburg courts. Reportedly, he owned the best residence in
Halberstadt.

And indeed the financial and agency roles of the Court Jews not
infrequently created opportunities to influence the course of
diplomacy proper. It is true that Christian states, in contrast to
Turkey or Morocco, did not appoint Jews as ambassadors or
representatives at international congresses, except perhaps for the
case of Dr Israel Conegliano, chosen to join the Venetian delegation
to the Congress of Karlowitz in 1698, owing to his unrivalled
knowledge of Turkish affairs. But in the early modern period important international dealings were not handled exclusively by the formal
representatives of the states concerned. On the contrary, it was an era
in which unobtrusive, backstairs diplomacy played a large and often
vital part. In the negotiations over the Dutch fleet for Sicily, in 1675,
for instance, it was Spain's Jewish 'agent-general' in Amsterdam,
Manuel de Belmonte, and not the Spanish ambassador in The Hague
who played the main role. Jerónimo Nunes da Costa, Portuguese
'Agent' in the United Provinces, effectively represented Portugal in
the Republic during the tense and difficult years 1651–8, when there
was no Portuguese ambassador in Holland and the two states teetered

---

[29] Lehmann, *Polnische Resident*, pp. 17–20, 30–1; Saville, *Juif de cour*, pp. 89–98.

on the brink of war over Brazil, Angola, and their differences in Asia.[30] He also played a central role in the making of the Dutch-Portuguese peace treaty of 1661. Again, after 1661, when there was usually no Portuguese ambassador in the Republic, Jerónimo routinely represented the Portuguese crown to the States General. But none of the Jewish diplomats made more of a splash than the intriguing figure of François van Schoonenbergh, a possibly baptized relative of Belmonte, whose name was merely a Dutch translation of that patronymic.[31] This personage stood high in the esteem of William III and represented him as a sort of unofficial ambassador for many years in both Madrid and Lisbon. His personality and taste for intrigue—the Austrian ambassador, Lobkowitz, described him as 'a very dangerous Jew'—caused no little scandal in Spain, but the efforts of Spanish ministers to be rid of him proved unavailing. Among other spheres, his influence was repeatedly felt in that of commercial relations between Spain and Holland and he was much involved in the 1690s in the arrangements for the slaving *asientos* whereby the Spanish Indies were supplied with slaves by the Dutch.

On a more routine level, many European states now found it useful to employ Jewish agents, especially in Amsterdam, Hamburg, Frankfurt, Vienna, and Livorno, to supply regular political and financial information as well as gold, silver, and jewels, and sign contracts on their behalf. The Amsterdam and Hamburg agents were also much involved in the procurement of military supplies and naval stores, those entrepôts being Europe's principal munitions exchanges. Besides the Spanish and Portuguese agents in Amsterdam and Hamburg, the Polish crown likewise employed Jews as factors in those cities. In the late 1640s, the Sephardi Isaac Pallache was acting simultaneously as agent in Amsterdam on behalf of the Polish king and the Moroccan sultan.[32] In the reign of Jan Sobieski, the Polish agent in Amsterdam was an Ashkenazi Jew, Simon de Pool.[33] Meanwhile, Daniel Abensur (d. 1711) served for decades as agent of the Polish crown in Hamburg, for part of that time simultaneously acting as a 'commissioner for commerce' of the Danish crown, which chiefly involved him in shipping silver for the royal mint in Copenhagen.[34]

---

[30] Israel, 'Diplomatic Career', pp. 174–6, 178–83.
[31] His real name was Jacob Abraham Belmonte, see Caro Baroja, *Judios*, ii. 167–9.
[32] ARH SG 6906, Isaac Pallache to States General, The Hague, 27 May 1647.
[33] Fuks, 'Simon de Pool', pp. 3–12.
[34] Kellenbenz, *Sephardim*, pp. 397–9.

The only Jew in Holland to accumulate German agencies was the merchant-jeweller, David Bueno de Mezquita, who at his height, in the 1670s and 1680s, was Amsterdam agent simultaneously of the duke of Brunswick and the margraves of Ansbach and Bayreuth.[35] But in Vienna, Samson Wertheimer, whilst co-ordinating the Austrian finances, at the same time acted, at the Imperial Court, as *Oberfaktor* for the Palatinate, the ecclesiastical electorates of Mainz and Trier, and Saxony. At Frankfurt, Aaron Beer and Jakob Kann acted as financial agents for various German princes. And, again, at Hamburg, several Jews, Sephardi and Ashkenazi, held official agencies for German states, notably André Henriques, Hamburg agent of Saxony from 1669 to around 1680, and Jeremias Fürst, Hamburg factor and supplier of silver to the court of Mecklenburg-Schwerin. However, these German agencies at Hamburg did not confer the same status as the agency for Portugal, held in Hamburg as in Amsterdam by the Nunes da Costa, or the commissions held by Hamburg Jews for Denmark. The Teixeira, by far the wealthiest Jewish family in Hamburg during the second half of the seventeenth century, enjoyed the highest standing of all but without holding a regular agency for any state, though after her abdication from the Swedish throne, Queen Christina of Sweden, in 1655, appointed Diogo Teixeira her personal 'resident' in Hamburg.[36] The Teixeira were responsible for handling her financial affairs and, when she stayed in Hamburg, as she did on a number of occasions, she generally lodged in the Teixeira residence which, indeed, became something of a hotel for visiting Catholic dignitaries. Before becoming a professing Jew, and moving to Hamburg, Diogo Teixeira had lived as a New Christian banker in Antwerp and been heavily involved in handling the payments from Spain for the Spanish army in Flanders. His flight from Antwerp, in 1646, had caused a sensation as well as considerable financial dislocation.[37] But none of this prevented him, or his son Manoel, subsequently, from becoming the key financial intermediary handling subsidies and other payments passing between Spain and Scandinavia, nor from acting as host to Spanish ambassadors stopping in Hamburg on their way to, or from, Copenhagen and Stockholm. And despite Manoel Teixeira's involvement

[35] GAA NA 4092, unpag. deed dated 23 Nov. 1679; Schutte, *Repertorium*, pp. 292–3, 377, 380.
[36] Kellenbenz, *Sephardim*, pp. 387–8.
[37] AGS Estado leg. 2066, *consulta*, Zaragoza, 27 Sept. 1646.

with Spain and the European bullion trade, he also endeavoured to cultivate links with the French.

Another significant function, at any rate of the Sephardi agents, was their role in state management of colonial trade outside Britain and France. As we have seen, the Nunes da Costa, in Amsterdam and Hamburg, were leading participants in the setting up of the Portuguese Brazil Company, and aided the colonial schemes of Duke James of Courland, while the Belmontes were intimately connected with the Spanish slaving *asientos* signed in favour of the Dutch. Many other indications of Jewish involvement in the evolution of colonial policy can be shown. The Danish Guinea, West India and East India Companies all relied quite heavily on Sephardi factors in Glückstadt, Hamburg, and Amsterdam.[38] Shortly after the founding of the Brandenburg Africa Company in 1682 (another organization in which Sephardi Jews were involved), the Great Elector's minister of marine, Raule, corresponded over the feasibility of setting up a Brandenburg East India Company, to be based in Emden, with Manoel Teixeira and Jorge Nunes da Costa, younger brother of Jerónimo and 'Agent' of Portugal in Hamburg.[39] As for Jerónimo, who regularly reported to the Portuguese colonial council in Lisbon, the *Conselho Ultramarino*, as well as to the Council of State, he from time to time functioned as a liaison officer between the Dutch colonial Companies, in which he was a prominent investor, and the Portuguese. In 1682, for instance, he had several meetings with directors of the Dutch East India Company, in Amsterdam, to discuss the possibility of Holland and Portugal swapping Cochin, in southern India, then held by the Dutch, for the Portuguese colony of Macao.

The aspect of courtly life most closely associated with Jewish activity was the purchasing of diamonds and jewellery. Because both the importing of rough diamonds into Europe, from India, and the cutting and polishing of diamonds were dominated by Jews, the distribution of jewellery to the European courts tended to be controlled by Jewish merchants, both Sephardi and Ashkenazi. In Germany and Poland the jewellery trade was almost entirely in Jewish hands.[40] Firms with branches in Holland as well as Germany, such as the Gomperz, played an especially prominent part in the

[38] GAA NA 4111B, pp. 196–7; Larsen, *Danske i Guinea*, pp. 20–8.
[39] Becher, *Politische Discvrs*, pp. 150–1.
[40] Yogev, *Diamonds and Coral*, pp. 124–60.

traffic. So important was this business that virtually all the Court Jews were expert in handling jewels. Jost Liebmann (1640–1702), who resided in Berlin as a court factor to the Great Elector from the 1670s, and was the Berlin agent of the house of Teixeira, apart from handling remittances and providing some silver, confined himself almost entirely to supplying jewels. In Amsterdam, Jerónimo Nunes da Costa was for many years one of the chief importers of rough diamonds and pearls which he supplied to local workshops for processing. He also sold finished jewellery and, in 1679, drew up a contract with Moses and Reuben Gomperz to export diamonds on a regular basis to Germany through the house of Gomperz in Cleves.[41] It is likely that David Bueno de Mezquita's German agencies were connected with his activity as a merchant-jeweller. A notable link between the selling of jewellery to courts and court finance more generally was the recurrent need of princes, in times of emergency, to pawn jewels bought in easier times for ready cash.

Another strand in the activity of the Court Jews, though a less universal one, was the farming of imposts and tolls. Like military contracting, this was a capital intensive business but one much less dependent on having a far-flung network of factors. There was therefore no specific reason for Jews to cultivate this line of activity except in underdeveloped regions, such as the eastern territories of Poland, where Jews held a preponderant share of available liquid capital. As we have seen, since the late sixteenth century Polish Jews had been accustomed to farm tolls on the estates of large land owners, while Portuguese New Christians, who were often crypto-Jews, were active farming customs duties, salt taxes, and the like in Spain from around 1620. But, generally speaking, the incidence of tax-farming among the Court Jews of central Europe, after 1650, was much less than in Poland or Spain. Even so, there were some notable instances. Israel Fürst, the merchant-jeweller who was the first Jew to settle in Copenhagen, in 1673, subsequently took to farming several Danish tolls. Bendix Goldschmidt and Reuben Fürst, of Hamburg, operated the state tobacco monopoly in Mecklenburg-Schwerin in the 1680s and 1690s. In 1698, Aaron Beer and Jacob Kann, of Frankfurt, took over the management of the state salt monopoly in the Palatinate.[42] Altogether exceptional was the allocation of a prestigious fiscal post to Reuben Elias Gomperz, around 1700, when King Frederick I of

---

[41] GAA NA 4089, pp. 345–6; Schnee, *Hoffinanz*, i. 83.
[42] Dietz, *Stammbuch*, p. 161.

Prussia appointed him receiver-general of the taxes of Cleves and Mark.[43]

The Court Jew is conventionally regarded as essentially a central European phenomenon. There is ample reason, though, to consider this too narrow an approach. As we have seen, the activities of the Jewish financial élite of Vienna, Frankfurt, and Hamburg were too closely tied to those of the Sephardi contractors and agents of Amsterdam, The Hague, and London, for it to make much sense to treat the two phenomena apart. It is clear, moreover, that several leaders of Polish Jewry, such as Moses Markowicz, who secured the confirmation of the privileges of Polish Jewry at the coronation of King Michael, in 1669, and subsequently had frequent dealings with the king and his ministers, also deserve to be categorized as 'Court Jews'.[44] The same is true, in Italy, in the case of Israel Conegliano or Isaac Avigdor of Nice, a prominent figure in Savoy in the 1650s and 1660s, who was often engaged in raising loans for the Duke, on one occasion contriving the speedy advance of 20,000 lire, by Jewish bankers, on the pledge of a diamond-encrusted sword.[45] In many parts of Italy, including Turin, Mantua, the Monferrato, and Rome, Jewish bankers and merchants were intimately involved in the provisioning of garrisons.

Account must also be taken of the continuing prominence of Marranos in Spanish state finance and military provisioning. During the Spanish–Portuguese war of 1640–68, all the Spanish garrisons and armies around Portugal were serviced by New Christian contractors.[46] The firm of Montezinos, which was probably crypto-Jewish, continued for many years supplying Spain's North African fortress of Ceuta and participating in the financing of the army of Flanders. Relatives of Manuel Cortizos—including Don Sebastian Cortizos, who, much to the amazement of Philip IV's courtiers, was appointed Spanish envoy to Genoa in 1657—also continued playing a key role in the payments for the army. Yet another leading participant in Spanish military finance was the 'Portuguese' Simon de Fonseca Piña, who also for many years farmed the duties on wool exports from Castile.[47] By the 1680s, however, the heyday of the 'Portuguese' financiers in Spain was definitely over, the bulk of Spain's military

[43]   Schnee, *Hoffinanz*, i. 86.
[44]   Meisl, *Juden in Polen*, ii. 28–31; Bałaban, *Historja*, ii. 119–22.
[45]   Foa, *Politica economica*, pp. 42, 57–9.
[46]   AGS Hacienda leg. 894, *consultas* 16 Oct. 1646 and 22 Sept. 1646.
[47]   Kamen, *Spain in the Later Seventeenth Century*, pp. 305, 363–4.

finance now being handled by Genoese, Catalans and others. The last major Marrano figure was Francisco Báez Eminente, who farmed the duties on trade between Spain and the Indies, at Seville, and provisioned the royal garrisons and fleets of Andalusia. He was arrested by the Inquisition as a Judaizer in 1689, though the firm continued under the direction of his son.

In the course of time, the Court Jews not only accumulated riches and honours but evolved a life-style to match. Gradually, they were exempted from many, though by no means all, of the irksome restrictions and curtailments which the Christian state imposed on the Jew. Many were granted the right to ride in carriages drawn by four, or six, horses and to be attended by liveried footmen. In Germany, they were also, in some cases, exempted from the prohibition on Jews buying land. A few titles of nobility were granted but obviously lower ones than the recipients would have received had they not been professing Jews. In May 1673, the Emperor Leopold made Manuel de Belmonte a count of the Empire, in recognition of his services, but hastily cancelled the patent on learning that he was a Jew. It was only in 1693 that Charles II of Spain finally made him a baron.[48] Jerónimo Nunes da Costa was a knight of the Portuguese royal household and 'Agent' of the Portuguese crown in the United Provinces but was pointedly never accorded the higher rank of 'resident' or a noble title. Antonio Lopes Suasso, for his appreciable services, was made 'Baron d'Avernas de Gras' and granted lands in the Spanish Netherlands,[49] but, as a Christian, he would undoubtedly have gained much more. In Hamburg, none of the Court Jews, except the Teixeira, had the right to own real estate outright: they were obliged, as Jews, to lease their homes from Christians.

In general, the Sephardi élite went further in adopting a fashionable, clean-shaven look and the refined cultural pursuits of the time than their Ashkenazi counterparts. This certainly made them more acceptable as hosts to royalty, princes, and ambassadors than the bearded Germans. If Queen Christina's sojourns in the Teixeira residence in Hamburg, and her use of Sephardi rather than Lutheran physicians whilst there, ensured a stream of lesser princely visitors to Hamburg Sephardi residences, Dom Duarte, younger brother of the duke of Braganza, afterwards John IV of Portugal, is known to have lodged with Jerónimo's father, Duarte Nunes da Costa, in Hamburg,

---

[48] Swetschinski, 'Portuguese Jewish Merchants', i. 270.
[49] Silva Rosa, *Geschiedenis*, p. 101.

as early as 1639, though it is true that he was then not yet a king's brother.[50] In 1679, the Duke and Duchess of Hanover, parents of the future George I of England, lodged for some time in Jerónimo's home whilst visiting Amsterdam. The Duchess, Sophia, writing to her brother, the Elector of the Palatinate, warmly approved of the cleanliness and refined manners of the Portuguese Jews; she contrasted them sharply with the German Jews, whom she and her brother clearly held in lower esteem.[51] On another occasion, whilst visiting Amsterdam, William III himself is said to have lodged for three days in the home of Jerónimo Nunes da Costa.

As regards the German *Hoffaktoren*, they seemingly remained remarkably conservative amid the luxury and temptation that now surrounded them. In this period, unlike the eighteenth century, they were inhibited not just by a still formidable piety but by their need to retain reputation and standing among the mainstream of their communities, as well as the respect of fellow Court Jews, collaboration and interdependence with other Jews being indispensable to their operations. Behrend Lehmann lived in a palatial town residence, rode in a six-horse carriage, and was the proud owner of several country villas. But he also dressed traditionally and insisted on retaining his beard. This reportedly so exasperated the Elector of Saxony that on one occasion, having unsuccessfully offered him 5,000 thaler to shave it off, the prince personally seized some scissors and removed it. Samson Wertheimer was immensely wealthy, possessed at least eight residences—in his birth-place Worms, in Frankfurt, Vienna, Prague, Eisenstadt, and Nikolsburg—and was popularly called the *Judenkaiser*. But he retained his beard and was said to have dressed 'like a Pole'. Certainly the inventory of his movable possessions, drawn up after his death, displays a monumental abstemiousness, his only appreciable collection being his books and old manuscripts.[52]

Still, it would be as wrong to conclude that the German Jewish élite made no effort to involve themselves in the courtly and bourgeois cultures around them as it would to assume that their more aristocratic Portuguese counterparts showed little real commitment to Jewish community life and tradition. Indeed, what is most special

---

[50] ANTT Misc. da Graça, cela O, caixa 17, tomo 4B, pp. 552–3: Duarte Nunes da Costa to Conde de Vidigueira, Hamburg, 27 June 1643.

[51] *Briefwechsel der Herzogin Sophie*, p. 369.

[52] Taglicht, *Nachlässe*, pp. 39–45.

about the German Court Jews of the seventeenth and early eighteenth centuries, in contrast to their descendants of the later eighteenth century, is precisely their determination to keep one foot in either world and sustain a balance between them. In their way, they became part of Europe's higher culture too. Their expertise in jewellery soon extended to the art market and all kinds of rarities and exotica, which they both dealt in and collected for their own homes. The house of Aaron Beer, in the Frankfurt ghetto, ressembled an art museum, containing a dozen landscapes and seven biblical scenes, in oils, besides portraits, Dutch flower-pieces, and woven tapestries.[53] Very likely he acquired many of these during his own visits to Amsterdam. Jacob Kann's household was less splendid, but he too had tapestries and at least five oil-paintings as well as an impressive collection of silverware and *objets*. Nor should we suppose that there was no contact socially between the princely class and German Court Jews, despite very real inhibitions on both sides. The account given by the diarist Glückel von Hameln of the wedding of her daughter Zipporah to Kossmann Gomperz, in Cleves, around 1685, reveals a glittering occasion at which the choicest food and drink was served to a mighty throng of guests, who included the Prussian Crown Prince Frederick, and the Stadhouder of Cleves, as well as lesser nobles and Portuguese Jews who had travelled for the occasion from Amsterdam.[54]

[53] Kracauer, *Juden in Frankfurt*, ii. 219–21.
[54] *The Life of Glückel*, pp. 78–80.

VII

The High Point (II): Jewish Society
(1650–1713)

I

THE climax of the European debate over Jewish readmission came during the third quarter of the seventeenth century. For a quarter of a century, conferences, commissions, petitions published and unpublished over whether or not to tolerate Jews, and if so on what terms, abounded from Poland to Portugal and from Hungary to Ireland. Why did the political and intellectual process of readmission culminate at this particular time? Several factors converged to intensify previous trends but what, almost certainly, was the most crucial was the widespread backlash in Germany, following the evacuation of the Swedish, French, and other foreign garrisons at the end of the Thirty Years War. The substantial gains made by the Jews of central Europe during the conflict, of Austria and the Czech lands as well as Germany, had aroused intense opposition and controversy, so that the coming of peace was almost bound to be accompanied by a formidable reaction. This, in turn, forced the princes of Germany to take a stand on a matter which previously, except in the case of the Emperor, had been outside their hands. They could go along with the populace and opt for re-expulsion, or else resist the pressure, which would mean taking decisive steps to protect the Jews from their foes. In fact, a good many princes, anxious to revive their territories ravaged in the recent fighting, and reduce the power of the towns, so as the better to enhance their own, chose the latter course. But such post-1648 controversy in Germany was not the only factor generating renewed debate. Also important was the sudden upsurge in Marrano and Sephardi immigration into western Europe, involving many hundreds of refugees in the years 1645–60, arising from the post-1645 Inquisition onslaught in Spain, which put an end to the period of less harshly intolerant policies which had begun in that country with the death of Philip II in 1598, and also from the collapse of Dutch rule in Brazil over the years 1645–54, which forced all openly professing Jews there to abandon their homes. A final factor stimulating debate over the Jewish question at this time was the state of flux in England, after the Civil War, which opened up new possibilities by disrupting previous patterns of commercial and church organization.

In central Europe, the post-1648 backlash followed more or less automatically on the withdrawal of the foreign garrisons. This new wave of anti-Jewish agitation emanated chiefly from the towns and at its head were the burgomasters, clergy, and guilds. As one would expect, the reaction was sharpest in the Imperial Free Cities, these being free from princely control.[1] Within the space of a few years, the Jews were re-expelled from Augsburg, Lübeck, Heilbronn, and Schweinfurt, while at Hamburg the bulk of the German Jews who had settled in the early 1640s were sent packing to Altona and Wandsbek, though some twenty families did remain as servants and employees in the homes of the Portuguese Jews. But a few princes also yielded to the pressure, the margrave of Baden-Durlach expelling the Jews who had drifted back into his territory and the duke of Neuburg acquiescing in re-expulsion from the town of Lauingen, in 1653, and from the entire palatine county of Pfalz-Neuburg by 1670.[2] There were also concessions to the agitation in Hesse, notably the expulsion from Giessen in 1662. But the most serious blow—apart from the expulsion from Vienna itself—was the decision in 1677 to drive out the bulk of the Jews of Fulda, one of the most ancient communities in Germany. In all some 300 Jews were expelled from the abbey-principality.

The Austrian lands were the focal point of the intensified anti-Semitism of the 1650s and 1660s. By 1648, Protestantism in Austria and Bohemia was a largely broken force. A militant, Counter-Reformationary Catholicism had arisen which was bound, sooner rather than later, given the outlook of the Counter-Reformation and the recent economic gains of the Austrian and Bohemian Jews, to turn heavily against Jewry. Until 1648, the Emperor had consistently favoured and protected the Jews because he needed their assistance. But in the changed circumstances of the 1650s, with Austria at peace and the Catholic Church triumphant, the young, inexperienced Emperor Leopold I, who succeeded his father in 1657, hesitated to block the prejudices of the clergy and people. The new era of

[1] Grünfeld, *Gang*, p. 46; Franke, *Geschichte*, p. 40; Baasch, 'Juden', p. 370; Grunwald, *Hamburgs deutsche Juden*, pp. 5, 8–10.

[2] Volkert, 'Juden in Fürstentum Pfalz-Neuburg', p. 589; Bodenheimer, 'Beitrag', pp. 14–15; Rosenthal, *Heimatgeschichte*, p. 196.

European peace was rung in for the Jews of Vienna (now one of the largest communities in Europe) by an upsurge of popular demonstrations against the *Judenstadt*, mostly incited by Jesuit students. More ominous still were the resolutions passed in the Estates of Bohemia and Moravia, in 1650, to drive out those Jews who, during the war, had settled in Bohemian and Moravian towns which had debarred Jews before 1618.[3] A substantial number of Jews were in fact re-expelled from Kaaden, Feldsburg, and other towns, though, apparently, most of these were able to settle, instead, in nearby villages belonging to great noblemen such as the Dietrichsteins and Liechtensteins, whose attitude, as always, differed markedly from that of the towns.

In Vienna, there was a ceaseless ferment until, in 1669, the Emperor bowed to the appeals of Bishop Kollonitsch and the city council, and consented to the setting up of a commission to report on the Jewish presence both in Vienna itself and in Lower Austria generally where, during the Thirty Years War, a network of communities had grown up along the Danube valley. Kollonitsch, the most implacable antagonist of the Jews, was appointed to chair the commission. Its findings were a foregone conclusion. The presence of the Jews was judged detrimental to the well-being, spiritual and temporal, of the Christian populace. Swayed by a promise of financial compensation from the Vienna city council, and the bigotry of his Spanish wife, Leopold finally gave the order for what was to be the largest and, for the Jews, most disastrous expulsion to have occurred in Europe since the Jews were driven from the Papal States (except Rome and Ancona), in 1569, precisely a century earlier. The elders of Vienna Jewry mobilized whatever counter-pressure they could, including, through the offices of the Hamburg Sephardi banker Manoel Teixeira, the intercession of ex-Queen Christina of Sweden. The Emperor was offered the handsome sum of 100,000 gulden to allow 1,000 Jews to remain. But the die was cast. The expulsion was carried out in stages, the bulk of the Viennese and outlying communities being ejected in 1669, a residue of wealthy Jews leaving in early 1670.[4] In all, approximately 4,000 Jews were exiled from Vienna, Krems, Langenlois, and neighbouring places, dispersing in all

[3] Stein, *Juden in Böhmen*, p. 59; Schwenger, 'Über die zweite Ansiedlung', pp. 37–40; Hoffmann, 'Juden in Kaaden', p. 303.

[4] Wolf, *Juden in der Leopoldstadt*, pp. 37–43; Kaufmann, *Letzte Vertreibung*, pp. 106–42; Moses, *Juden in Niederösterreich*, pp. 23, 84, 110.

directions especially to Prague, Nikolsburg, and Fürth. Simultaneously, there was also a temporary expulsion of the Jews from Eisenstadt and other communities of the Burgenland. The Swedish resident in Vienna remarked on the dignity of the exodus with, as far as he could ascertain, not a single Jew preferring to submit to baptism as the price of remaining.

But the Emperor, on the threshold of long and exhausting wars with France and the Turks, was soon to change his tune and despite the many local expulsions of the 1648–70 period, it remains true that most of the gains made by the Jews during the Thirty Years War, except in Vienna, were preserved and consolidated. For, on the whole, the tendency among the princes of central Europe was to forge Jewish policies which went flat against the inclinations of the populace and clergy. Even in Vienna, a Jewish community was soon reconstituted, in the late 1670s, and while this remained small compared with that of the *Judenstadt* in the 1621–69 period, it must be looked at in conjunction with Leopold's other post-1673 concessions to the Jews in Bohemia, Silesia, Hungary, Tyrol, and Trieste. In Silesia, where new communities formed at Breslau in 1657, and at Oels, Brieg, and neighbouring vicinities after 1673, the Jewish population rose from only two or three hundred in 1650, to around 800 by 1690.[5]

In Germany, the prince who stood out most strongly against the anti-Semitic backlash of the period was Frederick William of Brandenburg-Prussia (1640–88), known as the 'Great Elector'. It was this prince who first achieved a measure of centralization in the Prussian state, centring on Berlin, and launched Brandenburg-Prussia on the European scene as a major power. In line with his general strategy of weakening the towns and estates, Frederick William's policy toward the Jews developed in stages. First, in the years around 1650, he blocked the attempts of the Christian townsmen of his new acquisitions, Minden, Herford, and Halberstadt, as well as of Cleves and Mark, to go back to the *status quo ante* of 1618 and re-expel the Jews.[6] Next, this tireless enthusiast for grandiose mercantilist schemes lifted the restrictions on Polish Jews visiting the fairs at Frankfurt an der Oder, hoping thereby to divert part of the Polish-German overland trade from Breslau and Leipzig.

---

[5] Brilling, *Juden in Breslau*, pp. 70–1; Brilling, *Jüdische Gemeinden Mittelschlesiens*, pp. 4–5, 16.
[6] Krieg, 'Juden in der Stadt Minden', p. 119; Stern, *Preußischer Staat*, I/i. 9–10.   .

Then, in the 1660s, he embarked on a further phase of his Jewish policy, allowing readmission of certain limited categories of Jews to Brandenburg, Pomerania, and East Prussia, a project linked to his schemes for encouraging Rhinelanders, Dutchmen, and later Huguenots to settle in his eastern territories.

The introduction of Jews into East Prussia was hotly disputed by the towns, especially Königsberg, which, on this, as on other issues, spearheaded the opposition to the Great Elector's plans.[7] As late as 1700, there were only a few Jews settled in the province. Nevertheless, this tentative appearance of Jews in East Prussia was of some commercial and political significance. The Great Elector wanted to build up the port of Memel as a counterweight to Königsberg—a typically mercantilist project which fused political with economic goals—and to do this he invited a number of Jewish merchants to settle at Memel most notably the Dutch Ashkenazi Moses Jacobsen de Jonge and his son Jacob, who were to dominate Memel's foreign trade for some decades, down to 1720.[8] In the years 1694–6, the Jacobsens, who had close connections with Vilna and Grodno and imported a wide range of goods from Holland, especially salt, paid more customs duties to the Prussian treasury than the rest of Memel's citizenry put together.

Numerically much more significant though was the resettlement in Brandenburg. Landsberg seems to have been the first of the Brandenburg communities to be reconstituted, in the late 1650s.[9] Although the army supplier Israel Aaron was the first Jew to obtain a permit to live in Berlin, the real beginning of the modern Jewish community there lay in the Elector's decision, in 1670, to invite some of the wealthier families then being ejected from Vienna to settle on his territory. He instructed his resident in Vienna to find 'forty or fifty' families of suitable means who would be interested in such an offer. As a result, three Viennese Jewish elders came to Berlin to discuss terms with the Elector's ministers. They asked for a public synagogue, but this was refused on the grounds that such a concession would excessively inflame the already furious hostility of the townspeople to the Elector's policy. In contrast to Halberstadt, in Brandenburg the practice of Judaism was, at first, confined to the privacy of the Jews' homes. The Viennese duly arrived, the largest group settling in

[7] Ibid., I/i. 66–8; Krüger, *Judenschaft von Königsberg*, p. 7.
[8] Schnee, *Hoffinanz*, i. 106–9.
[9] Lassally, 'Zur Gesch. d. Juden in Landsberg', p. 405.

Berlin, others in Potsdam, Frankfurt an der Oder, and Landsberg.[10] Later, in the 1680s, the Elector initiated further readmissions of Jews when he added Halle and Magdeburg to his burgeoning state. Both of these cities which had rigidly excluded Jews since the fifteenth century, were now obliged to admit them and their right to practise Judaism, which, in the case of Halle, included, by 1700, the privilege of a public synagogue.[11] Berlin acquired its first public synagogue only at the close of the Spanish Succession war, in 1714.

The liberal Jewish policy of the Great Elector of Brandenburg-Prussia was matched or imitated by an appreciable number of other German princes. The dukes of Hanover were hesitant about placing Jewish readmission on a formal basis, but, under the leadership of Leffmann Behrends, Hanover Jewry grew to be several hundreds strong in the late seventeenth century and the city became a regular stopping-place for Jewish merchants travelling between Frankfurt and Hamburg.[12] In 1703, Behrends was given permission to build a proper synagogue in Hanover (which he paid for himself), this being a clear sign of the now entrenched position of the Jews in the electorate. Still more important, in the Palatinate, a territory particularly severely devastated during the Thirty Years War, Elector Karl Ludwig (1632–80), yet another keen mercantilist as well as a forthright absolutist, encouraged Jewish (and later also Huguenot) settlement in several places, including Heidelberg and especially Mannheim. Eager to develop the latter into a major Rhine depôt for the Low Countries trade, this prince issued a charter in 1660 granting Mannheim Jewry privileges which were among the most liberal in Europe and allowed work to commence on a public synagogue which was completed in 1664. He was especially eager to attract Portuguese Jews to Mannheim, but in this met with scant success, netting only three or four families. But Mannheim's German Jewish community grew rapidly from a mere fifteen families, in 1663, to seventy-eight families by the time of his death, in 1680.[13] It is a recurrent theme of early modern German history that the Jews received the best treatment from insecure Catholic rulers of predominantly Protestant states; under a charter of 1693, Karl Ludwig's Catholic successor, Johann Wilhelm von Neuberg, went even further, effectively remov-

---

[10] Ibid.; Ackermann. 'Gesch. d. Juden in Brandenburg', p. 66; Stern, 'Niederlassung d. Juden in Berlin', pp. 140–9.

[11] Stern, *Preußischer Staat*, I/i. 77.

[12] Löb, *Rechtsverhältnisse*, p. 6; Schnee, *Hoffinanz*, ii. 36–7, 42–3.

[13] Ibid., iv. 180–1; Stern, *Jud Süß*, p. 6.

ing what restrictions on Jewish commerce remained. By 1699, Mannheim Jewry consisted of 150 families and was one of the largest, freest, and most flourishing in the Holy Roman Empire.

Meanwhile, in Baden-Durlach, whence the Jews had been driven in 1648, small groups were readmitted in the 1670s and allowed to form communities in Durlach and Pforzheim.[14] In Anhalt, where the princes had allowed some Jewish settlement since the early seventeenth century, out of mercantilist motives, there was a notable acceleration in Jewish settlement in the principality's chief town, Dessau, especially from the 1680s, when Moses Benjamin Wulff became *Hoffaktor* there and a public synagogue was opened. Wulff was one of the most able and widely influential of the Court Jews ensconced in the lesser German states. A no less interesting, if more marginal example of German princely patronage of Jews in the late seventeenth century was Duke Christian August of Pfalz-Sulzbach's invitation to them to settle in his town of Sulzbach near Nuremberg. This occurred in 1666, the motives in this case, seemingly, being less the usual mercantilist calculations of the time than this prince's predilection for Hebrew studies and especially cabbala. Following the granting of a liberal charter to the Jews, in 1685, a house was converted into a synagogue. There were fifteen Jewish families in the town in 1699. It was owing to the patronage of Duke Christian August that Sulzbach developed into a major centre of Christian cabbalistic studies, the pre-eminent Latin compilation of cabbala to be published in early modern Europe, the *Kabbala Denudata*, compiled by Knorr von Rosenroth, being printed there in the years 1677–84.

When Altona passed under Danish rule in 1641, the Danish king had confirmed and extended the privileges of that community and later extended his protection also to the Jewish communities of Wandsbek and Moisling. The Jews continued for a time to be debarred from Denmark proper but, in 1673, after much deliberation in court circles in Copenhagen, it was resolved that Jews should be permitted to settle also on Danish soil. This reversal of Denmark's traditional exclusion of the Jews followed advice from the Danish Board of Trade, urging ministers that Jewish immigration would help stimulate Denmark's incipient commerce with Guinea and the Caribbean and revive her flagging links with the Iberian Peninsula.[15]

[14] Rosenthal, *Heimatgeschichte*, pp. 197, 200; Rosenthal, 'Aus den Jugendjahren', p. 207.

[15] Kellenbenz, *Sephardim*, pp. 73–4; Hartvig, *Jøderne i Danmark*, pp. 63–4.

It is clear from this that the Danish court was chiefly interested in drawing Portuguese Jews from Hamburg, perhaps with the help of the Teixeira and other great Sephardi families which had close financial ties with the court in Copenhagen, but the offer was open to the Ashkenazim also and it was they who were much the more responsive to it. By 1682, there was a community of eleven German Jewish families living in Copenhagen besides an assortment of tiny scattered groups in Fredericia, Aarhus, Nyborg, and other Danish towns. Admission to Denmark proper was followed by admission also to the Danish crown's recently acquired duchy of Oldenburg.[16] Meanwhile, though Lübeck persisted in its ancient policy of rigid exclusion of Jews, Hamburg notably liberalized its stance in the 1660s and, for the first time, permitted an organized German Jewish community to take root in the city proper, alongside the existing Portuguese Jewish community.[17] This fledgeling Hamburg German Jewish congregation was for many years under the dominance of the Fürst and Goldschmidt families.

For the Polish-Lithuanian monarchy, and its economy, the later seventeenth century was, by and large, a dismal period of decay and contraction. Poland's exports of grain and timber to the west steadily waned. Gradually, Polish agriculture was divested both of its profitability and of its previous high productivity while the nobility lost much of its former affluence. The German bourgeoisie of the Baltic coast progressively declined. Yet, for Poland's Jews, contrary to what is usually supposed, or how traditional Jewish historiography would have it, this period, though one of some difficulty in the luxury trades, was as much one of rapid expansion and strengthening of Jewish life as it was for the Jews of central and western Europe. The notion that the disruption of the 1648–60 period must have prefaced a century of despair, setback, and disintegration is, with the partial exception of the cultural sphere, as misconceived and misleading as are traditional accounts of the Chmielnicki massacres themselves. Indeed, in some respects, the expansion of Jewish life in Poland-Lithuania was now even more vigorous than in the pre-1648 period. Once again, the overriding factor was the patronage of the nobles and their urgent preoccupation with reviving and recolonizing Poland's eastern territories. But of considerable weight also was the pronouncedly mercantilist stance of the Polish kings of this period, especially John

---

[16] Trapp, *Oldenburger Judenschaft*, pp. 22–3.
[17] Baasch, 'Juden', pp. 371–2; Feilchenfeld, 'Älteste Geschichte', pp. 280–2.

Casimir (1648–68), Michael Wiśniowiecki (1669–73), and John Sobieski (1674–96), who all adopted policies favourable toward the Jews.[18] Indeed, the period of Poland's attempted, if largely unsuccessful, recovery from disruption and decline was precisely the time of closest collaboration between the Polish crown and Poland's Jews in the early modern period. 'Under John Sobieski', wrote an English clergyman who travelled extensively in Poland some decades later, 'they [the Jews] were so highly favoured, that his administration was invidiously called a Jewish junto: he farmed to the Jews the royal demesnes, and put such confidence in them as raised great discontent among the nobility.'[19]

Demographically and economically, if not culturally, Polish Jewry now staged a dramatic recovery throughout the Polish lands and at the same time continued to nourish the expansion of Jewish life elsewhere. There was a constant, if modest, trickle of Polish Jews westwards, as there had been since the 1570s, into Bohemia, Germany, and further west, and a rather more substantial flow south and south-east into Moravia, Hungary, and Romania. Plainly, the most impressive growth in Jewish population within the Polish Monarchy, after 1650, was in the east, especially Volhynia and Podolia. But there was also a marked strengthening in the position of the Jews in western and central Poland due essentially to the devastation wrought in those areas by the Swedish and Muscovite invasions of the 1650s and the waning of the German bourgeoisie along the Baltic littoral. Some royal towns, including Warsaw, Kielce, and Radom, continued to enjoy the privilege *de non tolerandis judaeis*, but others were now stripped of that right by the crown, usually at the instigation of local nobles, as well as Court Jews such as Markowicz. In the region of Białystok, four out of eight royal towns, including Augustów, now lost the right to exclude Jews and became foci of intensive Jewish settlement.[20] To help repair the havoc spread in the south by the Swedes, new concessions were granted the Jews of Tarnów, in 1670, and, in 1673, King Michael lifted almost all remaining restrictions on Jewish settlement and economic activity in Nowy Sącz; by the end of the century, almost all the trade and crafts of

---

[18] Meisl, *Juden in Polen*, ii. 27–35; Penkalla, 'Singagoa i gmina', p. 63; see also Dubnow, *Weltgeschichte*, vii. 86–7, 99.

[19] 'After his death', Coxe continued, 'an ancient law of Sigismund I was revived and inserted in the *Pacta Conventa* of Augustus II, that no Jew or person of low birth should be capable of farming the royal revenues', Coxe, *Travels into Poland*, i. 135.

[20] Leszczyński, 'Żydowski ruch osadniczy', p. 45.

this town, which had excluded Jews entirely down to a century before, were in Jewish hands.[21] At Zamość, there had been only a small community before 1648, partly Sephardi: it was precisely in the 1650s that began the large influx of Jews into Zamość's trade, crafts, and distilleries.[22] At Łuków, in 1659, and many other towns around this time, there were drastic modifications in guild regulations in favour of the Jews, reflecting a general weakening in the position of the Christian guilds discernible throughout the monarchy.[23] At Grodno, after decades of struggle, the Christian hat-makers were finally defeated in their efforts to keep the Jews out of their craft, in 1652. In other Lithuanian towns such as Vilna and, a decade or two later, in Pinsk and Slutsk, there was likewise a marked strengthening in Jewish involvement in urban crafts. Only in the largest Polish cities where Jews lived, notably Poznań, Cracow, and Lublin, can Christian guild restrictions be said to have remained a formidable obstacle to Jewish activity.

But nowhere was the expansion of Jewish life in the second half of the seventeenth century more evident than in the Dutch Republic. The influx from Spain and Brazil in the years around 1650 gave, as we have seen, a powerful boost to both the numbers and the resources of Dutch Sephardi Jewry. It is true that many of the refugees left again within a year or two to participate in colonizing ventures in the Caribbean, or settle in Italy or London. But others stayed, some migrating to Rotterdam and Middelburg, both of which Portuguese communities were notably strengthened in the 1650s.[24] But the most important factor was the influx of Ashkenazi Jews from Germany and (to a lesser extent) Poland, a much larger movement in terms of numbers if not in skills and resources. This migration from Germany was stimulated not only by the growing importance of Jewish trading links between Holland and Germany, and the liberal attitude of the Amsterdam and Rotterdam burgomasters, but also by the changing attitude on Jewish admission of other Dutch towns and cities, several of which now withdrew their fomer refusal to permit Jews to settle. Everywhere there was debate and discussion over both the economic and religious implications of Jewish admission. In some cases, Jewish settlement was resolved upon by lesser towns close to predominant

[21] Mahler, 'Z dziejów Żydów', pp. 3–6.
[22] Morgensztern, 'O działalności gospodarczej', pp. 25–30.
[23] Wischnitzer, 'Jüdische Zunftverfassung', pp. 439, 446–7; Nadav, 'Jewish Community of Pinsk', pp. 165–9.
[24] Zwarts, 'Joodse gemeenten', pp. 390–2, 395–6; Hausdorff, *Jizkor*, pp. 12–14, 24.

regional centres which continued to exclude Jews. Thus Jews were now admitted, in the 1650s, to Amersfoort, the second town of the province of Utrecht, and to Maarssen, but were kept out of the city of Utrecht itself until far into the eighteenth century.[25] In the province of Overijssel, Deventer debated Jewish readmission but decided against in 1654, as did Zwolle in 1657. But Kampen, the province's third town, decided to admit Jews, in 1661, while Zwolle reversed its previous stand in the 1680s. In the province of Groningen, there was a continuing increase in Jewish population in the villages whilst the provincial capital persisted in debarring Jews from settling until 1711. By contrast, at Leeuwarden, the provincial capital of Friesland, an Ashkenazi community began to form around 1670, as did several other communities at Workum and neighbouring places.[26] At The Hague, Jewish settlement also began in the 1670s.

The increasingly pivotal role of Dutch Jewry in the Jewish world generally was due also to the rise of new Dutch Sephardi colonies in the Caribbean. Jewish Amsterdam now became one corner of a trans-Atlantic triangle, tightly linked, as from the 1660s, with Curaçao and from the 1670s also with Surinam. Curaçao was the largest of the Sephardi communities which arose in the West Indies during the second half of the seventeenth century and acted as a hub for the lesser communities on Barbados, Jamaica, Martinique, Tobago, and other islands. Functioning as it did as the principal entrepôt in the direct transit trade between Holland and the Spanish Indies for about a century, from the late 1650s onwards, this small island, with its magnificent harbour, became a veritable Amsterdam of the Caribbean. By 1700, there were roughly 4,000 Sephardim in the West Indies, the majority in the Dutch colonies, and while this sizeable settlement was in part governed by the Amsterdam *parnasim*, it should not be forgotten that they were admitted, as a matter of policy, by the Dutch West India Company which had already collaborated closely with Jews in Brazil.[27] The community on Curaçao originated in contracts and patents for Jewish colonization signed and issued by the Company in 1651, 1652, and 1659.

Meanwhile, in 1653, shortly before the final collapse of Dutch Brazil, a government committee convened in Brussels to consider the

[25] Zwarts, 'Portugeesche Joden te Maarssen', pp. 50–1; Rijnders, *Van 'Joodsche Natiën'*, pp. 140–3.

[26] Beem, *Joden van Leeuwarden*, pp. 2–4, 10.

[27] Emmanuel, *History*, i. 40, 42, 45–6.

question of Jewish readmission to the Spanish Netherlands. This was done on the orders of the then governor, the Austrian Archduke Leopold, but without the knowledge of ministers in Madrid. This extraordinary procedure arose from an offer put to the Spanish ambassador in The Hague by a group of Dutch Sephardim, headed by Lopo Ramires, who were then at odds with the Amsterdam *parnasim*. The proposal consisted of a promise of a subsidy for the depleted Brussels treasury in return for the privilege of establishing an organized Jewish community in the Antwerp suburb of Borgerhout.[28] Moreover, the committee, headed by the primate of the Spanish Netherlands church, the Archbishop of Mechelen, decided that there was no legal or ecclesiastical impediment to Jewish readmission to Brabant. The Papacy, however, was determined to prevent the return of Judaism to the Spanish Netherlands and demanded of the Spanish King that he firmly block this initiative. Philip IV and his ministers were indeed horrified and ordered Leopold to desist. Yet, despite the shelving of the original scheme, the Archduke did admit Ramires, his associates, and their families, with special exemptions from the jurisdiction of the bishop of Antwerp which amounted to a government licence to practise Judaism in private. We know that this group continued, through the 1650s, to follow the observances of normative Judaism and that, from this point on, the existence of a clandestine Dutch synagogue in Antwerp, distinct from, but also interacting with, the vestigial crypto-Judaism of the Portuguese New Christians already there, was a more or less open secret.[29]

In North Italy the princely invitations to Jews of the post-1648 period once again reflect a determined assertion of the economic interest of the state over vested commercial interests. Here a special factor was the severe slump in trade and industry which set in throughout Italy following the 1630 outbreak of plague. This paralysis further stimulated the now traditional interest of the Italian princes in attracting Jewish immigration from abroad. Thus a wave of Italian charters inviting Jews coincided with the migrations of Marranos and Sephardim from Spain, Brazil, Holland, and North Africa in the period from 1645 down to the late 1660s. A high

[28] AGR SEG 257, protocole 11 Dec. 1653; AGS Estado 2185, *consulta* 7 Feb. 1654; Ouverleaux, *Notes et documents*, pp. 29, 38–41.

[29] GAA NA 2242A, fo. 14; Schmidt, *Hist. d. Juifs à Anvers*, pp. 44–5; Libermann, 'Découverte d'une synagogue secrète', pp. 38–43.

proportion of the newcomers were Portuguese New Christians who had been living, often for several decades, in Spain. Most of them arrived at Livorno and then stayed in Tuscany under the protection of the Grand Duke who now tolerated and condoned defection from Christianity on an unprecedented scale. Because of the wealth and skills possessed by a proportion of the new immigrants, the princes vied with each other more and more in their efforts to attract them. Venice acquired very few as its trade was still so severely hampered by the effects of the war with the Turks over Crete. But other states competed rather more successfully with Tuscany. The Duke of Modena issued no less than three charters in the years 1652–3 inviting foreign Jews to settle, proclaiming them 'wealthy people and very apt to introduce traffic and commerce' which the Duke thought especially needful 'in these present times when trade is in serious decline'. Illustrative of the success of his policy is a surviving list of sixty Sephardi families who settled in Modena and Reggio between 1652 and 1657.[30] The majority of these were former Marranos from Spain who had recently reverted to Judaism, usually in Tuscany, but it is interesting to note that no less than nine of these families had migrated from Amsterdam and Hamburg.

Meanwhile, in Savoy, Duke Charles Emmanuel II was eager to attract at least a certain sort of Sephardi Jew to his free port of Nice. He issued his invitations through his Court Jew, Isaac Avigdor. Again, it is noteworthy that quite a number of the Sephardim who settled in Nice in the 1650s were Dutch or from Dutch Brazil.[31] In 1669, the duke issued a fresh invitation through Avigdor, this time to the more than 400 Spanish Jews expelled that year from Spain's North African enclave of Oran. Nevertheless, Savoyard policy towards the Jews was distinctly more restrictive than that of Tuscany, and the majority of the exiles from Oran, those who were comparatively poor, were soon made to leave. The English envoy at Florence recounted the incident as follows:

For of the 470 Jewes banish'd from Oran in the Africa coast . . . all which came to Villa Franca [i.e. Nice], the Duke of Savoy has fix'd all the rich ones in that port and sent away 300 of the poor ones. Those Jewes which are full of ready mony there have wrote to the Jewes in Livorno, telling them of the benigne reception they found [there]. This letter the Jewes in Livorno sent to the Great Duke who made Count Bardi write another to them in Livorno,

---

[30] Balletti, *Gli ebrei e gli Estensi*, pp. 223–4.
[31] Menasseh ben Israel, *Esperança de Israel*, p. 108; Foa, *Politica economica*, pp. 52–5.

assuring them that their poor should be received here, and that the said Duke would treat all their nation with more regard then they should meet with from any other Prince.[32]

Still more indicative of the limits of Savoy's Jewish policy was the incident of 1685. In July of that year there arrived at Nice a ship full of escaped crypto-Jews fleeing from Mallorca where, since the 1670s, the local Inquisition had launched a fierce onslaught against them. The refugees threw themselves on the mercy of the duke beseeching his (tacit) permission for them to revert to open Judaism.[33] This placed the duke in an insoluble dilemma, being the first time the government in Turin was being asked to condone a mass defection from Christianity to Judaism. A fierce and widely publicized controversy erupted with the bishop of Nice rousing the clergy and populace against the crypto-Jews. The newcomers' lawyers maintained that the exiles could not be classified as having been 'real' Christians in Spain and that it was the privilege and duty of the Duke to decide their fate in accordance with the interest of the state. Here then was a classic instance of a clash of mercantilist *raison d'État* with established law, tradition, and papal policy. In the end, the duke found it best to fudge the issue. The Mallorcan refugees were first arrested and then released without any specific declaration in their favour. Most of them then moved on to other parts of Italy, especially Livorno.

In England, public debate over the readmission of the Jews erupted in 1655 on the arrival of Menasseh ben Israel in London and the publication of his *Humble Addresses* to the Lord Protector Cromwell. This was precisely the time when the influx of Marrano refugees from Spain, and Sephardi exiles from Brazil, into Holland, was at its height and Dutch Sephardi Jewry at its most preoccupied with schemes for Jewish colonization. The approach to the English government was, thus, part of a wider package including the negotiations in Brussels, and with the dukes of Savoy and Modena, as well as the schemes for settlement in the Caribbean. Menasseh was not in any formal sense an envoy of the Amsterdam Portuguese Jewish community but he can hardly have proceeded with his grandiose project without its collaboration. Cromwell for his part clearly inclined in favour of

[32] PRO SP 98/10, fo. 232. Sir John Finch to Lord Arlington, Florence, 15/25 June 1669; two Spanish sources which specify the number of Jews expelled from Oran in 1669 give 466 and 476 respectively, see Israel, 'Jews of Spanish North Africa', p. 71.

[33] Foa, *Politica economica*, p. 55; Bulferetti, *Assolutismo e mercantilismo*, pp. 227–8; Braunstein, *Chuetas of Majorca*, pp. 67–8, 77–8.

readmission. But most of the clergy and the entrenched mercantile élite of London, as well as the populace at large, were strongly against.[34] Menasseh, and those who supported him, ultimately succeeded essentially because the recent Civil War had disrupted Church, City, and traditional privilege to such an extent that the government had more or less a free hand, or at least a much stronger hand than had had the Stuart monarchs who preceded it. Admittedly, a fringe among the clergy, a number of radical Puritan ministers, were fervently in favour of readmission, believing that this would hasten the conversion of the Jews, judged in some quarters to be a precondition for the Second Coming, of which a few enthusiasts were now in excited expectation. But the influence of this fringe was slight and even they, in the interests of their cause, espoused the mercantilist arguments which Menasseh himself proclaimed, asserting that Jewish commerce would assuredly benefit the English nation overall even if it proved detrimental to the entrenched interests of London's élite.[35] Besides these few clergymen, certain elements of the mercantile community, such as the shipowners, who had done well during the Thirty Years War but who had lately lost much ground to the Dutch, especially in Iberian trade, probably supported readmission. Menasseh's efforts also gained from Cromwell's preoccupation at this time with expanding English power in the Carribean, the area where Jewish activity seemed likely to be most useful to the furtherance of English interests.

Allowing the Jews back into England was thus basically an act of *raison d'État* in the face of powerful theological and popular objections, inspired by a mixture of political and economic considerations. The millenarian factor was definitely subsidiary. The famous Whitehall Conference of December 1655 fully reflected both the clash of views and the preponderance of exclusionist opinion. To Cromwell's chagrin, the conference was wound up after a few weeks without reaching any firm conclusion. But it did not rule out the possibility that 'Jewes deservinge it may be admitted into this nation to trade and trafficke'.[36] Indeed, expecting the government to rule in favour, the conference recommended that drastic restrictions be imposed to prevent Jews 'seducinge the people of this nation . . . in matters of religion'. It was urged that the Jews 'be not allowed to print anything which in the least opposeth the Christian religion in our language'

[34] Katz, *Philosemitism*, pp. 225–9.   [35] Ibid.
[36] Wolf, *Menasseh ben Israel's Mission*, pp. lxxxiv–lxxxv.

and that 'some severe penalty be imposed upon them who shall apostatize from Christianity to Judaism'. But, without issuing any formal law of readmission, Cromwell provided informal guarantees which enabled a small Sephardi community to form in London thus keeping controversy to a minimum.

On the restoration of the Stuarts, in 1660, the City of London resumed its campaign against readmission, petitioning the new king, Charles II, to expel the newly formed and still insecure community. Various arguments were adduced to demonstrate that Jewish commerce was harmful to London, including the fact that Jews were selling English cloth on the continent more cheaply than established London merchants. Charles and his ministers rejected the appeal, perceiving clearly the disparity between the interest of the state, including the benefits of maximizing exports of what was England's principal product, and the privileged profits of the City's merchant oligarchy. But the issue of whether or not the Jews should be permitted into the country refused to die away. Commenting on the continuing opposition to the Jews on the part of most merchants, Sir Josiah Child wrote that the

subtiller the Jews are, and the more Trades they pry into while they live here, the more they are like to increase Trade, and the more they do that, the better it is for the Kingdom in general, though the worse for the English merchant . . . .[37]

In France, the process of resettlement, in progress since the end of the sixteenth century, continued during the early part of Louis XIV's reign.[38] But, as with much else, it was followed by a partial reaction after 1680. Admittedly, Louis showed his basic aversion to Jewish re-entry into France as early as 1663, when he rejected a proposal by a group of Amsterdam Jews to settle in Dunkirk which the French had recently captured from Spain, and draw trade to that port, if the king would authorize the public practice of Judaism there. But, generally speaking, the *politique* ideas of Richelieu and Mazarin remained the guiding principles of government policy. Indeed, the middle decades of the seventeenth century, down to 1680, were the crucial period for the shift from an essentially New Christian, or largely Christianized Marrano existence, to an essential Judaism so thinly veiled that even government ministers now switched to describing the Portuguese of

[37] Child, *New Discourse of Trade*, pp. 123–4.
[38] Vieira, *Obras escolhidas*, iv. 18.

Bordeaux, Bayonne, and Peyrehorade as 'Jews' in official correspondence. Colbert, Louis's great minister of commerce and finance, inclined in favour (at least initially) not only of protecting the Jews already in France but of encouraging more to follow. It was on his initiative that it was decided, in 1669, to permit a group of Livornese Sephardim to settle on a trial basis in Marseilles in the expectation that this would help stimulate French trade with North Africa and the Levant. A contract was signed with two Sephardi merchants, Joseph Váez Villareal and Abraham Athias, who brought their families and employees to Marseilles and were soon followed by other Jews from Nice and Avignon as well as Livorno. And they did establish a fairly substantial Levantine business.[39]

In the early years of Louis XIV, the situation in the French West Indies paralleled the position at home. The Sephardi *émigrés* from Brazil who had migrated to Martinique and Guadeloupe in the 1650s were permitted to stay and engage both in plantation agriculture and trade, exporting sugar and tobacco to Europe and importing slaves and cloth. For the time being, the fact that most of these settlers had intimate Dutch connections was ignored.[40] In the same way, the sizeable group of Portuguese Jews from Livorno, who had been settled in Cayenne under the auspices of the Dutch West India Company in the late 1650s, were allowed to remain when this territory was seized by the French in 1664.[41] The main Jewish colony, established at Remire, near Cayenne, stayed under French rule until 1667 when an English force raided the territory and removed the entire group of Jewish settlers to Surinam which was then still under the English. When Surinam, in turn, was captured by the Dutch a few months later, the Jewish colonists had turned full circle and mostly now remained under the Dutch.

The reversal of the pre-1680 trend, which began with increasing harassment and trials of Judaizers in and around 1680, and the stopping of Jewish migration into France from Avignon and Savoy, was doubtless prompted in the main by Louis's increasingly militant Catholic stance, though the Dutch connections of the Portuguese Jews in France and the West Indies certainly also played a role. The change in atmosphere was closely linked to Louis's mounting

[39] Crémieux, 'Établissement juif à Marseille', i. 121–6.
[40] GAA NA 2898, pp. 57–9, 185, 197 and NA 2901, deeds of 3 Jan. and 11 March 1670; Emmanuel, 'Juifs de la Martinique', pp. 511–16.
[41] Loker, 'Cayenne', pp. 111–16.

campaign against France's much more numerous Protestant community. But the king's prejudices and predilections were strongly reinforced by a whole crop of mercantilist arguments. Apart from the close involvement of France's Sephardim with the Dutch, it was alleged that the Jews of Marseilles were supplying information about the movements of French ships to the Barbary pirates in Algeria and were not above offering for resale in France goods auctioned off by their Sephardi associates in Livorno which had been transferred there by Algerians who had captured them in the first place from the French. After hearing a variety of evidence for and against the Jews, the king and his ministers began to edge towards a concerted anti-Jewish policy. The intendant of Marseilles was instructed by Colbert to investigate and report on the role of the Jews, taking care to discount the objections against them made by 'interested' Christian merchants and reach conclusions on the sole basis of whether or not Jewish activity in Marseilles was 'avantageux à l'Estat'.[42] The intendant's findings were presumably negative. At any rate, during 1682 the king made up his mind, and the Jews of Marseilles were expelled both from the city and from France.[43] The next year, Louis jettisoned what had previously been a major plank of France's colonial policy and (with vociferous encouragement from the Jesuits) decreed the expulsion of the Jews from Martinique, Guadeloupe, and Cayenne.[44] But the presence of a network of long-established Portuguese Jewish communities in the south-west of France which carried on a considerable trade with Spain, Portugal, Holland, and the Caribbean caused the king to hesitate. Following a case in which two Bordeaux Sephardim were arrested for sacrilege against the Catholic sacraments in 1682, Louis resolved to act but cautiously. In an instruction of January 1683, Colbert explained to the intendant of Bordeaux that

Sa Majesté connoist qu'il seroit dangereux de punir rigoureusement ce crime, parce que l'expulsion générale de tous les Juifs s'ensuivroit; et comme le commerce presque général est entre les mains de ces sortes de gens-là, Sa Majesté connoît bien que le mouvement qui en arriveroit au royaume seroit dangereux.[45]

Accordingly, Colbert continued, the king desired first to reduce the

---

[42] *Lettres, instructions et mémoires de Colbert*, vi. 159.
[43] Crémieux, 'Établissement juif à Marseille', i. 142–3.
[44] Cahen, 'Juifs', pp. 105–7;
[45] *Lettres, instructions et mémoires de Colbert*, vi. 188–9.

numbers and economic significance of the Jews in France, and gradually undermine their position, so that at a later date they could be expelled with impunity. Thus, the intendant was ordered to allow no more Portuguese Jews to settle in Bordeaux, to expel a few families in connection with the sacrilege and later a selection of other families 'et ainsy Sa Majesté croiroit qu'en huit ou dix années elle pourroit les chasser entièrement du royaume; et comme cette expulsion se feroit insensiblement, le commerce qu'ils font pourrait passer entre les mains des marchands françois sujets du Roy.'

Similar orders were sent to other intendants in the south-west, and during 1684 an initial list was drawn up of ninety-three Portuguese Jewish families deemed disloyal on account of contacts with Amsterdam or else poor and 'd'aucune utilité au commerce'.[46] Probably some of these families did leave, but there were appeals and a good deal of controversy and, finally, in January 1686, the order of expulsion on these families was lifted, mainly on account of the massive exodus of Huguenots from France which had begun the previous year with the revocation of the Edict of Nantes. The scale of the Huguenot flight was so great, as was the damage to the country's trade and industry, that the government was panicked into emergency measures to try to stem the flight of both Protestants and Jews. Thus the flight of so many Huguenots stopped the campaign against the Jews. The Sun King's drive against a people he despised collapsed after five years never to be revived. Even so, it is possible that the episode served to accentuate the tendency among the Jewish leadership in western and central Europe to align with William III and the Emperor against France in the great struggles of this period.

2   POPULATION GROWTH

The seventeenth century was a time of stagnant or falling population in much or most of continental Europe. In this respect, the baroque era contrasts sharply with the other centuries of modern times, the others being periods of steady and usually rapid growth. But the position was quite otherwise for Europe's Jews. Indeed, the seventeenth century was one of exceptionally rapid increase in almost all of the regions where the European states permitted them to live. Admittedly, some of this impressive demographic growth was due to

[46] Malvezin, *Juifs à Bordeaux*, pp. 132–3; Cirot, *Juifs à Bordeaux*, p. 6; Nahon, 'Inscriptions', ii. 356; Nahon, '*Nations' juives*, p. 3.

immigration from Poland and the Levant, but the main factor does seem to have been internal demographic increase from within western and central Europe. Before 1650, the principal Jewish centres in Europe, those with over 2,000 Jews, were mostly great inland metropolises such as Prague, Vienna, Frankfurt, Cracow, Lvov, Lublin, Mantua, and Rome. Among maritime centres, only the Jewish communities of Amsterdam and Venice could compare. But after 1650, while there arose only two or three new main communities, there was a definite shift in weight from the inland to the seafaring category. The Vienna *Judenstadt* was suppressed but for a few dozen souls. Prague did remain one of the foremost Jewish centres but nevertheless suffered some decline towards the end of the century owing to the fearful epidemic of 1680 and a major fire in 1689. The Frankfurt ghetto slowly recovered from the impact of the Thirty Years War but, as late as 1700, had barely regained the 2,000 mark, and, relative to other centres, was obviously losing ground throughout the century. Meanwhile Lvov, Cracow, and Lublin all tended to stagnate in size. In Amsterdam, the combined Sephardi–Ashkenazi population amounted to around 4,000 by 1650, but then expanded rapidly, as a result of the immigration from Germany, rising to around 8,000, perhaps slightly more, by 1700.[47] This amounted to approximately 4 per cent of the total population of Amsterdam and represented the largest concentration of Jews outside the Balkans, Amsterdam having outstripped Prague and Rome during the last third of the century. Meanwhile, Livorno moved forward to join the leading group, rising dramatically from around 1,000 Jews in 1640 to some 3,000 by 1665, as a result of the double influx of the 1650s and 1660s from Spain and Venice.[48] It is true that Venetian Jewry declined somewhat during the second half of the seventeenth century, but by 1700 it probably still amounted to around 3,000 or again some 4 per cent of the city's population. Figures are lacking for Hamburg–Altona–Wandsbek, except that we know that the Portuguese community numbered roughly 700 in the 1650s, but the combined Sephardi–Ashkenazi population would have exceeded that of Frankfurt by 1700 and become the largest concentration of Jews in the Empire after Prague.

But despite the steady growth and diffusion of Jewish communities in the west, there is no doubt that by far the greatest increase in numbers occurred in Poland-Lithuania, especially the eastern fringes

[47] Bloom, *Economic Activities*, p. 31.   [48] Toaff, 'Cenni storici', pp. 361, 368.

of the Polish monarchy. It is true that the Chmielnicki massacres temporarily halted the rapid accretion of Jewish population east of Lvov, but it is becoming increasingly clear that traditional Jewish historiography greatly exaggerated both the numbers killed and the demographic impact of the catastrophe on the Jews of Poland's eastern territories. Most Jews in the areas ravaged by Chmielnicki's bands were not in fact butchered but fled westwards and subsequently moved back again once the risings were suppressed.[49] Briefly, the refugee problem, in all the Polish and Lithuanian centres which survived intact, strained the communal fabric to the utmost; but this very cramming of the Polish ghettos with unsustainable, surplus population ensured a swift and massive trek back to the east as soon as conditions would allow. Admittedly, some of the refugees drifted further west, into Germany, Holland, Italy, and especially Moravia. But again the significance of this Polish Jewish migration westwards during the mid-seventeenth century has in the past been absurdly exaggerated.[50] For it is now clear that the great majority of Ashkenazi immigrants into the Dutch provinces and the Hamburg region in the 1650s and 1660s were 'High German' and not 'Polish' while the bulk of the newcomers to Livorno, Modena, and Venice were 'Spanish', or rather Portuguese Marranos from Castile. Of 252 Ashkenazi Jews who married in Amsterdam between 1635 and 1670 whose places of birth were registered, only thirty-five, or less than 14 per cent, were born in Poland or Lithuania.[51] Indeed, there were nearly as many Ashkenazi immigrants to Holland coming from Metz, Charleville, and elsewhere along France's eastern borders as there were from the whole of eastern Europe. There was a separate Polish Jewish community in Amsterdam in the years 1660–73, with its own synagogue, but it was diminutive compared with the 'High German' congregation which before long swallowed it up.[52] The fact is, the movement of Polish Jews to the west—except for Moravia where they were fairly numerous—was of little significance compared with the massive trek back to Volhynia, Podolia, and White Russia.

Notwithstanding the post-1650 decline of the Baltic grain trade, and the concomitant impoverishment of the nobles' estates, the Jewish role in Poland's decaying economy continued to grow. For

[49] Bałaban, *Historja*, i. 226–7; Nadav, 'Jewish Community of Pinsk', pp. 165–9.
[50] For examples, see Roth, *History*, p. 107; Feilchenfeld, 'Älteste Geschichte' pp. 275–7; Fuks, 'Amsterdamse Opperrabbijn', pp. 166–7.
[51] Vaz Dias, 'Nieuwe bijdragen', pp. 165–6.
[52] Sluys, 'Bijdrage', pp. 140–5.

what chiefly mattered from the Jewish point of view was not the weakness or strength of the Polish economy but the weakness or strength of the Christian guilds. And it was the virtual absence of such institutions east of Lublin, at any rate outside the city of Lvov, which made possible Jewish entry into a much wider spectrum of occupations in the eastern parts of the Polish monarchy than was feasible elsewhere. This broad occupation structure in turn paved the way for the rapid proliferation of large and largely Jewish communities, even in areas where there were only meagre possibilities for trade and industry. Weakness of Christian guilds, and nothing else, accounts for the steadily rising proportion of Jews to non-Jews in many Ukrainian and White Russian towns. Thus, despite the massacres, there is not a shadow of doubt that the Jewish population to the east of Lublin grew a good deal faster after 1650 than did that of central and western Poland. A census of all the Jews in Poland-Lithuania compiled in 1764–5 reveals that there were then 749,968 Jews in the Monarchy only about one third of whom lived in Poland proper. The Ukrainian provinces, even without White Russia, accounted for no less than 45 per cent of the total.[53]

Furthermore, it is evident that a vigorous demographic recovery was under way in the eastern territories almost as soon as the insurrections were suppressed. At Lutsk, Dubno, Brody, Belz, and many other places, appreciable increases over the figures for 1648 had been achieved as early as 1670.[54] At Tarnogród, near Lublin, one of the communities supposedly erased in 1648, Jews owned, as we now know, 20 per cent more houses in 1668 than they had done before the arrival of the Cossacks twenty years before! The building of a series of splendid stone synagogues at Zholkva, Tarnogród, and other places to the east of Lublin in the 1670s and 1680s tells the same story. Indeed, it may even prove that the decisive rise in the proportion of Jews to non-Jews in the towns of Poland's eastern territories was a phenomenon of the immediate post-Chmielnicki decades, or at any rate of the second half of the seventeenth century, rather than of the eighteenth century. At Pinsk there were approximately 2,000 Jews by 1700, as compared with about 1,000 in 1648, the eve of the massacres, the figure for 1700 representing well over 50 per cent of the town's total population.[55] And in towns such as Dubno, Brody, and Belz,

[53] Mahler, *Yidn in Amolikn Polyn*, statistical tables.
[54] Bałaban, *Studja Historyczne*, pp. 47–50; Horn, 'Skład zawodowy', pp. 15, 22.
[55] Nadav, 'Jewish Community of Pinsk', 190–6.

Jewish preponderance, before 1700, was even greater. At Berdichev, there were 1,220 Jews in 1765 out of a total population of 1,541, but this pattern of preponderance was certainly established many decades before.

Meanwhile, in ethnic Poland and old Lithuania, the Jewish population of the traditional centres—Poznań, Cracow, Lublin, Grodno, and Brest-Litovsk—did stagnate. But this does not signify that there was no expansion of Jewish activity and numbers in regions west of Lublin. On the contrary, despite the undoubted deterioration of the Polish economy, there was an appreciable growth of the Jewish communities especially in the extreme west along the borders with Silesia and Moravia. Most notable was the rise of Lissa and Kalisz, close to Germany, Lissa Jewry rising from a few hundred before 1650 to between two and three thousand by 1700, by which date this was one of the largest communities in Poland and indeed Europe.[56] The decline of the Christian guilds in western Poland and Lithuania everywhere stimulated Jewish entry into the crafts, generating a steady increase in the size of Jewish communities, if not in the old centres, where the Christian guilds were strongest, then certainly in Zamość, Nowy Sącz, Kraśnik, and numerous other secondary centres.[57]

There was also a constant increase in the size of Bohemian and Moravian Jewry after 1650 despite the slight contraction of Prague Jewry in the 1680s.[58] Many key communities grew spectacularly, by three or four times. Nikolsburg, the principal community of Moravia, expanded from 146 families in 1657 to more than twice this by 1690, and to 620 families by 1724. Prossnitz, the second community of Moravia, more than quadrupled from sixty-four families in 1669 to no less than 318 families by 1713. There is not a shadow of doubt that the Jews of Bohemia and Moravia, like those of Poland and Germany, were reproducing much faster in this period than was the rest of the population, and that sizeable increases were registered at Trebitsch, Austerlitz, Kremsier, Jamnitz, Ungarisch Brod, and elsewhere. At the same time Bohemia, and especially Moravia, supplied most of the settlers percolating into northern and western Hungary at this time, including the Burgenland region astride the Austro-Hungarian

---

[56] Lewin, *Gesch. d. Juden in Lissa*, pp. 28–9, 134.

[57] Morgensztern, 'O działalności', pp. 25–30; Morgensztern, 'Udział Żydow', pp. 18–24; Mahler, 'Z dziejów żydów', pp. 5–8.

[58] Gold, *Juden und Judengemeinden*, pp. 422–3, 491–2; Kestenberg-Gladstein, *Neuere Geschichte*, pp. 1–2, 10.

border. Expelled in 1670, Jews began to drift back into the district almost immediately. Under the protection of the Princes Esterhazy, who issued a notably liberal charter to the Jews in 1694, as part of their policy of developing the area, the so-called 'seven communities' of the Burgenland flourished.[59] By 1715, 600 Jews, about half the total belonging to this *Landjudenschaft*, dwelt in Eisenstadt, another 300 or so in Mattersdorf, and the final 300 in the five lesser congregations—Frauenkirchen, Lackenbach, Kittsee, Deutschkreutz, and Kobersdorf.

In the rest of western and northern Hungary and Slovakia, immigration from Bohemia and Moravia (and to a lesser extent from Poland) was substantial but sporadic, punctuated by two major reverses. These were the 1682–3 and 1703–11 Hungarian rebellions against Habsburg rule which engulfed several Jewries in sack and massacre. What was perhaps the worst slaughter occurred at Ungarisch Brod, in July 1683. But both revolts were followed by renewed immigration, in part drawn into the garrison supply network focusing on Budapest, Raab (Györ), and Pressburg, operated by the agents and representatives of Oppenheimer and Wertheimer. It was a case of expansion amid tremendous upheaval and disruption. In Ottoman Hungary, Jewish life had been largely urban in character but now the whole pattern was transformed by the Austrian advance.[60] Before the Austrian siege of 1686, Budapest Jewry had numbered around 1,000 but only a very small community arose in its place after the triumph of Austrian arms. When the Austrians took Székesfehérvár (Stuhlweissenburg) again the Jewish quarter was sacked and afterwards Jews were debarred from living there. The Emperor's authority remained much more limited in Hungary than in Austria or the lands of the Bohemian crown, and most of the Hungarian towns were able to obtain the right to exclude Jews completely which they continued to enjoy throughout the eighteenth century. Only in Budapest, Raab, and Pressburg were small communities allowed to take root. But many Magyar nobles followed the example of the Esterhazy and most of the expelled Jews from the towns, as well as the new immigrants, settled in the many new rural communities which arose at this time, notably in and around

---

[59] Markbreiter, *Beiträge*, pp. 20, 25, 47; Wachstein, *Urkunden*, pp. 557–9; Hodik, *Beiträge*, pp. 15, 17.

[60] Bergl, *Gesch. d. ungarischen Juden*, p. 65; Mandl, 'Zur Gesch. d. jüd. Gemeinde in Holitsch', pp. 180–3; Kaufmann, 'Joseph ibn Danon', pp. 287–9; Moses, *Juden in Wiener-Neustadt*, p. 96.

Tritschin, Nové Město, Holitsch, Prešov, Komárom, and further south around Nagykanizsa.

Like Polish Jewry, the Jews of Bohemia and Moravia during the later seventeenth century were spreading south and east rather than westwards. While a few Bohemian Jews did migrate to Germany and Holland, most of the evidence points to the conclusion that the rapid expansion of Ashkenazi Jewry in the west was principally due to a vigorous accretion in, and fanning out from, central Germany. The new communities around Hamburg, in Holland, and in Denmark were predominantly 'High German' in character. The same is true of the Ashkenazi congregation which formed in London around 1690. In Alsace, a combination of local increase and infusion from adjoining German lands boosted the Jewish population from around 2,000 in 1650 to more than three times as many, at least 6,500, by 1716.[61] Data indicating the dimensions of Jewish demographic growth exist for several German territories. In the duchy of Westphalia, for instance, the number of registered protected families rose from fifty-nine in 1672 to 136 by 1712, and besides these there was an increasing number of pedlars and other unregistered immigrants.[62] Officially, the *Landjudenschaft* of Münster more than doubled in only sixteen years from twenty-three families in 1667 to fifty families by 1683.[63] Berlin Jewry increased from a few dozen in 1671 to nearly 1,000 individuals by 1700. The Jewish community of Mannheim, as we have seen, increased from a handful in 1660 to nearly 1,000 by 1700. At Hanover, the Jews multiplied from scarcely a handful in 1650 to several hundred by the end of the century. Hildesheim Jewry nearly trebled from twenty-five families in 1633 to over seventy families by 1672. And many more examples can be given. As we have seen, Silesian Jewry approximately quadrupled during the second half of the seventeenth century, though admittedly in this case immigration from Poland was a preponderant factor. At Landsberg, in Brandenburg, the Jewish community rose from four or five families in 1671 to twenty-one families in 1690 and 417 individuals by 1717.[64] Halberstadt Jewry, which counted 669 souls in 1699, had at least doubled since 1650. Fürth Jewry, steadily increasing, reached around 400 families, some 2,000 souls, by 1675, while Hanau Jewry was 700

[61] Weill, 'Recherches', pp. 54–5.
[62] Holthausen, 'Juden im kurkölnischen Herzogtum', p. 132.
[63] Rixen, 'Geschichte und Organisation', pp. 8–9.
[64] Lassally, 'Zur Gesch. d. Juden in Landsberg', pp. 407, 410.

strong by 1700. It is also certain that there was vigorous growth in the Jewish population of the principality of Anhalt, particularly the town of Dessau, which was the nearest community to Leipzig with its great commercial fairs, a public synagogue being built as Dessau in 1687. At Minden, where there was also a notable increase, a list was drawn up, in 1700, giving the birthplaces as well as occupations of Jewish taxpayers in the territory; not only were virtually all the immigrants German but most were from neighbouring districts.[65]

Is it possible to estimate the size of European Jewry outside the Ottoman Empire in the late seventeenth century? The Jews of Poland-Lithuania are estimated to have numbered some 350,000 at the end of the century, and the Jews of Bohemia-Moravia around 50,000. To this 400,000, we should add 10,000 for Hungary and, at a very rough approximation, 60,000 for Germany. For Italy, Simone Luzzatto estimated 25,000 Jews, in 1637, a figure we can readily accept as we know that the five largest communities alone—Rome, Venice, Livorno, Mantua, and Ferrara—comprised over half this number of Jews. In the later seventeenth century there was some increase in a few places, notably Livorno, Modena, Casale, and in and around Trieste; however, at Rome, Venice, and Mantua there were probably slight falls while at Turin, where there were 700 Jews in 1630 and 763 in 1702, and other places, there was little or no change.[66] An acceptable estimate for Italy in 1700 would be 30,000. To this should be added around 18,000 for Dutch Jewry, including the Sephardim in the Caribbean colonies, some 12,000 for the Jews in France and possibly 2,000 for the Jews in England and the English West Indies. This yields a grand total of 532,000 without counting the remaining crypto-Jews in Portugal, or the Jews of the Balkans. If we throw in the Jewries of Salonika, Constantinople, and Dalmatia, as well as the Marranos, it emerges that we are dealing with a people numbering approximately three-quarters of a million, or somewhat over half of world Jewry.

3   THE JEWISH ECONOMY, 1650–1713

In 1550, apart from pawnbroking and money-changing in North Italy and central Germany, the Jews were all but eliminated from the

---

65   Krieg, 'Juden in d. Stadt Minden', p. 122.

66   Foa, *Politica economica*, pp. 80–1, 85; Milano, *Storia*, pp. 292, 298–9; at Mantua, the Jews declined from around 2,325 in 1610 to 1,758 in 1702: Simonsohn, *History*, pp. 191–3.

economic life of western and central Europe. At the same time, their trade in Poland-Lithuania and the Balkans was of rapidly increasing importance, a fact which of itself did much to prepare the ground for a new and enlarged Jewish role in the west. By the 1650s, the picture had changed dramatically. The Jews were now participating prominently in many sectors of international trade, as well as colonial commerce and industry, and had entered the main stream of economic life in many parts of continental Europe as far west as the United Provinces and the south-western corner of France. On one or two main routes, notably the overland trade between Poland and Germany, and the routes linking Italy with the Balkans, Jews actually predominated. In the second half of the seventeenth century, in contrast to the century 1550–1650, there was little further structural change. The characteristic forms of Jewish activity in Europe were now fixed. But the post-1650 period was a time of sustained expansion which marked the culmination of the Jewish economic role in early modern Europe. The Jewish economy fashioned in the century 1550–1650 now reached its point of fullest development, what one might term its apogee preceding subsequent decline.

The characteristics of the Jewish economy were, of course, reflected in the structure of Jewish society. Generally speaking, the latter conformed hardly at all to the Marxist notion of class differentiation and struggle. Almost always, the vertical ties which lent Jewish society its inner cohesion—commercial collaboration and the patronage network implicit in Jewry's institutions, charities, and welfare system—were of much greater significance than any occasional friction between rich and poor. It is nevertheless useful to differentiate horizontal strata determined by economic status. But to do this meaningfully it is necessary to identify some five or six classes. First, at the apex of the pyramid, stood the élite of financiers, Court Jews, and princely agents; next came the much more numerous body of substantial merchants, manufacturers, and factors; thirdly, and probably most numerous of all, was the mass of pedlars, hawkers, old-clothes men, and other petty tradesmen; fourthly and less numerous but, nevertheless, a substantial proportion of Jewish bread-winners, were the craftsmen and artisans; finally, at the base of the pyramid was a depressed mass of vagrants, beggars, and other unemployed and destitute.

From Court Jew to pedlar these divergent groupings penetrated and depended on each other economically, as well as in religious and communal life. It would be idle to deny that there was exploitation as well as collaboration and interdependence, but such exploitation existed at all levels and operated all ways. If the success of the Court Jews was based on the activity of lesser Jewish traders and artisans, it is equally true that the latter benefited from the operations of the Court Jews. In the same way, more generally, it is as true to say that Jews exploited Christians as it is to maintain that Christians oppressed Jews. While the Jews did make an appreciable contribution to the economic greatness of Amsterdam, particularly in the post-1650 period, they were at the same time helping to divert trade from other parts of Europe and, within Amsterdam, infiltrated sectors which would otherwise have been wholly in Christian hands. Jewish activity was frequently detrimental to Christians and their guilds; just as Christian society was perennially striving to repress the Jews. Absolutist monarchy and mercantilism tended to protect and favour Jews only because both trends were themselves fundamentally at odds with many features of traditional Christian society.

In Germany, the two main functions of the Jewish élite were court finance and army provisioning, and this very much reflects the orientation of Jewish trading generally. Most German Jews, urban or rural, dealt in the metal or money trades, handling gold, silver, copper, and iron, or else bought up rural produce (with the partial exception of wine) which they sold in the towns, or else retailed manufactures and luxuries imported from abroad. Jewellery, another main aspect of the activity of the Court Jews was likewise a central component of German Jewish commerce generally. In Lübeck, itinerant Jewish traders who entered the town were almost entirely involved in buying and selling gold and silver.[67] Dealing in horses and cattle remained one of the most characteristic occupations of Hessian and other central German Jews. Increasingly, Jews figured as distributors of foreign manufactures, especially metal goods and cloth.[68] It has often been remarked that there is a connection between the eclipse of the German textile industries (outside Silesia) after the Thirty Years War and the expanded activity of the Jews. At Frankfurt, clothmaking all but ceased in the 1630s, opening a gap as regards supply and distribution which in no small measure was filled by the Jews. The 1694 list of occupations of Frankfurt Jewry shows

---

[67] Baasch, 'Juden', pp. 370–2.
[68] Holthausen, 'Juden in kurkölnischen Herzogtum', pp. 103–4; Evers, *Juden in d. Stadt Warburg*, pp. 59–62.

that at that time cloth merchants were in fact the largest category of Jewish traders in the city.[69] The list also indicates that they mostly handled fabrics shipped up the Rhine from Holland, including a good deal of English cloth, or brought overland from Silesia via Leipzig. Thus the contention of Johann Becher, Germany's foremost mercantilist writer, that the Jews were eroding local industry and crafts by facilitating the penetration of foreign wares by no means lacked force.[70]

The main routes connecting eastern European Jewry with the west were, as we have seen, the overland trade linking Poland and Germany, via Breslau and Leipzig, and the trans-Balkan routes from Constantinople and Salonika to Italy, via Split and Dubrovnik. Of some significance also, from the 1670s, was the importing, by Jews, of Hungarian cattle, via the upper Danube valley, to the Rhine. Although Jews were not allowed to settle in Leipzig, or anywhere in electoral Saxony until the beginning of the eighteenth century, they attended the Leipzig Fairs in growing numbers and there was a flourishing community in nearby Dessau. In the 1650s, as we have seen, a community also formed in Breslau and, from this point on, there was a rapid expansion of the communities on the crossing-points between Poland and Silesia, particularly Lissa, Kalisz, and Gross-Glogau, communities which enjoyed their golden age during the latter half of the seventeenth and first third of the eighteenth century.

The essence of the Jewish overland trade between Poland and Germany was the exchange of Polish wools, flax, and leather, and also Russian furs, for Silesian and Dutch woollens and linens bought at Breslau and Leipzig.[71] The Polish raw materials were mainly for use in the flourishing Silesian woollen and linen industries and so were principally supplied to Breslau. From Breslau, Leipzig, and (to a lesser extent) Frankfurt an der Oder, Polish Jewry procured not just cloth but the expensive and exotic products of Europe's tropical colonies—spices, drugs, tobacco, and jewellery—which they then sold to the nobles and clergy throughout Poland, Lithuania, and the Ukraine.[72] While the tiny Jewish communities in Danzig, Memel, and other Baltic seaports participated during the later seventeenth

---

[69] Kracauer, *Juden in Frankfurt*, ii. 109–11.

[70] Becher, *Politische Discvrs*, pp. 218–19, 230.

[71] Lewin, *Gesch. d. Juden in Lissa*, pp. 28–31; Berger, *Zur Handelsgeschichte*, pp. 10–12, 20–1.

[72] Bałaban, *Historja*, i. 230–7; Horn, 'Żydzi przeworscy', pp. 21–2.

century in importing Dutch goods by the maritime route, the Baltic sea-trade continued to be handled mainly by the Dutch and the Lutheran Germans of the Baltic coast, this trade mattering chiefly to Polish Jewry as an outlet for the grain and timber transferred down the big rivers to Danzig and Königsberg.

From 1648 down to the high point, around 1710, there was a steady increase in the number of Jewish merchants visiting the Leipzig fairs.[73] The surviving data indicate that relatively few Polish Jews travelled as far as Leipzig, the bulk of the Jewish visitors to this key fair emanating from Dessau, Breslau, Halberstadt, Gross-Glogau, Berlin, and Prague. Polish Jews generally bought the merchandise obtained there in Breslau, Lissa, Kalisz, or Gross-Glogau, all of which were vibrant focuses of the overland trade between Poland and Germany. But, if most of the Jewish merchants visiting Leipzig came from neighbouring parts of Germany, there was also a substantial number who came from much further west. It was quite typical for German Jewish traders to move back and forth across Germany regularly taking in both the fairs, at Leipzig and Frankfurt am Main. Indeed, as we read in Glückel's Memoirs, it was by no means uncommon, especially for dealers in jewellery, to peregrinate ceaselessly between Hamburg, Frankfurt, Leipzig, and Amsterdam, stopping at dozens of small centres *en route*. Much of the importance of such Jewish communities as Hanover, Cleves, Dessau, Fürth, and Halberstadt derived from their location on the main roads between the great commercial entrepôts. There was also a constant stream of itinerant Dutch Jewish traders, including a handful of Amsterdam Portuguese, visiting Leipzig as well as Frankfurt.

Although the trans-Balkan trade via Split and Valona to Venice was frequently disrupted during the later seventeenth century by war between Venice and the Turks, this Venetian traffic, sporadically diverted via Dubrovnik and Ancona, remained crucial.[74] In the 1680s, for example, some 80 per cent of Venice's remaining cloth output was sold in the Balkans, chiefly by Jews. At the same time, Venetian Jewry continued to expand its role within Venice's declining economy. Though in the sphere of retailing and distribution, owing to Venice's laws against Jewish participation in shopkeeping, Jews figured prominently only in the selling of tobacco and old clothes, it is clear that they handled a large and rising proportion of

[73] Freudenthal, *Leipziger Meßgäste*, pp. 14–17, 21.
[74] Paci, *'Scala' di Spalato*, pp. 115–21; Milano, *Storia*, pp. 298–9.

the city's imports of grain, salt, and olive oil.[75] In particular, the Jews dominated shipments from Corfu and Zante which supplied over half of the Veneto's consumption of olive oil. This growing participation in the provision of basic foodstuffs acted in turn to broaden the role of the Jews in many towns of the Veneto which acted as distribution-centres for grain, salt, and oil imports from the southern Adriatic.[76] At Ferrara too, there was a notable broadening of the Jews' commercial role in the late seventeenth century, to encompass basic foodstuffs. At the same time, an increasing proportion of the transit traffic between the Balkans and Italy now by-passed Venice and the Veneto entirely, passing via Ancona, Pesaro, and Senigallia through Florence to Livorno, which by this period had become the most important and flourishing commercial entrepôt not just in Italy but in the entire Mediterranean. And the transit trade from Ancona, Pesaro, and Senigallia to Livorno was essentially a Jewish trade. Indeed, Livorno's status as the principal Dutch and English depot in the Mediterranean combined with the fact that 'les juifs . . . font presque tout le commerce du Levant', as the French agent at Livorno put it in 1692, enabled Livorno Jewry to play a much greater role in the organization of Mediterranean trade as a whole than is commonly realized.[77] Between one-third and half of all Dutch trade with the Mediterranean passed through the depot at Livorno in the century 1650–1750, as did a high proportion of English Mediterranean trade, and the resale of the manufactures, spices, and other goods stockpiled there, in North Africa and the Levant, was chiefly handled by Livornese Sephardi Jews.

But if the economic life of Italian Jewry—at any rate outside the Papal States—was transformed during the second half of the seventeenth century, it is scarcely to be doubted that there was also much that was still rooted in the past. Pawnbroking and loan-banks remained a typical feature of Italian Jewish life, especially in Piedmont and Modena, right through to the early eighteenth century. In Piedmont and the Monferrato there were loan-banks in most places where there were Jews, and down to around 1700 there was still a rough correlation between the number of loan-banks and the size of the Jewish population. The three largest Jewish communities in the

[75] BL MS Add. 10130, 'Relazione della città e republica di Venezia' (*c.* 1675), fo. 80–80ᵛ; Becher, *Politische Discvrs*, p. 219; Ciriacono, *Olio ed ebrei*, pp. 62–7.

[76] Luzzatto, *Cronache storiche*, pp. 73, 89–90; Angelini, *Ebrei di Ferrara*, pp. 62, 309.

[77] Wätjen, *Niederländer im Mittelmeergebiet*, pp. 122, 355; Milano, 'Sguardo sulle relazioni', pp. 143–5, 148–9.

Savoyard state—Turin, Nice, and Alessandria—were all exceptional in various ways; but if we take the next four largest Piedmontese communities—Vercelli, Asti, Cuneo, and Fossano—with Jewish populations ranging between 130 and 230 in the mid-eighteenth century, it is noticeable that all of these had been characterized by exceptionally large numbers of loan-banks, up to eight or nine in each case.[78] Even so, there is no doubt that pawnbroking and loan-banking finally ceased to be the mainstay of the inland Italian Jewish economy during the late seventeenth century. At Rome, the survival of Jewish loan-banks alongside, and in competition with, the *monti di pietà*, now became increasingly controversial until, in 1682, Pope Innocent XI took the signal step of suppressing the Jewish banks, first in Rome itself, and then, in the next year, at Ferrara and other localities where there were ghettos under his control. Then, through the 1680s and 1690s, the suppression of the Jewish loan-banks spread to Parma, the Mantovano, and many parts of the Veneto.[79] By and large, in northern Italy, the ending of Jewish loan-banking tended to hasten the drift of the Jews into general commerce and industry. In Rome, though, the abolition of the banks combined with the relentless rigidity with which the papal government excluded its Jews from shopkeeping and most sectors of trade and the crafts, combined to undermine the precarious economy of the ghetto. By 1720, Roman Jewry had been substantially reduced in size, markedly impoverished, and faced a mounting crisis of communal debt.

If the economic importance of German Jewry and, in some respects, that of Italian Jewry, greatly expanded during the second half of the seventeenth century, this is truer still of Dutch Jewry. As before, the essence of Dutch Jewry's role was the importing and processing of colonial wares, generally for re-export within Europe, and interaction in the precious metal and jewel trades with the Jews of central Europe. But within this framework there was now an extensive restructuring and reorganization as well as growth. Before 1648, Dutch Jewry's German trade was still of limited significance while most of its overseas trade was with the Portuguese colonies, especially Brazil, via the New Christian business communities of Lisbon and Oporto. But in the years after 1648, owing essentially to the influx of new immigration from Germany and the Marrano influx from

[78] Foa, 'Banchi e banchieri ebrei', pp. 525–9.
[79] Luzzatto, *Cronache storiche*, pp. 83–90; Poliakov, *Banquiers juifs*, pp. 249, 255–6; Colorni, 'Ebrie a Sermide', p. 42.

Spain, coupled with the rise of Caribbean sugar as a formidable competitor to the Brazilian product, the pattern changed rapidly and fundamentally.[80] Amsterdam Sephardi commerce with Portugal and the Portuguese colonies steadily contracted while contact with Spain, the Spanish colonies, and the non-Spanish Caribbean became the linchpin of their activity. It is true that there was a vigorous expansion in all Dutch trade with Spain after 1648 and that the Jewish share in this was never a dominant one. It has been estimated that in the 1650s Jews handled about 20 per cent of Dutch dealings with Spain, including the shipping of goods to Cadiz for re-shipment on the trans-Atlantic convoys to the Spanish Indies.[81] But 20 per cent was a very substantial part of what was one of the most important branches of Dutch trade during the second half of the seventeenth century. And such a proportion is evidence of Dutch Jewry's having made an outstanding contribution to Holland's economic golden age especially when we note that Dutch Sephardi Jews did play a preponderant role in Holland's other trade with Spanish America, the direct transit trade from Amsterdam, via Curaçao, with New Granada and Venezuela.[82] Dutch Jews were active on both routes in importing silver bullion to Amsterdam. At the same time, despite energetic attempts by the English and French to block Dutch economic penetration of their Caribbean colonies, the Sephardim of Amsterdam plied a lively trade with Barbados, Martinique, and other islands at any rate into the 1680s.[83] Subsequently, as the English and French measures began to bite, the Dutch developed Surinam as their prime source of sugar and other Caribbean cash crops. And here again Dutch Sephardi Jews played a major role, not only in trade to and from Surinam but also in the production of sugar and the running of the plantations. By 1694, there were 500 Jews in Surinam owning forty sugar plantations and 9,000 slaves.[84] By 1730, 115 of the 400 plantations in what was then Holland's most flourishing colony were Jewish, an appreciable stretch either side of the township known as Joden Savanneh—Savannah of the Jews—along the Surinam river constituting what was virtually a Jewish autonomous region.

[80]   Israel, 'Economic Contribution', pp. 521–4.
[81]   Swetschinski, 'Spanish Consul', p. 165.
[82]   See SRH WIC Curaçao books for the years 1700–10, and AGS La Haya xliii, fo. 94, xlvii, fo. 109, and fo. 115.
[83]   Emmanuel, 'Juifs de la Martinique', pp. 511–16.
[84]   Oudschans Dentz, *Kolonisatie*, p. 17.

In England and France, the Jewish role in commerce was, in general, a good deal less important than in central and eastern Europe, or than in Holland and Italy. Even so, the Sephardi involvement in the import–export trades of south-west France, especially to the Caribbean, Iberian Peninsula, and Holland, was substantial enough to make Louis XIV hesitate over his plan to expel them during the 1680s. And in London, the Sephardi immigrants did make an appreciable impact not only in the bullion trade and the importing of rough diamonds from India but also more generally in London's trade with Portugal, Spain, the West Indies, and Italy. Jewish prominence in London's silver market reflects the fact that several London Sephardi merchants, most notably Álvaro da Costa, who was pre-eminent among Jewish merchants in England during the 1660s and 1670s, shipped substantial quantities of light woollen cloth, especially *bays*, to Cadiz, as well as Bilbao, Málaga, and Bayonne (for Madrid), and imported from Spain sizeable amounts of American silver, cochineal, and indigo, as well as olive oil, wool, and wine from Málaga and the Canaries.[85] At the same time, London Jews imported a not insignificant proportion of England's sugar imports from the Caribbean, though this does seem to have declined from the early eighteenth century onwards if not before.[86] In addition, London Jews regularly imported linens from Hamburg and Amsterdam and red coral beads from Livorno with which to pay for their imports of colonial goods and, in the latter case, diamonds from India.

It seems clear that colonial trade, or rather the importing of colonial commodities into Europe by the Sephardi Jews of Amsterdam, Hamburg, London, and south-west France, was a factor of overriding significance in the post-1650 expansion and revitalization of Jewish commercial activity in every part of Europe. The grip of Ashkenazi Jewry over the jewel, precious metal, tobacco, and spice trades in central and eastern Europe would have been largely, or totally, unrealizable without Sephardi Jewry's far-reaching penetration of trans-Atlantic and Far Eastern trade. However, the role of colonial commodities in the post-1650 expansion and revitalization of Jewish crafts and industry seems to have been of somewhat less significance, at any rate outside Holland. At Amsterdam, certainly,

---

[85] On the role of London Jews in England's overseas trade in the 1660s and 1670s, I am indebted to Maurice Woolf for allowing me to see his lists of data extracted from the London Port Books.

[86] Yogev, *Diamonds and Coral*, pp. 63–4.

the colonial trades were the very basis of Jewish craft activity. Indeed, the size of Amsterdam's Jewish population, Sephardi and Ashkenazi, in the late seventeenth century, surpassing that of any other community in Christian Europe, was attained only because sizeable numbers of Jews found employment in processing Asian and American products. If most of the rough diamonds were imported, after 1670, in the first instance to London, extensive Jewish involvement in the cutting and polishing of jewels was largely confined to Amsterdam with only a token involvement of Jews in these crafts at London and Venice.[87] Chocolate-making, which became a major Jewish activity in Amsterdam from the 1660s, when Venezuelan cacao first began to be shipped in quantity via Curaçao to Holland, did spread to other parts of the western European Sephardi diaspora, notably Bayonne and Bordeaux,[88] and probably London, but also seems to have been chiefly a Dutch-Jewish activity. Sugar-refining never became a major Jewish industry, but what Jewish sugar-refining there was, at any rate outside Italy, was again mainly confined to Amsterdam. Amsterdam, finally, but not London or Hamburg, developed into a major centre for tobacco-spinning workshops. In these tobacco workshops, as in the diamond-processing establishments, Sephardi and Ashkenazi workers were to be found labouring side by side but usually with the latter occupying the more menial jobs.

Only in Holland, then, can colonial goods be said to have been the preponderant factor in the formation and growth of Jewish crafts. In Italy, where industry was as basic to Jewish life as anywhere, its structure and composition was much more diverse. This was partly because in Italy, unlike in northern Europe, governments had tolerated, indeed actively fomented, the silk-weaving and other textile manufacturing traditions of medieval Spanish and Sicilian Jewry. At Amsterdam, where Portuguese Jews had been the first to introduce a silk industry, in the early seventeenth century, they were subsequently squeezed out of business, in the 1650s, once the city's Christian silk-weavers were strong enough to organize a guild from which Jews could be excluded.[89] A Jewish silk-weaving establishment did survive for some years more, at Maarssen, but eventually this too lapsed. In Italy, by contrast, Jewish silk-weaving establishments

---

[87] Israel, 'Economic Contribution', pp. 513–15.
[88] Leon, *Juifs de Bayonne*, pp. 69–76.
[89] Zwarts, 'Portugeesche Joden te Maarssen', pp. 61–2.

were fairly numerous in towns such as Ferrara, Mantua, Padua, and Verona, though not in Venice or Rome.[90] At the same time, it is certainly true that Italian Jewry's industrial role was considerably enhanced by the addition of new crafts such as sugar-refining, tobacco-processing, and coral-polishing. Indeed, one of the principal themes pervading Italian princely charters to Jews in the seventeenth century was the presumption that Jews were useful to the state, as the Duke of Savoy expressed it, in 1652, as 'inventors and introducers of new crafts'.[91] At Nice, the Sephardi influx of the 1650s precipitated a proliferation of new factories, beginning with a sugar-refinery set up in 1649. The most widespread Jewish manufacture in Savoy was tobacco-spinning and blending based on the mixing of imported tobaccos with home-grown tobacco, the cultivation of which was apparently introduced into Savoy by Jews. Also of note were the Jewish workshops manufacturing soap and candles, typically Jewish products throughout not only Italy but much of central and eastern Europe as well. One of the workshops in Nice was producing 'Damascus soap', using a Near Eastern technique which was presumably novel in Italy.

In Tuscany, there were clusters of Jewish workshops at Pisa and Livorno. The former were chiefly set up around 1600 by Levantine Spanish Jews, concerned with producing specialized luxury fabrics, including silks, using techniques which, we may surmise, had been transferred from Salonika.[92] At Livorno, the leading Jewish industry was the polishing of red coral obtained from off Naples and the Tunisian coast. Some of this coral jewellery was on sale in the jewel boutiques of Rome, Frankfurt, and Prague but most was absorbed into the colonial trade network based on Amsterdam and London.[93] It was especially in demand as an export to India where it was greatly prized and regularly exchanged for diamonds. Indeed, Livorno coral was one of the main items dealt in by London Jews. At Venice, guild-restrictions were tighter than in the Tuscan centres and most poor Jews lived by *strazzaria*, selling rags and second-hand goods in the streets. Even so, there was an appreciable Jewish involvement in the local diamond and tobacco industries.[94] Tobacco-processing had

[90] Ciscato, *Ebrei in Padova*, pp. 110–13, 121.
[91] Foa, *Politica economica*, p. 43.
[92] Segre, *Ebrei, industria e commercio*, pp. 7–8.
[93] Yogev, *Diamonds and Coral*, pp. 103–7.
[94] It is striking that even in Holland, several of the more successful tobacco firms

been one of the main industries of Salonikan Jewry since the sixteenth century and was probably introduced to Venice by Balkan Jews. Through most of the seventeenth century there was also at least one Jewish workshop with a furnace and special privileges from the Venetian Senate, manufacturing sublimates and other chemical compounds.[95] In Rome, guild-restrictions were tighter still; nevertheless, most of the city's large Jewish population lived from crafts, mainly tailoring, the repairing of old clothes, and button-making.[96] There were also several silk and leather workshops in the ghetto, saddle-making being a well-established activity. Rome Jewry was also responsible for supplying barrack beds for the papal garrison. At Mantua and Ferrara the Jews had rather more scope for involvement in new industries as well as production of silk and other luxury fabrics. Abraham Haim Fano established a paper mill near Goito in 1690, receiving a monopoly for the manufacture of paper in the Mantovano. But the weaving of silk remained the main Jewish craft in towns such as Mantua, Padua, and Verona.[97]

Crafts were also central to the life of Bohemian and Moravian Jewry. According to the 1724 census and occupation statistics, some 19 per cent of Bohemian Jews outside Prague were involved in the crafts and in Prague the figure was around 30 per cent.[98] Unlike in Amsterdam, Rome, or Venice, Prague Jews enjoyed an unrestricted right of manufacture for Jewish customers, and this resulted in a more varied mix of activity than existed elsewhere in Europe. In a few cases, notably the processing of furs, they also possessed more general rights of manufacture. As in the major Polish communities, the Jewish artisans of Prague were grouped into guilds, on the lines of the Christian guilds, complete with their own insignia and welfare-system. Most of the Prague artisans were tailors, furriers, jewellers, cap-makers, and leather-workers. Outside Prague, and in Moravia, the principal Jewish industries, besides tailoring and tanning, were candle-making and the distilling of slivovitz and other spirits.[99] As in Poland, wealthy Jews frequently leased distilleries on the estates of

were established by Venetian Jews, Cohen, 'Zoogenaamde portugeesche gemeente', pp. 22–3.

[95] ASV CSM 1st ser., clv, fo. 157–157^v, clvii, fo. 107, and clviii, fos. 4^v–5; this factory belonged for many years to the Serfati family.
[96] Blustein, *Storia*, p. 181.   [97] Ciscato, *Ebrei in Padova*, pp. 110–13, 121.
[98] Kestenberg-Gladstein, *Neuere Geschichte*, pp. 4, 12–13.
[99] Flesch, 'Urkundliches, pp. 203–14; Grunwald, 'Contribution', pp. 439–49; Hodik, *Beiträge*, p. 34.

noblemen and numerous poor Jews were involved in servicing these establishments. In the Burgenland, where again some 20 per cent of employed Jews were in the crafts, brandy and slivovitz preparation seems to have been the second occupation after tailoring.

In western and central Poland, guild-restrictions were fairly extensive but there was a clearly defined Jewish craft sector, comprising tailoring, hat-making, book-binding, and leather-working, in some cases for the Jewish public only, and the processing of luxury products from abroad, especially jewellery, furs, drugs, tobacco, and confectionery. It is striking that the general economic decline of Poland in the mid-seventeenth century, and particularly the disruption spread by the Polish–Swedish war of 1655–60, tended to work in favour of the Jews, enabling them to penetrate the crafts more extensively than before in many western districts.[100] In the same way, further east, in the new territories, though Christian guilds had always been much weaker there, the upheavals and Muscovite invasions of the mid-century finally consolidated Jewish preponderance in the crafts at Pinsk and doubtless also a large number of other White Russian and Ukrainian towns.[101] In these furthermost territories of the Polish Monarchy the prime Jewish occupations were again tailoring, tanning, candle- and soap-making, and distilling spirits.

German Jewry fell heavily between the two stools of a weak guild-structure in the east and the new crafts based on colonial trade in the west. Jewish participation in industrial activity would seem to have remained more marginal in Germany, at least down to the beginning of the eighteenth century, than anywhere else. The outstanding contribution of Prussian Jews to the development of the textile industry in Berlin and other towns in Brandenburg was essentially a post-1713 phenomenon.[102] Before 1713, German Jews neither owned factories nor toiled as artisans in workshops. The 1694 list of occupations for Frankfurt Jewry, for instance, shows that the only artisans in the ghetto were butchers and bakers serving the ritual dietary requirements of the Jews themselves.[103] Much the same story is told by a surviving list of occupations for the Jews of Minden of 1700. At Hamburg, while the Portuguese community imported many of the

---

[100] Wischnitzer, 'Jüdische Zunftverfassung', pp. 438–9; Morgensztern, 'O działalności gospodarczej', pp. 25–30; Mahler, 'Z dziejów Żydow w Nowym Saczu' pp. 4–6.
[101] Nadav, 'Jewish Community of Pinsk', pp. 190–6.
[102] Stern, *Preußischer Staat*, I/i. 130.
[103] Bothe, *Beiträge*, pp. 159–65; Krieg, 'Juden in der Stadt Minden', p. 122.

same colonial wares as did their fellow Sephardim at Amsterdam, including sugar, cacao, spices, and jewellery, there was far less development of crafts based on such products, chiefly owing to the rigid attitude of the Hamburg Senate which proved immovable on the issue of allowing Jews into the crafts. The repeated efforts on the part of the Hamburg *Mahamad* to persuade the Senate to permit Hamburg Jews to set up sugar-refineries, for instance, proved unavailing despite the obvious benefit that would have accrued to the city from this.[104] It is true that there was more freedom outside Hamburg, especially at Glückstadt and Altona under Danish jurisdiction, and that Jewish sugar-refineries and soap factories were set up at Glückstadt in the 1620s. But it would seem that these failed to survive for very long. Presumably, the preponderance of Amsterdam was simply too great. Thus, while tobacco and jewel importers and retailers were among the principal categories of German Jewish traders in the later seventeenth century, the processing of the diamonds, pearls, and tobaccos they handled took place almost entirely in Holland.

[104] SAH JG 993/i. 88, Res. 16, Adar 5417; Feilchenfeld, 'Älteste Geschichte', pp. 326–7; Kellenbenz, *Sephardim*, p. 101.

VIII

The High Point (III): 'A Republic Apart'

POLITICALLY, as in other ways, the period 1650–1713 marked the culmination of a distinctive Jewish culture within Europe. While Jews, at least in many parts of Europe, had always tended to congregate in their own quarters, the need to live within walking distance of their synagogues encouraging this process, the changes of the sixteenth century—the vast expansion of Jewish life in Poland-Lithuania and in the Ottoman lands and the compulsory subjection to the ghetto system in Italy—combined to propagate a much more developed and intricate pattern of Jewish self-government than had existed previously.[1] And in the political as in the cultural sphere, perhaps the most striking feature of the general transformation was the large measure of conformity and cohesion applying across the continent. This is not to say that there were no significant divergences as between diverse parts of Europe, but by and large the essential similarities in the institutions of Jewish organized life held true everywhere. And there was a particularly notable uniformity regarding the chronology of the evolution of Jewish self-rule: practically everywhere the system reached its fullest development after 1650 and then gradually waned as from the early years of the eighteenth century. Possession of a viable and generalized system of interlocking and autonomous judicial, fiscal, and welfare institutions thus clearly distinguishes European Jewry of the baroque era from the dissolving political and cultural framework of the (later) eighteenth century as well as from the scattered, less structured pattern of the sixteenth.

In Poland-Lithuania, the typical elements of Jewish autonomy took shape between 1550 and the 1580s.[2] Under an edict of August 1551, King Sigismund II (1548–72) abandoned previous attempts to foist a royally-appointed chief rabbi on the Jews of his kingdom, conceding control over the administration of justice within the ghettos to the Jews themselves. This started a process which rapidly

---

[1] Bałaban, *Historja*, i. 326–7; Simonsohn, 'The Italian Ghetto', pp. 240–1.

[2] Schorr, *Rechtstellung*, p. 24; Bałaban, *Judenstadt von Lublin*, pp. 20, 36–7; Bencionas Teimanas, *L'Autonomie*, pp. 45–6.

gathered momentum along with the steady proliferation of Jewish communities throughout the Polish lands. In 1569, the king dropped his attempts to intervene in the selection of Jewish community leaders at Lvov, granting its Jews full control over the elections and procedures of its governing body as well as over its archives, communal property, and welfare provision. This much esteemed privilege was then acquired by a string of other major Polish Jewish communities. In the 1570s, additional edicts forbade Polish town governors and city councils to interfere in the passing of judgement and the imposing of punishments and fines within the Jewish communities. Finally, in 1581, the growing trend towards Jewish self-rule culminated in the establishment of a general Polish Jewish diet, or parliament, which to begin with convened annually, at Lublin. This assembly, known as the *Va'ad Arba Arzot*, or Council of the Four Lands, quickly succeeded in asserting itself in a supervisory capacity over the entire network of Jewish regional and communal organizations in Poland. From around 1590, it began to meet twice yearly, usually once at Lublin and once at Jarosław, at the times of the trade fairs held in those cities. Down to the early eighteenth century, the Council of the Four Lands remained a largely effective central agency for Polish Jewish life, after which the Council began to lose influence and to meet less frequently.

In Poland there was a crucial intermediate layer of institutions mediating between the *kehillot*, or communities, on the one hand, and the central diet, in Lublin and Jarosław, on the other. These were the regional assemblies of the 'Lands', provincial gatherings of delegates from the *kehillot* which as a rule were heavily dominated by the representatives of the largest and most powerful communities, whose overall ascendancy was reflected, in turn, in the workings of the Council of the Four Lands.[3] This lent a tightly oligarchic character to the system of Jewish self-rule in Poland which was probably unavoidable if the system was to work. The provincial assemblies of the four lands from which the central council of Polish Jewry took its name had likewise evolved during the course of the sixteenth century and were 'Great Poland' based on Poznán, 'Little Poland' headed by Cracow, 'Red Russia' which centred on Lvov and which included Podolia, and finally Volhynia. As the Lubin area, and later several other districts, had a separate status outside the 'four lands', the central council's designation was always something of a misnomer. There had also evolved during the sixteenth century a provincial

[3] Lewin, *Landessynode*, pp. 19, 31–2, 46.

assembly for Lithuania, headed by the community of Brest-Litovsk, which initially participated in the meetings of the Council of the Four Lands at Lublin. But then, in 1623, Lithuania separated from the Polish 'Lands' and began to function as a distinct judicial and fiscal entity though it did still occasionally convene in joint session with the diet in Lublin.[4] In all, the assembly of Lithuanian Jewry met forty-two times between 1623 and 1764, on nineteen occasions in Brest-Litovsk, eight times in Grodno, five in Pinsk, and the rest in Lublin, Slutsk, or Vilna. Although it met less frequently than the assemblies of the Polish 'Lands', or than the diet in Lublin, the Council of Lithuania nevertheless exerted a very tight control over Jewish life in the Grand Duchy, reflecting the again intensely oligarchic structure of Lithuanian Jewry.

In the Habsburg lands in central Europe, in contrast to Poland, no central agency with overall control ever emerged. But there was a closely related parallel trend towards autonomous institutions both at regional and local level. The two principal regional Jewries, or *Landjudenschaften* as they were called, were those of Bohemia and Moravia.[5] The jurisdiction of the Council of Moravia was subdivided into three areas each centring on a principal community, and whilst the *kehillot* of Nikolsburg and Prossnitz carried the most weight among the Moravian communities, there was a much wider distribution of influence and power in Moravia than in Bohemia or the Polish 'Lands'. Most frequently the council met at Nikolsburg, near the Austrian border, this ghetto also being the seat of the chief rabbinate of the Moravian *Landjudenschaft*. The Council of Bohemia was an altogether less cohesive force, chiefly owing to the absence of any possible counterweight to the overwhelming preponderance of Prague. Outside Prague, Bohemian Jewry was mostly scattered in tiny village communities which were generally much smaller than the typical Moravian community. From 1659, the Jews of Bohemia outside Prague took to meeting separately in order to achieve a measure of independence from the capital. From that point on there were in practice three administrative bodies supervising Jewish affairs in the Czech lands—the *Landjudenschaften* of Bohemia and Moravia and then Prague.

Meanwhile in Germany (as in medieval France), general synods of lay and rabbinic leaders had been characteristic of Jewish life since at

---

[4] Dubnow, *Weltgeschichte*, vi. 353–5; Tänzer, *Juden in Brest-Litowsk*, p. 38.
[5] Kestenberg-Gladstein, *Neuere Geschichte*, pp. 24–5.

least as far back as the eleventh century. Yet these medieval synods had tended to meet only occasionally, separated by long intervals, and are not really comparable with the regular assemblies of Jewish delegates meeting twice yearly in central and eastern Europe during the seventeenth century. During the sixteenth century, following the Reformation and the renewed drive towards expulsion which attended it, there arose a temporary trend towards more frequent meetings of the supra-regional type.[6] But then, as German Jewish life began to expand once more, after 1570, and with the growing political weakness of Charles V's successors, the convening of all-German synods came to make less and less sense. The last such general assembly convened at Frankfurt in 1603. By all accounts, it was a chaotic affair which abundantly demonstrated the unsuitability of such gatherings to the changed situation. From this point on, the emphasis switched to regional organization, the *Landjudenschaft*, the earliest instances of which, such as those of Cologne, Hesse, and Paderborn, reach back to the late sixteenth century.[7] Predictably, such a shift brought about a swift decentralization in the framework of German Jewish life and some reduction in the jurisdiction and influence of the chief rabbinical courts of Frankfurt, Worms, Friedberg, Fulda, Schnaittach, Günzburg, and Wallerstein. But the new pattern resulted in a more viable as well as more intricate edifice of institutions than had existed previously.

Thus there was nothing else comparable in scope in Jewish Europe to the Polish Council of the Lands. Its meetings were usually attended by some thirty lay representatives selected by election from the provincial assemblies and known as the *rashei ha-medinot*. The presiding figure was an elected president styled '*Parnas* of the House of Israel of the Four Lands' who was *ex officio* Polish Jewry's *shtadlan*, or lay representative entrusted to deal both with the king and the Polish national diet dominated by the nobility. At no stage was there a chief rabbi responsible for the whole of Poland but the Council of the Lands did comprise, in addition to the assembly of lay delegates, a bench of provincial chief rabbis, from Poznań, Cracow, Lvov, Lublin, and Ostrog, and this august body constituted the highest Jewish court in the Polish Monarchy. One of the principal tasks of the Council of the Lands was the appointment of annual tax-quotas among the 'Lands'

[6] Zimmer, *Jewish Synods*, pp. 102–6.
[7] Rixen, 'Geschichte und Organisation', p. 32; Baer, *Protokollbuch*, pp. 79–81; Cohen, 'The "Small Council" ', pp. 351–3.

and *kehillot*, a process which invariably generated much wrangling. Before the early eighteenth century, no royal officials attended these deliberations and the entire supervision of Jewish tax-collection was left to the Council. Besides its fiscal preoccupations, the diet regularly addressed itself to more general social issues especially questions of poor relief, relations with Polish town councils, and relations with the Catholic Church.[8] The Council also took responsibility for fixing guidelines on such problems as begging, vagabondage, gambling, settling disputes over jurisdiction between communities, and coping with disasters national and local. Yet, at times of major catastrophe, such as the Chmielnicki massacres, the Council of the Lands tended to be virtually paralysed by the extent of the disruption. In practice, at such times the task of administering relief and appealing for aid from abroad devolved largely on the main regional centres.[9]

In addition to an unquestioned ascendancy over Polish Jewry and the Silesian communities, as well as a certain influence in Lithuania, the Council of the Four Lands enjoyed a wider, if undefined, primacy within Ashkenazi Jewry generally. During the prolonged and bitter controversy at Frankfurt in the years 1615–28 over that community's procedures and methods of self-government, the Council of the Four Lands repeatedly intervened on the side of those who opposed the excessively oligarchic stance of the existing leadership, insisting on annual elections and short terms of office as was the practice among the principal Polish communities and Prague Jewry.[10] The Council at Lublin eventually placed the Frankfurt *parnasim* under a temporary ban until they submitted, acquiescing in the introduction of new constitutional procedures on the required lines. The unique standing of the Lublin diet was also on occasion reflected in the spiritual sphere. Although the Council of the Lands only belatedly condemned Shabbetai Zevi and his mystical following, in 1670, its ban was regarded as authoritative far beyond the confines of Poland.[11] Indeed, even in Amsterdam the voice of the Council of the Lands had a certain weight. In the years 1660–73, for example, whilst a separate 'Polish' congregation fought to maintain itself in Amsterdam, the Lublin diet was appealed to and sought to mediate between the 'Polish' and 'German' communities, though this failed to prevent the latter

---

[8] Bałaban, *Judenstadt von Lublin*, pp. 38–9.
[9] Halpern, 'Aid and Relief', pp. 338–40.
[10] Halpern, 'A Dispute', pp. 86–90.
[11] Bałaban, *Judenstadt von Lublin*, p. 41.

eventually absorbing the former.[12] The Council of the Lands again intervened in Amsterdam during an acrimonious quarrel in 1680–4 between rival 'German' and 'Polish' factions of the newly merged Ashkenazi community over its young and controversial Polish rabbi, David Lida. Not only the Ashkenazi but also the Sephardi *parnasim* of Amsterdam corresponded with Lublin over this prolongation of the 'Polish'–'German' split in Holland, though neither the one nor the other leadership was much impressed by Lublin's proffered solution—the imposing of draconian penalties on Lida's opponents. By 1684, it would seem, the prestige of the Council of the Lands among Dutch Jewry was decidedly on the wane.

The assemblies of the 'Lands' in Poland and Lithuania were prone to perpetual wrangling over allocation of representations and influence among the individual *kehillot*. As Polish Jewry proliferated, the initially iron grip of a few pre-eminent communities over the rest was increasingly challenged by newer up-and-coming communities so that a gradual but relentless shift towards further decentralization is constantly evident. The regional assembly of 'Great Poland' normally met once or twice yearly at Gniezno, but in the period down to 1650 was overwhelmingly dominated by Poznań.[13] But later, as the burgeoning overland trade with Germany drew thousands of Jews to settle in Lissa and Kalisz, near the German border, these towns surged to the fore and to some extent eclipsed Poznań. While the provincial chief rabbi continued to reside in Poznań, from the 1670s onwards Lissa and Kalisz each carried more weight than the older community in determining regional Jewish policy in 'Great Poland'. In 'Little Poland', by contrast, Cracow never lost its preponderance, but the number of recognized major communities in the region increased during the seventeenth century and the Cracow *parnasim* and rabbinate were forced to make concessions to communities such as Opatow and Pinczów, Opatów for two short periods being the seat of the provincial chief rabbinate.[14]

In the large region of Lvov-Podolia, or 'Red Russia', the community of Lvov virtually monopolized the formulation of provincial policy (and representation at Lublin) over many decades. It was only after a protracted struggle that Brody, Zholkva, and Buczacz eventually succeeded in securing permanent seating on the provincial

[12] Sluys, 'Bijdrage', pp. 140–5; Fuks, 'Amsterdamse Opperrabbijn', pp. 169–73.
[13] Lewin, *Landessynode*, pp. 51–2; Lewin, *Juden in Lissa*, pp. 37, 46.
[14] Horowitz, 'Jüdische Gemeinde Opatow', pp. 11, 15.

council and altering procedures for choosing the region's delegates to the Council of the Lands.[15] Later, there was renewed friction as Brody increasingly pulled ahead of the others in numbers and importance and by the early eighteenth century rivalled Lvov itself. Brody by this time was one of the pre-eminent Jewish centres of Europe. Volhynia meanwhile was no less prone to power struggles than Red Russia. Originally, control over the region's affairs had rested firmly with the community of Ostrog, the seat of the chief rabbinate of the 'Land'. After 1650, though, Ostrog gradually lost its former standing as 'first and leading' community of the region, yielding ground to its principal rivals Dubno and Lutsk. Like Brody, the largely Jewish town of Dubno had by the early eighteenth century emerged as one of the most prestigious Ashkenazi communities in Europe. Flourishing under the rule of the Princes Lubomirski, 'Dubno the Great' became renowned far and wide as a centre of Jewish life unobstructed by Christian guilds or municipality.

Like the assemblies of the Polish 'Lands', the Council of Lithuania divided its territory into zones subordinated in matters of rabbinical authority, jurisdiction, and tax-collection to its chief communities. Originally these were only three—Brest-Litovsk, which had much the largest jurisdiction, extending eastwards as far as Mogilev and the Muscovite frontier, and then Grodno and Pinsk.[16] Eventually, after much wrangling, Vilna and Slutsk, also acquired the status of 'chief communities' and were allocated zones of jurisdiction. Even so, Vilna never seems to have obtained a jurisdictional role commensurate with its position as the most flourishing of the Lithuanian communities in the late seventeenth century. At any rate only one meeting of the Council of Lithuania was ever held in Vilna.

The individual *kehillot* of Poland-Lithuania were headed by elected executive committees, or boards, which exhibited many of the characteristics of early modern city councils which, in many ways, they were. They took care of the poor, supervised trade and markets, regulated begging and vagrancy, enforced the authority of the Jewish clergy and paved and cleaned the Jewish quarters.[17] They appointed the heads of the educational and charitable fraternities of the community and upheld the regulations of the Jewish guilds. Each major community also had an elected *shtadlan* whose job it was to represent

[15] Bencionas Teimanas, *L'Autonomie*, pp. 80–9.
[16] Dubnow, *Weltgeschichte*, vi. 354–5; Tänzer, *Juden in Brest-Litowsk*, pp. 39–41.
[17] Perles, *Ges. d. Juden in Posen*, pp. 68–71.

the community in negotiations with burgomasters, bishops, and other Christian authorities. It is true that in great cities such as Lvov, Poznań, Cracow, or Lublin, the role of the community leadership did not compare with that of the Christian city councils in the overall shaping of social and economic life. But in some respects the power of the Jewish councils was greater. For the burgomasters of the Christians were obliged to defer in matters touching faith and education, and in much that concerned poor relief and charity, to the dictates of the Church, whilst they were obliged to share the administration of justice with the crown and the national Diet. The *parnasim*, by contrast, appointed and paid the Jewish clergy, enjoyed full autonomy in matters of taxation and justice, and exercised sole control over Jewish schools, hospitals, and charities. Furthermore, the frequent need to co-ordinate responses to emergencies gave rise to a far-flung correspondence between the *kehillot* which ranged not only right across Poland-Lithuania but Germany, Holland, Italy, and the Holy Land as well.

By and large, the communities of Poland-Lithuania, like those of western Europe and the Near East, were dominated by tight cliques of affluent patricians, together with a sprinkling of university-trained physicians.[18] Status within the *kehillot* was the exclusive preserve of the rich and the highly educated. Yet, narrowly oligarchic though these communal structures were, ordinary folk played a prescribed part in the processes of community politics and all the communities evolved highly complex consultative and electoral procedures, though none of the Polish community constitutions quite rivalled the astounding intricacy of those of the Prague *Judenstadt*.[19] In Poland, Germany, Bohemia, and Moravia, the usual pattern of *kehilla* government among the large communities was for annual election by the tax-payers of a community council of elders which might consist of thirty, forty, or a hundred members.[20] From this council were elected each year an executive board or college of seven to twelve elders consisting usually of four full *parnasim* and three to five lesser *parnasim* or *tovim*. Chairmanship of the executive alternated month by month among the full *parnasim*, the presiding *parnas* being known as *Parnas ha-hodesh* or '*parnas* of the month'. The exact balance of power between

[18] Bałaban, *Historja*, pp. 299–308.

[19] Spiegel, 'Prager Juden', pp. 147–50; Kestenberg-Gladstein, *Neuere Geschichte*, pp. 23–4.

[20] Bencionas Teimanas, *L'Autonomie*, p. 57; Kaufmann, 'Extraits', pp. 116–17.

the councils, executive boards, and tax-payers varied somewhat from place to place. Prague, for instance, was considered more democratic than Frankfurt. It was not uncommon for the appointment of rabbis and cantors to be decided by mixed committees chosen from among the *parnasim*, the elders, and non-council members according to the most elaborate procedures.

In Germany, Jewish self-government was essentially a mix of autonomous main communities, such as Frankfurt, Hamburg-Altona-Wandsbek, Fürth and so forth, and territorial entities, the *Landjudenschaften*, which organized the affairs of the many small rural congregations. The territorial jurisdiction of the German *Landjudenschaften* was much less extensive than those of Bohemia or Moravia, or of the Polish 'Lands', as they corresponded to the political boundaries of the principalities where Jews were permitted to live. For not only was each principality a self-regulating fiscal unit which meant that Jewish tax-collecting had necessarily to conform to such boundaries,[21] but there was also a growing tendency in the second half of the seventeenth century, on the part of absolutist princes, to forbid Jewish litigants to appeal to rabbinic courts outside their principalities. The Elector of Mainz came to insist on this even in the case of his Jewish community at Aschaffenburg which was situated on the other side of Frankfurt from the rest of his territory.[22] Since the number of Jews living in any one state was usually quite small, the assemblies of the German *Landjudenschaften* did not consist of elected delegates, like those of Bohemia, Moravia, and the Polish 'Lands', but were eventually open to all the householders living in that principality. In the margravate of Ansbach, an evolution can be traced reaching back to 1603 when the few families then living there (having previously dealt individually with the treasury) obtained recognition as a self-administering fiscal corporation under a council of six representatives. In the 1620s, the system was broadened into assemblies of the 'most eminent' Jewish residents of the principality. Regular assemblies of all the Jewish house-holders of the principality of Ansbach began in 1677.

Among the *Landjudenschaften* which drew up statutes and commenced regular assemblies around the middle of the seventeenth century were those of Paderborn (1649), Cleves (1650), Münster (1650s), Mainz (1661), Trier, Bamberg, Hesse-Darmstadt, and

---

[21] Baer, *Protokollbuch*, pp. 80–1; Cohen, 'The "Small Council" ', pp. 350–6.
[22] Schaab, *Diplomatische Geschichte*, pp. 223–4.

Jülich-Berg. As the evidence from Mainz, Ansbach, and Münster clearly shows, the princes played a key role in the evolution of the *Landjudenschaften*. In the bishopric of Münster, it was Prince-Bishop Christoph-Bernard, through his court Jew, Nini Levi, who gave the decisive impetus to the emergence of a Jewish territorial organization in his principality with its centre in the village of Warendorf. In some cases, as with the cluster of Jewish communities to the south of Würzburg, in and around Mergentheim and Weikersheim, no *Landjudenschaft* developed owing to this group's cutting across political borders.[23] Yet it would be wrong to see the *Landjudenschaft* as primarily a product and instrument of German princely policy. For princely influence was more or less limited to determining the territorial make-up of the organization; it scarcely touched the *Landjudenschaft*'s inner processes. Thus Jewish self-government was inherent in the circumstances of the time and would have developed within one territorial framework or another irrespective of princely intervention. In the case of Cleves, it would seem that the *Landjudenschaft* was in fact organized by the communities who merely sought permission from the Elector in Berlin.[24]

The *Landjudenschaften* were headed by elected executive committees which met several times yearly to regulate the affairs of the 'Land'.[25] In the electorate of Trier—where there were some 170 Jewish families by 1700, the largest *kehilla* at Koblenz—the governing board consisted of twelve *parnasim*, seven representing Koblenz and five the western part of the territory, around the town of Trier. The boards kept the records of the *Landjudenschaft*, collected its taxes, and supervised its court in conjunction with the *Landesrabbiner*, the rabbi for the principality. Leading families, such as the Wallich family of Koblenz, perennially strove to increase their influence over the workings of the boards. Indeed, in some *Landjudenschaften*, a single family did manage to secure an unbreakable grip on Jewish life in the territory over several generations. In Cleves, the Gomperz dynasty wielded hegemony for over a century. In this situation, the offices of *shtadlan*, *Landesrabbiner*, chief *parnas*, and treasurer tended to converge within one family or even a single individual. In 1653, the Court Jew Mordechai Gomperz, already chief *parnas*, also became *Landesrabbiner*

[23] Sauer, *Jüdischen Gemeinden*, pp. 40, 70, 188–9.
[24] Baer, *Protokollbuch*, pp. 81, 85.
[25] Ibid., p. 93; Kober, 'Kurtrierer "Jüdisch Ceremonial Verordnung" ', pp. 103, 106–8

and treasurer of the *Landjudenschaft*. In Hanover, Leffmann Behrends, who was an accomplished Talmudist as well as a financier, presided over the religious, political, and financial life of the community, the main synagogue being in his home. Though he lacked the title, he was in effect *Landesrabbiner* for the duchy until he gained the right to appoint one with this title in 1687.

The group of seven communities headed by Eisenstadt and Mattersdorf in the Burgenland represent something of a variant of the central European *Landjudenschaft*. All seven *kehillot* came under the same set of privileges and all were located on the territory of the princes Esterhazy. The Eisenstadt *parnasim* and rabbinic court were always dominant within the group and this *kehilla* regularly paid nearly three-fifths of the contributions levied on the seven.[26] At the beginning of the eighteenth century, Samson Wertheimer, one of whose homes was in Eisenstadt and who built a synagogue there, exercised both rabbinic and lay dominance over the community and the group as a whole. Under the patronage of the Esterhazy, the Burgenland *kehillot* achieved something near to complete autonomy.

However, the large communities of central Europe, including Vienna, Berlin, and, after 1659, Prague, stood outside the *Landjudenschaft* system. These, like the Polish *kehillot*, were governed by elaborate electoral procedures which balanced factions one against another, generally preventing excessive accumulation of power within any one individual or family. Their intricate constitutions provided an elaborate forum for the pent-up tensions and rivalries of ghetto life but they also excessively nourished internal frictions and strife.[27] At Prague, the system of dividing tax-payers into three classes—rich, middling, and poor—each voting for a fixed proportion (weighted in favour of the rich) of an electoral college of 200 which in turn elected a small college of thirty-five which, finally, proceeded to select the executive council, proved an infallible recipe for almost perpetual turmoil. In 1635, the Emperor had been obliged to intervene and insist on constitutional reforms but, despite some changes, the system remained highly complex and prone to disputes.

At Hamburg, the situation was uniquely intricate owing to the division of the Jewish population into Ashkenazi and Sephardi groupings, and its further division between Hamburg proper and the suburbs of Altona and Wandsbek under Danish rule. The Altona

---

[26] Markbreiter, *Beiträge*, pp. 36–7, 47; Wachstein, *Urkunden*, pp. 557–9, 568.
[27] Spiegel, 'Prager Juden', pp. 149–54, Kracauer, *Juden in Frankfurt*, ii. 47–9.

community retained its original primacy over all the Ashkenazi Jews in and around Hamburg but was prone to fierce internal squabbles which more than once led to the intervention of the Danish king.[28] By and large, the Portuguese community conducted its affairs in a more dignified manner, but here too there were strong undercurrents of rivalry between various patrician clans, notably between the de Lima with their connections with the Danish court and the Nunes da Costa with their links with the Portuguese crown. Traditionally, ever since their rise in the years around 1600, the western Sephardi communities were even more rigidly exclusive than their Ashkenazi counterparts. At both Amsterdam and Hamburg, the governing boards consisted of 'colleges' of seven *parnasim* nominated annually by their outgoing predecessors, no one else having a say in the matter. To resolve a major dispute in 1662, the Hamburg *Mahamad*, in conjunction with a consultative assembly of former *parnasim*, did agree to broaden the procedure somewhat, switching to a system whereby householders voted for a short list of candidates from which each outgoing executive selected the members of its successor.[29] This more democratic method of choosing the community leadership persisted until 1678 but then lapsed when the householders themselves voted to revert to the original closed system. Meanwhile, in 1669–70, negotiations between the Hamburg Portuguese and Altona 'High German' *parnasim* produced an agreement which henceforward governed the entire structure of Jewish life on the Lower Elbe. Provision was made for various forms of collaboration including a joint supply of kosher meat.[30] The Portuguese now recognized the authority of the Altona *parnasim* over the German Jews in Hamburg proper—these having previously come under the protection of the Portuguese—as well as over the community as Wandsbek. The Hamburg *Mahamad*, it was agreed, should be responsible for the group of Portuguese living in Altona as well as for the larger Sephardi congregation at Glückstadt.

In Italy, the institutions of Jewish self-government before 1500 had been mostly rudimentary and undefined, even 'primitive'.[31] This was true even in the case of the largest community, Rome. The trend which developed in the fifteenth and sixteenth centuries toward occasional synods of delegates from all over Italy proved temporary,

---

[28] *The Life of Glückel*, pp. 18–19.
[29] SAH JG 993/i. 233–4 and SAH JG 993/ii. 151–3.
[30] Feilchenfeld, 'Älteste Geschichte', pp. 281–2, 322–3.
[31] Simonsohn, *History*, p. 319.

the last such general congress being, apparently, that of 1586.[32] By the second half of the sixteenth century, the emphasis lay increasingly on elaboration of community institutions at local rather than regional or supra-regional level, though communities such as Padua and Mantua did also govern the small outlying congregations of the Padovano, Mantovano, and other such limited districts.[33] The only real parallel to the *Landjudenschaft* pattern of central Europe was the regional organization of the duchy of Savoy where there were many communities within one state. Although the evolution of new and more elaborate local institutions began before ghettoization, as we see in the cases of Rome, Mantua, Padua, and other centres, there is little doubt that the ghetto greatly stimulated the process by forcing Jewish social life to turn inwards and by pressing the Jews entirely in on one another. How far this process may also have been influenced by 'Spanish', 'Sicilian', and 'German' immigrants remains unclear.

At Rome, the constitutions which shaped Jewish self-rule throughout the early modern era were drawn up in 1524 amid arguments between the 'Italian', 'Spanish', 'Sicilian', and 'German' elements as to how to achieve greater co-ordination in communal life.[34] Henceforward, the community was ruled by a general council of sixty which in turn elected each year a small executive consisting of three *parnasim* and several treasurers and other officials. Essentially, the system adopted at Rome was similar to that evolving among the *kehillot* in Poland, except for the intricate rules at Rome for balancing power between the groupings, basically in the proportion of two to one, in favour of the 'Italians' and 'Sicilians' as against the 'Spaniards' and 'Portuguese', with the 'Germans' playing a much inferior role. At Mantua, where the Jewish institutions, apart from the synagogues, hardly existed before 1500, the intricate structure characteristic of the early modern period came into existence during the middle decades of the sixteenth century.[35] Again, there was a general council which varied in size between fifty and one hundred members which, in turn, annually elected an executive, headed by three *parnasim*, and a number of intermediate councils and committees. At Padua, where the constitutions were drawn up in 1577, a

[32] Shulvass, *Jews in the World of the Renaissance*, p. 90.
[33] Ibid., p. 110; Carpi, *Pinkas*, pp. 470, 480.
[34] Blustein, *Storia*, pp. 118–20, 122, 178.
[35] Simonsohn, *History*, pp. 322, 325–6, 340–2.

community council of twenty-three, elected by the higher tax-payers, in turn annually elected the *parnasim* and governing board.[36]

In Venice, the division of the Jewish population into three 'nations' arising from the special circumstances of the 1580s persisted from then on throughout the early modern era.[37] This unique triangle of 'Ponentine', 'Levantine', and 'German' communities dwelt together, as in so many other places, in severely overcrowded conditions but with a rough segregation of the 'Germans' into the so-called New Ghetto and the rest in the adjoining Old Ghetto. In fact, there were four principal synagogues and community boards—the Ponentine, Levantine, German, and 'Italian'—the last being mainly a grouping of less recently arrived 'Germans' who continued to be grouped officially with the latter although they prayed separately. Of the three nations, the Ponentines were the wealthiest, comprising some 60 per cent of the ghetto's higher tax-payers in the early seventeenth century, but the Germans the most numerous. As at Rome, there was a fixed balance between the 'nations' in the co-ordination of policy for the ghetto as a whole. The ghetto was ruled by the so-called *Va'ad katan*, or small council, which, as from 1645, consisted of ten *parnasim*, or *capi* as they were known in Italian. Of the ten, the Ponentines and Germans each had four representatives, the Levantines the remaining two.

In contrast to Rome and Venice, the Jewish community of Livorno was overwhelmingly Portuguese in character and its institutions were modelled on those of the Ponentine community at Venice. Although Livorno Jewry was different from that of the other large Italian communities in that it was not confined to a closed ghetto, in practice the Jews were concentrated in their own sections of the town and for most purposes were segregated from the Christian population. Despite the lack of ghetto regulations, the *parnasim*, or *Massari*, ruled Jewish life in Livorno with just as stringent a hand as they did elsewhere. In contrast to the Livorno community, which kept its records in Portuguese, the Levantine community at Pisa kept its records in Spanish and modelled its institutions on those of Balkan Jewry.[38]

At Amsterdam, unlike Venice and Rome, there was never any form of joint executive. From 1639 onwards, there were just two community governing boards—the Portuguese and the 'High German'—except during the years 1660–73 when there was also a separate 'Polish' community. The constitutions of the Portuguese community,

[36] Carpi, *Pinkas*, p. v.   [37] Roth, *History*, pp. 127–9.
[38] Toaff, 'Il "Libro Nuovo" ', pp. 232–43.

like those of Livorno, and indeed of Hamburg and London, were expressly modelled on those of the Ponentine community of Venice.[39] The Amsterdam Portuguese *Mahamad*, nominated each year from among the 20 per cent or so wealthiest members of the community by their seven predecessors, was probably the most powerful, as well as exclusive, Jewish executive of early modern times, carrying real influence with the city burgomasters and the States of Holland of a sort which was often remarked on by foreign diplomats,[40] and exercising a general hegemony over the other Portuguese Jewish communities in the Dutch Republic—Rotterdam, The Hague, Middelburg, Maarssen, Amersfoort, and Naarden. The Amsterdam *Mahamad* also exerted a strong influence over the actions of the two large Dutch Sephardi colonies in the Caribbean—Curaçao and Surinam—and to some extent over the *Mahamad* at Hamburg. Unlike the Jewish leadership in Poland and Germany, the community councils of Dutch Jewry were not required to collect taxes for the state, but in other respects their role was identical to that of Jewish governing boards elsewhere. They controlled charity, sick-care, and education, exercised moral and intellectual censorship, and maintained a generally formidable grip over Jewish life-style.

That Jewish self-rule in the seventeenth and early eighteenth centuries was oligarchic, authoritarian, and not infrequently despotic is undeniable. In the constitutions of the Amsterdam, London, and other Sephardi communities it was laid down that the gentlemen of the governing board 'shall have authority and supremacy over everything', and this was no idle boast.[41] The universal precariousness of Jewish life militated strongly in favour of subjection to discipline and authority. It was not simply a question of upholding the Torah and pursuing the moral ideals of Judaism. Anything likely to exacerbate the ever-present reality of popular hatred was deemed a threat to the community. Unseemly conduct, licentiousness, extravagance, the presence of too many beggars, any sort of provocative behaviour was liable to be promptly suppressed. The boards of elders kept a vigilant eye on costume, morals, and every aspect of life-style and this congregants had no choice but to accept. In December 1663, the Hamburg *Mahamad* actually forbade the use of sleighs and sledges

---

[39] *Libro de los Acuerdos*, p. 3; Swetschinski, 'Portuguese Jewish Merchants', i. 368.

[40] See, for instance, AGS Estado 2091, Vincent Richard to Philip IV, The Hague, 3 Sept. 1658.

[41] GAA PJG xix. 106–11; SAH JG 993/i. 1–10; *Libro de los Acuerdos*, p. 4.

during the winter snows by any member of the community lest they 'provoke Christian neighbours' or cause injury to themselves: in cases of emergency, permission to ride a sleigh had to be sought from the chief *parnas*.[42] The right to admit or refuse admittance to newcomers to the community was exercised everywhere. In 1673, the gentlemen of the London *Mahamad* decreed that they would admit no one who could not satisfy them as to his or her financial circumstances.

The intellectual censorship exercised by the governing boards was, of course, much tighter in Poland and the Balkans than in the west. In countries such as Germany, Holland, and England, the *parnasim* could not stop their congregants reading books which were freely available in vernacular languages, and in Holland and (after 1695) in England there was considerable freedom of the press. This meant that in western countries Jews were potentially subjected to precisely the same heterodox, freethinking, and philosophical ideas as anyone else. Even so, a vigilant censorship was exercised on everything published, or distributed, in Hebrew, Yiddish, Spanish, and Portuguese and these were the languages that western, as well as east European Jewry, normally used. It was not until the early eighteenth century that the Sephardi population in Holland can be said to have been more familiar with Dutch than with Spanish or Portuguese.[43] The medieval compilation of erotic Hebrew poetry by Immanuel of Rome was universally prohibited. Yoseph Delmedigo encountered several censorship problems, especially in Amsterdam, in 1629.[44] Quite a number of Spanish and Portuguese works were wholly or partially censored, ranging from Uriel da Costa's 1624 tract assailing rabbinic authority, which was prohibited *in toto*, to the works of the historian and poet Daniel Levi de Barrios, whose various writings were subjected to repeated expurgation.[45] In 1656, the year of Spinoza's expulsion from the Amsterdam Sephardi community, a book of poems in Spanish by Jacob de Pina , a Marrano who had reverted to Judaism in Amsterdam, was condemned as 'lascivious' by the *Mahamad*, the stock of copies being seized and publicly burned. Moreover, the action was promptly repeated by the gentlemen of the Hamburg *Mahamad*.[46] When an influential cousin of the author happened to come on to the Amsterdam *Mahamad* some years later,

---

[42] 'Hamburg Protokollbuch' *JJLG* x. 232.
[43] Hirschel, 'Cultuur en volksleven', pp. 59–60.
[44] Swetschinski, 'Portuguese Jewish Merchants', i. 414–20.
[45] Revah, 'Les écrivains', pp. lxxv–lxxvii.
[46] Ibid.; 'Hamburg Protokollbuch', *JJLG* vii. 181, 183.

the ban was solemnly revoked only to be reimposed two years later when the patrician in question had come off the governing body. Somewhat perplexed, no doubt, the Hamburg *parnasim* dutifully followed Amsterdam's example on both occasions. Yet, in many respects, the Sephardi boards of elders proved more liberal than their Ashkenazi counterparts, especially as regards frequenting musical recitals, plays, and opera which most German Jewish *kehillot* prohibited at all times except at Purim and one or two other especially joyful festivals. It was not until the early eighteenth century that there was some relaxation in the rules.[47]

The Jewish community boards of elders were likewise perpetually at pains to enforce modesty in dress and public demeanour. There were rules against groups gathering in their sabbath best outside synagogues. The sumptuary laws, or enactments on matters of costume, decreed by the *kehillot* generally entered into a host of restrictive minutiae often seemingly of the most trivial kind. Doubtless these rulings were constantly breached in practice but, in view of the immense zeal which went into enacting them, there is reason to suppose that they had an appreciable impact in imposing outward restraint and modesty at any rate down to the middle of the eighteenth century when a marked relaxation set in. The result was that a certain sumptuousness of dress was displayed by the better-off, in synagogue and in the home, which was largely veiled outside. Thomas Coryat glimpsed something of this veiled splendour when he visited the synagogues of Venice at the beginning of the seventeenth century, noting especially the finery of the women

whereof some were as beautiful as ever I saw, and so gorgeous in their apparel, jewels, chaines of gold, and rings adorned with precious stones, that some of our English countesses do scarce exceede them, having marvailous long traines like princesses that are borne up by waiting women.[48]

Without exception, Jewish women were subjected to a high degree of seclusion. There were strict rules against their walking in the streets, or to and from synagogue, unaccompanied by relatives or other women. We can readily believe the numerous references in the travel literature of early modern Europe to the beauty of Jewish women and their unimpeachable chastity in view of the fact that they were given not the slightest opportunity to mix with Christian men or engage in any unseemly or frivolous activities with their own. The menfolk, inevitably, were less tightly restricted; but they too were forbidden to frequent inns and taverns or attend Christian carnivals or any common festivities where bawdy scenes and lewd behaviour were to be expected.[49] Brothels were generally excluded from the ghettos, though in Italy this was not invariably the case. Jewish prostitutes did exist, but mainly in Italy and the Balkans and then only very sporadically. There is no evidence of Jewish harlots as a regular feature at Venice, which until the rise of Amsterdam was Europe's most noted centre for numbers and variety of prostitutes. While it was universally true, even in Amsterdam, that public and civic law forbade sexual relations between Jews and Christians, there were many places where Jewish men clearly did frequent Christian women of easy virtue. A report on the Jews of Split, of the year 1638, asserts that liaisons between Jews and Christian girls were frequent and that it was not uncommon for Jewish youths to parade publicly through the streets of the town in the company of loose women and girls.

The primary concern of the community boards in the area of sexual conduct was to minimize extra-marital liaisons within the Jewish quarters, such relationships being prevalent both in the overcrowded, cramped conditions of the ghetto and in the more relaxed atmosphere of Amsterdam and Livorno. In particular, the presence of maid-servants in the homes of the wealthy, and the defencelessness of such girls at the hands of the master of the house, or of his sons, gave rise to a constant stream of illegitimate births. In such cases, the community boards needed to know who the father was and, where it proved difficult to discover this, it was not uncommon for committees of enquiry to be set up to investigate.[50] When the culprit's name was known, he would be required to pay towards the cost of the girl's confinement and the subsequent upkeep of the infant. In Holland (though not in Hamburg), and sometimes elsewhere, notably in the Balkan countries, there were often Christian maidservants and wet-nurses in the homes of the Jewish well-to-do and here again seduction, rape, and extra-marital pregnancy were fairly common.[51] It was no

---

[49] Grunwald, 'Luxusverbot der Dreigemeinden', pp. 229–30; though here again, for inns, as for plays and opera, there was a notable relaxation of the rules as applied at Hamburg–Altona–Wandsbek, at least as far as men were concerned, following the revision of the Ashkenazi communal statute-book in 1725; see Graupe, *Statuten der drei Gemeinden*, pp. 86–8; Paci, '*Scala*' *di Spalato*, p. 138.

[50] Simonsohn, *History*, p. 544.

[51] See the many examples in Koen, 'Notarial Records'; Paci, '*Scala*' *di Spalato*, p. 139.

idle flourish which led the eighteenth-century Dutch Jewish *philosophe* Isaac de Pinto to list 'passion des femmes' as one of the chief failings of Dutch Sephardi Jewry.[52] Numerous written agreements were drawn up before Amsterdam notaries whereby Portuguese Jews undertook to pay compensation to Christian mothers (often German or Scandinavian immigrants) of their illegitimate children.

For all its shortcomings, it would be wrong to dismiss Jewish self-rule as just another instrument of social repression, adding unwanted extra burdens to the daily lot of the early modern Jew. Until the eighteenth century, there is no evidence of significant opposition to the rule of the Jewish patricians and, despite the inequalities and wide differences of means in the ghettos, there were rarely, if ever, any true instances of class friction. The former Marrano Isaac Cardoso, who, in later life, dwelt under the vigilant eye of the wardens of Venice and Verona, devotes several passages in his book *Excelencias de los Hebreos* (1679) to what he calls the 'inner beauty' of Jewish life, accounting Jewish political autonomy a universally prize consolation for the humiliations and hardships imposed on Jews by Christians. As he saw it, Jewish self-rule was an integral and essential part of Jewish culture: 'the Jews are not the serfs of the nations', he wrote, 'but a Republic apart which lives and governs itself by its laws and precepts which God gave them at Sinai.'[53]

One of the chief tasks of the community boards, in conjunction with the charitable societies which had begun to flourish since the end of the sixteenth century, was to dispense aid to the Jewish poor. In every European country which tolerated Jews it was expressly understood that responsibility for the Jewish destitute lay with the Jews alone as was also the case with Jewish orphans, unmarried mothers, and the sick. Thus every *kehilla* from London to Mogilev maintained a community poor-chest which consumed a great part of the revenue the community boards levied from their congregations for communal purposes. This Jewish community revenue was raised through a combination of obligatory taxes levied on those able to pay, graded according to means, and voluntary donations given regularly as part of routine piety and as bequests to the 'Jewish poor' which were a common feature of the wills of the wealthy. Inevitably, all the *kehillot* were under constant pressure from their members to limit the number of poor on the books. The lists of eligible needy were constantly

[52] De Pinto, *Lettres de quelques Juifs*, i. 16–17.
[53] Cardoso, *Excelencias*, pp. 374–6; Yerushalmi, *From Spanish Court*, p. 469.

scrutinized by the community treasurers, and impoverished new-comers and vagrants frequently sent packing. Many communities also assisted the passage of widows and able-bodied poor from one region to another, at times even from one end of Europe to the other, where family circumstances or opportunities were judged to be better. In the case of Amsterdam's Portuguese community this amounted to a systematic policy of colonization, whole shiploads of Sephardi poor, sometimes sent on from Livorno or Venice, being sent out, at the expense of the community, to settle in Curaçao or Surinam.[54]

The community chests thus provided basic aid, often including ritual bread and pretzels on the eve of sabbath or festivals, and assisted the passage of the needy. But in the field of poor relief the governing boards worked extensively in conjunction with the burgeoning charitable societies. Of these there were many, especially in the larger communities, and they tended to follow fixed patterns. The most common and oldest were the societies for burial, which helped pay the costs of funerals for the poor. To these were gradually added a variety of other poor-relief fraternities such as those devoted to supplying firewood and fuel to the poor or for providing marriage portions for poor girls. In Mantua, the society *Mazal Bethula* (Maiden's fortune) held a lottery each year on the first day of the Feast of Tabernacles, the winners receiving the collected money. The societies for endowing poor Sephardi girls established at Venice and Amsterdam, in 1613 and 1615 respectively, were remarkable institutions which conducted an extremely wide-ranging correspondence, having associate members not only in Pisa, Livorno, and Hamburg but among the New Christian communities of Antwerp, the French ports, and even Brazil.[55] As regards eligibility for their annual lotteries no distinction was made between Marrano girls living where Judaism was forbidden and Sephardi Jewish girls. Indeed, one of the chief purposes of these fraternities was to proselytize, offering dowries to New Christian girls who came to 'places of Judaism' to contract Jewish marriages. Later, the dowry societies of Curaçao and Surinam were also affiliated to the parent body in Amsterdam.

A universal feature of the system was the provision of professional medical care for the poor. After 1550, it became usual for the larger *kehillot* to employ university-trained physicians to tend impoverished or orphaned sick who were unable to pay. Many of the foremost

[54] Zwarts, 'Joodse gemeenten', p. 390–2; Emmanuel, *History*, i. 47.
[55] Revah, 'Le premier règlement imprimé', pp. 651–2, 659–61.

Jewish intellectuals of the seventeenth century were to be found in the post of community physician, and in this connection it happened frequently that prestigious Sephardi doctors were signed on by the larger Ashkenazi communities. Thus Yoseph Shlomo Delmedigo signed on as community physician at Frankfurt in 1631, and Moseh, son of Eliau Montalto, settled and died at Lublin, in Poland.[56] Isaac Cardoso, invited to come from Venice to fill the post of community physician in Verona, in 1653, was unusual, we learn from the community records, in that he took 'it upon himself to visit the sick among the poor in the ghetto for nothing'.[57] Of course, the usual arrangement was a communal salary. In 1673, the London Sephardi community, 'considering the necessity for a doctor to tend the sick of the poor of the nation', agreed to appoint Dr Abraham Perez Galvão to this position at an annual salary of ten pounds sterling to be paid at fifty shillings per quarter 'for which the said doctor shall be bound to attend and visit at due times as may be needful in service and care for the poor'. The larger *kehillot* generally had reserve doctors or even two full-time physicians in their employ.[58] Thus Isaac Bacharach was community physician for many years at Poznań where he worked together with his Sephardi father-in-law, Dr Judah de Lima (who in 1629 was also a delegate for Poznań to the regional assembly of Great Poland), and later with the latter's son, Moseh de Lima. Typically, these physicians prescribed drugs for destitute patients at the expense of the community—but only after obtaining signed chits for this from the *parnasim*. Nor could a community physician leave town for more than two days without the permission of the chief *parnas*.

To supplement the funds and care provided by the community boards, the societies known as *Bikur Holim* (Visiting the Sick) were a universal feature of Jewish community life throughout Europe. These fraternities were allowed to set up collection boxes in public places in the ghettos and practise various forms of fund-raising on behalf of the sick. As their name implies, members took it upon themselves to visit and comfort the sick and dying as well as assist with money. In what may well be an indication of how all the charitable societies spread across Europe, these *Bikur Holim* confraternities are known to have originated in late medieval Spain and been introduced by Spanish exiles in Italy and the Balkans during the sixteenth century, from where they spread to the rest of Europe.

---

[56] Barzilay, *Yoseph Shlomo Delmedigo*, p. 83; Bałaban, *Judenstadt von Lublin*, pp. 26–7.
[57] Yerushalmi, *From Spanish Court*, p. 214. [58] Lewin, 'Jüdische Ärzte', p. 374.

Education was another constant concern of the Jewish governing boards. In theory, all adult Jewish males were literate and grounded in the rudiments of Jewish law, and so the boys, and some girls below the age of puberty, received their primary education in community schools. In Amsterdam, Sephardi boys began school at the age of four. All the *kehillot* had primary teachers in their employ. The lessons were invariably given in Judeo-German, Spanish, Portuguese, or Italian. The larger communities also maintained religious colleges, or *yeshivot*, where more advanced Talmudic and rabbinic learning was dispensed. Following the setbacks of the fifteenth century, hardly any *yeshivot* survived in central Europe outside Frankfurt and Prague and, in the sixteenth century, it became customary for substantial numbers of German Jewish youth to trek to Poland for their higher studies. After the Thirty Years War, however, with the rapid re-expansion in German Jewish life, *yeshivot* proliferated at Hamburg, Fürth, Halberstadt, where Berend Lehmann founded the community college in 1687, Nikolsburg, where the college was founded by David Oppenheim, Eisenstadt, where Samson Wertheimer founded a college in 1707, and Mannheim, where the college was established by Lemle Moses, again in 1707.[59] The best equipped of the Jewish religious colleges was that of Ets Haim, at Amsterdam, founded in 1639. This renowned institution, administered by an annually elected board of six governors, attracted some sizeable bequests and amassed a highly important library and collection of manuscripts.

Finally, all the European *kehillot* raised regular annual subsidies for the Jews of the Holy Land and for the redemption of Jewish captives taken by Muslims or Christians in the Mediterranean, ransomed through a special fund administered in Venice. There was also wide-ranging collaboration in the raising of special disaster funds at times of emergency in one part of Europe or another. In 1627, for instance, the Sephardim of Holland, alerted from Venice to the disruption of Jewish life in Jerusalem at the hands of the despotic Turkish governor Muhammad ibn Farruk, collected a subsidy to mitigate the 'great calamity and misery in which our breathren dwelling in the holy city of Jerusalem now find themselves.'[60] Both the Sephardi and Ashkenazi communities in the west contributed liberally to the disaster relief programme in Poland-Lithuania following the Chmielnicki massacres. At the time of the terrible epidemic of 1680, which is said

[59] Unna, 'Verordnungen', pp. 133–45.
[60] GAA PJG xiii, fo. 19ᵛ, termo 7 Feb. 1627.

to have killed 3,000 Jews in the *Judenstadt* of Prague, funds were remitted to Bohemia from all over Europe, Ashkenazi community treasurers working hand in hand with their Sephardi counterparts.[61] The same occurred during the emergencies of 1686 and 1688, when first Budapest and then Belgrade were captured and sacked by the armies of Austria. Thousands of Jewish captives were ransomed in Hungary and Moravia, the money being channelled from all sides via Prague, Vienna, Livorno, and Venice.[62]

But the most important remittances were those to the Holy Land. Every year contributions flowed, usually via Venice, Constantinople, and later also Livorno, for the upkeep of the so-called 'four holy communities', namely Jerusalem, Safed, Tiberias, and Hebron. Many of the major communities in the west had annually elected 'treasurers for the Holy Land' who collected the subsidy and arranged for its remittance. As there were Polish, German, Italian, Spanish, and Portuguese colonies in all of the four holy *kehillot*, the provisions governing the distribution of the funds were highly intricate. Various Italian communities experimented with different methods of dividing their contributions between diverse groupings. The Sephardim in the west generally distributed their contributions through the hands of trusted Portuguese representatives. Thus, in 1682, the Sephardi subsidy from Holland was remitted, via Livorno, to Rabbi Simson Gomes Pato and two other Portuguese in Jerusalem, who were probably all of recent western origin, for distribution.[63] The Dutch Sephardi subsidies included the contributions sent by the Portuguese Jewish colonies in the New World; thus, in 1639, the subsidy, sent through the hands of the banker Abraham Aboab in Venice, included the proceeds from a consignment of sugar shipped to Holland on behalf of the poor of Jerusalem by the Dutch Sephardi congregation in Brazil.[64]

---

[61] SAH JG 993/ii. 292–3, 297, 301.

[62] GAA PJG xix. 408 and v. xx 131, 134.

[63] GAA PJG xx. 31, 56, 87.

[64] GAA PJG xix. 98; the Curaçao Jewish community regularly sent its contributions for the Holy Land to Amsterdam each year from at least as early as 1671, if not before: Emmanuel, *History*, i. 154.

IX

High Point (IV): Spiritual Crisis
(1650–1713)

I

DURING the latter half of the seventeenth century, the Jewish world was shaken spiritually more profoundly than at any time since the expulsions of the late fifteenth century. A mounting turmoil of inner pressures erupted in the 1650s and 1660s in a drama which was to convulse world Jewry for decades. Furthermore, although this Jewish upheaval had some separate and independent roots, unconnected with the current intellectual preoccupations of Christian Europe, it took place during, and shared some causes with, the deepening crisis besetting seventeenth-century European culture as a whole. Inevitably, the ferment within the Synagogue interacted on the wider upheaval within European devotion and thought, the one chain of encounters pervading the other in a remarkable process of cultural transformation.

Ultimately, the upheaval is perhaps best understood as a cultural reaction to the immense disruptions and migrations of the previous two centuries and the many unresolved contradictions the vast treks, first to the east and then to the west, had given rise to. The expulsions, and especially the experience of 1492 in Spain, had had an immensely unsettling effect, creating a uniquely mobile, shifting society, despite its cohesion of language and institutions. The question of the meaning of Jewish exile and separateness had now been posed in a new and more urgent form.[1] And yet, paradoxically, whilst the new Jewish culture was an entity cut adrift from its old geographical moorings, detached from rootedness in any specific locality, in some respects Jewry, from the end of the sixteenth century onwards, was being reintegrated into the life and civilization of the west. It may be true that this reintegration was more economic than cultural, yet the rifts and disintegrative tendencies within western Christendom had placed the age-old confrontation of Christianity and Judaism on a

[1] Scholem, *Sabbatai Sevi*, pp. 18–20.

totally new basis. The west was no longer wholly Christian. The west had lost its doctrinal unity and self-assurance and become prey to scepticism and philosophic perplexity. It was precisely this which enabled European Jews to become part of western civilization; but the corrosive forces at work generally now also entered the body politic and spiritual of Jewry.[2]

Foremost among the unsettling pressures which now beset the Jewish world was the sudden vast upsurge of messianic expectations. Of course, yearnings for redemption and the ingathering of the Jewish people from exile, together with the reconstitution of mankind in a new age of peace, had always been basic to Judaism and Jewish tradition. Intermittently, through the Middle Ages, and in the early sixteenth century, there had also been disturbing outbreaks of messianic frenzy centring around one or another popular religious leader. But these had been short-lived and local. The Shabbatean movement which arose in 1665 was much the most enduring and widespread phenomenon of this type within Judaism since the rise of Christianity. From the end of the sixteenth century, Lurianic cabbala, emanating from Galilee, and its idea of imminent redemption which could be hastened by personal acts and piety, spread far and wide, pervading every corner of Jewish life and awareness. It was diffused through preaching, through the *yeshivot*, and through the proliferation of pious societies and fraternities which now spread across Europe. About half a century after Lurianic cabbala had first become an active force in Italy and the Balkans it began to achieve its greatest impact. In 1648, Naphtali ben Jacob Bacharach published his *Emeq ha-Melekh* (Valley of the King), at Frankfurt, a work which popularized Luria's teaching, imparting to it a decisive new impetus in the lands north of the Alps. Bacharach's work was suffused with a mystical exaltation perceiving Luria's system as an instrument of the general uplifting of the Jewish people from the depths and degradation into which it had been pushed by Christendom and Islam.[3] It was a mystical theology, tinged with elation, deriving ultimately, perhaps, from the lessening of Christian pressure since the end of the sixteenth century and the palpable gains which Jewry had made since that time.

The messianic turmoil of the mid-seventeenth century also exuded a strong strain of mystical Zionism. Another of the cabbalistic writers of the time, Nathan Shapira, who published his *Goodness of the Land* at

[2] Kracauer, *Juden in Frankfurt*, ii. 46–9.
[3] Scholem, *Sabbatai Sevi*, pp. 69–71.

Venice in 1655, stressed the pivotal role of the Holy Land in bringing about the redemption of the Jews, and therefore of mankind, insisting that it was in the promised land that the true preparations for redemption were taking place. Nor did such effusions originate from a purely Jewish milieu. Very close in spirit was the book *Du Rappel des Juifs* by the French Calvinist of Marrano extraction, Isaac de la Peyrère, published at an unknown place in 1643. La Peyrère, admittedly, tried to synthesize Christian and Jewish messianism, claiming that the imminent Messiah would be Christ on his second coming and that the Jews would at last acknowledge Christ. But what he chiefly emphasized was that the redemption of the Jews, which he insisted must be physical and political as well as spiritual, their ingathering to Jerusalem and the Holy Land, was the prerequisite and instrument of the salvation of all mankind which, clearly, he did not believe Christ's first appearance had achieved.[4]

Shabbatai Zevi (1626–76) was born into an affluent family at Smyrna, trained as a rabbi, and early on took to withdrawing for long spells into mystical seclusion. He suffered from an acute manic-depressive illness, long bouts of depression alternating with periods of exaltation which increasingly led him to commit extravagant and blasphemous acts. A strikingly handsome man, burdened by some sexual impediment, he contracted two marriages whilst in his twenties, both of which remained unconsummated and were dissolved. Banished from Smyrna for his sporadic outbursts of wild behaviour, he wandered to Salonika, Constantinople, Jerusalem, and Cairo. He eventually married a Podolian Jewess, a refugee from the Chmielnicki massacres, who had lived in Amsterdam and Livorno and is said to have been a prostitute. The crucial point in Shabbatai's life occurred early in 1665 when he travelled to Gaza, to visit Nathan of Gaza (1643–80), a cabbalist locally renowned for his visions, who he hoped would cure him of his mental sickness. It was Nathan, a much more energetic mystic and propagandist than Shabbatai himself, who effectively created the movement by fanning Shabbatai's delusions, finally leading him to proclaim himself the Messiah of the Jews, in May 1665.

Notwithstanding determined opposition from the rabbis of Jerusalem, Nathan soon overawed the communities of Gaza and Hebron, skilfully promoting Shabbatai's 'miracles' and rituals. Nathan of Gaza, at once the John the Baptist and the Paul of the

[4] La Peyrère, *Du Rappel des Juifs*, pp. 11–13, 78–9, 149, 374–5.

Shabbatean movement, showed a rare, uncanny grasp of how to arouse the religious emotions of the common people. He particularly stressed individual repentance and 'inner renewal' as the way to prepare and precipitate mankind's salvation, exploiting for messianic purposes what was a central feature of Luria's method of mystical communication with God. Nathan took to sending letters of joyful tidings to Constantinople and Cairo, rapidly widening the dimensions of the movement. Moving back to Smyrna, soon after the launching of his Messiahship, Shabbatai was able to place himself at the head of that community.

Word of the coming of the Messiah, buoyed by a wave of reports of prophecies, visions, and miracles, swept western Europe in October 1665. Letters from the Near East were read out in the Portuguese synagogues, the fervour being heightened by a spate of Dutch and German news-sheets reporting the agitation and the strange events afoot in the Levant. Though it was the Sephardim who received the missives from the Holy Land and Constantinople, via Venice and Livorno, German Jews in Venice, Hamburg, and Amsterdam flocked to the Portuguese synagogues to hear the word and proved no less susceptible to the general intoxication.[5] From the main centres, and the Balkans, the ferment rapidly spread across Germany, Bohemia-Moravia, and Poland-Lithuania. Not only was there no split in responses along Sephardi–Ashkenazi lines, but neither was there any rift according to wealth or social status. It is true that the writings of Bacharach, Shapira, and other messianic authors of the period were tinged with criticism of the rich and that the legends and penitential fervour of the movement appealed strongly to the poor and downtrodden. But it is no less true that the intoxication gripped many, or most, of the Amsterdam and Hamburg Portuguese and German Jewish patriciate, including the super-wealthy Pereira and Nunes da Costa.[6] Everyone donned their best clothes to which they attached green silk ribbons (green being the colour of Shabbatai Zevi) and vowed repentance and a new striving for moral perfection. Many or most of the leading rabbis joined in. Yair Haim Bacharach (1638–1702), outstanding among late seventeenth-century German rabbis in learning and renown, took to meeting daily with a circle of Shabbatean enthusiasts to help hasten the day of redemption.

No less astonishing, for approximately six to eight months virtually all the governing boards and assemblies were swept up in the

[5] *The Life of Glückel*, pp. 45–6.   [6] Scholem, 'An Italian Note-Book', p. 66.

fervour.[7] At Amsterdam, the *Mahamad* fiercely condemned the perpetrators of a printed tract circulating among the Jews deriding the pretensions of the presumed Messiah, threatening opponents of the movement with excommunication. Everywhere, the *parnasim* sanctioned the penitential upsurge and, in a good many cases, authorized the use of musical instruments in synagogue on *Shabbat* and the major festivals, something forbidden by rabbinic tradition, accompaniment by musical instruments having previously been allowed only in some Sephardi synagogues on *Simchat Torah*, the most joyful festival of the year. To make communal decisions in these exceptional circumstances, the *parnasim* convened large councils of past and present office-holders or mass assemblies of all the householders. Lvov, Livorno, and other communities sent envoys to Smyrna to bow down before 'our king' as he is called in Jewish community records. At Hamburg, the leadership split. First, the council of elders decided that an 'embassy' should be sent out to the Levant on behalf of the community.[8] Then, under pressure from a crowd of non-elders, it was agreed that major decisions should now be made by mass assembly. Later both decisions were suspended.

Christian reactions ranged from initial perplexity and curiosity to widespread popular indignation at the insolence of the Jews in believing that their Messiah had come. No doubt the more hostile manifestations were in some measure provoked by gleeful insinuations on the part of Jews that the boot would soon be on their foot. There were riots in Vilna, Pinsk, and Lublin, and right across southern Germany. The students of Cologne University marched on nearby Deutz and set about sacking the Jewish quarter, though eventually they were driven off, apparently with the aid of the villagers.[9] Inevitably, the Jews' suddenly inflated pretensions were universally derided. In Germany, the blowing of trumpets at night outside Jewish homes became a favourite taunt. The Jewish governing boards became seriously alarmed at the prospect of further violent outbreaks, such anxiety being one reason why the Hamburg *Mahamad* chose to cancel its delegation to the Near East. The same anxiety moved the Hamburg *parnasim* to petition the city senate to stop the printing and distribution of news sheets reporting the Shabbatean upsurge to the German public. They also dispensed large tips to the

---

[7] Kracauer, *Juden in Frankfurt*, ii. 46–7; Kaplan, 'Attitude of the Leadership', p. 202.
[8] 'Hamburg Protokollbuch', *JJLG* x. 292–3, 295 and *JJLG* xi. 5–6.
[9] Brisch, *Gesch. d. Juden in Cöln*, p. 121.

city militia in return for a tightening of the guard on the Jewish quarter. Elsewhere alternative forms of preventive action were taken. In February 1666, the Bamberg *parnasim* obtained from the Prince-Bishop a decree forbidding Christians publicly to mock and throw stones at Jews under pain of a hefty fine.[10] Meanwhile, the feverish state of the Jews everywhere aroused the Christian clergy.[11] The Jesuits, in particular, were much exercised as to how to meet the challenge. But they were by no means alone. At a gathering of the Calvinist church council of Utrecht, in May 1666, it was agreed to mount a 'powerful' effort now that the Jews were in such a frenzy over their supposed Messiah and were 'in the midst of great expectations, to bring them over to Christ'.

But for the moment nothing could damp down the messianic excitement among the Jews. It was a mass movement which gripped rich and poor alike from one end of Europe to the other. At Amsterdam and Hamburg, wealthy Sephardi patricians began selling off their possessions and houses and preparing for the journey to the Holy Land. Among them was the wealthy mystic and benefactor Abraham Pereira who at this time published at Amsterdam a fiercely penitential work, entitled *La Certeza del Camino* and then travelled overland to Venice where he waited months, in vain, for shipping to take him and his family to Palestine. João de Yllan, who formerly had led a Jewish colonizing expedition to Curaçao, now prepared at Amsterdam to ship fifty poor families to the Holy Land since, as he wrote, 'God in his mercy has begun to gather in his scattered people'.[12] It was just the same in southern Europe. Sir John Finch reported to London from Florence, in April 1666, that 'many families of Jewes have come to Livorno from Rome, Verona, and Germany to embarque to find their Messia'.[13] It is evident also that the temporary paralysis of shipping in the Mediterranean, caused by the second Anglo-Dutch War (1665–7), which was then at its height, caused immense frustration and congestion among the Jews at Livorno, Venice, and doubtless elsewhere.

Finally the bubble burst in September 1666 when the Sultan, tiring of the commotion, summoned Shabbatai to Constantinople. Shabbatai was presented with the choice of death or conversion to

[10] Eckstein, *Gesch. d. Juden in Bamberg*, p. 21.

[11] Buchenroeder, *Eilende Messias-Juden-Post*, Biii; Brugmans, 'Houding van staat en kerk', p. 635.

[12] Emmanuel, *History*, i. 42–3.

[13] PRO SP 98/6. Finch to Arlington, Florence, 2/12 Apr. 1666.

Islam. He chose the latter, his apostasy taking place on 15 September 1666. Within weeks the entire Jewish diaspora was reduced to dejection and shock as total as had been the previous euphoria. The governing boards quickly moved to restore everything to the *status quo ante*, but, by this time, no small damage had been done spiritually. The Jews were so blind to truth, thundered Protestant and Catholic clergy alike that they could be led hopelessly astray by a ridiculous impostor while all the while they spurned the true redeemer, Christ, who stood before them. In Holland, there was a flurry of conversionist tracts.[14] The derision and mockery reached a crescendo. There were many hundreds of conversions to Christianity, especially in Italy but also in many other parts.[15]

But if the Shabbatean movement momentarily collapsed and never regained its former supremacy, it remained a potent force within Judaism. The feelings of inner renewal experienced by countless enthusiasts had, in many cases, run so deep that it proved impossible to accept the non-validity of what had transpired. It is this which explains Nathan of Gaza's astonishing success over the next few years in generating a widespread heretical belief in Shabbatai, the 'apostate Messiah'. On hearing of Shabbatai's acceptance into Islam, Nathan had set off with a large entourage and travelled, via Damascus, to see him. On the way, he defended the apostasy as a deep mystery, to be penetrated only by the paths of cabbala. He claimed that the apostasy was a necessary sign of Shabbatai's messianic mission. After meeting the would-be Messiah, in Adrianople, and renewing their collaboration, Nathan started out on a tour through Greece, Corfu, and Italy, preaching a progressively more elaborate heresy, honouring those of Shabbatai's adherents who had followed him into Islam, but not requiring further conversions. On visiting Venice, in March 1668, Nathan spent two weeks debating with the rabbis. His 'errors' were sharply condemned, but both in Venice, and in Livorno and Rome, where he went subsequently, before returning to the Near East, he found numerous believers whose faith he reinforced.

Shabbatai and those of his adherents who had become Muslims, followed the Islamic faith in public but, in private, they continued to practise Jewish ritual and immerse themselves in cabbala. Nor did they seek to propagate Islam among Jews. In 1673, the Turks forced

[14] Bovenkerk, 'Schrijvers', pp. 130–1.
[15] Morosini, *Via della Fede*, i. 76–8; Yerushalmi, *From Spanish Court*, pp. 348–9; Graupe, *Rise of Modern Judaism*, p. 55.

Shabbatai to retire to a remote place in Albania and there, in 1676, he died. His death, followed by that of Nathan, in 1680, precipitated a fresh crisis among believers, but this too was surmounted, Shabbatai's decease being interpreted as a necessary preliminary to his second coming. Indeed, Nathan's cabbalistic, messianic heresy continued to show great vitality almost everywhere. Through the 1680s and 1690s, Shabbatean seers and visionaries were active throughout Jewish Europe, insisting on provisional loyalty to rabbinic law but also on the imminent return of Shabbatai Zevi and pending redemption of the Jewish people and mankind as a whole. A key heretic, for whom the Torah 'as it now exists' will soon be 'no longer necessary', was the former Marrano Abraham Cardoso (1626–1706), brother of the rationalist apologist Isaac Cardoso. Abraham wandered ceaselessly throughout the Near East, being expelled from community after community, propagating his own mystical interpretation of Shabbatai's mission. Despite the closeness of several of his formulas to Christian modes of thought, he attacked both Christianity and the rationalist tradition in Judaism, especially the anti-Shabbatean views of his brother, and those who thought like him, with fierce passion. Others went still further in their departure from traditional Judaism. In 1683, after fresh revelations, in Salonika, a large group of 300 families converted to Islam, merging with Shabbatai's original fellow converts to form a crypto-Jewish sect, known as the Dönme, which survived, preserving a rich mystical literature, almost down to the present day. Around 1700, a splinter group of the Dönme, under Baruchiah Russo, carried what was previously only a sporadic revolt against the obligatoriness of the moral law to an extreme, discarding many Mosaic precepts regarding sexual conduct and relationships. This was presaged in the writings of Abraham Cardoso which contain more than a hint of imminent release from the sexual code of the Torah. Erotic imagery had always been integral to the language of cabbalistic speculation but was now emerging as an instrument of radical change at least among a coterie at the extreme fringe of the Shabbatean movement.[16] Orgiastic rituals involving exchange of wives and incestuous liaisons became part of the tradition of the Dönme.

In Ashkenazi Europe, the pre-eminent Shabbateans in the years after 1680 included some notable figures. Heschel Zoref (1633–1700), a Vilna silversmith who had been one of the leading Lithuanian

---

16 Scholem, *The Messianic Idea*, pp. 74–5.

enthusiasts in 1665–6, gathered a fervent circle to whom he revealed the 'secrets' of the first and second coming. Haim Malakh (c.1660–1716) of Kalisz, a child at the time of the original eruption, emerged as a powerful popular preacher and ascetic, a precursor of the eighteenth-century hasidic leaders except for the heretical messianic theology to which he adhered and which, in his later years, he propagated in Podolia.[17] Judah Leib Prossnitz (1670–1730), a Moravian pedlar, underwent spiritual rebirth around 1696 and took to wandering through Moravia and Silesia preaching renewal through penitence and the imminence of redemption and Shabbatai's return. Another notable enthusiast for self-mortification, fasts, and pending salvation through the second coming of Shabbatai Zevi—which he believed would take place in the year 1706—was Judah Hasid (c.1660–1700) of Dubno.[18] These and other leaders of the heretical movement met at a secret congress at Nikolsburg, in 1699, which precipitated a fresh wave of excited frenzy. A remarkable mass migration of some 1,500 Polish, Moravian, and German Jews to Jerusalem took place in the following year. This *aliyah* to the Holy Land, in 1700, has been described as the largest Ashkenazi ingathering to that date and a landmark in the history of spiritual Zionism. But once again the excitement ended in disillusionment and internal splits, partly owing to the death of the immigrants' leader, Judah Hasid, a few days after his arrival in Jerusalem. Some of his flock stayed on but most returned to Europe. A few of the disillusioned converted to Islam, many more to Christianity.

Meanwhile, in western Europe, the post-1666 messianic controversy persisted under the surface. For a time, the governing boards prevented overt manifestations of Shabbatean belief and, indeed, encouraged the circulation of tracts condemning the mystical frenzy.[19] The *parnasim* strove to restore faith in tradition and authority in place of the spent frenzy and shattered hopes. But controversy over the messianic claims of Shabbatai Zevi continued to simmer. In 1713, Nehemiah Hiyya Hayon (c.1655–c.1730), a Balkan Shabbatean, having succeeded in publishing, at Berlin, the only overtly Shabbatean tract to be printed after 1666, brought his stock of copies to Amsterdam for distribution. Initially, Hayon succeeded in enlisting the support of the Portuguese congregation for his venture, as the then

---

[17] Krauss, 'Die Palästinasiedlung', pp. 56–66.   [18] Ibid., pp. 62–6.

[19] Fuks, 'Sebastianisme in Amsterdam', pp. 20–8; Kaplan, 'Attitude of the Leadership', pp. 212–16.

leading Sephardi rabbi in Amsterdam, Selomoh Ayllon, was himself a Shabbatean. He met with stiff opposition, though, from the Ashkenazi rabbi, Zevi Hirsch Ashkenazi (1660–1718), echoes of the ensuing controversy reaching far beyond the confines of Holland. Tracts attacking the heretical views of Hayon issued forth from Livorno and London, as well as Amsterdam, together with adverse rabbinic judgement from Constantinople and Salonika. Hayon was forced to return to the Levant in disgrace; but Zevi Hirsch Ashkenazi, who had offended the Amsterdam Portuguese *parnasim*, was also forced to leave, and there is no doubt that the cells of Shabbatean heresy in Holland, as in Italy and Germany, remained largely intact.

2   THE SPINOZIST REVOLT

While there were sceptics and doubters among the Marrano diaspora of the early seventeenth century, the most notable of whom was Uriel da Costa, a sustained revolt against the intellectual foundations of rabbinic Judaism began only in the 1650s among a small circle in Amsterdam who gathered initially around the figure of Dr Juan de Prado (c.1615–c.1670).[20] This Sephardi coterie included a schoolmaster, Daniel de Ribera, but its most notable member was the budding philosopher Spinoza. Prado, a physician trained at the Universities of Alcalá and Toledo, had joined the exodus from Spain of the 1640s and then spent some years in France, still as a New Christian. He arrived in Amsterdam, in 1655, and nominally reverted to normative Judaism but, almost at once, joined Spinoza in rejecting the pretensions of the rabbis. Spinoza may already by that date have been close to the Amsterdam Socinians and other anti-Trinitarian Christians of whom he was soon to be seeing a great deal, as well as the ex-Jesuit freethinker Franciscus van den Enden, and it is unclear how far Prado can be said to have influenced him.[21] What is clear is that, together with Ribera, they now systematically denied that the Torah and Jewish tradition had any divine origin or sanction and, thus, came directly into collision with the authority of the rabbis and *parnasim*. Spinoza refused to compromise his views and, after several warnings and lesser penalties, was expelled from the community on 27 July 1656. Prado at first recanted and then relapsed before finally being

[20] Revah, 'Aux origines', pp. 368–9, 379; Revah, *Spinoza*, pp. 22–8; Kaplan, *From Christianity to Judaism*, pp. 114–33.
[21] Méchoulan, 'Morteira et Spinoza', pp. 54–9.

expelled in 1657. In the years 1657–9, Prado and Spinoza remained in
close proximity, in Amsterdam, meeting for example at the house of a
certain Spaniard, named José Guerra, together with both Chistian
dissenters and Jewish sceptics, one of whom was a former Marrano
confectioner from Seville, well known in Amsterdam, named Samuel
Pacheco.

What was new in the Spinozist revolt was assuredly not its
intellectual content; for the revolt began long before Spinoza formulated the more original parts of his system. What defined the 'sect',
as it was commonly known at the end of the seventeenth century and
beginning of the eighteenth,[22] was the denial of all revealed religion,
the claim that God did not exist other than 'philosophically', that is as
a First Cause which did not intervene in the affairs of men, and a
thoroughgoing materialism which denied the immortality of the
soul.[23] All these elements had been articulated by some Marranos, as
well as non-Jewish sceptics and deists, long before 1655. What was
new was the peculiar circumstances which prevailed in Holland after
1650. It was the unprecedented degree of freedom of expression and
assembly encountered in the Dutch Republic in the later seventeenth
century which made it possible for groups opposed to conventional
religion, Christian or Jewish, to meet, co-ordinate, and propagate
their views in print. The adherents of this 'atheistical' philosophy
were, from 1670 until after 1700, commonly known as 'Spinozists' in
France, England, and Germany, as well as in Holland, and were the
first wave of a flood of radical pantheism and deism which swept
north-western Europe in the eighteenth century.

Around 1660, Spinoza settled in Rijnsburg, near Leiden, then, in
1664, he moved to Voorburg, near The Hague, and finally, in 1670, to
The Hague itself. Much of his early effort went into a long manuscript
which was a direct, systematic attack on rabbinic Judaism—and only
by implication on Christianity—a justification for his break with the
Synagogue, which, for whatever reason, remained unpublished and
largely unknown, and is now lost.[24] Parts of it were incorporated,
however, into his *Tractatus Theologico-Politicus*, which he published
unsigned, in Latin, in 1670. This work was a watered-down version of
his real critique, but nothing like it had been published before and it
made a tremendous impact among the learned. Then, in 1678, three

---

[22] Bayle, *Dictionnaire historique*, iv. 253–71; Toland, *Letters to Serena*, pp. 134–6.
[23] Strauss, *Spinoza's Critique of Religion*, pp. 67–8, 263; Revah, *Spinoza*, pp. 27, 32, 36.
[24] Bayle, *Dictionnaire historique*, iv. 255; Revah, *Spinoza*, p. 35.

simultaneous French editions appeared, at Amsterdam, Leiden, and 'Cologne', and Spinoza, at a stroke, became a sensation among the courts and higher nobility of Europe, though he himself had died the year before. Despite the widespread hostility that he provoked, and the furious campaign of vilification directed against him, his works, and his followers, much of the reaction to the French edition of his *Tractatus* was enthusiastic, though it was not considered decent to express approval openly.[25] The clergy thundered but a great many of the thinking laity silently applauded.

Though the *Tractatus* was, in essence, a critique of Judaism, and only secondarily of Christianity, its initial effect, in some quarters, was to enhance the standing of Judaism and rabbinic learning. For Spinoza's barbs, if valid, struck at the roots of both Judaism and Christianity, so that to rebut Spinoza one had to stress the validity and sanctity of the Hebrew Bible. However, idealizing the ancient Israelites, which now suddenly came into fashion, proved to be perfectly compatible with perpetuating anti-Semitic attitudes toward their descendants, as we see from such conservative Catholic replies to Spinoza as Huet's *Demonstratio evangelica*, sections of Bossuet's *Universal History*, and the Abbé Fleury's *Les Mœurs des Israelites* (1681). According to the Abbé Fleury, in a book which served Europe as the classic account of the ancient Hebrews until well into the eighteenth century, ancient Israelite society had been the most admirable and excellent on earth, but the Jews had subsequently suffered an 'entière reprobation' and were now the most 'sordid, despicable people' known to man.[26]

It is true that Spinoza's *Tractatus* momentarily further focused attention on the Hebrew language, that he refers frequently to earlier Jewish philosophers such as Maimonides and Ibn Ezra, who gained greater currency among Christians as a result, and that there was a certain affinity between aspects of his metaphysics and Lurianic cabbala. But it was Spinoza himself who forcefully stressed the limitations of the Hebrew tongue and cast doubt on rabbinic readings and renderings of the ancient texts.[27] This, in turn, contributed to the growing reaction, evident in the late seventeenth century, against the existing Hebrew Bible, and the validity of Hebrew studies generally, in favour of a renewed confidence in the Septuagint, the Greek

[25] *Briefwechsel der Herzogin Sophie*, pp. 351, 353, 368.
[26] Fleury, *Mœurs des Israelities*, pp. 1–3, 196–7.
[27] Spinoza, *Tractatus*, pp. 108, 140–4, 165.

versions of Scripture.[28] At the same time, Spinoza's biting scorn for the observances and ceremonies of Judaism which, as he saw it, had 'emasculated the minds of the Jews', helped stoke up the deep-seated animosity towards Judaism which eventually pervaded almost the entire output of the European Enlightenment.

There is, of course, no way of quantifying the drift into Spinozism, or philosophic deism generally, among Portuguese and other Jews in north-west Europe at the end of the seventeenth century. But there is little reason to doubt that Spinoza struck a chord among many Jews just as he did among non-Jews. It is clear, at any rate, that the apologists for official Judaism in Amsterdam, London, and Hamburg soon became acutely sensitive to the Spinozist threat. Initially, in the 1660s, the drive to combat philosophic deism among the Jews was directed chiefly against Juan de Prado. But after the publication of his *Tractatus*, in 1670, Spinoza himself was usually the main target. Just as several Dutch Protestant clergymen fell foul of charges of Spinozism in the years around 1700, so this happened in the case of at least one rabbi. In 1703, dispute erupted in London after the Sephardi rabbi, David Nieto, delivered an address to his students demolishing the philosophic deists but also employing, or seeming to employ, some of Spinoza's terminology, designating Nature as God working through his Providence.[29] Nieto had already contrived to antagonize several groups in London, in particular owing to his anti-Shabbatean views, and now charges that he was a 'Spinozist' rang about his ears. He responded with the pamphlet *De la Divina Providencia* (1704), a vigorous rebuttal of Spinozism, but it took years of further controversy, and the intervention of the Ashkenazi rabbi, Zevi Hirsch Ashkenazi, before he was finally freed from the taint of Spinoza's heretical ideas. But, especially in western Sephardi society, elements of Spinozism were now firmly embedded.

3   APOLOGETICS

Anxious to stabilize Jewish life once more, in the aftermath of the Shabbatean fiasco, and counter the ridicule, derision, and shaken self-confidence of the later 1660s, European Jewry now strove to

---

[28] Lebram, 'Streit um die Hebräische Bibel', pp. 21–5; Le Clerc, *Sentimens de quelques théologiens*, pp. 94–5, 330–1.

[29] Petuchowski, *Theology of Haham David Nieto*, pp. 15–16; see also the opening pages of Nieto's *De La Divina Providencia*.

reassert itself, its traditions, and its arguments. Given the countless
restrictions on the Jews' freedom of expression, this could mostly be
done only by word of mouth, in manuscript, and, to a limited extent,
in print. But at Amsterdam in the early 1670s, the Jews, both the
Ashkenazi and Sephardi communities, received permission, for the
very first time in the history of Europe, to express themselves,
relatively free from restriction, in stone; that is, to build tall, splendid
new synagogues with façades which reflected not just growing wealth
but renewal, reviving confidence, and even claims to grandeur. These
two new synagogues built at Amsterdam in the early 1670s were not
just revolutionary structures in the history of synagogue design, they
were a revolutionary landmark in the long, slow, history of the
liberation of the Jews from Christian oppression. The great Portuguese synagogue, designed by Elias Bouman, built at a cost of
185,000 gulden, and inaugurated amid great splendour, in 1675, was,
with its grandiose allusions to what was thought to have been the
shape of Solomon's Temple, one of the largest and most imposing
buildings in Amsterdam and caused a sensation among foreign
visitors. The papal nuncio at Cologne who visited Amsterdam the
following year, was appalled that so 'vile' a people should be allowed
to erect so splendid a structure, while in his *Travellours Guide*, around
1680, William Carr, English consul in Amsterdam, remarked that the
'Jewes, who are verie considerable in the trade of this citie have two
synagogues, one whereof is the largest in Christendom, and as some
say in the world, sure I am, it far exceeds those in Rome, Venice, and
all other places where I have been'.[30]

The need to restate their case now produced an efflorescence of
Jewish polemics directed against all the ideological movements, old
and new, which seemingly threatened Judaism. Tradition may have
been under assault from every side but, for roughly half a century or
so after the fiasco of 1665–6, the Jewish leadership succeeded by and
large in restoring a viable framework of intellectual cohesion, tradition, and authority. The Jewish polemics of the post-1666 period were
thus defensive and therapeutic in origin. But in their sweep, vigour,
and vehemence they far outstripped what had gone before. David
Nieto's struggle with heretical messianism and Spinozism was, in
fact, a mild example of the increasingly outspoken apologetic

---

[30] Carr, *The Travellours Guide*, p. 23; the papal nuncio at Cologne, Opizio Pallavicino,
wrote 'fra i nuovi edificii viddi la synagoga degl' hebrei, fabrica veramente magnifica e
della quale non e degna quella gente vile', see *BMHG* xxxii (1911), p. 91.

effusions which now poured forth on all sides. Besides assailing Cartesianism, Spinozism, Socinianism, and Shabbateanism, the new crop of Jewish polemics contributed to, and pervaded, the widening revolt against traditional Christian belief, a revolt which laid the foundations of the European Enlightenment.

Each of the specific challenges confronting traditional Judaism elicited its own response among the polemical replies of the period. But there was also a constant interweaving and overlapping of the various strands. Saul Levi Morteira (*c.*1596–1660), whose life and intellectual endeavour spanned the gap between Montalto and the new ideological phase which begins in the 1650s, typifies this remarkable interplay. None of his four or five polemical tracts (written in Spanish) was ever published; but they circulated widely in western Europe and thoroughly pervaded the western Sephardi milieu. In the manner of Montalto, Morteira assails Christian teaching as contrary to reason and common sense; but, after 1650, mixes this with polemics against radical scepticism and Socinianism.[31] Morteira was perhaps the first Jewish writer to realize that a Gentile ideology which rejected the divinity of Christ, along with the Trinity and the Cross, and which urged that nothing should be believed which was not readily evident to reason, was just as antagonistic to Judaism as the pretensions of the churches. And, indeed, as we know, there was a very close connection between Spinoza, Prado, and their circle, and the Amsterdam Socinians in the 1650s.

After Morteira came a host of younger Jewish controversialists. Among the most notable was Jacob Sasportas (*c.*1610–98), for many years Sephardi rabbi at Hamburg, a fierce opponent of the Shabbateans, who frequently compared Shabbateanism with Christianity. Isaac Cardoso, physician at Verona, engaged in bitter controversy with Shabbateans, sceptics, and Christians, strenuously disputing the low esteem in which modern Jews were held by most contemporary authors in his *Excelencias de los Hebreos* published at Amsterdam in 1679. Moseh Raphael d'Aguilar (d.1679), a Dutch Sephardi rabbi who spent some years in Brazil, circulated various Portuguese tracts in manuscript assailing materialism, scepticism, and Christianity. But the most important of the new controversialists was Isaac Orobio de Castro (1620–87), a former Marrano who had studied medicine and philosophy at Alcalá and Salamanca before falling foul of the Inquisition, being made to abjure at an *auto da fé* in Seville, in 1656,

[31] Méchoulan, 'Morteira and Spinoza', p. 59.

and finally fleeing to France. Briefly, still as a New Christian, he taught as Professor of Pharmacy at Toulouse. Finally, in 1662, he settled in Amsterdam, reverted to normative Judaism (he claimed always to have been a Jew at heart) and at once took up his pen against the philosophic deism of Prado and, later, Spinoza. In 1665–6, his reputation as an opponent of the Shabbateans spread beyond Italy to the Levant. Later, in the 1680s, he was chiefly known as an opponent of Christianity.

But while it is possible to discern stages in the development of Orobio's polemical writing, all the elements were present at the outset and continued to interact throughout. In Orobio's mind, scepticism and unbelief were a particular vice of the Iberian New Christians which he saw in large measure as a microcosm of a Christian Europe unable to believe in its own professed faith. He accepts that most Europeans are sincere Christians and that the Almighty has not destined this majority to damnation. But, according to Orobio, what excuses the Christian belief of the masses is their illiteracy and ignorance, their honest incapacity to reason. The position was quite otherwise, he averred, in the case of men of learning whether New or Old Christian. These he sees as 'culpable and fit for punishment, for they wilfully stifle their own reason . . . and whilst very erudite in other sciences, do not wish to understand what they believe, nor believe what they understand, and seek to justify with sophisms and meaningless forms of words what they do not perceive through reason.'[32] For Orobio, the post-1666 drift of many Jews into Christianity was not a sign of changed belief but of scepticism and apathy. In his mind, the political supremacy of the Christian churches was little more than a cover, even a stimulus, for the spread of unbelief. Orobio's writing is suffused with deep veneration for 'reason'. To believe in a Messiah who is at once human and divine and who has supposedly come, but has not significantly changed the world for the better, is, he says, unreasonable. This means that what is, in the case of the untutored masses, a partial monotheism, albeit heavily tinged with superstition and idolatry, is in the case of the Christian learned unadulterated idolatry.

Apart from Spinoza, Orobio was the most systematic opponent of Christianity in late seventeenth-century Holland, and therefore Europe, as well as being one of Spinoza's foremost critics, and the

---

[32] Orobio de Castro, *Carta al hijo*, pp. 50–2; Revah, *Spinoza*, pp. 36–40; see also Kaplan, *From Christianity to Judaism*, pp. 132–7.

question arises as to how far his critique surfaced outside a specifically Jewish milieu. Most of his writing was too outspoken to be published, even in Holland. Furthermore, whilst his manuscripts circulated widely they were written in Spanish or Portuguese. Yet despite this, and despite the Amsterdam *Mahamad*'s efforts to prevent Jews arguing religion with Christians, following a protest by the Dutch Calvinist clergy to the States of Holland, in 1676, over the freedom with which Jews were speaking against Christianity, Orobio did debate with Christians, and his views became a recognizable strand in the spreading anti-Christian revolt characteristic of early Enlightenment Holland.

Orobio's most notable face-to-face encounter was his disputation with the liberal Christian theologian Philippus van Limborch, at the house of Dr Egbert Veene, before an audience of scholars, in the mid 1680s.[33] Subsequently, Limborch published a Latin account of the discussion which appeared at Gouda, in 1687, giving considerable publicity to Orobio's views. Most of the debate centred on the messianic issue, many pages being devoted to Orobio's assertions that it is unreasonable to believe in a Saviour at once human and divine who has failed to change mankind in any significant way. 'Neither in conducting their lives, nor in the disposition of their hearts, nor in the practice of their religion, do I see Christians manifesting a higher spirituality than other peoples, though assuredly they pride themselves on doing so.'[34] Orobio points out that there were still many parts of the world where the inhabitants were pagan, and God unknown, and that Israel was now just as dispersed, if not more so, as it had been before Jesus's coming.

Limborch's published account of his encounter with Orobio was reviewed at length, by John Locke, in Jean le Clerc's *Bibliothèque universelle et historique* vii (1687), Locke being unsympathetic to Orobio's opinions but giving them additional currency.[35] Later, the contents not only of this Latin text but of Orobio's own anti-Christian tracts began to percolate into the literature of the Enlightenment. The Huguenot pastor and historian Jacques Basnage maintained in his *L'histoire et la religion des Juifs* (1706–11) that the honest Christian had to face up to the arguments of Jewish controversialists, acknowledging in particular the force of Cardoso and Orobio de

---

[33] Kaplan, *From Christianity to Judaism*, pp. 243–7.

[34] Limborch, *De Veritate religionis*, pp. 67, 70–9.

[35] *Bibliothèque*, vii. 289–330.

Castro.[36] Several of Orobio's manuscripts circulated in French translation, both in France and England, well before the Baron d'Holbach
published one of his most vehement pieces, under the title *Israël Vengé*,
at London, in 1770.

4   PHILOSEMITISM

The wave of philosemitism that manifested itself in Europe during the
mid and late seventeenth century is assuredly a most striking
phenomenon and a most revealing one. It is best seen as a product of
the drift away from an exclusively Christian culture and as characteristic of the transitional phase preceding the later ascendancy of
philosophic deism and the Enlightenment. Those who had departed
from a firm faith in Christ often, like Bodin (who in some respects was
a precursor of the movement) still immersed themselves in Biblicism
and messianic expectations. Even among those who remained
Christians, there were many who were prey to spasmodic doubt. The
age-old theological tension between Christianity and Judaism was
surfacing in new ways. As Pascal expressed it, 'il faut que les Juifs ou
les Chrétiens soient méchants'.[37] It was the increasing difficulty of
being sure 'which' that made the Jews an object of growing fascination for many Europeans at this time.

More than anything it was the mood of messianic expectancy
which swept England and Holland, in particular in the 1640s and
1650s, which generated the phenomenon of philosemitism. The idea
that the conversion of the Jews to Christianity was a prerequisite for
the redemption of mankind, and that this was now at hand, became
suddenly widespread in certain circles. It is true that expectation that
the Jews were about to acknowledge Christ does not in itself imply
philosemitism, but the notion certainly generated interest in, and the
desire for involvement with, the Jews, and it was from this that
philosemitism evolved. In Isaac de la Peyrère's *Du Rappel des Juifs*
(1643), the Christian content is reduced to a minimum and the whole
stress is placed on the reconciliation of Christians and Jews, their
underlying brotherhood, and the imminence of the ingathering of the
Jews to the Holy Land.[38] And although La Peyrère was probably of
Marrano extraction, it would be wrong to dismiss his books as

[36] Basnage, *Histoire*, ix. 736–8, 1017–25, 1043–55.
[37] Pascal, *Pensées*, p. 287.
[38] La Peyrère, *Du Rappel*, pp. 78–9, 149, 374–5.

untypical of the broader trend. The Latin letter of Nathaniel Holmes and Henry Jesse to Menasseh ben Israel, of 1649, exudes a longing for reconciliation, mutual forgiveness, and common redemption. And while contemporary Jews had strong reservations about the vestigial Christian content in such outpourings, this Gentile messianism did coincide in time with the mid-century upsurge in Jewish messianism and there clearly was some scope for collaboration of the sort that led to Menasseh ben Israel's mission to London. Both sets of messianists believed that universal redemption was at hand. Both de-emphasized, or dismissed, the role of the historical Jesus, the whole emphasis being placed on a future and supposedly imminent messianic event.

A key instance of this intertwining of Christian and Jewish messianism was the compilation entitled *Bonum Nuncium Israeli* published by Paul Felgenhauer, at Amsterdam, in 1655. Felgenhauer was a Bohemian pietist and mystic of fiercely anti-Catholic and anti-Calvinist views. He dedicated his book to none other than Menasseh ben Israel, who, in turn, contributed a discreet postscript. Felgenhauer, a fervent messianist whose overwrought mind discerned tokens of pending salvation at every turn, longed for the reunification of Christian and Jew in one church.[39] But the new messianism was not confined to dissenting Protestant circles. The most notable of all the mid-century messianists was the Portuguese Jesuit mystic, preacher, and mercantilist, António Vieira.[40] Vieira, who spent many months in Holland in the late 1640s, taking the opportunity to frequent the synagogues and Jewish homes, like other Christian messianists of the period,[41] fused elements of the Protestant–Sephardi messianic mix, which he encountered in Amsterdam, with Sebastianism or traditional Portuguese messianic folklore, itself a *mélange* of Old Christian and Judaic components. Though the Inquisition never managed to pin him down as a heretic, owing to his impeccable connections in Rome, Vieira's theology was highly unconventional, not to say eccentric. It was also uniquely philosemitic and couched in the most masterly Portuguese prose of the age. Vieira's philosemitism was theological, practical as we see from his many contacts with Jews— and vigorously mercantilist. Several English millenarians, it is true, also employed mercantilist arguments in pressing for closer contact

---

[39] Felgenhauer, *Bonum Nuncium Israeli*, pp. 5–9; Schoeps, *Philosemitismus*, pp. 20–3.
[40] Saraiva, 'António Vieira', pp. 42–50.
[41] *Cartas do Padre António Vieira*, pp. 161–8, 183, 187.

with Jews, but only as a debating device to advance their theological preoccupations. In Vieira, philosemitic mercantilism ran deeper. The pre-eminent Portuguese mercantilist writer of the mid-seventeenth century, during the 1640s and early 1650s the great Jesuit also carried considerable personal influence with the Portuguese King. His political objective was to harness the financial potential of Portugal's New Christians, and of the Portuguese Jewish diaspora in northern Europe, behind his country's desperate struggle for independence (and survival as a colonial power) against Spain and Holland.[42] Beyond this, he aimed to recall the Jews to Portugal and Brazil to live as New Christians once more but this time with the Inquisition bridled and on conciliatory terms. Ultimately, as we discern from his mystical *História do Futuro*, Vieira envisaged the political rebirth of Portugal and its empire as the harbinger of the Second Coming, it being the mission of the Portuguese, according to his vision, to finally accomplish the calling of the Jews to Christ.

Philosemitic messianism involved mixing with Jews, collaborating with them, and learning about them. It therefore also demanded a willingness to shock and scandalize contemporary opinion. La Peyrère's *Praeadamitae* published at Amsterdam in 1655, and in London the following year, caused a sensation on account of its totally novel construings of Scripture, its cutting across all accepted theological barriers, and its stress on the centrality of modern Jewry in the affairs of men.[43] Among those who applauded was that most provocative of baroque ladies, Queen Christina of Sweden, who had recently abdicated the Swedish throne and was residing in Antwerp in 1654 when La Peyrère passed through the city *en route* to Amsterdam. She greeted him and his ideas enthusiastically. Queen Christina, as well as being something of a Hebraist herself, is well-known for having cultivated amicable relations with Jews; not only with her agent in Hamburg, Teixeira, but with several others including the Hamburg Sephardi physician Bento de Castro who treated her illnesses whilst she was in Hamburg, was seen riding with her in her carriage, and was widely rumoured to have been taken into her bed. In part, Christina's cultivation of Jews derived from her delight in shocking conventional opinion and, in particular, her loathing of Lutheran

---

[42] Boxer, 'Padre António Vieira', pp. 474–80; Hanson, *Economy and Society*, pp. 88–90, 116; Saraiva, 'António Vieira', pp. 42–50.

[43] La Peyrère, *Praeadamitae*, ii. 49–58, 64–70; Popkin, 'Menasseh ben Israel', pp. 62–3.

divines. She once put on a firework display to celebrate the enthrone-
ment of a new pope, in Protestant Hamburg, which, not surprisingly,
provoked a full-scale popular tumult. But there was a serious side to
her studies, as her interest in Hebrew and La Peyrère shows. She also
had dealings with Menasseh ben Israel who came to visit her whilst
she was in Antwerp, where she stayed in the house of the Portuguese
New Christian financial baron, García de Yllan, a cousin of the João
de Yllão who later led Jewish colonizing expeditions to Curaçao and
the Holy Land.[44] Menasseh came to Antwerp primarily to claim
payment for Jewish books he had procured for Christina; but doubtless he also indulged her taste for messianic and theological speculation. Later, in Rome, the former Queen of Sweden had much to do
with Vieira, whom she greatly admired. She remained true to her
philosemitic proclivities, submitting a protest to the Emperor on the
occasion of the expulsion of the Jews from Vienna.

The de-Christianizing tendencies, already implicit in La Peyrère
and Felgenhauer, came progressively to the fore as the century
progressed. In 1688, the Swedish messianist Anders Pedersson
Kempe published his *Israels erfreuliche Botschaft* at Hamburg , dedicat-
ing it to Christina's Jewish agent there, Manoel Teixeira, who
(wisely) disowned the work, since in it Kempe outspokenly
denounced Lutheran, Calvinist and Catholic Christians alike as
'Godless heathens'.[45] Oliger Pauli, a Danish messianist who
gravitated to Amsterdam in 1695, proclaimed the return of the Jews
to Zion as the key to universal salvation and submitted petitions
asking (in turn) King William III of England, the Danish monarch,
and the French Dauphin to support his schemes for returning the
Jews to the Holy Land and rebuilding the Temple in Jerusalem.[46]
Pauli called himself and his followers 'Jehovanists'. After a time, his
preaching against conventional Christianity proved too much even
for the Amsterdam burgomasters and he was sent unceremoniously
back to Denmark. In the 1690s, several German messianists and ex-
Socinians in Holland jettisoned the last vestiges of allegiance to Christ
and openly converted to Judaism. Three or four such joined the
Sephardi community in Amsterdam, the most noteworthy being
Johann Pieter Späth (1644–1701), also known as Moses Germanus.

---

[44] Denucé, 'Koningin Christina', pp. 31–6; Katz, 'Menaseh ben Israel's Mission',
pp. 57–9.
[45] Valentin, *Judarnas Historia*, p. 36; Schoeps, *Barocke Juden*, pp. 35–42.
[46] Gelber, *Vorgeschichte*, pp. 14–23; Schoeps, *Philosemitismus*, pp. 53–67.

An Augsburg Catholic who spent most of his life sampling the varieties of Protestantism, Späth finally became a Jew in 1697 and in the last four years of his life achieved notoriety throughout Europe as an anti-Christian controversialist, attacking Christianity in print as well as in debate.[47] One of his memorable encounters in Amsterdam was with the fiery Lutheran divine Johann Georg Wachter, who subsequently denounced him in print as a 'Spinozist', pantheist, and atheist, as well as cabbalist and Jew. For his part, Späth attributed to the Socinians, Mennonites, 'Coccejans', and 'Philadelphians' praiseworthy Judaizing tendencies which, however, none of these groups had properly followed through.[48] Other German messianists, stopping short of the Synagogue, likewise discarded Christ, embracing Pauli's biblical 'Jehovanism', a quasi-Judaism stripped of rabbinic law. One of these personages, Heinrich Bernhard Küster, published the philosemitic Jehovanist work *Hebräer Schechinah* at Amsterdam in 1701.

The roots of philosemitism, then, lay in conflict with official Christianity as shows through in numerous seventeenth-century contexts. Späth's 'Socinians, Mennonites, Coccejans, and Philadelphians' were all groups in revolt against the orthodoxies of Calvin, Luther, and the Papacy. To those in doubt concerning the teaching of the churches, and that of the Greek and Latin Fathers of the Church on which it was based, the Jews were precious as a lifeline, a thread leading back to a purer, pre-church, biblical spirituality. 'Ce peuple', as Pascal put it, 'est le plus ancien qui soit en la connaissance des hommes: ce qui me semble lui attirer une vénération particulière et principalement dans la recherche que nous faisons, puisque, si Dieu s'est de tout temps communiqué aux hommes, c'est à ceux-ci qu'il faut recourir pour en savoir la tradition.'[49] The great artist Rembrandt epitomized this process. His revolt against Calvinism, his consorting with Mennonites and Socinians, went hand in hand with his intense Biblicism and rubbing shoulders with contemporary Jews. His house in Amsterdam was located right in the Jewish quarter. Similarly, John Milton, whose *De Doctrina Christiana* (1658–60) shows strong messianic and anti-Trinitarian leanings, combined an intense Biblicism with a marked interest in Talmud and cabbala, all of which elements infuse his poems.

---

[47] Wachter, *Spinozismus im Jüdenthumb*, preface; Schudt, *Jüdischer Merkwürdigkeiten*, iv. 309–10.
[48] Wachter, *Spinozismus im Jüdenthumb*, preface; Schoeps, *Barocke Juden*, pp. 83–91.
[49] Pascal, *Pensées*, p. 237.

The mid- and late seventeenth-century preoccupation with the Old Testament was so strong that in Rembrandt, Milton, and Racine themes from ancient Jewish history rival, even at times take precedence over, scenes from Gospel and classical mythology. This development was paralleled by the expansion and intensification of Old Testament, Talmudic, cabbalistic, and other Hebrew studies. Assuredly, many or most post-1650 Christian Hebraists were orthodox Protestants or Catholics just as their predecessors had been. The objective of using Hebrew to promote the conversion of the Jews remained habitual. Nevertheless, Hebrew studies now attained an altogether higher level of priority and sophistication. For the first time, powerful interest was shown in the Lurianic as well as the Old Cabbala, as well as in the Karaites, a medieval Jewish heretical group, and many other facets of Jewish spirituality and history. If both conservative churchmen, and the Spinozists, were busily undermining the standing of the Hebrew Bible, a school of liberal Christian Hebraists, of whom the Dutchmen Johannes Cocceius (1603–69) and Johannes Leusden (1624–99) were leading representatives, emphasized its centrality and the necessity of studying Talmud and post-Talmudic rabbinic literature to understand it properly.[50] At the same time, in parts of Europe, such as Sweden, where Hebrew studies had not previously percolated, there was now a remarkable flowering of interest, particularly in the last two decades of the century.[51]

Two results of the new Hebraism were the increasingly systematic classification of rabbinic literature by Christian scholars and the rendering of more of the salient writings into Latin. Guilio Bartolocci (1613–87), Professor of Hebrew at the *Collegium Neophytorum*, a college for Jewish converts in Rome, and keeper of the Vatican Hebrew Collection, was certainly a faithful Catholic, devoted to the conversion of Jews. But his *Bibliotheca Magna Rabbinica* (4 vols., Rome, 1675–93) was the first detailed bibliography about Jews and Judaism and frequently reflects a more objective, as well as sympathetic, attitude than Catholic scholars had been apt to show in the past. Johann Christoph Wolf (1683–1739), a professor at Hamburg, later built on the foundations laid by Bartolocci, using what was then the foremost Jewish library in Europe, that of David Oppenheimer, housed at Hamburg, producing a more complete bibliography, his monumental

---

[50] Lebram, 'Streit um die hebräische Bibel', pp. 47–54; Hirschel, 'Johannes Leusden', pp. 30–5.
[51] Schoeps, *Philosemitismus*, pp. 157–62.

Bibliotheca Hebraea (4 vols., Hamburg, 1715–33). Another salient instance of Christian–Jewish scholarly collaboration was the historic Amsterdam Hebrew Bible of 1667, produced by Leusden, Professor of Hebrew at Utrecht, and the Sephardi printer of bibles, Joseph Athias, who obtained access for him to the oldest Iberian Hebrew medieval bibles possessed by the Sephardim in Holland.[52] Willem Surenhuis (1666–1729), Professor of Hebrew at Amsterdam, compiled the monumental *Versio Latina Mischnae* (6 vols., 1698–1703), a bilingual rendering in Hebrew and Latin which for the first time introduced what was the most essential part of the Talmud to the non-Hebrew reading learned public.

Interest in Lurianic cabbala, which, as has become increasingly evident, attracted more than passing attention from such central figures as Henry More, Milton, and Isaac Newton, was cultivated in many parts of Protestant Europe. Its foremost interpreter within European culture was the Silesian mystic and Hebraist, Christian Knorr von Rosenroth (1636–89). A devotee of the pietism of Jakob Boehme (whose mysticism shows an uncanny kinship to that of Isaac Luria), Knorr studied with numerous Ashkenazi cabbalists both in Germany and Holland. From 1668, he resided at Sulzbach, as an adviser and intellectual adornment to the court of Duke Christian-August. He was the chief compiler of the monumental *Kabbala Denudata* (Sulzbach, 1677–84), a key anthology of Latin renderings of Lurianic writings, sections from Naphtali Bachrach, and, most influential of all, an abridged version of Abraham Cohen Herrera's *Puerta del Cielo*. However, most non-Jews who preoccupied themselves with matters cabbalistic, including More and Knorr's associate, the Flemish mystic Frans Mercurius van Helmont (1614–98), evinced no further interest in Judaism and principally saw cabbala as a mystical aid to the general reconciliation and reunification of Protestants, Catholics, and Jews.[53]

A more definite parallel to the bibliographical and textual endeavours of the new Hebraists, including Knorr, was the rise of scholarly interest, for the first time, in post-biblical Jewish history and folklore, and in Yiddish. These trends were almost totally new. A central figure here was Johann Christoph Wagenseil (1633–1705), who opened up several new fields of study. Wagenseil assembled the first comprehensive study by a Christian of Jewish observances and

---

[52] Franco Mendes, *Memorias*, p. 63; Basnage, *Histoire*, x. 1026.
[53] Schulze, 'Einfluß der Kabbala', pp. 78–83, 97.

ceremonies. It is true that much of what he investigated he accounted superstitious and absurd. It is true also that he was motivated in part by his desire to bring the Jews to Christ. But for all that an unmistakable admiration for Jewish life and life-style insistently creeps through. 'It is undeniable', he wrote,

that they show far more care, zeal, and constancy in all this (their religious duties) than Christians do in practising their true faith, and that, fur-thermore, they are far less given to vice; rather they possess many beautiful virtues, especially compassion, charity, moderation, chastity, and so forth, so that at the Last Day they will shame and see damned many Christians—for, unquestionably, as regards compassion and charity, they far, far surpass Christians in that they give generously to the poor and destitute, as far as they can, and all this, by God's grace, I can attest to by my own experience.[54]

Wagenseil's study of Jewish life extended also to the vernacular of Ashkenazi Jewry, Judaeo-German, or Yiddish, which he was the first to investigate systematically, assembling a unique collection of Yid-dish tracts and manuscripts. Others, especially in Germany and Scandinavia, followed up aspects of Wagenseil's pioneering researches. One of his pupils, Johann Jakob Schudt (1664–1722), in his *Jüdische Merkwürdigkeiten* (1714–18), compiled what is still a valuable compendium of Frankfurt Jewish folklore, customs, and prayers, even if occasionally marred by anti-Semitic comment. Meanwhile, in Holland, the Huguenot refugee pastor and historian Jacques Basnage composed the first serious Christian history of the post-biblical Jews in his *L'Histoire et la religion des Juifs depuis Jésus-Christ jusqu' à present* (5 vols., 1706–11). Among other noteworthy features of this work, it is striking that Basnage draws his readers' attention to the anti-Christian arguments of Morteira, Cardoso, and Orobio de Castro, pointing out that the honest Christian has to face up to them.[55]

5   THE NEW ANTI-SEMITISM

European anti-Semitism during the age of the Court Jews was a *mélange* of traditional ecclesiastical and popular hostility mixed with several novel elements. A new age was dawning intellectually, an age which has aptly been termed the 'Crisis of the European Mind', and it was from this ferment that the Enlightenment was to emerge. Where

[54] Wagenseil, *Der Jüden Glaube und Aberglaube*, pp. 184–5; Wagenseil, *Belehrung*, foreword.
[55] Basnage, *Histoire*, ix. 736–8, 1017–25, 1043–55.

Bossuet and the Abbé Fleury echoed the traditional doctrine of the Church, accounting the Jewish people as 'autrefois le plus heureux du monde, maintenant la fable et la haine de tout le monde',[56] the Spinozists and other pantheists and deists who pioneered the ideological terrain of the Enlightenment deemed the Mosaic Law itself a 'yoke' of superstition which had not just stunted the development of the Jews but, what was a good deal more deplorable, also that of much of the rest of mankind. The notion that Judaism was a tenacious, as well as ancient, superstition, a device of priests to promote their own power, which, in some measure, still held modern minds in thrall, so thoroughly permeated Enlightenment thought that it may, without exaggeration, be described as one of its fundamental principles. Some of the later _philosophes_, such as Voltaire, may have been given to personal anti-Semitism, but, fundamentally, animosity towards Jewish tradition was ingrained in the ideology of philosophic deism from the outset.

Spinoza, who, in his anti-Judaism, as in so much else, was a true precursor of much of the spirit of the Enlightenment, believed that the Jews' adherence to the Mosaic Law had blocked and imprisoned their minds.[57] And so it was with the Spinozists generally. While John Toland (1670–1722) is generally classified as a 'philosemite', owing to his opposition to religious and racial prejudice, and to intolerance of Jews as people, as well as his judging Jews to be useful economically, in fact he followed Spinoza not only in his pantheism, rejection of revealed religion, and contempt for priests, but in his basic anti-Judaism. In Toland's eyes not only was the entire corpus of Talmudic and rabbinic literature 'useless' but it acted as a perennially 'deforming and distorting' influence.[58] The appraisals of Judaism to be found in the works of Toland's fellow deists, Collins, Tyndal, and Trenchard, were by and large still harsher.

Richard Simon, the outstanding French biblical critic of the late seventeenth century, moved from an initial philosemitism to an anti-Semitism which was a curious blend of old and new elements. His

---

[56] Truchet, _Prédication de Bossuet_, ii. 31–2.

[57] Spinoza, _Tractatus Theologico-Politicus_, p. 56.

[58] Toland, _Christianity not Mysterious_, pp. 51, 115, 151–2; Toland, _Letters to Serena_, p. 39; Pierre Bayle, another key precursor of the Enlightenment fully shared this new 'rationalist' aversion to Judaism and Jewish tradition: 'L'antijudaisme de Bayle', M. Yardeni has written, 'procède d'une vision du monde, dont le point de départ est une nouvelle morale fondée non pas sur la religion, mais sur la raison', Yardeni, 'Vision des Juifs'. (Pierre Bayle), p. 86.

stress on the centrality of the Hebrew Bible, and the necessity of studying rabbinic literature in order to cope with it, was rejected from opposite standpoints by deists and conservative churchmen alike. Simon also recognized certain qualities in the Jewish way of life. 'Il semble', he wrote, 'qu'on voit éclater dans la compassion qu'ils ont pour les pauvres, l'image de la charité des premiers Chrestiens pour leurs frères.'[59] Simon's antipathy to the Jews arose from his conviction that their faith in their ways and tradition had totally closed their minds to modern science and literature, leaving them proud, aloof, and adrift from the rest of mankind. Moreover, he believed that they nurtured hidden longings to dominate Christians and their society. Even their charity, which they reserved for their own people, and their pride in a special relationship to God derived, as he saw it, from this supposed Jewish quest for ascendancy. Thus, Simon's anti-Semitism, at bottom, emphasized the suspected cultural and social traits of the Jew rather than the theological objections of the Church.

The populace, however, adhered to more traditional modes of anti-Semitism. If there were no further expulsions after 1670, apart from those from Fulda, Marseilles, and the French Caribbean, this was only because European states were now firmly set against the pressure. The city of Trieste repeatedly petitioned the Emperor to clear the Jew from its vicinity, but Leopold refused; indeed, in 1694–6, the Austrian government imposed a ghetto on Trieste over the objections of its city council.[60] In 1683–4, during and after the Turkish siege of Vienna, and at the start of the Austrian advance into Hungary, a wave of anti-Jewish violence swept central Europe, with riots in Bohemia, Moravia, and as far afield as Padua.[61] In 1699, in the bishopric of Bamberg, bread shortages precipitated months of peasant unrest which led to a few attacks on noble landowners but which mainly took the form of pogroms on defenceless village Jewries.[62] Certainly the Emperor was prepared to curb the worst excesses. The *shtadlan* of the Bamberg *Landjudenschaft* was a brother-in-law of Samson Wertheimer, and his, and the Bishop's, appeals to Vienna were vigorously acted upon. Troops were raised throughout Franconia and the risings suppressed. Yet the court at Vienna remained a hotbed for the dissemination of Catholic anti-Semitism,

---

[59] Yardeni, 'Vision des Juifs' (Richard Simon), pp. 201–2.
[60] Cervani and Buda, *Comunità israelitica di Trieste*, p. 8.
[61] Ciscato, *Ebrei di Padova*, pp. 202–3.
[62] Eckstein, *Juden im Fürstbistum Bamberg*, pp. 25–37.

the most inflammatory preacher of anti-Semitism in all Europe at the close of the seventeenth century being the Austrian court preacher Abraham a Sancta Clara (1646–1709). It was typical of the sermons of this immensely influential Augustinian that, even though both the Turks and the Lutherans were each of them a much more tangible and visible menace to Catholic supremacy of the Danube than were the Jews, his fury against Islam and Protestantism was moderation itself compared with the savage virulence and appalling abuse he heaped upon the Jews.[63]

But the most notable anti-Semitic happening around the turn of the eighteenth century was the furore over the infamous diatribe against Jewry compiled by Johann Andreas Eisenmenger (1654–1704), Professor of Hebrew at Heidelberg. Like so many other violent effusions of the day, Eisenmenger's attack was, at bottom, the result of shaken confidence. On a visit to Amsterdam in 1680–1, Eisenmenger had been profoundly shocked to discover the openness with which Jews in Holland spoke against Christianity and by the sensational conversion at that time, in Amsterdam, of three former German Protestants to formal Judaism. He poured his rage into a vast, 2,000-page attack, entitled *Entdecktes Judenthum*, which he had printed at Frankfurt in 2,500 copies, in 1699. Eisenmenger's object was to defame the Jews by convincing the public of the truth of the medieval blood-libel that Jews had killed Christian boys to use their blood for ritual purposes and by vindicating the charge that they had poisoned the wells during the Black Death and perpetrated all manner of other vile and insidious deeds. To support his case, this Heidelberg professor compiled a farrago of falsehood and twisted constructions, massively citing Talmud out of context and falsely translated. To stop Eisenmenger, the Frankfurt *parnasim* turned, like their colleagues at Bamberg, to the 'Judenkaiser', Samson Wertheimer, who interceded with the Emperor. Leopold duly forbade distribution of the book until its contents had been investigated by a mixed commission of Jesuits and rabbis. But the Frankfurt city council, indignant with the *parnasim* for appealing to Vienna over their heads, agreed to lend Eisenmenger firm backing. The stage was set for a sensational *cause célèbre* which spread ripples throughout German-speaking Europe.

The Court Jews once more demonstrated their cohesion, pooling their influence to mobilize the machinery of the Empire against

[63] Kann, *A Study*, pp. 74–9.

Eisenmenger.[64] Leffman Behrends besought the Elector George of Hanover (afterwards George I of England), first in the name of the *Landjudenschaft* of Hanover, and then in that of all the Jews of the Empire, to intercede with the Emperor. This he did through his resident in Vienna, as did the Archbishop-Elector of Mainz, and several other princes. But the Elector of the Palatinate backed his academic protégé, as did King Frederick I of Prussia, who was generally less friendly towards the Jews than had been his father. These princes pressed the Emperor to permit publication. Privately, Eisenmenger himself was ready to call the whole thing off—in return for an appropriate payment from the Jews; but they preferred to confront his challenge politically. On Eisenmenger's death, in 1704, his heirs fought on, eventually securing permission, from the Prussian monarch, to print and distribute a new edition of 3,000 copies, in Berlin. Thus the book finally appeared in 1711, the title-page of this second edition falsely stating Königsberg as the place of publication, that city lying outside the jurisdication of the Empire. However, Leopold, and his successor, Joseph I, maintained their ban on the compilation as being 'prejudicial to the public and to the Christian religion, and especially to the unlearned'.

Eisenmenger's text was a disreputable and turgid fabrication but his outrage at the seepage of Jewish polemics against Christianity into the mainstream of European life and thought was symptomatic of the times. By the 1690s, Europe's theologians were everywhere on the defensive and there was no denying that the writings of Isaac of Troki, Montalto, Morteira, and Orobio de Castro, as well as of men like Späth, were compounding the impact of the burgeoning mass of anti-Christian doctrine heralded by Spinoza and the Spinozists. In central Europe, it was Wachter and Wagenseil who took the lead in taking up cudgels against the rising tide of irreligion, Spinozism, and Jewish 'blasphemy'. [65] Wagenseil, a Lutheran but, as we have seen, not in any traditional sense an anti-Semite, launched into a powerful crusade against Jewish intellectual influence. But, paradoxically, his tactics in trying to persuade Protestant rulers to bridle the Jews and stop the diffusion of their anti-Christian arguments, by showing how shocking several of their writings were, only served to lend such

---

[64] Wiener, 'Des Hof- und Kammeragenten Leffmann Berens Intervention', pp. 52–4; Kracauer, *Juden in Frankfurt*, ii. 104–6; Ettinger, European Society, pp. 208–9.

[65] Wachter, *Spinozismus in Judenthumb*, foreword; Wagenseil, *Tela Ignea Satanae*, foreword; Dietrich, 'Jüdisch-christliche Religionsgespräch', pp. 2, 10, 15–17.

literature wider currency than before. By re-translating, from Hebrew into Latin, Isaac of Troki and other controversial pieces, collected in Germany, Holland, and as far afield as Gibraltar, and publishing them in his *Tela Ignea Satanae* (1689) and *Denunciatio Christiana de Blasphemiis Judaeorum* (1703), Wagenseil sought to equip Christians to confront Jewish denials of Christ. He also advocated a generally tighter repression of Jewish life, and a more determined effort to convert the Jews to Christianity, though he refused to sanction the use of force. But the only result of his endeavours was to add impetus to the very propositions he strove with all his might to combat.

X

Decline (1713–1750)

DURING European Jewry's age of expansion (1570–1713), the increase and fanning out of Jewish population was virtually universal and all the more remarkable for being totally out of phase with European demographic trends generally. For in most of Europe (other than Britain and Ireland) population stagnated or actually declined during the seventeenth century. This arrestation of population growth, so untypical of the modern era otherwise, was particularly noticeable in Spain, central Europe, Poland, and Italy, countries where New Christians and Jews were able to achieve a much expanded role. Thus, during the seventeenth century, not only was European Jewry steadily increasing but, almost everywhere where they were permitted to live, they were a rapidly growing proportion of the population. In many parts of Poland, Germany, Bohemia, and Moravia, the increase was nothing less than dramatic. The same is true of Venice, Livorno, and Amsterdam, where the Jewish population roughly trebled in the period 1640–1700, rising from around 2 per cent to some 6 per cent of the city's total population. Much the same occurred in Hamburg. In Alsace, the number of Jewish families rose by 150 per cent, from 522 families in 1689, to 1,269 families by 1716. Virtually everywhere there was a vigorous increase in Jewish numbers.

The period 1713–50, by contrast, was one of sharp deterioration in European Jewry's demographic position. It is true that a steady, if usually considerably slower, increase persisted in many parts, but, from the second decade of the eighteenth century onwards, the population of Europe as a whole began to burgeon once more so that, generally speaking, other than in the eastern territories of Poland, Jewish population growth now lagged well behind that of the rest. Furthermore, and a more immediately relevant factor in the economic and cultural decline of European Jewry during the eighteenth century, practically all the leading Jewish urban centres, including those of Poland, displayed a marked incapacity for growth. Most of what increase in Jewish numbers there was, west of Vilna and

Lublin, tended to disperse geographically, extending the scope of Jewish settlement into the countryside and small towns, especially in Poland, Germany, and Holland, and south-eastwards into Hungary and Romania, but, at the same time, contributing to the decline of the Jewish role in the main centres.

The faltering of the principal Jewish urban centres after around 1713 is a key historical phenomenon which has certainly not attracted the scholarly attention it deserves. To some extent, the shrinking process is noticeable everywhere. In the Balkans, the economic and cultural waning of the Jewish communities went hand in hand with appreciable reductions in the size of the main Jewish communities. That of Salonika is estimated to have fallen from 30,000 to around 25,000. Similarly at Constantinople, Sofia, Adrianople, and Belgrade. Meanwhile Venice, now in full decay, lost something like half her Jewish population in the period 1700–66, the number of Jews falling to around 1,700 by the latter date. The collapse of Venetian Jewry was fully evident to the Florentine Jewish traveller, Moseh Cassuto, when he visited the city in 1735.[1] Rome Jewry similarly shrank, by approximately half, during the eighteenth century, down to about 3,000 by 1800, due both to migration away from Rome and a continuing high level of conversions to Christianity. It is true that the disastrous losses at Venice and Rome were untypical and are partly to be accounted for by migration to other parts of Italy induced by changes in patterns of commerce.[2] Trieste, for instance, now took over much of Venice's former trade in the Adriatic. But the growth of Trieste Jewry, which in the nineteenth century was to be the fourth largest in Italy, was painfully slow during the first half of the eighteenth century, rising from a mere 103 Jews in 1735 to only 120 in 1748. The fact is, and this was indeed a sign of the times, the Jews played little part in the rise of Austria's entrepôt in the Adriatic. Admittedly, Livorno did continue to attract Jews from elsewhere and remained a flourishing business centre throughout the century, and yet the further growth of Livornese Jewry after 1700 was slight compared with that of the previous half-century, rising from over 3,000 in 1700 to 3,476 in 1738, and just 4,327 as late as 1784. Otherwise, the general trend in Italy was one of stagnation. Mantuan

---

[1] *The Travels of Moses Cassuto*, pp. 97–8.

[2] Pavoncello, *Ebrei in Verona*, pp. 44–5; Cervani and Buda, *Comunità ebraica di Trieste*, pp. 20, 52–3; on the decline of Ancona Jewry in the eighteenth century see Laras, 'Notizie storiche', pp. 87–8.

Jewry stood at 1,758 in 1702, and only 1,842 in 1747; and the pattern was much the same at Ferrara, Modena, Verona, and Padua.[3] Relative to the rest of the population, which was then rapidly increasing, all this added up to a pattern of irreversible decline.

Meanwhile, in Bohemia, rapid increase in Jewish numbers continued down to the issuing of the so-called Familiants Law of 1726, which imposed a ceiling of 8,541 families (around 35,000 souls), the then pertaining level, above which Bohemian Jewry was not permitted to increase. The Jewish population now began to decline, in relation to the rest of the population, moving from stagnation to absolute decline as a result of the policies of the Empress Maria Theresa, a zealous Catholic with strong feelings of dislike, amounting to physical aversion, for Jews. Her official anti-Semitism culminated in the famous episode in 1744, when she banished the Jews from Prague, arousing a storm of protest in much of Europe, as well as practical difficulties which finally induced her to cancel the expulsion in 1748. While most of those whom she had expelled then returned, they did not all do so. By 1754, Bohemian Jewry was down to around 29,000, of whom about one-third lived in Prague. In Moravia, under restrictive laws issued in 1725, the number of Jewish families was held down to 5,106, or some 20,000 people, condemning Moravian Jewry to zero growth at a time of otherwise rapid demographic increase. As late as 1803, the Jews of Moravia still numbered only 28,396. Jewish population growth likewise slowed, or ceased, in the Burgenland; Eisenstadt, for instance, had 600 Jews in 1700 and only 650 in 1750 which is especially remarkable in view of the emigration from Bohemia and Moravia.

In Germany, the pattern was one of little or no increase in the principal centres, representing a fast dwindling percentage of the population of the major cities, combined with a further dispersion into the countryside. This was partly a matter of increases in the village communities of areas such as Hesse, Franconia, and Münster, where Jewish village life was already well established, and partly an extension of this rural existence into the Palatinate, Baden, and Württemberg, where Jewish settlement had previously been sparse.[4] The number of Jewish families in the villages of the bishopric of Münster more than doubled from 61 in 1720 to 126 by 1749.

---

[3] Simonsohn, *History*, p. 193.

[4] Arnold, *Juden in der Pfalz*, p. 11; Pfeifer, *Kulturgeschichtliche Bilder*, 2–6; Rixen, 'Geschichte und Organisation', pp. 8–9; Kahn, *Juden in Sulzburg*, 17–22.

Meanwhile all the principal Jewish centres in Germany either decayed or, very exceptionally, achieved a slight growth. Frankfurt Jewry, after a spurt of growth during the War of the Spanish Succession, when Jews flooded into the *Judenstadt* to escape the fighting, bringing the number of inhabitants of the ghetto up from around 2,300 to 3,000, then stagnated at that level for the rest of the century, still numbering 3,000 in 1800.[5] Hanau Jewry dwindled from 700 in 1700 to only 540 in 1805. The community at Friedberg shrank from 72 families in 1729 to 42 by 1805. In the new city of Mannheim, where the Jewish population had grown by leaps and bounds during the late seventeenth century, reaching 200 families by 1717, there was very little further growth, the community standing at only 225 families as late as 1761. The picture was much the same at Worms, Speyer, Hildesheim, Halberstadt, and Bamberg. At Hamburg, while the Ashkenazi community continued to grow, the Sephardi community certainly declined both in numbers and even more in commerce. Even Berlin, now emerging as one of the foremost centres of German Jewish life, failed to attract much new Jewish settlement owing to stringent government restrictions, including the expulsion of 387 poor Jews from the city in 1737. Having reached around 1,000 in the first thirty years of its renewed existence, and well over 1,000 by 1713, Berlin Jewry reached only 1,945 as late as 1743.

One principal cause of the unbalanced pattern of Jewish demographic development in post-1713 Germany was the increasingly negative stance adopted by the Prussian Crown.[6] Retreating from the policy of the Great Elector, and of King Frederick I (1688–1713), Frederick William I (1713–40) embarked, from 1714, on a series of measures to restrict Jewish immigration into Brandenburg-Prussia. In 1730, a revision of the Jewry laws actually reduced the quotas of tolerated Jews stipulated from particular localities and reinforced guild privileges excluding Jews from the crafts. Thus, Jewish life ceased expanding almost everywhere in Prussia, except Berlin and in Silesia, which Frederick the Great forcibly annexed in 1740. This reaction against the more liberal trends of the second half of the seventeenth century was especially harsh in East Prussia, where the sprinkling of Polish Jews who had previously percolated into villages were re-expelled in the 1720s. Meanwhile the position of the communities in Königsberg and Memel steadily deteriorated.

---

[5] Kracauer, *Juden in Frankfurt*, ii. 106–7; Dietz, *Stammbuch*, p. 433.
[6] Stern, *Preußischer Staat* II/i. 11, 21–3; Krüger, *Judenschaft von Königsberg*, pp. 4, 7.

In Poland-Lithuania, the demographic power-house of modern European Jewry, the increase in Jewish numbers continued but, as in Germany, this took the form of dispersal, and especially dispersal towards the east and south-east, rather than growth of the main communities. For Lublin province, we possess statistics for a number of small communities which show startling increases over the ninety years 1674–1764, that of Bilgoray, for instance, up from 40 Jews to 644, Kurow from 61 to 904, and Kraśnik from 52 to 901.[7] But, in this same period, the major communities of Lublin, Poznań, Grodno, and Pinsk scarcely increased at all. The Jewish population of Cracow, estimated at 2,060 in 1578 had reached only 3,458 by 1764, almost two centuries later. And according to the census of 1764, there were only five other communities in the whole of Poland-Lithuania which exceeded the 3,000 mark in size—Brody (7,198), Lvov (6,159), Lissa (4,989), Vilna (3,390), and Brest-Litovsk (3,175).[8] Thus there were in the entire monarchy only three communities which surpassed that of Livorno in size and not one that approached that of Amsterdam.

In Amsterdam, also, the growth of the Jewish population virtually ceased after 1713. Thereafter it stagnated for decades at around the 12,000 mark.[9] In the Netherlands as a whole, however, as in parts of Germany, but in contrast to the Balkans and Italy, there was a continuing expansion of Jewish life with appreciable growth in the communities of Rotterdam, The Hague, Amersfoort, Leeuwarden, Zwolle, and Groningen.[10] As a sign of this continuing vitality, three imposing synagogues were completed in successive years, in 1725–7, at Rotterdam, The Hague, and Amersfoort. But whilst Dutch Jewry as a whole still grew, the Sephardi community in Amsterdam not only stagnated but even dwindled somewhat in numbers, and much more in its trade and general vitality.

The unbroken flow of German Jewish immigrants into Holland, after 1700, was paralleled by a steady trickle also into England, Denmark, and Alsace. And yet the dimensions of this movement in the eighteenth century, at any rate into England and Denmark, remained modest, even meagre. Britain was now outstripping the Netherlands as Europe's economic leader. Her trade throughout Europe and the wider world, and her industrial output, were

---

[7] Weinryb, *Jews of Poland*, p. 319.

[8] Mahler, *Yidn in Amolikn Poyln* i. 29–46.

[9] Bloom, *Economic Activities*, p. 31.

[10] Zwarts, 'Joodse gemeenten', pp. 399–400, 413–14; Beem, *Joden van Leeuwarden*, pp. 13–17.

burgeoning. Yet the role of the Jews in England's rise to economic dominance was surprisingly restricted and solidly anchored in the past. Apart from dominating the trade in diamonds and coral, a central strand in Britain's commerce with India, and participating prominently in the trade with the Spanish Indies via Cadiz (the Jews handling a not inconsiderable slice of Britain's silver imports), Jewish activity counted for relatively little.[11] Lack of scope in retailing and the crafts depressed Ashkenazi immigration into England to an almost negligible trickle. Outside London, Jewish communities simply failed to take root. What was probably the oldest provincial congregation, at Portsmouth, was not formed until 1746. There was no community in Liverpool until after 1750. And as regards London Jewry, not only did its growth totally fail to compare with that of Amsterdam, during the previous century, it remained notably sparse. There was a sizeable influx of Marrano immigrants into northern Europe in the 1720s, when a last wave of intense Inquisition persecution of crypto-Jews swept both Spain and Portugal; but, after 1730, the flow of refugees from the Iberian Peninsula dried up. By 1750, except in a few remote parts of northern Portugal, Iberian Marranism had all but ceased to be a living force and was certainly no longer capable of lending sustenance to the Jewish role within Europe as a whole. It is true that much of the influx of the 1720s came to London, and that there was some Sephardi migration to England from Holland and Italy. Yet despite all this the London Sephardi community remained relatively weak. It rose in numbers from 1,050 souls in 1720 to around 1,700 by 1740, but then fell back noticeably during the middle decades of the century, owing to a high rate of re-emigration to the Caribbean and a substantial level of conversions to Christianity.[12]

Not only was Jewish immigration into England and Denmark decidedly sluggish but, in the years after 1713, there were very few attempts to seek admission to new regions of settlement and still fewer princely initiatives to attract Jewish settlement. From Stuttgart, where the dukes of Württemberg had allowed a Jewish community to form around 1700, there was a partial re-expulsion following the fall of the Court Jew Joseph Süss Oppenheimer in 1739: by 1770, there were only four Jewish families living there, compared with seven in 1721. Jewish settlement in Dresden and Leipzig, in electoral Saxony,

[11] Samuel, 'Jews in English Foreign Trade', pp. 134–9.
[12] Diamond, 'Problems', pp. 40–1.

was only marginally more buoyant. Even the Jewish community of
Karlsruhe, the newly established capital of Baden, founded in 1715,
and something of an exception among eighteenth-century German
Jewish communities, grew vigorously only at first, rising from nine
families in 1720 to fifty families by 1733.[13] As late as 1770, Karlsruhe
Jewry had risen to just eighty families. Outside Germany, there was a
similar loss of momentum. In 1745–6, the King of Sweden did try to
attract Sephardi Jews to Gothenburg as part of a scheme to revitalize
Swedish colonial enterprise.[14] It was hoped to set up a Swedish West
India Company which, with the help of Jewish investment and
connections, would carve a niche in Caribbean commerce and
establish a Swedish colony in the vacant area between the Dutch and
Spanish settlements in the Guyanas. But the Swedish Crown's letters
of invitation to the Sephardi communities of Amsterdam, Hamburg,
and London fell flat, eliciting virtually no response. In Sweden,
Jewish settlement began only belatedly, in the 1770s, and then on the
part of a handful of Ashkenazim. All the signs were that the old
dynamism had gone out of European Jewry.

Following the signing of the treaty of Utrecht, in 1713, a prolonged
period of peace descended on most of Europe and, as a consequence,
the role of the Court Jews sharply declined. A wave of damaging
bankruptcies set in continuing down to the 1720s, the most disastrous
being that of the sons of Leffmann Behrends, at Hanover in 1721. The
standing of the Court Jews did revive somewhat during the War of the
Austrian Succession, in the 1740s, but it was never again to attain its
pre-1713 levels. The co-ordinated response to Maria Theresa's expulsion of the Jews from Prague in 1744, and her simultaneous threat to
expel the Jews from Moravia, demonstrates that there was still a
measure of cohesion between the Court Jews of central Europe and
collaboration between them and the Jewish financiers of Holland and
England.[15] But leading Jews were now involving themselves less
closely in Jewish community affairs and, increasingly, there was a
drift away from relying on other Jews as associates, correspondents,
and factors. This loosening of seventeenth-century patterns is particularly noticeable among the Sephardim, who, in most cases, now

[13] Rosenthal, 'Aus den Jugendjahren', pp. 207–8.
[14] Valentin, *Judarnas historia*, pp. 121–7; Barnett, 'Correspondence', pp. 22–3.
[15] Mevorah, 'Jewish Diplomatic Activities', pp. 146–51; the Court Jews arranged
protests against the Empress's policy from the Dutch government, the kings of
England, Denmark, and Poland, the Sultan, the Senates of Hamburg and Venice, and
the Archbishop of Mainz.

lost their former zeal for community service. After 1713, it became increasingly common in the Portuguese community in Amsterdam for members of leading families elected to the *Mahamad* to refuse office.[16] This loosening of ties with the community, and with tradition, is clearly discernible also in England. The withdrawal of the Marrano financier Joseph da Costa Villareal from the London Sephardi community and his cancelling of his project to bequeath large sums to Jewish charities was only one of a series of dramatic defections. The Jewish ties of Samson Gideon (1699–1762), the most important Jewish financier in mid-eighteenth-century England, had ceased to mean much, even with regard to his business, long before he formally withdrew from the synagogue in 1753.[17] Gideon's ambition, like that of increasing numbers of Jews of his generation, was not for Jewish status but for standing in Gentile society. He married a Protestant Englishwoman and had his children baptized into the Anglican Church. Even so he himself was repeatedly refused a title, despite major services to the English Crown, though finally, in 1759, he did obtain a baronetcy for his eldest son.

At Vienna, no one figure inherited the position of Samson Wertheimer, but even in peacetime, the court needed the services of Jewish bankers, purveyors, and agents, not least to supply their snuff, tea, coffee, confectionery, and jewellery, and a mixed bag of Court Jews evolved which was partly traditional in life-style and partly of a new type. Bernard Gabriel Eskeles (1692–1753), son of the *landesrab-biner* of Moravia, was a highly learned and strictly orthodox Jew, as well as being a court supplier and munitions dealer. His ambition was definitely backward-looking. In 1725, he succeeded to Wertheimer's former title of 'Chief Rabbi of Hungary'. The next generation of Eskeles, by contrast, were altogether more assimilated, indeed fashionable courtiers. Emmanuel, son of Samuel Oppenheimer, was an early representative of the clean-shaven, fashionably dressed fraternity.[18] However, another leading Viennese dynasty, that established by Isaac Aaron Arnstein, who hailed from Arnstein near Würzburg, and his son, Adam Isaac Arnstein (1721–85), remained bulwarks of conservatism, retaining their beards and a modest black attire down to, and beyond, the middle of the century.[19] Another of the clean-shaven was Moseh Lopes Pereira (Diego d'Aguilar)

---

[16] GAA PJG 334, 'Taboa dos ssres que servirão cargos neste Kaal Kados'.
[17] Sutherland, 'Samson Gideon', p. 85.
[18] Stern, *Jud Süß*, p. 18.   [19] Spiel, *Fanny von Arnstein*, pp. 71–2.

(*c*.1699–1759), one of the Marranos who fled Spain in the 1720s. After settling in Vienna, Pereira leased the Austrian state tobacco monopoly from the government in the years 1723–39 at a price of seven million florins yearly; meanwhile, a London Sephardi firm, in which he was a partner, regularly imported large amounts of bullion from Spain and Portugal into England. His role in raising Anglo-Dutch loans for the Austrian treasury, in the 1740s, afforded him a certain leverage even with the arch-bigot Maria Theresa and he was at the centre of the efforts to block the expulsion from Prague. In 1749, however, the Empress co-operated with moves to extradite him to Spain, to face trial by the Inquisition as a lapsed Spanish Catholic. He promptly abandoned Vienna and retired to London giving up his involvement in state finance for a notoriously miserly life of leisure.

The most courtly Court Jew of the early eighteenth century, and a figure decidedly representative of the trend away from traditional Jewish values and culture, was Joseph Süss Oppenheimer (1699–1738), whose father, a relative of Samuel Oppenheimer, had been a *Hoffaktor* of the Palatinate, at Heidelberg. 'Jud Süss', as he became known, combined a successful business, which he established at Frankfurt, with a sophisticated knowledge of the state finances of Austria and the Palatinate. In 1732 he was appointed court 'agent' of the duke of Württemberg, swiftly rising to become a Württemberg state councillor and then, in 1734, being placed virtually in charge of the finances and economic policy of the duke. He was placed in this unprecedented position by the Catholic Duke Karl Alexander, a confirmed absolutist, as well as a foreigner, profoundly at odds with the mass of his Lutheran subjects. While serving the court as an official, Oppenheimer still continued his business, both in Frankfurt and Stuttgart where he concentrated on supplying the court with jewellery. His life-style and attitudes mirrored the rapidly changing outlook of the European Jewish élite.[20] A deist who did not trouble to conform to the more onerous demands of his faith, he dressed as a nobleman and was accustomed to have non-noble Christians rise to their feet in his presence. His library consisted almost entirely of German works on politics, history, and law. His two residences, at Frankfurt and Stuttgart, were crammed with paintings, mainly Flemish and Dutch, including a Rembrandt, several copies of Rembrandts and four van der Velde seascapes. He pursued women with zest, bedding an impressive number of both noble ladies and

[20] Stern, *Jud Süß*, pp. 130–7, 293–6.

servant-girls. But he never sought to conceal or deny his Jewishness and in certain situations enjoyed dramatizing the fact of his Jewish allegiance. In fact, he was a complex double-being, the courtier in him coexisting uneasily with his Jewish background. He was well aware that his polished manners and elegant attire both smoothed his path and added to his enemies. When Duke Karl Alexander suddenly died, in 1737, Oppenheimer was arrested and tried for collusion in subverting the constitutions of the state. Condemned and sentenced to death, he was beheaded before a jeering crowd of thousands.

While some German Court Jews were becoming more aristocratic in life-style and less observant Jews, the waning prestige of their Sephardi counterparts was mirrored in the lapsing of their diplomatic agencies. By the 1690s, there were no longer any Jewish agents of major courts at Hamburg. While Manoel Teixeira was provisionally appointed Danish 'resident' at Hamburg, in 1697, the Senate, under heavy pressure from the populace, refused to recognize him as such.[21] The Amsterdam agencies of Spain and Portugal were transferred from Jewish hands, seemingly as a result of the anti-Semitic outburst in the Peninsula of the 1720s. Manuel de Belmonte was succeeded as Spain's 'resident' in Amsterdam, by a nephew, Baron Francisco de Ximenes Belmonte, who held the agency in the years 1706–13;[22] his successor, Manuel Levi Ximenes, was the last of the series. Around 1725, a Catholic Spaniard was appointed to the post and from then on Jews were rigorously debarred. The agency for the crown of Portugal remained in the hands of the Nunes da Costa, down to the death of Jerónimo's youngest son, Álvaro, in 1737. Ministers in Lisbon then refused to transfer the title to the latter's heir on the grounds that he was 'a Jew'. From then on, Jews were excluded from that post too.

In the economic sphere, the Portuguese community of Amsterdam did not decline as seriously, or as rapidly, as the Sephardi communities of Hamburg and Venice, but there too stagnation and loss of dynamism were unmistakable. By 1750, the wealthy Portuguese Jews in Holland were mainly leisured *rentiers* who participated less and less in active trade, enjoying a luxurious existence on the interest of their accumulated investments in the Dutch colonial companies and an assortment of Dutch, English, and Venetian public funds. One should not exaggerate the falling-off in their business activity. While their links with Portugal were now greatly reduced, owing to the

[21] Schudt, *Jüdischer Merckwürdigkeiten*, iv. 58; Kellenbenz, *Sephardim*, p. 394.
[22] Schutte, *Repertorium*, p. 611.

virtual extirpation of the Marrano business class in Lisbon and Oporto, in the 1720s and 1730s, and their trade with Italy and the Levant also much diminished, they continued to ship goods to Cadiz for re-export to the Spanish Indies on an appreciable scale and maintained a lively trade with the Caribbean, at least with the Dutch colonies, down to the 1780s. Still, in general terms, the picture was one of slow eclipse.

In Germany, Jewish commerce little by little lost its former centrality in the economic life of the country. It is true that the marked falling-off in the number of Jewish merchants attending the Leipzig fairs after 1710 was largely compensated for by an increasing attendance at the fairs at Frankfurt an der Oder and that the German–Polish transit trade remained buoyant.[23] Poland still sucked in an abundance of manufactures and luxuries, despite the progressive impoverishment of the Polish nobility, stripped of much of their grain business; and Polish raw materials—wool, flax, and leather—were still much in demand, indeed more so, in Silesia and Brandenburg. But the new phase in Prussian mercantilism, after 1720, with the ban on wool and other raw material exports, heavy duties on non-raw-material imports, and an increasing emphasis on stimulating home manufactures (an industrial mercantilism imitated, from the 1720s, by Württemberg and other states), now played havoc with traditional patterns of trade. The prosperity of Hamburg, Frankfurt, and Mannheim Jewry, and to some extent that of all German Jewry, depended essentially on imports from, and through, Holland and England. And it was precisely Dutch cloth and other Dutch manufactures, which figured large in German Jewish trade, which were now hardest hit by the new economic strategy.

This is not to say that Germany as a market suddenly broke free of dependence on the more developed western economies, or that the position of Hamburg, Frankfurt, and Mannheim Jewry was completely undermined. Germany continued to be supplied with sugar, tobacco, tea, coffee, and a host of other colonial goods through London and Amsterdam, and Jewish merchants remained prominent in such trade. But in place of the vigorous growth of the late seventeenth century, there was now stagnation and this, combined with the eclipse of Jewish army provisioning, tended to narrow the commercial base of German Jewry at a time when numbers were increasing. Despite the fact that nearly all the increase in the size of

[23] Freudenthal, *Leipziger Meßgäste*, pp. 14–15; Stern, *Preußischer Staat*, II/i. 72.

the German Jewish population was sucked out of the main centres, as much by lack of opportunities as by government restrictions, a steadily growing proportion of German Jewry was pressed down into destitution, vagrancy, and begging.[24] In Frankfurt, though there was no increase in the number of Jews between 1713 and 1750, the number receiving charity, and too poor to pay taxes, steadily mounted. The position was much the same, or worse, among both the Ashkenazi and Sephardi Jews in Holland. The Dutch Sephardi *philosophe* and deist Isaac de Pinto calculated that, in the quarter of a century down to 1743, the number of impoverished Portuguese families on poor relief in Amsterdam quadrupled from 115 to 415, amounting by the 1740s to 40 per cent of the community.[25] And the position was scarcely better among the Ashkenazim whether in Amsterdam or elsewhere. In response to the crisis, there was a definite tendency on the part of the Jewish wealthy, especially in Brandenburg-Prussia and in Italy, to transfer capital from trade into industry. Unlike Jewish élites of the seventeenth century, the upper crust of Berlin Jewry, during the middle decades of the eighteenth century, consisted not of merchants and financiers but of financiers and industrialists, especially silk-manufacturers.[26] But whereas the Jewish crafts of seventeenth-century Amsterdam, Prague, Cracow, and Rome were all-Jewish as regards capital and work-force, hardly any of the workers in the factories of the Berlin Jewish manufacturers were Jews, owing to tough government regulations and restrictions favouring Christians.

More pronounced than either Jewish economic or demographic decline in the eighteenth century was the gradual dissolution of traditional communal structures and authority, and with it, the virtual disintegration of early modern Jewish culture. Historians have postulated various explanations for the 'crisis of authority' experienced throughout European Jewry in the eighteenth century;[27] but what, ultimately, these boil down to is that the whole intellectual and cultural outlook of Enlightenment Europe was totally at odds

---

[24] Kracauer, *Juden in Frankfurt*, ii. 145, 295–301; Evers, *Juden in Warburg*, p. 67.

[25] Mendes dos Remédios, *Judeus portugueses*, pp. 46–8; in 1738, the city of Leeuwarden raised the question of the increasing number of Jewish poor in Friesland in the provincial estates; in 1754, 48 out of 140 Jews in Leeuwarden, or more than a third of the community, were on the communal poor list and in receipt of charity: see Beem, *Joden van Leeuwarden*, pp. 14–15.

[26] Stern, *Preußischer Staat*, II/i. 89–97.

[27] Abramsky, 'Crisis of Authority', pp. 13–15.

with the essentials of Jewish tradition. It is not simply that one or two leading *philosophes*, notably Voltaire, were themselves anti-Semitic and identified Jewish 'superstition' as being of the root and essence of the priestly obscurantism they so passionately desired to sweep away. With very few exceptions, the dismissing of Jewish erudition and observance as archaic, obscurantist, and barbaric was part and parcel of the Enlightenment itself. English, French, and German deists alike reacted strongly against the philosemitic Biblicism of the preceding century. Even publicists such as John Toland, generally categorized as philosemites on account of their defence of Jewish rights and liberties, invariably disdained Jewish learning and post-biblical literature as something 'useless' and derelict. And this prevailing attitude of mind was absorbed not only by the odd Court Jew such as Joseph Süss Oppenheimer, or by an occasional Sephardi sophisticate such as Isaac de Pinto, but by the ordinary western Jew in the street. A high rate of conversion to Christianity during the eighteenth century may have been more typical of Italian and western Sephardi than of German or Bohemian Jewry, but the conventional Ashkenazi middle-class Jew of the mid-eighteenth century frequently combined a loyal adherence to Jewish ritual and dietary observance with a sarcastic contempt for rabbis and traditional Jewish learning.[28] The prevailing characteristic of later modern German Jewish history, from the second half of the eighteenth century onwards, was the almost total rejection, even on the part of observant Jews, of their own traditions and values.[29]

The collapse of Jewish political and institutional autonomy in eighteenth-century Europe was a virtually universal phenomenon. It affected Sephardim and Ashkenazim, east and west, more or less simultaneously. This process is perhaps best understood as the outcome both of creeping inner decay, arising from profound changes in culture and outlook, and of the progressive secularization and centralization of the European state itself. The waning of the chief communities of Poland and Lithuania not only reflected the general economic malaise but greatly contributed to the increasing disruption of the traditional institutions of Polish-Lithuanian Jewry. Reflecting the demographic shift away from the main communities, the latter now lost their grip over the proliferating number of small communities which not infrequently took to resorting to the protection of local

---

[28] Yogev, *Diamonds and Coral*, pp. 267–8.
[29] Scholem, *Jews and Judaism in Crisis*, pp. 74–7.

nobles in challenging the supremacy of the major *kehillot*. Another factor which helped undermine the viability of the *kehillot* was the mounting burden of indebtedness to which the principal and many lesser communities became subject due to the increasing numbers of impoverished claiming relief. Nor was the primacy of the old-established élite families so readily accepted by the mass of the Polish Jewish population in the eighteenth century as had been the case previously. Numerous damaging disputes erupted, especially between the governing boards and the Jewish guilds. Eventually, in 1764, after decades of decline, both Polish Jewry's Council of the Four Lands and the Council of Lithuanian Jewry, were suppressed under a decree of the Polish Sejm forbidding the convening of such Jewish general assemblies in future. The final elimination of Jewish self-government in Poland-Lithuania took place under Russian, Austrian, and Prussian occupation, following the successive partitions of Poland. This began with the abolition of the *kehillah* as a secular institution in the eastern parts of the Polish Monarchy which came under Russian rule as a result of the first partition of Poland. Under Catherine II's municipal reforms of 1775–9, the Jews of these regions, principally White Russia, were legally released from the fiscal and juridical jurisdiction of the Jewish communities.

Within the Austrian empire, which, as a result of the first partition of Poland in 1772, included Lvov and a large part of Galicia, the parallel to Catherine II's emasculation of the *kehillot* on the eastern fringes of old Poland was the reforms of Joseph II. This Emperor, in conformity with the 'enlightened' ideas of his age, wished to remove the prejudice and discrimination which had traditionally segregated his Jewish from his non-Jewish subjects. His prime object was to render the Jews 'useful' citizens of the state. To do this, he believed, it was necessary to dismantle the intricate network of institutions which seemed primarily responsible for imparting a distinct national character to the Jews of his empire. Integrating the Jews into Austrian society, education, and the army meant sweeping away Jewish self-rule and the autonomy of Jewish society. This was accomplished in stages, beginning with the removal of the fiscal powers of the Jewish community organizations. Finally, under decrees of 1785 and 1788, the *Landjudenschaften* and juridical autonomy of the communities of Bohemia and Moravia were abolished.

In western and central Europe there was no sudden dissolution or removal of the institutions of Jewish self-rule before the French

Revolution. What there was was an inexorable process of slow decay, a loss of grip over the basic mechanisms of Jewish life resulting from an irreversible loss of prestige and standing on the part of *parnasim* and rabbis alike. All this was fully evident well before 1750 in the German as well as the western Sephardi communities. If the European Enlightenment and its later offshoot, the ideology of the French Revolution, proclaimed that Jewish tradition and Jewish separateness were obstacles to human progress having neither dignity nor value, rapidly increasing numbers of 'enlightened' western Jews were inclined to agree. The prostration before the intellectual and social ideals of the Enlightenment was complete. The French Revolution, furthermore, went well beyond the Enlightenment in its rejection of Jewish culture and tradition. In the eyes of the revolutionary assembly in Paris, the 'Jews should be denied everything as a nation, but granted everything as individuals'. And this uncompromising style of emancipation, not of a people but of its component individuals, was gratefully accepted by many, or most, Jewish leaders from Berlin and Vienna westwards. Acquiescence in the process of dissolution took a multiplicity of forms. In Bordeaux, in February 1790, the elders of the Sephardi community simply noted, at the conclusion of their minutes, that 'since the Jews of Bordeaux can no longer be considered a national community', the community as a political, judicial, and fiscal body had dissolved itself. But such strokes of the pen were mere belated acknowledgement of what everyone could see: that an era of Jewish life and experience was at an end.

XI

Conclusion

No doubt not a few readers will be somewhat bemused, if not shocked, to find the eighteenth century in European Jewish history characterized as an epoch of 'decline'. The whole weight of traditional historiography seems to lean heavily against such a designation. We are so used to thinking of Jewish integration into modern western civilization as an accelerating process, fed by the increasingly secular tone, tolerant atmosphere, and vibrant economic life which we all tend to associate with the eighteenth century that to speak of the 'decline' of European Jewry in the era of Enlightenment seems a virtual contradiction in terms. One contemporary historian who did give a new twist to traditional views on the subject, Ellis Rivkin, shifted the emphasis in his analysis from 'liberating ideas' which most previous scholars identified as the crucial factor, to the beneficial impact of what he calls 'developing capitalism'; but he too still saw the eighteenth century, a period of accelerating economic growth in the west, as an era which immeasurably strengthened the position of European Jewry. Rather than growing freedom of expression and toleration of their religion, Rivkin stressed increasing freedom of economic opportunity and movement. And while not everyone will be willing to accept that 'developing capitalism is the prime factor in the liberation and emancipation of the Jews',[1] few will dispute that intellectual developments do indeed have to be looked at in their economic context. But the basic question remains: taking all the new eighteenth-century freedoms together, intellectual and economic, is it true that these nourished and enhanced the Jewish role in the west? The answer, I believe, at any rate as regards Europe before 1800, is no.

In fact, much of the evidence for decline is well known to scholars, but the indications for the various parts of Europe are rarely brought together and looked at *in toto*. The economic deterioration of whole networks of Jewish communities during the Age of Enlightenment and of the early, pre-1800 Industrial Revolution, accompanied by the

---

[1] Rivkin, *The Shaping of Jewish History*, p. 160.

pauperization of the Jewish masses, is obvious enough in specific instances, being well known, for instance, to specialists in Dutch, German, Italian, and Polish Jewish history. Yet there has long been a curious reticence, or unwillingness, to gather the strands together and draw conclusions about the overall situation. Could it be that the facts simply do not fit in with the entrenched assumptions and prejudices of nineteenth- and early twentieth-century Jewish historiography, infused as it is with a powerful, at times excessive, reverence for the forms and processes of political and legal emancipation? It is hard to deny, in any case, that what was an age of tremendous economic vitality and increasing opportunity was, generally speaking, for the Jews an era of stagnation, decay, and impoverishment, both economic and cultural.

It is of course perfectly true that, as a specifically Jewish intellectual movement, expressed in Hebrew and Yiddish, the Enlightenment, or *Haskalah*, surfaced only very late in the eighteenth century and at the beginning of the nineteenth. The founding father of this movement, Moses Mendelssohn (1729–96), was steeped to an altogether exceptional, almost unique degree, in both traditional Jewish learning and the new culture of the Enlightenment and strove with all his being to find a viable basis for contact and reconciliation between the two. A passionate defender of Judaism against the sneering denigration of the *philosophes*, a man who adhered strictly to at least the essentials of Jewish observance in his personal life, Mendelssohn was also highly critical of many aspects of traditional Jewish society, education, and community regulation and became, among the Jews, a highly controversial as well as an admired figure. Yet for all his achievements, and he was a central figure of the German Enlightenment, it has to be said that in the essential task of mediation and reconciliation which he set himself he totally failed. Even within his own circle and family there took place, soon after his death, a rapid drift into complete assimilation and conversion to Christianity. It is not surprising, therefore, that those who have tended to look with disfavour upon the prevalent trends towards denationalization and assimilation among the mass of Jews, through the nineteenth and early part of the twentieth century had often found little good to say of Mendelssohn. But from a historical point of view much of the controversy about Mendelssohn and the *Haskalah* rests on a fallacy. For it is certainly wide of the mark to imagine that European Jewish society was only marginally infiltrated by the Enlightenment until towards the end of the eighteenth century. Long before Mendelssohn, the drift away from traditional Judaism was already a mass movement.

Large-scale defections from the restraints of Jewish communal life began with the collapse of the Shabbatean movement, in 1666, which led to thousands of conversions in Italy, Germany and elsewhere, not to any sincere Christianity but simply away from a derided and seemingly discredited Judaism. From the end of the seventeenth century onwards withdrawal from the Synagogue, usually accompanied by conversion to one or another form of Christianity, was visibly sapping the demographic strength of many western communities. And among those who did not convert, or had not yet converted, large numbers went over to deistic beliefs and a less and less observant life-style, whether leading intellectuals, such as Isaac de Pinto, Court Jews such as Jud Süss, great financiers such as Samson Gideon, or simply those ordinary Ashkenazi businessmen of Metz who by 1740 had shaved off their beards, taken to dressing like fashionable Frenchmen, and become publicly casual about their drinking habits and attentiveness to women.[2] By the early eighteenth century, as we see from the revision of the Ashkenazi statute-book of the three communities of Altona, Hamburg, and Wandsbek, in 1725, the rabbis themselves were sanctioning a certain liberalization of life-style by way of adapting to fast-changing circumstances. Among other points, the ban on visiting Hamburg's theatres and opera-house was lifted.[3] But such marginal concessions as traditional Judaism could countenance were not enough to stem the tide. Even the conventional German Jew who went regularly to *shul* and ate only kosher meat now took less and less notice of communal regulations and laughed at rabbinical pretensions to scholarship. And among intellects such as Isaac de Pinto, a man proud of his Sephardi descent and disdainful of Christianity, the signs of decay of Jewish culture are all too evident. In his varous writings, de Pinto virtually never refers to the Bible, Talmud, or any part of rabbinic literature, concurring in the general judgement of his time that Jewish books contained nothing useful to the needs of 'enlightened', eighteenth-century man. And then again, as we see from his vehement rebuttal of Voltaire's attack on the Jews, which he published in 1762, de Pinto, instead of defending the honour, worth, and standing of all Jews, as Simone Luzzatto, Menasseh ben Israel, Isaac Cardoso, and Daniel Levi de

---

[2] Hertzberg, *French Enlightenment*, p. 164.
[3] Graupe, *Statuten der drei Gemeinden*, i. 86–7.

Barrios had been at pains to do, during the seventeenth century, concedes that only the westernized, beardless, Portuguese Jews were worthy of respect and that the rest, the mass of Ashkenazi Jewry, were indeed lamentably lacking in refinement, culture, and intellect, though he is careful to attribute their defects to a persecuting, oppressive, Christian society rather than to any intrinsic short-comings of the Jews themselves. Some of his remarks suggest that de Pinto continued to adhere to the Jewish community chiefly out of his sense of honour.

It is impossible to doubt the collapse of Jewish political autonomy in the eighteenth century but this, it would seem, has rarely been regretted either at the time or among modern historians. And yet there is something inherently paradoxical in this situation. It is curious that in an age such as our own which has witnessed the rise of organized political Zionism, so little sympathy should be shown to the forms and procedures of early modern Jewish self-government. It may be that Jewish self-rule was oligarchic and that its zeal for regulating life-style ill accords with twentieth-century ideas on per-sonal freedom. It is also true that early modern Jewish autonomy was partly a product of enforced segregation and the fiscal convenience of the state. But the positive side of its influence deserves attention also. While conferring a tightly cohesive social system and an obligatory life-style, unequivocally based on rabbinic law and tradition, Jewish self-rule also created one of the most remarkable and elaborate educational and welfare systems of early modern Europe and a richer, more varied Jewish culture than had existed previously. It also assisted the involvement of the Jewish leadership in state finance, army contracting, and state regulation of international trade. Nor should we forget the central role of the European community network in raising resources for the upkeep of a grouping of Jewish communi-ties in the Holy Land at a time when the Jewish minority in Palestine was facing great economic hardship and was incapable of sustaining itself. If, indeed, European Jewry was (in a purely secular sense) relatively more important, and commanded relatively greater resources, in the period 1570–1713 than either for some time before or subsequently, then assuredly the new and extensive network of Jewish community government was one of the prime factors which accounts for this.

But what precisely was the significance of the Jews in seventeenth-century Europe? It is not easy to arrive at a succinct but comprehensive formulation and not many attempts at this have been made. It is clear enough, though, that their general significance has to be appraised under two heads—the economic and the cultural. The problem is to identify the exact nature of their role. It would be quite wrong, it is now clear, to suggest that they introduced any economic innovations, let alone lent any novel or special impetus to the progress of capitalism as Sombart believed. The techniques of Jewish trade, finance, and industry differed not a jot from other trade, finance and industry except in that an oppressive stystem of state, municipal, and guild restrictions cut the Jews out of much, or most, retail trade and most crafts. What made the Jews important, given that in the fifteenth and early sixteenth century their role, everywhere west of Poland, had become more and more marginal, was the simultaneous penetration, from the end of the sixteenth century, on the part of both Ashkenazi and Sephardi Jews, as well as of Portuguese Marranos, into several crucial east–west transit, colonial, and precious-metal trades. This simultaneous penetration, linking the Spanish and Portuguese colonial empires with the trade routes of Germany, Poland, and the Levant, combined with the uniquely close interaction between the Jewish communities scattered across Europe and the Near East, provided them with the means to circulate precious metals and loans internationally more quickly and efficiently than any other network or grouping. If one or two other groups, such as the Genoese bankers and their factors, could muster greater financial power than the Jews on a localized basis, in that case the western Mediterrancan, no other grouping could match the Jews in the vast scope and range of their operations. And this at a time of empty, over-stretched state treasuries was bound to become a major factor in all European statecraft and army upkeep from Portugal to Poland and from Ireland to Hungary. This does not mean that the Jews necessarily possessed a large part of Europe's capital resources. It means only that they were uniquely well placed to control precious metal circulation in central and eastern Europe, to influence the flow of both gold and silver in and out of Holland—Europe's financial as well as commercial entrepôt—and to transfer capital from one part of Europe to another. The great Jewish financiers and contractors, Ashkenazim such as Samuel Oppenheimer and Samson Wertheimer, as well as Sephardim such as Antonio Lopes Suasso and Diogo Teixeira, were what they were, key intermediaries in the contest of states, only because they could draw on the assistance and resources of a host of money-changers, metal-dealers, colonial wholesale merchants and brokers who, in turn, depended on droves of poor Jewish pedlars and hawkers whose activity, despite their modest means and often unkempt, outlandish appearance, nevertheless had a decisive influence on the circulation of gold and silver not only between different parts of Germany, Austria, and Hungary but also in and out of Holland.[4] And if the Jewish leadership could offer financial services of a kind that others could not, they were doubly inclined to respond to the pleas of rulers for assistance, having no other means than their financial and commercial power to extract the much needed favours, concessions, and security they lacked.

It was neither an accident, nor some deep and hidden mystery, that Sephardim and Ashkenazim should have gained ground, reached the peak of their importance, and then declined, hand in hand, as it were *pari passu*. For both were interacting with, and responding to, a common set of European circumstances, political, economic, and cultural. Fernand Braudel puts forward the astounding notion that the European Sephardim declined in the later seventeenth century—when in fact they were at their peak—and that there was then a period of 'relative decline for Jewish merchants everywhere' before the rise of the Ashkenazim which, according to him, began in the eighteenth century[5] But then Braudel, on the subject of the Jews (as on so much else), diverges so far from what the data show that we scarcely need apologize for dismissing his remarks, without more ado, as nonsense. The reality could not have been more different from what he claims. Sephardim and Ashkenazim rose and fell together.

But the importance of the Jews in early modern European life is not to be measured solely in terms of their economic role, vital as this was to their position. If, by 1760, even Jewish intellectuals felt impelled to apologize for, and explain away, what they perceived as the cultural backwardness of the mass of their brethren, this was a state of affairs of comparatively recent origin. Part of the price for Jewish self-government, censorship, and the elaborate educational structure European Jewry created in the sixteenth century, and sustained through the seventeenth, was a creeping intellectual paralysis which by 1700 or shortly after had drained the vitality and dynamism of sixteenth- and seventeenth-century Jewish scholarship and creative

---

[4] Attman, *Dutch Enterprise*, p. 38.
[5] Braudel, *Wheels of Commerce*, p. 159.

writing. But less than two centuries separated the universal contempt for Jewish learning prevalent in the mid-eighteenth century from the remark, by one of Europe's foremost scholars at the end of the sixteenth, Joseph Justus Scaliger, that the Jews should be retained in the west not just for economic reasons but because 'we need to learn from them', a point echoed by Grotius. The baroque culture of seventeenth-century Europe was one in which Old Testament imagery, Hebrew language, and post-biblical literature, and the new cabbala emanating from Safed, exerted a profound influence on art, literature, and scholarship, as well as liberal Protestant thought. One has only to recall the impact not just of Old Testament themes, but of rabbinic literature, contemporary Jewish scholarship, and cabbalistic concepts on Scaliger, Grotius, Vieira, Rembrandt, Coccejus, Milton, Newton, Pascal, Racine, and Richard Simon, to name but a few, to see how pervasive this influence was. It is true that Spinoza, a Jewish heretic ejected by his community in Amsterdam, was the only Jewish cultural figure of sufficient stature to stand alongside the great names of Europe's seventeenth century. But Spinoza was a product of a vibrant Jewish cultural and intellectual milieu. The collective impact of the Jews' spiritual and intellectual leaders, men such as Luria, Judah Loew, Herrera, Montalto, Leone Modena, Levi Morteira, Menasseh ben Israel, and Orobio de Castro did leave many traces in the European culture of the age.

Finally, there is the question of what it was that released the Jews into the mainstream of European life suddenly, at the end of the sixteenth century, after centuries of enforced marginality. I have argued that the key factor was not 'developing capitalism' but the weakening of Christian allegiance in the west following the deadlocked Wars of Religion and the rise of *politique* attitudes to statecraft and economics. In other words, the sudden involvement of the Jews in a major and creative way in western civilization must be seen as part and parcel of the simultaneous process of making room, from the end of the sixteenth century, for a proliferating assortment of sceptics, Jehovanists, deists, and other anti-Trinitarians and non-Christians of every hue. It may be that believing Catholics and Protestants cannot, in the nature of things, fully share in the view that the undermining of Christian allegiance was the vital factor in the shift to a freer, more open, and more tolerant Europe during the early modern era. Final agreement, no doubt, is hardly to be expected. Even so, some of the more blatant misconceptions still current on

Jewish-Christian relations in early modern times really should now be thoroughly eradicated. One scholar, in a recent book on the rise of toleration, wrote that Rome under papal government 'allowed complete freedom to its Jewish community', a claim which would be too preposterous to require further comment were it not for the insulting unconcern it shows for the generations who suffered from an oppressive system of restrictions designed to pile the greatest possible discomfort and pressure upon them.

Today probably only a minority of professional historians are believing Christians. Yet there is still, it seems to this writer at any rate, an almost universal disinclination to focus attention on the progressive weakening of Christian belief in early modern times or to consider its consequences and implications. And yet how can it be denied that the progressive undermining of what had once been universally dominant in the west is a historical development of the very first order of importance?

Works Cited

I. PRIMARY PRINTED SOURCES

Aboab, Imanuel, *Nomologia, o discursos legales* (Amsterdam, 1629)

Aveiro, Fray Pantaleão d', *Itinerario da Terra Sancta e todas svas particvlaridades* (Lisbon, 1600)

Barrios, Daniel Levi (Miguel) de, *Triumpho del govierno popular en la Casa de Jacob* (Amsterdam, 1683)

Basnage de Beauval, Jacques, *Histoire des Juifs depuis Jésus-Christ jusqu'à présent*, 12 vols. (The Hague, 1716)

Bayle, Pierre, *Dictionnaire historique et critique*, 4 vols., 5th edn. (Amsterdam, 1740)

Becher, Johann Joachim, *Politische Discvrs von den eigentlichen Ursachen des Auf- und Abnehmens der Städte, Länder und Republicken* (Frankfurt, 1673)

Bodin, Jean, *Discovrs de Iean Bodin svr le rehavssement et diminution des monnoyes, tant d'or que d'argent* (Paris, 1578)

—— *Colloque Heptaplomeres* trans. from Latin and ed. by R. Chauviré (Paris, 1914)

Bondy, G., and Dworsky, F. (eds.), *Zur Geschichte der Juden in Böhmen, Mähren, und Schlesien von 906 bis 1620*, 2 vols. (Prague, 1906)

Briefwechsel der Herzogin Sophie von Hannover mit ihrem Bruder dem Kurfürsten Karl Ludwig von der Pfalz, (ed.) E. Bodemann (Leipzig, 1885)

Broughton, Hugh, *Ovr Lordes Familie, and many other Poinctes depending vpon it, opened against a Iew Rabbi David Farar: who disputed many houres with hope to overthrow the Gospel* (Amsterdam, 1608)

Buchenroeder, M., *Eilende Messias Juden-Post* (Nuremberg, 1666)

Buxtorf, Johannes, *Synagoga Ivdaica. Das ist Jueden Schul* (Basel, 1604)

Cantero Vaca, Pedro, 'Relación de Oran' (*c.*1637), ed. F. Jiménez de Gregorio in *Hispania* xxii (1962)

Cardoso, Isaac, *Las Excelencias de los Hebreos* (Amsterdam, 1679)

Carew, Sir George, *A Relation of the State of Polonia and the United Provinces of that Crowne*, ed. C. H. Talbot (Rome, 1965)

Carpi, Daniel (ed.), *Pinkas Va'ad k.k. Padovah* (The Hebrew Minutes Book of the Council of the Jewish Community of Padua) (Jerusalem, 1973)

Carr, William, *The Travellours Guide and Historian's Faithful Companion* (London, 1691)

Cartas do Padre António Vieira, (ed.) J. Lúcio de Azevedo, 3 vols. (Coimbra, 1925–8)

Child, Sir Josiah, *A New Discourse of Trade* (London, 1692)

Coryat, Thomas, *Coryat's Crudities; Reprinted from the Edition of 1611*, 3 vols. (London, 1776)

Costa, Uriel da, *Exemplar Humanae Vitae* trans. into French with critical introduction by A. B. Duff and P. Kaan (Paris, 1926)

Coxe, William, *Travels into Poland, Russia, Sweden and Denmark* (London, 1784)

Felgenhauer, Paul, *Bonum Nuncium Israeli* (Amsterdam, 1655)

Fleury, Claude, *Les Mœurs de Israelites* (4th edn. The Hague, 1683)

Franco Mendes, David, *Memorias do estabelicimento e progresso dos judeus portuguezes e espanhões nesta famosa citade de Amsterdam* in *SR* ix

Gans, David, *Zemach David* (1593), trans. into German by G. Klemperer (Prague, 1890)

Gomes Solís, Duarte, *Mémoires inédits de Duarte Gomes Solís* (1621), (ed.) L. Bourdon (Lisbon, 1955)

—— *Discursos sobre los comercios de las dos Indias* (1622), (ed.) M. Bensabat Amzalak (Lisbon, 1943)

González de Cellorigo, Martín, *Alegación en que se funda la iusticia y merced que algunos particulares del reyno de Portugal piden a S.M.* (Madrid, 1619)

Graupe, Heinz Mosche (ed.), *Die Statuten der drei Gemeinden Altona, Hamburg und Wandsbek. Quellen zur jüdischen Gemeindeorganisation im 17. und 18. Jahrhundert*, 2 vols. (Hamburg, 1973)

Grotius, Hugo, *De Jure Belli ac Pacis* (Amsterdam, 1631)

—— *Remonstrantie nopende de ordre dije in de landen van Hollandt ende Westvrieslandt dijent gestelt op de Joden* (1614), ed. Jaap Meijer (Amsterdam, 1949)

Halperin, Israel, *Acta Congressus Generalis Judaeorum Regni Poloniae (1580–1764)* (Jerusalem, 1945)

'Hamburg Protokollbuch', 'Aus dem ältesten Protokollbuch der portugiesisch-jüdischen Gemeinde in Hamburg', (ed.) I. Cassuto, in instalments in *JJLG*

Hannover, Nathan Nata, *Yeven Mezula* (1653), trans. into German by S. Kayserling (Hanover, 1863)

'Journal de Joselmann', The Journal of Rabbi Josel of Rosheim, trans. and ed. by J. Kracauer in *REJ* xvi (1888), 84–105

Jüdische Privatbriefe aus dem Jahre 1619, ed. A. Landau and B. Wachstein (Vienna, 1911)

Kaufmann, David (ed.), 'Extraits de l'ancien livre de la communauté de Metz', *REJ* xix (1889), 115–30

Kober, Adolf (ed.) 'Documents selected from the Pinkas of Friedberg', *PAAJR* xvii (1947/8), 19–59

Koen, E. M. (ed.), 'Notarial Records pertaining to the Portuguese Jews in Amsterdam up till 1639', in instalments in *SR*

La Peyrère, Isaac de, *Du Rappel des Juifs* (n.p., 1643)

—— *Praeadamitae* (Amsterdam, 1655)

Le Clerc, Jean, *Sentimens de quelques théologiens de Hollande sur l'histoire critique du Vieux Testament composée par le P. Richard Simon* (Amsterdam, 1685)

Le Clerc [*cont.*], *Bibliothèque universelle et historique de l'année 1687* (n.p. 1687)

Lettres, instructions et mémoires de Colbert, (ed.) P. Clement, 10 vols. (Paris, 1861–2)

Libro de los Acuerdos: Being the Records . . . of the Spanish and Portuguese Synagogue of London, 1663–1681, (ed.) L. D. Barnett (Oxford, 1931)

The Life of Glückel of Hameln, 1646–1724, trans. and ed. B. Z. Abrahams (London, 1962)

Limborch, Philip van, *De Veritate religionis Christianae amica collatio cum erudito Judaeo* (Gouda, 1687)

Livro de Bet Haim do Kahal Kados de Bet Yahacob, (ed.) W. C. Pieterse (Assen, 1970)

Luther, Martin, *Von den Juden und iren Luegen* (Wittenberg, 1543)

Luzzatto, Simone, *Discorso circa il stato de gl'hebrei et in particolar dimoranti nell'inclita città di Venetia* (Venice, 1638)

Mémoires du Maréchal de Bassompierre, 4 vols. (Amsterdam, 1723)

Menasseh ben Israel, *The Humble Addresses*, reprinted in L. Wolf, *Menasseh ben Israel's Mission to Oliver Cromwell* (London, 1901)

—— *Mikveh Israel. Esto es, Esperança de Israel* (Amsterdam, 1650)

Modena, Leone, *Historia di gli riti hebraici* (Paris, 1637)

Montalto, Eliahu, 'Quatre Lettres d'Elie de Montalto. Contribution à l'histoire des Marranes', (ed.) C. Roth, *REJ* lxxxvii (1929), 137–65

Montchrétien, Antoine de, *Traicté de l'Œconomie Politique* (1615) (Paris, 1889)

Morosini, Giulio, *Via della Fede mostrato a' gli Ebrei*, 3 vols. (Rome, 1683)

Müller, Johannes, *Judaismus oder Judenthumb, das ist ausfürhrlicher Bericht von des jüdischen Volckes Unglauben* (Hamburg, 1644)

Nahon, Gérard (ed.) *Les 'nations' juives portugaises du Sud-Ouest de la France (1684–1781), Documents* (Paris, 1981)

Nieto, David, *De La Divina Providencia* (1704; 2nd edn., London, 1716)

Orobio de Castro, Isaac (Baltasar), *Carta al hijo de el Doctor Prado*, printed in I. S. Revah, *Spinoza et le Dr Juan de Prado* (Paris–The Hague, 1959)

Pascal, Blaise, *Pensées*, ed. M. L. Brunschvicg and C. M. des Granges (Paris, 1961)

Pinto, Isaac de, *et al. Lettres de quelques Juifs portugais et allemands à M. de Voltaire* (2 vols. Paris, 1772)

Plessis-Mornay, Philippe du, *Advertissement avx Ivifs svr la venve dv Messie* (Saumur, 1607)

Pribram, A. F., *Urkunden und Akten zur Geschichte der Juden in Wien* (Vienna, 1918)

Report of the Commissioners for Taking, Examining, and Stating, the Publick Accounts of the Kingdom with the Depositions at Large of Sir Solomon Medina, Kt., John Montgomery, Esq., and Captain William Preston (London, 1711)

Schudt, Johann Jakob, *Jüdische Merkwürdigkeiten*, 4 vols. (Frankfurt, 1714–18)

Simonsohn, Shlomo (ed.), *The Jews in the Duchy of Milan. Documents*, 3 vols. (Jerusalem, 1982)

Spinoza, Baruch de, *Tractatus Theologico-Politicus*, trans. and ed. by R. H. M. Elwes in *Works of Spinoza* (New York, 1951)

Toaff, R. (ed.), 'Il "Libro Nuovo" di statuti della nazione ebrea di Pisa (1637)', in *Scritti sull'ebraismo in memoria di Guido Bedarida* (Florence, 1966)

Toland, John, *Christianity not Mysterious* (London, 1696)

—— *Letters to Serena* (London, 1704)

Travels of Moses Cassuto, The, extracts ed. by Richard Barnett in *Remember the Days. Essays on Anglo-Jewish History presented to Cecil Roth*, ed. J. M. Shaftesley (London, 1966), 73–121

Ulrich, J. C., *Sammlung jüdischer Geschichten welche sich mit diesem Volk in dem XIII und folgenden Jahrhunderten bis auf MDCCLX in der Schweiz von Zeit zu Zeit zugetragen* (Basel, 1768; repr. 1969)

Usque, Samuel, *Consolaçam as tribulaçoens de Israel*, 3 vols. (Coimbra, 1906–7)

Vieira, António, *Obras Escolhidas*, ed. A. Sergio and H. Cidade, 12 vols. (Lisbon, 1951–4)

Wachstein, B., *Urkunden und Akten zur Geschichte der Juden in Eisenstadt und die Siebengemeinden* (Vienna–Leipzig, 1926)

Wachter, Johann Georg, *Der Spinozismus im Jüdenthumb* (Amsterdam, 1699)

Wagenseil, Johann Christoph, *Tela Ignea Satanae* (Altdorf, 1681)

—— *Belehrung der jüdisch-teutschen Red- und Schreibart* (Koenigsberg, 1699)

—— *Der Jüden Glaube und Aberglaube* (Leipzig, 1705)

Weensche Gezantschapsberichten van 1670 tot 1720, ed. G. von Antal and J. C. H. de Pater, 2 vols. (The Hague, 1929–34)

Zorattini, Pier Cesare Ioly (ed.), *Processi del S. Uffizio di Venezia contro ebrei e giudaizzanti (1548–1560)* (Florence, 1980)

2. SECONDARY WORKS

Abramsky, Chimen, 'The Crisis of Authority within European Jewry in the Eighteenth Century', *Studies in Jewish Religion and Intellectual History Presented to Alexander Altmann*, ed. S. Stein and R. Loewe (Alabama, 1979)

Ackermann, A. *Geschichte der Juden in Brandenburg an der Havel* (Berlin, 1906)

Adler, Israel, *La Pratique musicale savante dans quelques communautés juives en Europe aux XVIIᵉ siècles* (Paris, 1966)

—— *Musical Life and Traditions of the Portuguese Jewish Community of Amsterdam in the Eighteenth Century* (Jerusalem, 1974)

Agt, J. J. F. W. van, 'De Joodse gemeente van Nijmegen en de 18e eeuwse synagoge in de Nonnenstraat', *SR* iii (1969), 168–92

Alcalá-Zamora y Queipo de Llano, José, *España, Flandes y el mar del Norte (1618–39)* (Barcelona, 1975)

Altmann, Alexander, 'Eternality of Punishment: a theological controversy within the Amsterdam rabbinate in the thirties of the seventeenth century', *PAAJR* xi (1972), 1–88

—— *Moses Mendelssohn. A Biographical Study* (London, 1973)

Anfossi, M. D., *Gli ebrei in Piemonte* (Turin, 1914)

Angel, M. D., *The Jews of Rhodes. The History of a Sephardic Community* (New York, 1978)

Angelini, W., *Gli ebrei di Ferrara nel settecento* (Urbino, 1973)

Anklam, K., *Die Judengemeinde in Aurich* (Frankfurt, 1927)

Arendt, Hannah, *Rahel Varnhagen. The Life of a Jewess* (London, 1957)

Arnheim, A., 'German Court Jews and Denmark during the Great Northern War', *Scandinavian Economic History Review* xiv (1966), 117–33

Arnold, Hermann, *Von der Juden in der Pfalz* (Speyer, 1967)

Asaria, Zvi, *Die Juden in Niedersachsen von den ältesten Zeiten bis zur Gegenwart* (Leer, East-Friesland, 1979)

Attman, A., *Dutch Enterprise in the World Bullion Trade, 1550–1800* (Gothenburg, 1983)

Azevedo, João Lúcio de, *História de António Vieira*, 2 vols. (Lisbon, 1918–21)

—— *História dos cristãos-novos portugueses* (2nd ed. Lisbon, 1975)

Baasch, Ernst, 'Die Juden und der Handel in Lübeck', *VSW* xvi (1922), 370–98

Baer, Fritz (Yitzhak), *Das Protokollbuch der Landjudenschaft des Herzogtums Kleve* (Berlin, 1936)

Bałaban, Meir, 'Die Krakauer Judengemeinde-Ordnung von 1595 und ihre Nachträge', *JJLG* x (1913), 296–308

—— *Die Judenstadt von Lublin* (Berlin, 1919)

—— *Studja Historyczne* (Warsaw, 1927)

—— *Historja Żydow w Krakowie i na Kazimierzu, 1304–1868*, 2 vols. (Cracow, 1931–6)

Balletti, A., *Gli ebrei e gli Estensi* (Modena, 1913)

Balslev, B., *De danske jøders historie* (Copenhagen, 1932)

Barnett, Richard, 'The Correspondence of the *Mahamad* of the Spanish and Portuguese Congregation of London during the 17th and 18th Centuries', *TJHSE* xx (1964)

Baron, Salo W., *A Social and Religious History of the Jews*, 18 vols. thus far (Philadelphia, 1957–)

Barzilay, Isaac E., 'The Italian and Berlin Haskalah', *PAAJR* xxix (1960/1) 17–54

—— *Between Reason and Faith. Anti-Rationalism in Italian Jewish Thought, 1250–1650* (The Hague, 1967)

—— *Yoseph Shlomo Delmedigo (Yashar of Candia). His Life, Works and Times* (Leiden, 1974)

Baxter, C. R., 'Jean Bodin's Daemon and his Conversion to Judaism', *Jean Bodin. Verhandlungen der internationalen Bodin Tagung in München* ed. H. Denzer (Munich, 1973)

Beem, H., *De Joden van Leeuwarden*, 2 vols. (Assen, 1974)

Beinart, Haim, 'La venuta degli ebrei nel Ducato di Savoia e il privilegio del 1572' (Hebrew with Italian appendices) in *Scritti in memoria di Leone*

Carpi: saggi sull'ebraismo italiano, ed. D. Carpi *et al.* (Jerusalem, 1967), 72–119

Bencionas Teimanas, D., *L'Autonomie des communautés juives en Pologne aux XVIe et XVIIe siècles* (Paris, 1933)

Ben-Sasson, Haim Hillel, 'The Reformation in Contemporary Jewish Eyes', *Proceedings of the Israel Academy of Sciences and Humanities* iv (Jerusalem, 1971), 239–327

Berger, M., *Zur Handelsgeschichte der Juden in Polen im 17. Jahrhundert* (Berlin, 1932)

Bergl, J., *Geschichte der ungarischen Juden* (Kaposvar, 1879)

Berliner, A., *Geschichte der Juden in Rom*, 2 vols. (Frankfurt, 1893)

Bloch, Ph., 'Ein vielbegehrter Rabbiner des Rheingaues, Juda Mehler Reutlingen', *Beiträge zur Geschichte der deutschen Juden. Festschrift zum siebzigsten Geburtstage Martin Philippsons* (Leipzig, 1916), 114–34

Bloom, Herbert I., *The Economic Activities of the Jews of Amsterdam in the 17th and 18th Centuries* (1937; repr. Port Washington, New York, 1969)

Blumenkranz, B., 'Les Juifs dans le commerce maritime de Venise (1592–1609)', *REJ* cxx (1961), 143–51

Blustein, G., *Storia degli ebrei in Roma* (Rome, 1921)

Bodenheimer, R., 'Beitrag zur Geschichte der Juden in Oberhessen von ihrer frühesten Erwähnung bis zur Emanzipation', *ZGJD* iv (1932), 11–30

Bonfil, Roberto, 'Some Reflections on the Place of Azariah de'Rossi's *Meor Enayim* in the Cultural Milieu of Italian Renaissance Jewry', in *Jewish Thought in the Sixteenth Century*, ed. B. D. Cooperman (Harvard, 1983), 23–48

Bothe, F., *Beiträge zur Wirtschafts- und Sozialgeschichte der Reichstadt Frankfurt* (Leipzig, 1906)

Bovenkerk, H., 'Nederlandse schrijvers tijdens de Republiek over de Joden', *GJN*, 714–71

Boxer, C. R., 'António Vieira S. J. and the Institution of the Brazil Company in 1649', *Hispanic American Historical Review* xxix (1949), 474–97

Boyajian, J. C., 'The New Christians Reconsidered: Evidence from Lisbon's Portuguese Bankers, 1497–1647', *SR* xiii (1979), 129–56

Braudel, Fernand, *Civilization and Capitalism 15th–18th Century, vol. II: The Wheels of Commerce* (London, 1982)

Braunstein, Baruch, *The Chuetas of Majorca. Conversos and the Inquisition of Majorca* (Scottsdale, Pa., 1936)

Breuer, Mordechai, 'Modernism and Traditionalism in Sixteenth-Century Jewish Historiography: a Study of David Gans' *Tzemach David*', in *Jewish Thought in the Sixteenth Century*, as above (see Bonfil) pp. 49–88

Brilling, B., 'Die frühesten Beziehungen der Juden Hamburgs zu Palästina', *JJLG* xxi (1930), 19–38

—— *Geschichte der Juden in Breslau von 1454–1702* (Stuttgart, 1960)

—— *Die jüdischen Gemeinden Mittelschlesiens. Entstehung und Geschichte* (Stuttgart, 1972)

Brisch, Carl, *Geschichte der Juden in Cöln und Umgebung aus ältester Zeit bis auf die Gegenwart* (Mulheim, 1879)

Brugmans, H., 'De houding van staat en kerk ten opzichte van de joden', *GJN*, pp. 617–42

Brunschvigg, Léon, *Les Juifs de Nantes et du pays nantais* (Nantes, 1890)

Bulferetti, L., *Assolutismo e mercantilismo nel Piemonte di Carlo Emanuele II (1663–1675). Memorie dell'Accademia delle scienze di Torino*, 3rd ser., vol. ii.

Burmeister, K. H., *Sebastian Münster. Versuch eines biographischen Gesamtbildes* (Basel-Stuttgart, 1963)

Cahen, Abraham, 'Les Juifs de la Martinique au XVIIᵉ siècle', *REJ* x (1881), 93–122

Cantera Burgos, F., 'Dos escritos inéditos y anónimos sobre los judíos y España durante el siglo XVII', *Scritti . . . in memoria di G. Bedarida* (Florence, 1966), pp. 33–47

Carlebach, S., *Geschichte der Juden in Lübeck und Moisling* (Lübeck, 1898)

Caro Baroja, Julio, *Los judíos en la España moderna y contemporánea*, 3 vols. (2nd ed., Madrid, 1978)

Carpi, D., 'Alcune notizie sugli ebrei a Vicenza (sec. XIV–XVIII)', *Archivio Veneto*, 5th ser., lxxiii (1961), 17–23

Carsten, F. L., *Princes and Parliaments in Germany from the Fifteenth to the Eighteenth Century* (Oxford, 1959)

Cassandro, M., *Gli ebrei e il prestito ebraico a Siena nel cinquecento* (Milan, 1979)

Cassuto, Alfonso, 'Die portugiesischen Juden in Glückstadt', *JJLG* xxi (1930), 287–317

—— 'Neue Funde zur ältesten Geschichte der portugiesischen Juden in Hamburg', *ZGJD* iii (1931), 58–72

Cassuto, Umberto, *Gli ebrei a Firenze nell'età del Rinascimento* (Florence, 1918)

—— 'La famille des Medicis et les juifs', *REJ* lxxvi (1923), 132–45

Castro y Rossi, Adolfo de, *Historia de los judíos de España* (Cadiz, 1847)

Cervani, G. and Buda, L. *La comunità israelitica di Trieste nel secolo XVIII* (Udine, 1973)

Ciriacono, Salvatore, *Olio ed ebrei nella Repubblica Veneta del settecento* (Venice, 1975)

Cirot, G., *Les Juifs de Bordeaux* (Bordeaux, 1920)

Ciscato, A., *Gli ebrei in Padova (1300–1800)* (Padua, 1901)

Cohen, A. and Lewis, B., *Population and Revenue in the Towns of Palestine in the Sixteenth Century* (Princeton, 1978)

Cohen, D. E., 'De zoogenaamde portugeesche gemeente te Nijkerk', *BGJW* iii (1925), 20–7

Cohen, J., 'The "Small Council" of the Jewry of Brandenburg-Ansbach' (Hebrew), *Yitzhak F. Baer Jubilee Volume* (Jerusalem, 1960), pp. 351–72

Cole, W. C., *French Mercantilist Doctrines before Colbert* (New York, 1931)

—— *Colbert and a Century of French Mercantilism*, 2 vols (New York, 1939)

Coleman, D. C., *Revisions in Mercantilism*, (London, 1969)

Colorni, Vittore, 'Gli ebrei a Sermide, cinque secoli di storia', *Scritti in memoria di Sally Mayer (1875–1953)*. *Saggi sull'ebraismo italiano* (Jerusalem, 1956), pp. 35–72

Crémieux, A. 'Un établissement juif à Marseille au XVIIᵉ siècle', *REJ* lv (1908), 119–45 and lvi (1908), 99–123

Davidsohn, D., *Beiträge zur Sozial- und Wirtschaftsgeschichte der Berliner Juden vor der Emanzipation* (Berlin, 1920)

Denucé, Jean, 'Koningin Christina van Zweden te Antwerpen (1654) en Don García de Yllan', *Antwerpsch Archievenblad* (1927), pp. 31–6

Diamond, A. S., 'Problems of the London Sephardi Community, 1720–1733—Philip Carteret Webb's Notebooks', *TJHSE* xxi (1968), 39–63

Dietrich, E. L., 'Das jüdisch-christliche Religionsgespräch am Ausgang des 16. Jahrhunderts nach dem Handbuch des R. Isaak Troki' *Judaica* (Basel) xiv (1958), 1–39

Dietz, A., *Stammbuch der Frankfurter Juden* (Frankfurt, 1907)

——*Frankfurter Handelsgeschichte*, 4 vols. (Frankfurt, 1910–25)

Dillen, Johan G. van, 'Vreemdelingen te Amsterdam in de eerste helft der zeventiende eeuw, 1. De portugeesche joden', *Tijdschrift voor Geschiedenis* l (1935), 4–35

Domínguez Ortiz, A. *Política y hacienda de Felipe IV* (Madrid, 1960)

Dubnow, Simon, *Weltgeschichte des jüdischen Volkes von seinen Uranfängen bis zur Gegenwart*, 10 vols. (Berlin, 1925–9)

Eckstein, A., *Geschichte der Juden im ehemaligen Fürstbistum Bamberg* (Bamberg, 1898)

—— *Geschichte der Juden im Markgrafentum Bayreuth* (Bayreuth, 1907)

Emmanuel, I. S., *Histoire des Israélites de Salonique* (Paris, 1936)

—— and Emmanuel, S. A., *History of the Jews of the Netherlands Antilles*, 2 vols. (Cincinnati, 1970)

—— 'Les Juifs de la Martinique et leurs coreligionnaires d'Amsterdam au XVIIᵉ siècle', *REJ* cxxiii (1964), 511–16

Ettinger, S., 'Jewish Participation in the Colonization of the Ukraine' (Hebrew), *Zion* xxi (1956), 107–42

—— 'The Beginnings of the Change in the Attitude of European Society towards the Jews' *Scripta Hierosolymitana* vii (Jerusalem, 1961), 193–219

Evans, R. J. W., *The Making of the Habsburg Monarchy, 1550–1700* (Oxford, 1979)

Evers, M., *Geschichte der Juden in der Stadt Warburg zur fürstbischöflichen Zeit* (Warburg, 1978)

Fabião, L. C., 'Subsídios para a história dos chamados 'judeos portugueses' na indústria dos diamantes em Amsterdão nos séculos XVII e XVIII', *Revista da Faculdade de Letras da Universidade de Lisboa*, ser. 3, xv (1975), 455–519

Feilchenfeld, A., 'Anfang und Blüthezeit der Portugiesengemeinde in Hamburg', *Zeitschrift für Hamburgische Geschichte* x (1899), 199–240

Feilchenfeld [cont.], 'Die älteste Geschichte der deutschen Juden in Hamburg', *MGWJ* xliii (1899), 271–82, 322–8, 370–81

Feilchenfeld, L., *Rabbi Josel von Rosheim. Ein Beitrag zur Geschichte der Juden in Deutschland im Reformationszeitalter* (Strasbourg, 1898)

Ferro Tavares, Maria José Pimenta, *Os judeus em Portugal no século XV*, 1 vol. thus far (Lisbon, 1981)

Flesch, Heinrich, 'Urkundliches über jüdische Handwerker in Mähren', *MGWJ* lxxiv (1930), 197–216

Foa, Salvatore, 'Banchi e banchieri ebrei nel Piemonte dei secoli scorsi', *RMI* xxi (1955), 38–50, 85–97, 127–36, 190–201, 284–97, 325–36, 471–85, 520–35

—— *La politica economica della casa savoia verso gli ebrei. Il portofranco di Villafranca (Nizza)* (Rome, 1961)

Franke, H., *Geschichte und Schicksal der Juden in Heilbronn* (Heilbronn, 1963)

Frankl, H., 'Die politische Lage der Juden in Halberstadt von ihrer ersten Andsiedlung an bis zur Emanzipation', *JJLG* xix (1928)

Freudenthal, M., *Leipziger Meßgäste. Die jüdischen Besucher der Leipziger Messen in den Jahren 1675 bis 1764* (Frankfurt, 1928)

Fuks, Lajb, 'Simon de Pool—faktor króla Jana Sobieskiego w Holandii', *BZIH* xxi (March 1957), 3–12

—— 'De Amsterdamse Opperrabbijn David Lida en de Vierlandensynode (1680–1684)', *SR* vi (1972), 166–79

—— 'Sebastianisme in Amsterdam in het begin van de 18e eeuw' *SR* xiv (1980), 20–8

Galanté, Abraham, *Hommes et choses juifs portugais en Orient* (Constantinople, 1927)

Gans, Mozes H., *Memorboek. Platenatlas van het leven der joden in Nederland van de middeleeuwen tot 1940* (Baarn, 1971)

—— 'Don Samuel Palache. Rabbi and Pirate' (Hebrew), *SHDJ* i, 33–9

García de Proodian, L., *Los judíos en América* (Madrid, 1966)

Gelber, N. M., *Zur Vorgeschichte des Zionismus* (Vienna, 1927)

Gindely, Anton, *Geschichte der Gegenreformation in Böhmen* (Leipzig, 1894)

Gold, Hugo, *Die Juden und Judengemeinden Mährens in Vergangenheit und Gegenwart* (Brunn, 1929)

—— 'Zur Geschichte der Juden in Pirnitz', *ZGJT* i (1930/1), 51–2

—— (ed.), *Geschichte der Juden in der Bukowina bis zum Jahre 1919*, 2 vols. (Tel Aviv, 1958)

Graupe, H. M., *The Rise of Modern Judaism. An Intellectual History of German Jewry, 1650–1942* (New York, 1978)

Gross, Benjamin, *Le Messianisme juif. L'éternité d'Israel du Maharal de Prague (1512–1609)* (Paris, 1969)

Grünfeld, R., *Ein Gang durch die Geschichte der Juden in Augsburg* (Augsburg, 1917)

Grunwald, Max, *Portugiesengräber auf deutscher Erde* (Hamburg, 1902)

—— *Hamburgs deutsche Juden bis zur Auflösung der Dreigemeinden, 1811* (Hamburg, 1904)

—— *Samuel Oppenheimer und sein Kreis. Ein Kapitel aus der Finanzgeschichte Österreichs* (Vienna–Leipzig, 1913)

—— 'Luxusverbot der Dreigemeinden (Hamburg–Altona–Wandsbek) aus dem Jahre 1715', *JJV* (1923), 227–34

—— 'Contribution à l'histoire des impôts et des professions des Juifs de Bohême, Moravie et Silesie depuis le XVIᶜ siècle, *REJ* lxxxii (1926), 439–49

Gundersheimer, W. L., 'Erasmus, Humanism, and the Christian Cabala', *Journal of the Warburg and Courtauld Institutes* xxvi (1963), 38–52

Haenle, S., *Geschichte der Juden im ehemaligen Fürstenthum Ansbach* (Ansbach, 1876)

Haller, Ernst, *Die rechtliche Stellung der Juden im Kanton Aargau* (Aargau, 1901)

Halpern, I., 'Aid and Relief for the Polish Communities following the Massacres of 1648/9', *Yitzhak F. Baer Jubilee Volume* (Hebrew), pp. 338–50

—— 'A Dispute over the Election of the Community Council at Frankfurt am Main and its Repercussions in Poland and Bohemia' (Hebrew), *Zion* xxi (1956), 64–91

—— 'The Jewish Refugees of the Thirty Years War in Eastern Europe' (Hebrew), *Zion* xxvii (1962), 199–215

Hanson, C. A., *Economy and Society in Baroque Portugal, 1668–1703* (Minnesota, 1981)

Hartvig, M., *Jøderne i Danmark i tiden 1600–1800* (Copenhagen, 1951)

Hasselmeier, Hans-Heinrich, *Die Stellung der Juden in Schaumburg-Lippe von 1648 bis zur Emanzipation* (Bückeburg, 1967)

Hassinger, H, *Johann Joachim Becher, 1635–1682. Ein Beitrag zur Geschichte des Merkantilismus* (Vienna, 1951)

Hausdorff, D., *Jizkor, Platenatlas van drie en een halve eeuw geschiedenis van de joodse gemeente in Rotterdam* (Baarn, 1978)

Heckscher, E. F., *Mercantilism*, revised edn., 2 vols. (London, 1955)

Henriquez Pimentel, M., *Geschiedkundige aanteekeningen betreffende de Portugeesche Israelieten in Den Haag* (The Hague, 1876)

Hertzberg, Arthur, *The French Enlightenment and the Jews. The Origins of Modern Anti-Semitism* (New York, 1970)

Herzog, M. S., 'Geschichte der Juden in Stupava (Stampfen)', *ZGJT* ii (1931/2)

Hirschel, L., 'Cultuur en volksleven', *GJN*, 454–97

—— 'Johannes Leusden als Hebraist', *SR* i (1967), 23–50

Hodik, F. P., *Beiträge zur Geschichte der Mattersdorfer Judengemeinde* (Eisenstadt, 1975)

Hoffmann, J., 'Geschichte der Juden in Kaaden', *ZGJT* ii (1931/2), 110–17

Holthausen, M., 'Die Juden im kurkölnischen Herzogtum Westfalen', *Westfälische Zeitschrift* xcvi (1940), 48–152

Horn, Maurycy, 'Zydzi województwa bielskiego w pierwszej połowie XVII w.' *BZIH* xxvii (1958)

—— 'Żydzi przeworscy w latach, 1583–1650' *BZIH* lxxvi (1970), 3–79

—— 'Skład zawodowy: rozwarstwienie majątkowe żydow tarnogródzkich w świetle inwentarzy z lat 1650–1686', *BZIH* lxxviii (1971), 11–29

—— 'Działalność gospodarcza i pozycja materialna Żydów czerwonoruskich w świetle lustracji i unwentarzy z lat 1564–1570', *BZIH* lxxxii (1972), 15–26

Horowitz, H., 'Die jüdische Gemeinde Opatow und ihre Rabbiner', *MGWJ* lxxiv (1930), 10–23

Israel, Jonathan I., 'Spain and the Dutch Sephardim, 1609–1660', *SR* xii (1978), 1–61

—— 'The Jews of Spanish North Africa, 1600–69', *TJHSE* xxvi (1979), 71–86

—— *The Dutch Republic and the Hispanic World, 1606–1661* (Oxford, 1982)

—— 'The Economic Contribution of Dutch Sephardi Jewry to Holland's Golden Age, 1595–1713', *Tijdschrift voor Geschiedenis* xcvi (1983) 505–36

—— 'Central European Jewry during the Thirty Years' War, 1618–48', *Central European History* xvi (1983), 3–30

—— 'The Diplomatic Career of Jeronimo Nunes da Costa: an Episode in Dutch–Portuguese Relations of the Seventeenth Century', *BMGN* (1983), 167–90

Kahn, Ludwig D., *Die Geschichte der Juden in Sulzburg* (Mülheim, 1969)

Kann, R. A., *A Study in Austrian Intellectual History. From Late Baroque to Romanticism* (London, 1960)

Kaplan, Josef, 'The Attitude of the Leadership of the Portuguese Community in Amsterdam to the Sabbatian Movement, 1665–71' (Hebrew), *Zion* xxxix (1974), pp. 198–216

—— 'Rabbi Saul Levi Morteira's Treatise "Arguments against the Christian Religion" ', (Hebrew) *SHDJ* i, 9–31

—— *From Christianity to Judaism. The Life and Work of Isaac Orobio de Castro* (Hebrew) (Jerusalem, 1982)

—— 'The Curaçao and Amsterdam Jewish Communities in the 17th and 18th Centuries', *American Jewish History* lxxii (1982), 193–211

Kardaszewicz, S., *Dzieje Dawniejsze miasta Ostroga. Materyały do historyi Wołynia* (Warsaw, 1913)

Katz, David S., *Philosemitism and the Readmission of the Jews into England 1603–1655*, (Oxford, 1982)

—— 'Menasseh ben Israel's Mission to Queen Christina of Sweden, 1651–1655', *Jewish Social Studies* xlv (1983), 57–72

Kaufmann, David, *Samson Wertheimer, der Oberfaktor und Landesrabbiner (1658–1728) und seine Kinder* (Vienna, 1888)

—— 'Les Marranes de Pesaro et les represailles des Juifs Levantins contre la ville d'Ancone', *REJ* xvi (1888), 61–5

—— *Die letzte Vertreibung der Juden aus Wien und Niederösterreich. Ihre Vorgeschichte (1625–1670)* (Vienna, 1889)

—— *Dr Israel Conegliano und seine Verdienste um die Republik Venedig bis nach dem Frieden von Carlowitz* (Vienna, 1895)

—— *Urkundliches aus dem Leben Samson Wertheimers*, (Vienna, 1892)

—— 'Contributions à l'histoire des Juifs de Corfou', *REJ* xxxii (1896), 226–43

—— 'Joseph ibn Danon de Belgrade', *REJ* xxxvii (1898), 284–91

—— 'Die Vertreibung der Marranen aus Venedig im Jahre 1550', *JQR* xiii (1901), 520–32

—— 'Die Verbrennung der Talmudischen Litteratur in der Republik Venedig', *JQR* xiii (1901), 533–8

Kayserling, Meyer, *Biblioteca Española–Portugueza–Judaica* (Strasbourg, 1890)

Kellenbenz, Hermann, *Sephardim an der unteren Elbe* (Wiesbaden, 1958)

—— *As relações econômicas entre o Brasil e a Alemanha na época colonial* (Recife, 1961)

Kestenberg-Gladstein, Ruth, *Neuere Geschichte der Juden in den böhmischen Ländern* (Tübingen, 1969)

Kober, Adolf, 'Die Reichsstadt Köln und die Juden in den Jahren 1685–1715', *MGWJ* lxvii (1931), 412–28

—— 'Eine Kurtrierer "Jüdisch Ceremonial Verordnung" aus der Wende des 17. und 18. Jahrhunderts', *MGWJ* lxxvii (1933), 100–13

Köhn, G., 'Ostfriesen und Niederländer in der Neugründung Glückstadt von 1620 bis 1652', *Hansische Geschichtsblätter* xc (1972), 81–3

Krabbenhoft, K., 'Structure and Meaning of Herrera's *Puerta del Cielo*', *SR* xvi (1982), 1–20

Kracauer, I. *Geschichte der Juden in Frankfurt am Main*, 2 vols (Frankfurt, 1925)

Krauss, S., 'Die Palästinasiedlung der polnischen Hasidim und die Wiener Kreise im Jahre 1700', *Abhandlungen zur Erinnerung an Hirsch Perez Chajes* (Vienna, 1933) pp. 51–94

Krieg, Martin, 'Die Juden in der Stadt Minden bis zum Stadtreglement von 1723', *Westfälische Zeitschrift* xciii (1937), 113–96

Krüger, H. J., *Die Judenschaft von Königsberg in Preusen, 1700–1812* (Marburg, 1966)

Kühler, W. J., *Het Socinianisme in Nederland* (Leiden, 1912)

Laras, Giuseppe, 'Notizie storiche e prammatica degli ebrei di Ancona nel sec. XVIII', in *Scritti sull'ebraismo a memoria di Guido Bedarida* (Florence, 1966)

—— 'Diego Lorenzo Picciotto: un delatore di Marrani nella Livorno del seicento', *Scritti in memoria di Umberto Nahon*, ed. R. Bonfil et al. (Jerusalem, 1978), pp. 65–104

Larsen, K., *De Danske i Guinea* (Copenhagen, 1918)

Lassally, O., 'Zur Geschichte der Juden in Landsberg a. d. Warthe', *MGWJ* lxxx (1936), 403–15

Lebram, J. C. H., 'Ein Streit um die Hebräische Bibel und die Septuaginta', in *Leiden University in the Seventeenth Century*, ed. Th. H. Lunsingh Scheurler *et al.* (Leiden, 1975), pp. 21–63

Lehmann, E., *Der polnische Resident Berend Lehmann, der Stammvater der israelitischen Religionsgemeinde zu Dresden* (Dresden, 1885)

Lemos, Maximiano, *Zacuto Lusitano: a sua vida e a sua obra* (Oporto, 1909)

Léon, Jacob H., *Histoire des Juifs de Bayonne* (Paris, 1893)

Leszczyński, Anatol, 'Żydzi w Choroszczy od połowy XVI w. do 1795 r.', *BZIH* lxxxviii (1973), 3–31

—— 'Żydowski ruch osadniczy na ziemi bielskiej do 1795 r.', *BZIH* xcii (1974), 31–58

Lewin, Louis, *Geschichte der Juden in Lissa* (Pinne, 1904)

—— 'Jüdische Ärzte in Großpolen', *JJLG* ix (1912), 367–420

—— *Die Landessynode der großpolnischen Judenschaft* (Frankfurt, 1926)

Libermann, K., 'La découverte d'une synagogue secrète à Anvers à la fin du dix-septième siècle', *REJ* c (1935), 36–48

Löb, A., *Die Rechtverhältnisse der Juden im ehemaligen Königreiche und der jetzigen Provinz Hannover* (Frankfurt, 1908)

Loker. Z., 'Cayenne—a Chapter in the Jewish Settlement of the New World in the 17th Century' (Hebrew), *Zion* xlviii (1983), 107–16

Löwenstein, Leopold, 'Zur Geschichte der Juden in Fürth', *JJLG* vi (1908), 153–233 and viii (1910), 65–213

Luzzatto, Federico, 'La Comunità ebraica di Rovigo', *RMI* vi (1932), 509–23

—— *La Comunità ebraica di Conegliano Veneto ed i suoi monumenti* (Rome, 1957)

—— *Cronache storiche della università degli ebrei di San Daniele del Friuli* (Rome, 1964)

Maczak, Antoni, 'Money and Society in Poland and Lithuania in the 16th and 17th Centuries', *Journal of European Economic History* v (1976), 69–104

Mahler, Raphael, 'Z dziejów żydów w Nowym Sączu w XVII i XVIII wieku', *BZIH* lv (1965), 3–32

—— *Yidn in Amolikn Poyln in Likht fun Tsifern* (Yiddish) (Warsaw, 1958)

Malvezin, Theophile, *Histoire des Juifs à Bordeaux* (Bordeaux, 1875)

Mandl, B., 'Zur Geschichte der jüdischen Gemeinde in Holitsch, *ZGJT* i (1930/1), 180–3

Markbreiter, M., *Beiträge zur Geschichte der jüdischen Gemeinde Eisenstadt* (Vienna, 1908)

Marmorstein, A., 'Zur Geschichte der Juden in Jamnitz', *MJV* xiii (1910)

Marwedel, Günter, *Die Privilegien der Juden in Altona*, (Hamburg, 1976)

Marx Alexander, *Studies in Jewish History and Booklore* (New York, 1944)

Mattiesen, O. H., *Die Kolonial- und Überseepolitik der kurländischen Herzöge im 17. und 18. Jahrhundert* (Stuttgart, 1940)

May, J., 'Die Steuern und Abgaben der Juden im Erzstift Trier', *ZGJD* vii (1937), 156–79

Méchoulan, H., 'Morteira et Spinoza au carrefour du socinianisme', *REJ* cxxv (1976), 51–65

Meijer, Jaap, *Zij lieten hun sporen achter. Joodse bijdragen tot de Nederlandse beschaving* (Utrecht, 1964)

—— '*Moeder in Israël*'. *Een geschiedenis van het Amsterdamse Asjkenazische Jodendom* (Haarlem, 1964)

Meinecke, Friedrich, *Machiavellism. The Doctrine of Raison d'État and its Place in Modern History* (London, 1957)

Meisl, Josef, *Geschichte der Juden in Polen und Russland*, 2 vols. (Berlin, 1921)

Mendes dos Remédios, Joaquim, *Os judeus portugueses em Amsterdam* (Coimbra, 1911)

Mevorah, B., 'Jewish Diplomatic Activities to prevent the Expulsion of Jews from Bohemia and Moravia in 1744–5' (Hebrew), *Zion* xxviii (1963), 125–64

Milano, Attilo, 'Ricerche sulle condizioni economiche degli ebrei a Roma (1555–1848)', *RMI* v (1931), 446–65, 545–66, 629–50

—— *Storia degli ebrei in Italia* (Turin, 1963)

—— 'Uno sguardo sulle relazioni tra la Livorno ebraica e i paesi della Berberia', *Miscellanea di studi in Memoria di Dario Disegni* (Turin, 1969)

Morgensztern, J., 'Udział Żydów w życiu gospodarczym Kraśnika i włości kraśnickich do połowy XVII w.', *BZIH* xxxvi (1960), 3–40

—— 'O działalności gospodarczej żydów w Zamościu w XVI i XVII wieku', *BZIH* liii (1965), 3–32

Morreale, M., 'El Sidur ladinado de 1552', *Romance Philology* xvii (1963–4), 332–8

Moses, Leopold, *Die Juden in Wiener-Neustadt. Ein Beitrag zur Geschichte der Juden in Österreich* (Vienna, 1927)

—— *Die Juden in Niederösterreich. Mit besonderer Berücksichtigung des XVII. Jahrhunderts* (Vienna, 1935)

Moulinas, R., *Les Juifs du Pape en France. Les communautés d'Avignon et du Comtat Venaissin aux 17e et 18e siècles* (Paris 1981)

Müller, G. 'Christlich-jüdisches Religionsgespräch im Zeitalter der protestantischen Orthodoxie—Die Auseinandersetzung Johann Müllers mit Rabbi Isaac Troki's "Hizzuk Emuna", in *Glaube, Geist, Geschichte. Festschrift für Ernst Benz* (Leiden, 1967), pp. 513–24

Nadav, M., 'The Jewish Community of Pinsk from the Khmelnitsky Massacres to the Peace of Andruszów (1648–1667)' (Hebrew), *Zion* xxxi (1966), 153–96

Nahon, Gérard, 'Inscriptions funéraires hébraïques et juives à Bidache, Labastide-Clairence (Basses-Pyrenées) et Peyrehorade (Landes)', I. *REJ* cxxvii (1968), 347–65 and II. *REJ* cxxviii (1969), 349–75

Nehama, J., *Histoire des Israélites de Salonique*, 4 vols. (Salonika, 1931–6)

Neher, André, *David Gans (1541–1613)* (Paris, 1974)

Netanyahu, B., *The Marranos of Spain from the late XIVth to the early XVIth Century according to Hebrew Sources* (New York, 1966)

Nordmann, A., 'Histoire des Juifs à Genève de 1281 à 1780', *REJ* lxxx (1925), 1–41

Novak, G., *Židovi u Splitu* (Split, 1920)

Oberman, Haiko A., *Wurzeln des Antisemitismus* (Darmstadt, 1981)

Oelman, Timothy, *Marrano Poets of the Seventeenth Century* (London–Toronto, 1982)

Oestreich, Gerhard, *Neostoicism and the Early Modern State* (Cambridge, 1982)

Oudschans Dentz, F., *De kolonisatie van de Portugeesch Joodsche natie in Suriname en de geschiedenis van de Joden Savanne* (Amsterdam, 1927)

Ouverleaux, Emile, *Notes et documents sur les Juifs de Belgique sous l'ancien régime* published in sections in *REJ* xii (1883), viii (1884) and ix (1884)

Paci, Renzo *La 'Scala' di Spalato e il commercio veneziano nei Balcani fra cinque e seicento* (Venice, 1971)

Panova, Snezhka, 'On the Social Differentiation of the Jewish Population in the Bulgarian Lands during the XVIth–XVIIIth Centuries', *Annual of the Social, Cultural, and Educational Association of the Jews in the People's Republic of Bulgaria* xii (1977), 135–45

Patinkin, D., 'Mercantilism and the Readmission of the Jews to England', *JJS* viii, (1946)

Paulo, Amilcar, *Os criptojudeus* (Oporto, 1970)

Pavoncello, J., *Gli ebrei in Verona dalle origini al secolo XX* (Verona, 1960)

Penkalla, A., 'Synagoga i Gmina w Szydłowie', *BZIH* cxxi–ii (1982), 57–70

Perles, J., *Geschichte der Juden in Posen* (Breslau, 1865)

Petuchowski, J. J., *The Theology of Haham David Nieto. An Eighteenth-Century Defender of Jewish Tradition* (New York, 1954)

Pfeifer, S., *Kulturgeschichtliche Bilder aus dem jüdischen Gemeindeleben zu Reckendorf* (Bamberg, 1897)

Plochmann, R., *Urkundliche Geschichte der Stadt Markbreit in Unterfranken* (Erlangen, 1864)

Pohl, Hans, *Die Portugiesen in Antwerpen (1567–1648)* (Wiesbaden, 1977)

Polak-Rokycana, J., 'Die Häuser des Jakob Bassewi von Treunburg', *ZGJT* i (1930/1).

Poliakov, Leon, *Histoire de l'Antisémitisme. Du Christ aux Juifs de Cour* (Paris, 1955)

—— *Les banquiers juifs et le Saint Siège du XIII^c au XVII^c siècle*, (Paris, 1965)

Pollack, Hermann, *Jewish Folkways in Germanic Lands (1648–1806). Studies in Aspects of Daily Life* (Cambridge, Mass., 1971)

Popkin, Richard H., *The History of Scepticism from Erasmus to Descartes* (New York, 1964)

—— 'Menasseh ben Israel and Isaac la Peyrère', *SR* vii (1974), 59–63

Prins, J. H., 'Prince William of Orange and the Jews' (Hebrew), *Zion* xv (1950), 93–106

Pullan, Brian, *Rich and Poor in Renaissance Venice* (Oxford, 1971)

—— *The Jews of Europe and the Inquisition of Venice, 1550–1670* (Oxford, 1983)

Rabinowicz, O. K., *Sir Solomon de Medina* (London, 1974)

Rau, Virginia, 'A embaixada de Tristão de Mendonça Furtado e os arquivos notariais holandeses', *Anais da Academia Portuguesa da História*, 2nd ser. viii (1958), 95–151

Ravid, Benjamin, *Economics and Toleration in Seventeenth-Century Venice: the Background and Context of the Discorso of Simone Luzzatto* (Jerusalem, 1978)

—— 'The Socioeconomic Background of the Expulsion and Readmission of the Venetian Jews, 1571–1573', *Essays in Modern Jewish History. A Tribute to Ben Halpern* (London–Toronto, 1982), pp. 27–55

Reinach, S., 'Joseph Scaliger et les Juifs', *REJ* lxxxviii (1929), 171–6

Revah, I. S., 'Les Marranes', *REJ* cxviii (1959), 29–77

—— *Spinoza et le Dr Juan de Prado* (Paris–The Hague, 1959)

—— 'Autobiographie d'un Marrane', *REJ* cxix (1961), 41–130

—— 'Le premier règlement imprimé de la "Santa Companhia de dotar orfans e donzelas pobres" ', *Boletim internacional de Bibliografia Luso-Brasileira* iv (1963), 650–91

—— 'Aux origines de la rupture spinozienne', *REJ* cxxii (1963), 359–431

—— 'Les ecrivains Manuel de Pina et Miguel de Barrios et la censure de la communauté judeo-portugaise d'Amsterdam', *Otzar Yehude Sefarad* (*Tesoro de los Judíos Sefardíes*) viii (1965), lxxiv-xci

Rexhausen, Anton, *Die rechtliche und wirtschaftliche Lage der Juden im Hochstift Hildesheim* (Hildesheim, 1914)

Rijnders, Carolus, *Van 'Joodsche Natiën' tot joodse Nederlanders* (Amsterdam, 1970)

Rivkin, Ellis, *Leon de Modena and the Kol Sakhal*, (Cincinatti, 1952)

—— *The Shaping of Jewish History. A Radical New Interpretation* (New York, 1971)

Rixen, Carl, 'Geschichte und Organisation der Juden im ehemaligen Stift Münster', *Münstersche Beiträge zur Geschichtsforschung*, new ser., viii (Münster, 1906)

Roellenbleck, G., *Offenbarung, Natur und jüdische Uberlieferung bei Jean Bodin. Eine Interpretation des Heptaplomères* (Gütersloh, 1964)

Roorda, D. J., 'De joodse entourage van de koning-stadhouder', *Spiegel Historiael* (May, 1979), 258–66

Rosenthal, B., *Heimatgeschichte der badischen Juden seit ihrem geschichtlichen Auftreten bis zur Gegenwart* (Bühl, 1927)

—— 'Aus den Jugendjahren der jüdischen Gemeinde Karlsruhe', *MGWJ* lxxi (1927), 207–20

Rosenthal, L., *Zur Geschichte der Juden im Gebiet der ehemaligen Grafschaft Hanau* (Hanau, 1963)

Roth, Cecil, 'Immanuel Aboab's Proselytization of the Marranos', *JQR* xxiii (1932/3), 121–62

—— 'Les Marranes à Venise', *REJ* lxxxix (1930), 201–23

Roth [*cont.*], *History of the Jews of Venice* (3rd edn., New York, 1975)

Rubens, Charles, 'Joseph Cortissos and the War of the Spanish Succession', *TJHSE* xxiv (1975), 114–33

Salfeld, S., *Bilder aus der Vergangenheit der jüdischen Gemeinde Mainz* (Mainz, 1963)

Salomon, H. P., 'The "De Pinto Manuscript". A 17th Century Marrano Family History', *SR* ix (1975), 1–62

—— 'Haham Saul Levi Morteira en de Portugese Nieuw-Christenen', *SR* x (1976), 127–41

—— 'The Portuguese Background of Menasseh ben Israel's Parents', *SR* xvii (1983), 105–46

—— *Portrait of a New Christian: Fernão Alvares Melo (1569–1632)* (Paris, 1982)

Samuel, Edgar R., 'Portuguese Jews in Jacobean London', *TJHSE* xviii (1958), 171–230

—— 'The Jews in English Foreign Trade—A Consideration of the 'Philo Patriae' Pamphlets of 1753', in J. M. Shaftesley (ed.) *Remember the Days. Essays on Anglo-Jewish History Presented to Cecil Roth* (London, 1966), 123–43

—— 'Sir Thomas Shirley's "Project for Jews"—the Earliest Known Proposal for the Resettlement', *TJHSE* xxiv (1975), 195–97

—— 'Manuel Levy Duarte (1631–1714): an Amsterdam merchant jeweller and his trade with London', *TJHSE* xxvii (1982), 11–31

Sander, Erich, 'Die Juden und das deutsche Heerwesen 1. Von den Anfängen bis zum Aufkommen des Hofjudentums', *Deutsches Archiv für Landes und Volksforschung* vi (1942), 632–46

Saraiva, A. J., *Inquisição e cristãos-novos* (2nd edn. Oporto, 1969)

—— 'António Vieira, Menasseh ben Israel et le cinquième empire' *SR* vi (1972), 24–56

Sauer, Paul, *Die jüdischen Gemeinden in Württemberg und Hohenzollern* (Stuttgart, 1966)

Saville, Pierre, *Le Juif de Cour. Histoire du resident royal Berend Lehman (1661–1730)*, (Paris, 1970)

Schaab, K. A., *Diplomatische Geschichte der Juden in Mainz* (1855; reprinted Wiesbaden, 1969)

Schmidt, Ephraim, *L'histoire des Juifs à Anvers* (2nd edn. Antwerp, 1969)

Schnee, Heinrich, *Die Hoffinanz und der moderne Staat*, 3 vols (Berlin, 1955)

Schoeps, Hans-Joachim, *Philosemitismus im Barock* (Tubingen, 1952)

—— *Barocke Juden, Christen, Judenchristen* (Berne–Munich, 1965)

Scholem, Gershom, *Sabbatai Sevi, the Mystical Messiah (1626–1676)* (London, 1973)

—— 'An Italian Note-Book on the Sabbatian movement in 1666' (Hebrew), *Zion* x (1945), 55–66

—— *Major Trends in Jewish Mysticism* (New York, 1961)

—— *The Messianic Idea in Judaism. And Other Essays on Jewish Spirituality* (New York, 1971)

Schorr, M., *Rechtsstellung und Innere Verfassung der Juden in Polen. Ein geschichtlicher Rundblick* (Berlin–Vienna, 1917)

Schulze, W. A., 'Der Einfluß der Kabbala auf die Cambridger Platoniker Cudworth und More', *Judaica* xxiii (1967), 75–126 and 136–60

Schutte, O., *Repertorium der buitenlandse vertegenwoordigers residerende in Nederland, 1584–1810*, (The Hague, 1982)

Schwenger, H., 'Über die zweite Ansiedlung der Juden in Lundenburg', *ZGJT* i (1931/1), 37–40

Seeligmann, S., 'Het marranen-probleem uit oekonomisch oogpunt', *BGJW* iii (1925), 101–36

—— *Bibliographie en historie. Bijdrage tot de geschiedenis der eerste Sephardim in Amsterdam*, (Amsterdam, 1927)

Segre, Alfredo, *Ebrei, industria e commercio in Pisa* (Pisa, 1907)

Segre, Renata, *Gli ebrei lombardi nell'età spagnola* (Turin, 1973)

Sherwin, B. L., *Mystical Theology and Social Dissent. The Life and Works of Judah Loew of Prague*, (London–Toronto, 1982)

Shulvass, M. A., 'The Jewish Population in Renaissance Italy', *Between the Rhine and the Bosphorus. Studies and Essays in European Jewish History* (Chicago, 1964)

—— *From East to West. The Westward Migration of Jews from Eastern Europe during the Seventeenth and Eighteenth Centuries* (Detroit, 1971)

—— *The Jews in the World of the Renaissance*, trans. E. I. Kose (Leiden–Chicago, 1973)

Silva Rosa, J. S., *Geschiedenis der portugeesche joden te Amsterdam, 1593–1925* (Amsterdam, 1925)

—— 'Joseph Athias (1635–1700). Ein berühmter jüdischer Drucker', *Soncino-Blätter* iii (1930; *Festschrift Heinrich Brody*), 107–12

Simonsohn, Shlomo, 'The Italian Ghetto and its Administration' (Hebrew), *Yitzhak F. Baer Jubilee Volume* (Jerusalem, 1960), 270–86

—— *History of the Jews in the Duchy of Mantua* (Jerusalem, 1977)

Skinner, Quentin, *The Foundations of Modern Political Thought*, 2 vols. (Cambridge, 1978)

Sluys, D. M., 'Bijdrage tot de geschiedenis van de Poolsch-Joodsche gemeente te Amsterdam', *BGJW* iii (1925), 137–58

Spiegel, K., 'Die Prager Juden zur Zeit des dreißigjährigen Krieges', in S. Steinherz (ed.), *Die Juden in Prag* (Prague, 1927)

Spiel, Hilde, *Fanny von Arnstein oder die Emanzipation. Ein Frauenleben an der Zeitenwende, 1758–1818* (Frankfurt, 1962)

Spooner, F. C., 'Venice and the Levant: an aspect of monetary history (1610–1614) in *Studi in onore di Amintore Fanfani* v (Milan, 1962), 645–67

Stein, A., *Die Geschichte der Juden in Böhmen* (Brünn, 1904)

Stein, S., *Geschichte der Juden in Schweinfurt* (Frankfurt, 1899)

Stern, Selma, *Der preußische Staat und die Juden*, 6 vols. (Berlin, 1925)

Stern [*cont.*], *Josel von Rosheim. Befehlshaber der Judenschaft im Heiligen Römischen Reich Deutscher Nation* (Stuttgart, 1959)

—— *Jud Süß. Ein Beitrag zur deutschen und zur jüdischen Geschichte* (Munich, 1973)

Stow, K. R., *Catholic Thought and Papal Jewry Policy, 1555–1593* (New York, 1977)

Strauss, L., *Spinoza's Critique of Religion* (1930; English version, New York, 1965)

Sutherland, L. S., 'Samson Gideon: Eighteenth-Century Jewish Financier', *JHSE* xvii (1953)

Swetschinski, Daniel, 'The Spanish Consul and the Jews of Amsterdam', in *Texts and Responses: Studies Presented to Nahum N. Glatzer* (Leiden, 1975), 158–72

—— 'The Portuguese Jewish Merchants of 17th century Amsterdam: a Social Profile' (unpublished Ph.D. thesis, Brandeis University, 1979)

Switalski, Z., 'Przyczyny wycofania sie Zydów tureckich, uchodźców z Hiszpanii, z handlu lewantyńskiego Rzeczypospolitej w ostatnich latach XVI wieku', *BZIH* xxxvi (1960), 59–65

Taglicht, J., *Nachlässe der Wiener Juden im 17. und 18. Jahrhundert* (Vienna, 1917)

Tänzer, A., *Die Geschichte der Juden in Tirol und Vorarlberg* (Meran, 1905)

—— *Geschichte der Juden in Brest-Litowsk* (Berlin, 1918)

Tenenti, A., *Naufrages, corsaires et assurances maritimes à Venise, 1592–1609* (Paris, 1959)

Ten Raa, F. J. G., *et al.*, *Het Staatsche Leger, 1568–1795*, 11 vols. (The Hague, 1911–)

Tishby, I., 'The Confrontation between Lurianic Cabbala and Cordoverian Cabbala in the Writings and Life of Rabbi Aaron Berechiah of Modena' (Hebrew), *Zion* xxxix (1974), 8–85

Toaff, Alfredo, 'Cenni storici sulla communità ebraica e sulla sinagoga di Livorno', *RMI* xxi (1955), 355–430

Toaff, Ariel, 'Nuova luce sui Marrani di Ancona (1556)' in E. Toaff (ed.), *Studi sull'ebraismo italiano in memoria di Cecil Roth* (Rome, 1974), 261–80

Trapp, L., *Die Oldenburger Judenschaft* (Oldenburg, 1973)

Truchet, J., *La prédication de Bossuet. Étude de thèmes*, 2 vols. (Paris, 1960)

Ullmann, Salomon, *Studien zur Geschichte der Juden in Belgien bis zum XVIII Jahrhundert* (Antwerp, 1909)

Unna, Isaak, 'Die Verordnungen für die Lemle Moses Klausstiftung in Mannheim', *JJLG* xvii (1926), 133–45

Valentin, Hugo, *Judarnas historia i Sverige* (Stockholm, 1924)

Vaz Dias, A. M., 'Nieuwe bijdragen tot de geschiedenis der Amsterdamsche hoogduitsch-joodsche gemeente', *BGJW* vi (1940), 153–81

Verd, G. M., 'Las Biblias romanzadas: criterios de traducción, *Sefarad* xxxi (1971), 319–51

Volkert, W., 'Die Juden im Fürstentum Pfalz-Neuburg', *Zeitschrift für bayerische Landesgeschichte* xxvi (1963), 560–605

Wätjen, H. *Die Niederländer im Mittelmeergebiet zur Zeit ihrer höchsten Machtstellung* (Berlin, 1909)

Weill, G., 'Recherches sur la démographie des Juifs d'Alsace du XVIᶜ au XVIIIᶜ siècle', *REJ* cxxx (1971), 51–89

Weill, Julien, 'Nicolas Antoine', *REJ* xxxvii (1898), 161–80

Weinryb, Bernard D., *Texts and Studies in the Communal History of Polish Jewry* (New York, 1950)

—— *The Jews of Poland. A Social and Economic History of the Jewish Community in Poland from 1100–1800* (Philadelphia, 1972)

Weiss, C. T., *Geschichte und rechtliche Stellung der Juden im Fürstbistum Strassburg*, (Bonn, 1896)

Welder-Steinberg, A., *Geschichte der Juden in der Schweiz*, 2 vols. (Goldach, 1966)

Wiener, Meir, 'Die Juden unter den Braunschweigischen Herzögen Julius und Heinrich Julius', *Zeitschrift des historische Vereins für Niedersachsen* (1861), pp. 244–306

—— 'Des Hof- und Kammeragenten Leffmann Berens Intervention bei dem Erscheinen judenfeindlicher Schriften', *MWJ* (1879), 48–64

Wijler, Jacob Samuel, *Isaac de Pinto. Sa vie et ses œuvres*, (Apeldoorn, 1923)

Wilhelm, Peter, *Die jüdische Gemeinde in der Stadt Göttingen von den Anfängen bis zur Emanzipation*, (Gottingen, 1973)

Wischnitzer, M., 'Die jüdische Zunftverfassung in Polen und Litauen im 17. und 18. Jahrhundert', *VSW* xx (1928), 433–51

Wiznitzer, Arnold, *The Jews of Colonial Brazil* (New York, 1960)

Wolf, Gerson, *Ferdinand II und die Juden nach Aktenstücken* (Vienna, 1859)

—— *Zur Geschichte der Juden in Worms*, (Breslau, 1862)

—— *Die Juden in der Leopoldstadt im 17. Jahrhundert in Wien*, (Vienna, 1864)

Wolff, Egon and Frieda, *A Odisséia dos judeus de Recife* (São Paulo, 1979)

Woolf, Maurice, 'Foreign Trade of London Jews during the Seventeenth Century', *TJHSE* xxiv (1973)

Yardeni, M., 'La vision des Juifs et du judaisme dans l'œuvre de Richard Simon', *REJ* cxxix (1970), 179–203

—— 'La vision des Juifs et du judaisme dans l'œuvre de Pierre Bayle', in M. Yardeni (ed.), *Les Juifs dans l'histoire de France* (Leiden, 1980)

Yates, Frances, *Giordano Bruno and the Hermetic Tradition* (London, 1964)

Yerushalmi, Yosef, *From Spanish Court to Italian Ghetto. Isaac Cardoso, A Study in Seventeenth-Century Marranism and Jewish Apologetics* (2nd edn. Seattle and London, 1981)

Yogev, Gedalia, *Diamonds and Coral. Anglo-Dutch Jews and Eighteenth-Century Trade* (Leicester, 1978)

Zimmels, H. J., *Die Marranen in der rabbinischen Literatur* (Berlin, 1932)

Zimmer, Eric, *Jewish Synods in Germany during the Late Middle Ages (1286–1603)* (New York, 1978)

Zivier, E., 'Jüdische Bekehrungsversuche im 16. Jahrhundert', *Beiträge zur Geschichte der deutschen Juden. Festschrift zum Siebzigsten Geburtstage Martin Philippsohns* (Leipzig, 1916), 96–113

Zuckermann, M., 'Übersicht über den jüdisch-geschichtlichen Inhalt des königlichen Staatsarchivs zu Hannover', *Mitteilungen des Gesamtarchivs der deutschen Juden* (Leipzig, 1910)

Zuiden, D. S. van, *De Hoogduitsche Joden in 's-Gravenhage*, (The Hague, 1913)

—— 'Over de relaties van Prins Willem van Oranje en diens broeders met de joden', *BGJW* v (1933), 211–24

Zwarts, Jacob, 'Portugeesche Joden te Maarssen en Maarsseveen in de 17de eeuw', *Jaarboekje 1922 van het oudheidkundig genootschap 'Niftarlaken'*, (Utrecht, 1922)

—— *De eersten rabbijnen en synagogen van Amsterdam naar archivalische bronnen* (Amsterdam, 1929)

—— 'De joodse gemeenten buiten Amsterdam', *GJN*, 382–453

Index

Aboab, Immanuel (*c.*1555–1628), anti-Christian proselytizer among the Marranos, 83

absolutism, and the Jews, 75, 145–56, 148, 150, 172, 245

Aguilar, Moseh Raphael d' (d. 1679), Dutch rabbi and anti-Christian polemicist, 221

Albania, Jews in, 32, 48, 214

Alessandria (Spanish Lombardy; later part of the Savoyard state), Jews of, 23, 176

aliyah, to the Holy Land, 212, 215, 224, 255; *see also* Zionism

Alsace, Jews of, 8–9, 102–3, 169, 237

Altona (Hamburg), 43, 92, 96, 146, 151; Ashkenazi *kehilla* organization at, 195, 254

Amersfoort, 105, 155, 198, 241

Amsterdam, Jewish policy of city council, 62–4, 66, 154; Sephardi settlement at, 51, 63, 80, 93, 111, 154; German Jews at, 104–5, 106, 124, 154, 169, 179; Polish Jews at, 165, 188–9, 197; Jewish population of, 51, 164, 237, 241; Jewish emigration from, 66, 105–6, 156–7; Jewish institutions at, 197–9, 223, 244; construction of synagogues at, 63–4, 220; as Jewish cultural centre, 76–7, 80, 220; trade of Jews of, with Portugal, 62, 108–9, 176–7, 246–7; with Spain, 107–8, 176–7, 247; with the Caribbean, *see* Caribbean trade; with Germany, 174, 176, 257; *yeshivah* Ets Haim, 205; Shabbatean movement at, 211, 215–16

Ancona (Papal States), Jews of, 17, 19, 21, 45, 49, 72, 174–5, 238 n.

Ansbach, Jews of, 67, 99, 127, 192

Antoine, Nicholas (1603–32), French pastor converted to Judaism, burnt at the stake in Geneva, 82

Antwerp, Portuguese Marranos at, 16, 50–1, 62, 156, 203, 227; attempts to settle German and Dutch Jews in, 50, 156

arenda, 30, 165–6

army contracting, involvement of Jews in, 123–32, 247

art collecting, 144, 245

Aschaffenburg (electorate of Mainz), 192

Ashkenazi, Zevi Hirsch (1660–1718), Amsterdam Ashkenazi rabbi, 216

Asti (Piedmont), Jews of, 47, 176

Augsburg, 13, 15, 101, 146

Augustów (Białystok), 153

Aurich (East Friesland), 43

Avigdor, family of Court Jews in Piedmont, 115, 141, 157

Avignon (Papal States), Jews of, 22, 23, 47, 55, 161

Bacharach, Naphtali ben Jacob (first half of seventeenth century), German cabbalist, 208, 210, 230

Bacharach, Yair Haim (1638–1702), German rabbi, 210

Bacon, Francis (1561–1626), 2, 54

Baden-Durlach, 69, 146, 151, 239

Balkans, trade of, 33–4, 45, 48, 61, 113, 171, 173–5, 256

Bamberg, bishopric and town of, 16, 143, 98–9; *Landjudenschaft* of, 192–3, 212, 233

banking, 205–6, 244, 256; petty loan-banking, 27, 40, 175–6; *see also* state finance

baptism, forced, 24–7, 121

Barbados, 107, 155

Barrios, Daniel Levi (Miguel) de, (1635–1701), Dutch Sephardi chronicler, 199, 254

Bartolocci, Giulio (1613–87), Professor of Hebrew at the Collegium Neophytorum at Rome, 229

Basel (Basle), 20, 56, 105

Basnage de Beauval, Jacques (1653–1725), Huguenot historian of the Jews, 223, 231

Bassevi von Treuenberg, Jacob (1570–1634), Court Jew of Prague ennobled by the Emperor Matthias, 89–90

Bavaria, 6

Bayle, Pierre, 233 n.

Bayonne, Sephardi Jews of, 51–2, 108, 116, 161, 178

Bayreuth, 98

Becher, Johann Joachim, German mercantilist agent and writer, 173, 175 n.

Beer, Aaron (late seventeenth century), Frankfurt Jewish banker, 133, 138, 140, 144

Behrends, Leffmann (1634–1714), Hanover Court Jew, 135, 150, 194, 235, 241

Belgrade 32, 125, 206, 238

Belmonte, Baron Manuel de (Isaac Nunes; d. 1705), Sephardi 'Agent' of Spain at Amsterdam, 134, 136, 142, 246

Berlin, expulsion of Jews from (1510 to 1573), 8, 10, 11, 13; resettlement of Jews in, 149–50; public practice of Judaism at, 149, 194; Jewish population of, 169, 240; Jews and the textile industry at, 182, 248; expulsion of poor Jews from (1737), 240; publication of Eisenmenger's *Entdektes Judenthum* at, 235

Białystok, 153

Bikur Holim confraternities, 204

Bilgoray (Lublin), 241

Bodin, Jean (1530–96), 2, 37–8, 53–4, 56, 82, 224

Bohemia, Jews of, 38–40, 89, 99, 104, 147, 169, 233; Jewish population of, 39, 170, 237, 239; *Landjudenschaft* of, 186, 191–2, 250

Bologna, 21, 22

Bordeaux, Sephardi Jews of, 51–2, 116, 161–3, 251

Bossuet, Bishop Jacques Benigne (1627–1704), French theologian and polemicist, 218, 232

Brandenburg, electorate of, 8–9, 11, 13, 97, 148–50, 182

Brandenburg Africa Company, and the Hamburg Sephardim, 139

Braudel, Fernand, 257

Brazil, 91, 106–7, 203; Jewish population of Netherlands Brazil, 106; collapse of

Netherlands Brazil and the Jews, 145–6, 154, 156–7, 158, 161

Brazil Company (1649), Sephardi participation in, 109–10, 119, 139

Breisach (Breisgau), 96, 100, 102

Breslau (Wrocław), 148, 173–4

Brest-Litovsk, 167, 186, 190; Jewish population of, 241

Brody (Lvov), 120, 166, 180–90; Jewish population of, 241

Broughton, Hugh (1549–1612), English Puritan Hebraist and controversialist, 67, 84

Bruno, Giordano, 37–8

Brunswick, expulsion of Jews from, 12

Bucer, Martin (1491–1551), Protestant reformer at Strasbourg, 10, 12

Budapest, 125, 168, 206

Bueno de Mezquita, David, Amsterdam 'Agent' of the Duke of Brunswick (late seventeenth century), 138, 140

Bulgaria, 29, 32, 34

Burgau, the (Ulm), migration of Jews from, 100–1

Burgenland (Austro-Hungarian border), 167, 182, 194, 239

burial societies, 203

Buxtorf, Johannes (1564–1629), Professor of Hebrew at Basel, 56

cabbala, 73, 78–81, 213–14; Christian, 18, 151, 228–30; Lurianic, 79–80, 85, 208, 229–30

Cadiz, Dutch, English, and Hanseatic trade to, 108, 178, 242, 247

Calvin, Jean, 13–14, 228

Calvinists, and the Jews, 13–14, 41–2, 63–4, 68

candle-making, 180, 182

Cansino, Jacob (d. 1666), Jewish leader at Oran, 112

Capito, Wolfgang, Protestant reformer and Hebraist, 14

Cardoso, Abraham (Miguel; 1626–1706), Sephardi mystical messianist, 214

Cardoso, Isaac (Fernando; 1604–81), Sephardi physician and controversialist, 202, 204, 214, 221, 223, 231, 254

Caribbean trade, Sephardi involvement in, 107, 151, 161, 177–8, 243, 247

Carpentras (Papal states in France), 22

Casale Monferrato, Jews of, 115, 170, 175

Castro, Bento de (Baruch Nehamias; 1597–1684), Hamburg Sephardi physician and Shabbatean, 226

Catherine II, the 'Great', Empress of Russia, 250

Cayenne, Sephardi settlement in, 161–2

censorship, Jewish communal, 198–200

charity, organized, in the Jewish communities, 73, 231–3

Charles V, Holy Roman Emperor (1518–56), 11, 15–16, 17, 38

Charleville, 165

Child, Sir Josiah, English mercantilist writer, 160

Chmielnicki, Bogdan (1595–1657), Ukrainian insurgent leader, and the slaughter of Jews in the Ukraine, White Russia and south-east Poland, 121–2, 152, 165, 188, 205

chocolate-making, 179, 182

Christian IV, king of Denmark (1596–1648), and the Jews, 65–6, 92–3

Christianity, in the west, weakening of in the early modern era, 35–8, 207–8, 222–3, 224

Christina, Queen of Sweden (1632–54), and the Jews, 142, 147, 226–7

class-structure, of early modern Jewish society, 171–2

Clement VIII, Pope (1592–1605), and the re-expulsion of the Jews from the Papal States (1593), 22

Cleves, Duchy of, 101–2, 144, 148, 174; *Landjudenschaft* of, 192–4

cloth trade, 160, 172–3, 178, 247

Coccejus, Johannes (1603–69), Dutch Hebraist and founder of the theological school of 'Coccejans', 228–9, 258

Colbert, Jean-Baptiste (1619–83), and the Jews, 117, 161–3

Cologne, electorate of, 9, 42, 65, 97, 126, 128; Portuguese New Christians in, 50; *Landjudenschaft* of, 187

colonization, Jewish, in the Ukraine 28–9, 122, 165, 166–7; in Thirty Years' War Germany, 98–9; in the Caribbean, 107, 151, 154, 158, 170, 198, 203, 242–3

Constantinople, 26, 29, 32, 33–4, 113, 209–10, 212

conversion, of Jews to Christianity, 55, 213, 236, 238, 242, 248, 254, *see also* baptism, forced; of Jews to Islam,

213–14; of Christians to Judaism, 19, 21, 47, 49, 51–2, 82–5, 227–8, 234

Copenhagen, 151–2

coral trade, *see* Livorno

Cordovero, Moses (1522–70), Safed cabbalist, 78–9

Corfu, Jews of, 19, 49, 114, 175

Cortizos, family of Marrano financiers in Spain, 111, 124, 141

Cortizos, Joseph (1656–1742), Sephardi army contractor, 130–2

Cosimo I, Grand Duke of Tuscany, 20

Cosimo II, Grand Duke of Tuscany, 61

Costa, Alvaro de, London Sephardi merchant, 178

Costa, Uriel da (1585–1640), Marrano sceptic, 199, 216

Council of the Four Lands, see Poland

Counter-Reformation, the, and the Jews, 10, 17–23, 45, 47, 49, 72–3, 88, 146

Courland 27, 118–19, 139

Court Jews, the, 40–1, 89–90, 108–9, 123–44, 193–4, 233–5, 243–6

Cracow, Jews of, 28, 33, 154, 164, 167, 185, 187, 189, 248; Jewish population of, 241

crafts, Jewish, 26–7, 31, 40, 62, 65–6, 178–83; *see also* Amsterdam and Prague

Cremona, 23

Crete, Jews of, 19, 48; War of (1645–69), effects of on Venetian Jewry, 113, 157

Cromwell, Oliver, and the Jews, 158–60

Curaçao (Dutch West Indies), Sephardi Jews of, 107, 155, 177, 179, 203, 206 n., 212

Danzig (Gdańsk) 27–8, 30, 173

David, Michael (late seventeenth century), Hanover Court Jew, 135

deism, 249, 254–5, 258, *see also* Bodin, Spinoza, Spinozists, and Enlightenment

Delmedigo, Yoseph Shlomo (1591–1655), Cretan Jewish physician, philosopher and cabbalist, 78, 199, 204

Denmark, and the Jews, 65–6, 92–3, 135, 140, 195, 227; Ashkenazi settlement in, 151–2, 169, 241

Dessau, 97, 151, 170, 173–4

Deutz (Cologne), Jewish community of, 23, 74, 211; *see also* Wendel of Deutz diamond trade, Jewish preponderance in, 40, 62, 126, 137, 139–40, 174, 178, 182–3, 245

distilleries, producing vodka and slivovitz, leasing of, 30, 181–2

Dominicans, role of in sixteenth-century persecution of the Jews, 7

Dönme, the, Shabbatean mystical sect in the Balkans, 213–14

dowry societies, Jewish, 117, 203

Dubno (Volhynia), 120–1, 166, 190

Dunkirk, proposal for Sephardi settlement in (1663), 160

Dutch Republic, Jewish population of, 170; *see also* Holland, Amsterdam, Rotterdam, etc.

East Friesland, 43, 51

East India Company (Dutch), 62, 139

East Prussia, Jews in, 149, 240

education, Jewish community, 184, 198, 205, 225

Eisenmenger, Johann Andreas (1654–1704), Professor of Hebrew at Heidelberg and anti-Jewish polemicist, 234–5

Eisenstadt (Burgenland) 143, 168, 194; Jewish population of, 168, 239; Samson Wertheimer and, 194, 205

Emden, Jews of, 43, 65

Emmerich (Cleves), Ashkenazi settlement in, 101

Endingen (Aargau), German Jews settle in, 105

England, and the Jews, 5, 57, 158–60, 170, 241–2, 232

Enlightenment, the, anti-Judaism of, 219, 223, 232, 253–4, *see also* Spinoza

ennoblement, of Jews, 41, 90, 130, 142–3, 244, 245

Erasmus, and the Jews, 14–15, 18, 36

eroticism, in Jewish mysticism, 214; among Dutch Sephardim, 201–2

Essen, 42

Este, Italian princely house, and the Jews, 9, 20–1, 22, 45

Esterhazy, Hungarian noble family, and the Jews, 168, 194

Feldsburg (Bohemia), 147

Felgenhauer, Paul (mid-seventeenth century), Moravian Christian pietist and messianist, 225

Feltre, Bernadino da (1439–1494), Franciscan preacher against the Jews, 7

Ferdinand I, Holy Roman Emperor (1556–64), and the Jews, 38–9

Ferdinand II, Holy Roman Emperor (1619–37), and the Jews, 88–90, 103, 120, 194

Ferdinand III, Holy Roman Emperor (1637–57), and the Jews, 103–4

Ferrara, Jews in, 9, 19, 20, 22, 45, 47, 70, 73; Jewish population of, 114, 239; economic activity of the Jews of, 175–6, 180–1

Ferrara Bible (of 1553), the, 21

Fettmilch, Vincent (d. 1616), Frankfurt anti-Jewish guild leader, 68–9

Fleury, the Abbé Claude, French prelate and historian of the ancient Hebrews, 218, 232

Florence, and the Jews, 9, 19, 61, 113, 114

France, and the Jews, 5, 36–8, 51, 67–8, 82–3, 85, 116–18; Jewish population of, 170

Franconia 99, 233, 239

Frankfurt am Main, ghetto of, 16, 41–2, 50, 58, 66, 74, 93, 96, 144, 174; Jewish population of, 41, 66, 94, 164, 240; rabbinic courts at, 44, 187, 192; and the Fettmilch rising, 68–9; lack of Jewish crafts at, 182; Jewish leadership at, 16, 90, 188, 191, 234

Frankfurt an der Oder, 10, 148, 150, 173, 247

Frederick I, king of Prussia (1688–1713), and the Jews, 235, 240

Frederick William, the 'Great Elector' of Brandenburg-Prussia (1640–88) and the Jews, 102, 126, 139, 148–50

Frederick William I, king of Prussia (1713–40), anti-Jewish policy of, 240

Friedberg (Hesse), Jewish community of, 44, 67, 74, 93–5, 188; decline of, 240

Friesland, Jews of, 105, 155; Jewish poverty in, 248

Fulda (Hesse), Jewish community of, 16, 44, 94–5, 146, 187

Fürst, Jeremias (late seventeenth century), Hamburg Court Jew 138, 152

Fürth (Franconia), Jewish community of, 42–3, 98–9, 148, 174, 199; Jewish population of, 169

Galilee, 26, 29, 32, 72, 78–9, 206

Gans, David (1541–1613), Prague Jewish chronicler, 39, 74–5

Gaza, 26, 210

Gaza, Nathan of (1643–80), mystical messianist, founder of the Shabbatean movement, 209–10, 213–14

Gelderland, 16

Geneva, 8, 13, 82

Genoa, and the Jews, 46

ghetto, the, and ghettoization, 17, 64, 72–4, 114–15, 176

Gideon, Samson (1699–1762), Anglo-Jewish financier, 244, 254

Glückel of Hameln (1645–1724), Hamburg Yiddish diarist and business-woman, 144, 174, 210 n.

Glückstadt (Holstein), Jewish settlement in, 65–6, 91–3, 96, 124, 139, 183, 195

gold bullion, and the Jews, 172, 178, 256–57

Gomes Solís, Duarte (early seventeenth century), Portuguese New Christian mercantilist writer, 56–7

Gomperz, family of Court Jews, 101–2, 124, 140, 144

Gomperz, Mordechai (d. 1664), Court Jew and Landesrabbiner of the duchy of Cleves, 193–4

Gomperz, Reuben Elias (1655–1705), Court Jew in Cleves, 126, 140

Gonzaga, Italian princely family, and the Jews, 9

Gothenburg, 243

grain trade (Adriatic), 175; (Polish) 28, 30, 174, 247

Grodno (Grand Duchy of Lithuania) 149, 154, 167, 186, 190, 241

Groningen, Jewish settlement in, 51, 155, 241

Gross-Glogau (Silesia), Jews of, 13, 96, 120, 173

Grotius, Hugo (1583–1645), 53–4, 55, 64, 259

guilds, Christian, and the Jews, 27, 40, 43, 62, 68–9, 119, 154, 166–7, 172, 179; Jewish, 181–2, 250

Guinea trade, 139, 151

Günzburg (Ulm), Jewish community of, 44, 74, 187

Gustavus Adolphus, king of Sweden (1611–32), 93–4, 99

Haarlem, debate over Jewish admission to (1604), 63

Hague, The, Jewish settlement in, 127, 155, 198, 217, 241

Halberstadt, bishopric of, Jews in, 16, 42, 65, 97, 148–9, 174, 205; Jewish population of, 169, 240; anti-Jewish riots at (1621), 90

Halle, 8

Hamburg, Sephardi settlement in, 43–4, 58, 62, 65, 91–3, 96, 107, 110, 164, 240; German Jews at, 92, 146, 152, 165, 169, 240, 254; Sephardi population of, 164; Polish Jews at, 165; Bank of, 92; Court Jews at, 135, 137–9, 142–3; lack of Jewish crafts at, 65–7, 182; Shabbatean movement at, 211–12; *see also* Altona and Wandsbek

Hanau, Jews of, 66–7, 90, 93–4, 96; Jewish population of, 169–70, 240

Hannover, Nathan Nata (d. 1683), Ukrainian Jewish mystic and chronicler, 121 n., 261

Hanover, Jews of, 12, 97, 135, 150, 169, 194, 235

Hansa, The, 43

Hasid, Judah, of Dubno (c.1660–1700), Ukrainian Jewish mystic and colonizer in the Holy Land, 215

Haskalah, the (The Enlightenment in Hebrew literature), 253–4

Hayon, Nehemiah Hiyya (c.1655–c.1730), Shabbatean mystic and polemicist, 215–16

Hebraists, Christian, 14–15, 36, 54–6, 229–30, 258

Hebrew Bible, the, controversies over, 218–19, 233

Hebron, 26, 206, 209

Heidelberg, 150

Heilbronn, and the Jews, 103, 146

Henri IV, king of France (1589–1610), 38, 51–2

Herford, 97, 148

Herrera, Abraham Cohen (c.1570–1635), Sephardi cabbalist and philosopher, 80, 230

Hesse, Jewish communities of, 44, 87, 146, 172, 187, 192, 239

Hildesheim, bishopric of, Jews in, 42, 96, 97, 169, 240

Hirschel, Lazarus (late seventeenth century), Austrian Court Jew, 125–6

Hohenems (Vorarlberg), 100
Holbach, Baron d', 224
Holland, Ashkenazi migration to, 104–5, 154–5, 165, 169, 241; exceptional freedom of thought and speech in, 84 n., 217, 222–3, 234; States of, 64, 198, 223, 243 n.; *see also* Amsterdam, Haarlem, Rotterdam, etc.
horse-trade, 95, 127, 172
hospitals, Jewish, 191
Huguenots, 37, 133, 150, 163
Hungary, Jews of, 125, 148, 153, 168–9, 206; Jewish population of, 170, 238; chief rabbinate of, 244; export of cattle from, 173

illegitimacy, 201
Imperial Free Cities, of the Holy Roman Empire, 23, 43, 58, 101, 146
Index, the Papal (1564), 20
Innocent XI, Pope (1676–89), and the suppression of Jewish loan-banking in the Papal States, 176
Inquisition, the, in Italy, 19, 49; in Mallorca, 158; in Spain 25, 58–9, 112, 145, 242, 245; in Portugal, 25, 58, 82, 110, 225–6, 242
Ireland, and the Jews, 57, 256
Isserles, Moses (*c.*1530–72), Polish Talmudist, 78
Italy, Jewish population of, 5, 170; *see also* individual Italian states and cities, Papcy, and Counter-Reformation

Jamnitz (Jemnice), Moravia, 100, 167
Jassy (Romania), 34
Jerusalem 26, 32, 70, 205–6, 209, 215
Jesuits, and the Jews, 147, 162, 212; *see also* Vieira, António
jewellery trade, *see* diamonds
Joachim II, elector of Brandenburg (1535–71), and the Jews, 9, 11
Joden Savanneh, *see* Surinam
John IV, king of Portugal (1640–56) and the New Christians, 108–10, 142
John Sobieski, king of Poland (1674–96), favourable policy of toward Jews, 136–7, 153
Josel of Rosheim (also Joselmann or Joseph ben Gershon of Rosheim; *c.*1478–1554), leader of German Jewry, 11–13, 16

Joseph II, Emperor of Austria (1780–90), and the Jews, 250

Kaaden (Kadeň), Bohemia, 99, 147
Kalisz, Great Poland, 120, 167, 173, 190
Kampen (Overijssel), admission of Jews to, 155
Kann, Jacob (late seventeenth century), Frankfurt Jewish financier, 133, 138, 140, 144
Karaites, Jewish anti-rabbinic sect in Eastern Europe, 32, 230
Karlsruhe, Jewish settlement in, 244
kehilla (Jewish community), organization of, 185, 188, 189–2, 194–8, 200–2, 249–51
Kempe, Anders Pedersson (late seventeenth century), Swedish religious controversialist, 227
Kielce, exclusion of Jews from, 28, 153
Knorr von Rosenroth, Christian (1636–89), Christian cabbalist, 230
Koblenz, electorate of Trier, Jews of, 193
Kolin (Bohemia), 100
Kollonitsch, Cardinal Leopold (1631–1707), leader of the anti-Jewish agitation in Vienna, 126, 147
Königsberg (East Prussia) 28, 30, 149, 174, 235, 240
Kraśnik (Lublin), Jews of, 167, 241
Krems (Lower Austria), 147

Labastide-Clairence (south-west France), Sephardi settlement at, 68, 116–17
Ladino language (Balkan and Turkish Judaeo-Spanish), 31–3
Landjudenschaften 186–7, 192–4, 250–1
Landsberg an der Warthe (Brandenburg), Jews settle in, 150; Jewish population of, 169
Lauingen (Pfalz-Neuburg), Jews readmitted to, 101; Jews re-expelled from, 146
Leeuwarden, Jews of, 105, 155, 241, 248 n.
Lehmann, Behrend, of Halberstadt (1661–1730), German Court Jew, 136, 143, 205
Leipzig 148, 170, 173, 242
Lengnau (Aargau), Jewish community of, 105
Leopold I, Holy Roman Emperor (1657–1705), and the Jews, 146, 148, 234–46

Lerma, duke of, chief minister of Spain (1598–1618), and the Portuguese New Christians, 59–60

Leusden, Johannes (1624–99), Professor of Hebrew at Utrecht, 230–1

'Levantine' Jewish communities in Italy, 45–7, 63, 180, 198

Levi, Behrend, of Bonn (mid-seventeenth century), German Court Jew, 102, 109

libraries, Jewish, 143, 205, 299, 245

Lida, David (late seventeenth century), Polish rabbi in Amsterdam, 189

Liebmann, Jost (*c.*1640–1702), Berlin Court Jew, 135, 140

Lima, Judah de (early seventeenth century), Sephardi physician at Poznań, 204

Limborch, Philip van (late seventeenth century), Dutch liberal theologian, 223

Lipsius, Justus, 2, 37–8, 40, 53–4

Lisbon, 51, 59, 62, 84, 107, 111, 176, 247

Lissa (Leszno), Great Poland, expansion of Jewish life at, 120, 167, 173–4, 189; Jewish population of, 167, 241

Lithuania, Grand Duchy of, Jewish autonomy in, 184, 186, 190–1; *see also* Brest-Litovsk, Vilna, Grodno, Pinsk, Slutsk and Courland

Liverpool, 242

Livonia, exclusion of Jews from, 27, 118

Livorno (Leghorn), Sephardi settlement at, 49, 58, 61, 73, 113, 115, 157–8, 165; statistics of Jewish population of, 113, 164, 238, 241; Levant trade of Sephardi community of, 161–2, 175, 206; Jewish institutions at, 197; coral industry and trade at, 178, 180; Shabbatean movement at, 211–13; Dutch Sephardi links with, 161, 175, 203, 206

Locke, John, 223

Loew, Rabbi Judah (the 'Maharal' of Prague; *c.*1525–1609), 40, 80–1, 258

London, slow growth of Jewish population of, 160, 169, 242; Jewish institutions at, 198–9; *see also* England

Lopes Pereira, Moseh (Diego, Baron d'Aguilar; *c.*1669–1759), Sephardi Court Jew at Vienna, 244–5

Lopes Suasso, Antonio (Isaac), 1st Baron d'Avernas de Gras (late seventeenth century), Dutch Sephardi financier, 128, 133, 142, 256

Lopes Suasso, Francisco (Abraham), 2nd Baron d'Avernas de Gras, 133–4

López, Alphonse (early seventeenth century), political agent of Richelieu, 116

López Pereira, Manual (1582–*c.*1650), Marrano protegé of Olivares and mercantilist writer, 112

Louis XIV, king of France (1643–1715), and the Jews, 127, 129, 133, 161–3

Lübeck, 65, 146, 152, 172

Lublin, 29, 33, 154, 164, 167, 187, 211, 241; and the Council of the Four Lands, 185–7

Lubomirski, Princes, and the Jews, 190

Lugo, ghetto of, 114

Luria, Isaac (1534–72), mystic and holy man of Safed, 78–80, 81, 208, 210; *see also* cabbala, Lurianic

Luria, Solomon (*c.*1510–74), Polish Talmudist, 78

Luther, Martin, and the Jews, 10–13, 82, 228

Lutsk (Volhynia) 166, 190

Luzzatto, Simone (1583–1663), Venetian rabbi, 113, 170, 254, 262

Maarssen (Utrecht), Sephardi community of, 155, 179, 198

Machado, Antonio (Moseh) Alvarez (late seventeenth century) Dutch Sephardi army contractor, 127–8, 130–1

Madrid, 59, 107–8, 111, 116, 178

Mainz, electorate of, Jews in, 6, 9, 42, 93, 97–8, 103, 192, 235, 243 n.; *Landjudenschaft* of, 192–3

Malaga 59, 108, 178

Mallorca, Marranos of, 3, 25, 158

Mannheim, Jewish settlement at, 150–1, 169, 205, 240, 247

Mantovano, the, 176, 181

Mantua, Jews of, 9, 20, 50, 58, 68, 73, 76–7, 79, 170, 180; Jewish population of, 50, 116, 238–9; Jewish institutions at, 196, 203; sack of (1630), 115–16

Margarita, Antonius (b. *c.*1490), Jewish apostate and anti-Jewish polemicist, 11–12

Maria Theresa, Empress of Austria (1740–80), and the Jews, 239

Markowicz, Moses (mid-seventeenth century), Polish Court Jew, 141, 153

Marlborough, duke of (John Churchill), 130–2

Marranos 3–4, 18, 20, 43, 47, 58–9, 82–5, 111, 116–17, 141–2, 145; desecration of Christian rites by, 68; burning of, at Ancona (1555), 19; *see also* Spain, Portugal, and Mallorca

Martinique, Sephardi settlement on, 107, 155; expulsion of Jews from (1683), 161–2

Mattersdorf (Burgenland), 168; *see also* Burgenland

Maximilian II, Holy Roman Emperor (1564–76), and the Jews, 38–9, 87

meat, provision of *kosher*, 195

Mecklenburg, 8

Medici family, Jews and, 9, 20, 49, 61, 157–8

Medina, Sir Solomon de (c.1650–1730), Dutch Sephardi army contractor, 130–1

Melanchton, Philipp (1479–1560), German Protestant Reformer, 14

Memel (East Prussia), 149, 173, 240

Menasseh ben Israel (1604–57), Dutch Sephardi rabbi, 86, 158–9, 224, 227, 254, 258

Mendelssohn, Moses (1729–96), 253–4

Mennonites 44, 228

Mergentheim (Würzburg), 98, 193

metal trade, 172, 176, 257

Metz, Jews of, 52, 102, 116, 165, 254

Meysl, Markus, of Prague (1528–1601), Prague Court Jew, 41

Michael, Simon (late seventeenth century), Austrian Court Jew, 125–6

Middelburg, 50, 154, 198

Milan, duchy of, expulsion of the Jews from (1597), 22–3

Milton, John, 228–9, 258

Minden, Jews of, 16, 42, 97, 148, 182

Modena, Jews of, 73, 79, 114, 157, 158, 165, 175, 239

Modena, Leone da (1571–1648), Venetian rabbi and controversialist, 77, 83, 258

Mogilev, White Russia, Jews of, 119, 122, 190, 250

Moisling, village on Danish territory near Lübeck, Jews of, 151, 172

Momigliano, Jewish loan-banking family in Piedmont, 115

Montaigne, M. de, 2, 36, 53

Montalto, Eliahu (Felipe Rodrigues; c.1550–1616), Sephardi anti-Christian polemicist and medical writer, 76, 83–5, 204, 221, 235, 258

Montalto, Moseh (early seventeenth century), Sephardi physician in Poland, 204

Montchrétien, Antoine de (early seventeenth century), French mercantilist writer, 56

Montezinos, Portuguese New Christian banking family of Madrid, 111, 141

monti di pietà, 7, 176

Moravia, Jews of, 6, 125, 147, 153, 165, 170, 181–2, 233, 237; Jewish population of, 239; *Landjudenschaft* of, 186, 191–2, 206, 252

Morosini, Giulio (Samuel ben David Nahmias 1612–83), convert to Catholicism and anti-Jewish polemicist, 17 n., 213 n., 262

Morteira, Saul Levi (c.1596–1660), Dutch Sephardi rabbi and anti-Christian polemicist, 85, 221, 231

Moses, Lemle, of Mannheim (late seventeenth century), Palatine Court Jew, 127, 205

Müller, Johannes (mid-seventeenth century), Hamburg Lutheran anti-Jewish polemicist, 84, 262

Münster, Sebastian, (1489–1552), Professor of Hebrew at Basel, 14

Münster, peace congress at, 102, 109; bishopric, Jews of, 44, 97, 135; Jewish population of, 168, 239; *Landjudenschaft* of, 192–3

music, in synagogues, controversies over, 77, 211; in early modern Jewish culture, 73, 200

mysticism, see cabbala

Naples, viceroyalty of, expulsion of Jews from (1510 and 1541) 16–17, 24

Narol (south-east Poland), 122

Navarre, viceroyalty of, expulsion of Jews from, 7; Bayonne Sephardim trade through, to Madrid, 108, 116

Nazi historiography, and the Jews, 95–6, 103

Neuburg, Palatine county of, Jews in, 95–6, 103

Nice, Sephardi settlement at, 47, 157–8, 176; Jewish factories at, 180

Nieto, David (1654–1728), London

Sephardi rabbi and controversialist, 219–20

Nikolsburg (Mikulov), head Jewish community of Moravia, 143, 148, 186, 205; Shabbatean congress at (1699), 215

Nowy Sącz, Jews of, 28, 153–4, 167

Nunes da Costa, Alvaro (Nathan Curiel) (d. 1737) 246

Nunes da Costa, Duarte (Jacob Curiel; 1587–1664), Sephardi 'Agent' of Portugal at Hamburg, 92, 109, 110, 119, 124, 142–3

Nunes da Costa, Jerónimo (Moseh Curiel; 1620–97), Sephardi 'Agent' of Portugal in the United Provinces, 109, 129, 136–7, 139–40, 142–3, 210

Nuremberg 8, 42–3, 65

Olivares, Conde-Duque de, chief minister of Philip IV of Spain (1621–43), 110–12

Oppenheimer, Emmanuel (d. 1721), Austrian Jewish army contractor, 125–6, 244

Opppenheimer, Joseph Süss (1699–1738), Württemberg Court Jew, 242, 245–6, 249, 254

Oppenheimer, Samuel, of Heidelberg and Vienna (1630–1703), Austrian Jewish army contractor, 123–7, 131, 256

Oran (Spanish North Africa), Jews of, 112; expulsion of Spanish Jews from (1669), 157–8

Orobio de Castro, Isaac (Balthasar; 1620–87), Dutch Sephardi controversialist 221–3, 231, 258

Orvieto (Papal States), expulsion of Jews from (1569), 21

Ostrog, head Jewish community of Volhynia, 29, 120–1, 187, 190

Ostrogski, Polish noble family, and the Jews, 29

Ottoman Empire, the, and the Jews, 26, 31, 45–6, 58, 63, 70, 82, 168, 212–13, 243 n.

Overijssel, 155

Paderborn, bishopric of, Jews of, 16, 42, 44, 65, 97, 102, 187

Padua, Jews of, 49, 73, 180, 233; Jewish institutions at, 196, 239; Jewish population of, 115

Palatinate, the, and the Jews, 13, 124, 133–4, 140, 150, 235, 239

Pamplona, *see* Navarre

Pantaleão d'Aveiro, Fr. (late sixteenth century), Portuguese traveller in the Near East, 26

Papacy, the, and the Jews, 9, 17–23, 45, 67, 70, 114, 156

Papal States, Jews in, 9, 21, 46, 114, 147, 175

paper-making, 181

Parma, duchy of, Jews in, 22, 176

parnasim, see kehilla organization

Pascal, Blaise, 224, 228, 258

Paul IV, Pope, anti-Jewish campaign of, 17–19, 20–1

Pauli, Oliger (late seventeenth century), Danish messianist, 227–8

pawnbroking 27, 40, 175–6

pedlars, Jewish, 40, 171–2, 174

Pereira, Abraham (Tomás Rodríguez Pereyra; mid-seventeenth century), Sephardi merchant, moralist and Shabbatean, 210, 212

Pereira, Jacob (late seventeenth century), Dutch Sephardi army contractor, 127–8, 130

Pereira, Isaac (early eighteenth century), Dutch Sephardi army contractor, 129

Pesaro, Jews of, 19, 45, 49; Jewish population of, 114

Peyrehorade (south-west France), Sephardim in, 68, 116–17, 160; Jewish population of, 117

Peyrère, Isaac de la (c.1595–1676), French Calvinist millenarian and controversialist, 209, 214–15, 226

Philip II, king of Spain (1556–98), antipathy of to Jews and Marranos, 22, 47, 59

Philip IV, king of Spain (1621–65), and the Portuguese New Christians, 110–12, 141, 154, 156

physicians, 191, 203–4

Piedmont, *see* Savoy

Pimentel, Manoel de, Marrano courtier, 52

Pina, Jacob de, Dutch Sephardi merchant poet, 199

Pina, Paulo de (Reuel Jeshrun; c. 1575–1634), Marrano poet and polemicist, 76

Pinsk, Grand Duchy of Lithuania, Jews of, 119, 154, 166, 182, 186, 190, 211, 241; Jewish population of, 119

Pinto, Isaac de (1717–1787), Dutch Sephardi *philosophe* and economist, 248–9

Pinto Delgado, João (Moseh; d. 1653), Marrano poet of Rouen, 76, 83

Pisa, Sephardi community of, 45, 46, 49, 61, 84, 180, 197, 203

Pius IV, Pope (1559–65), hostility of to Marranos, 20

Pius V, Pope (1566–72), and the expulsion of the Jews from the Papal States (1569), 21–2

plague, 94, 115, 164, 205–6

Podolia (Ukraine), Jews of, 120–2, 165–6, 185, 189–90, 215

Poland, Jewish life in, 6, 26–31, 106, 152–4, 164–7; migration of Jews from to the west, 40, 106, 153, 165, 169; Jewish population of, 5, 27, 166, 170, 241; regional rabbinic courts of, 187, 189; Jewish institutions of, 184–91, 249–50, 255; overland trade of with Germany, 167, 171, 173–4, 247, 256; *see also* Cracow, Poznan, etc.

politiques, and politique attitudes to government, 2, 51–2, 59, 116–17, 160–1, 258

poor-relief, among the Jews, 73, 202–3, 231

Portsmouth, 242

Portugal, Marrano emigration from, 3, 7, 17, 24–5, 58–9, 62, 82, 242; Dutch and Hanseatic trade with, 91–3, 107–8, 151, 247

poverty, 176, 247, 253

Poznan (Posen), Great Poland, Jews of, 29, 120, 154, 185, 187, 189, 241

Prado, Dr Juan de (*c*.1615–*c*.1670), Marrano sceptic, 216–17, 221, 222

Prague, Jews of, 5, 38–40, 41, 58, 88–90, 104, 148, 164; as Jewish cultural centre, 77, 80–1, 89; Jewish population of, 40, 104, 164, 239; Jewish institutions at, 90, 104, 186, 188, 191–2, 194; Jewish crafts at, 40, 181, 248; and plague of 1680, 164, 206; expulsion of Jews from (1557), 38–9 and (1744–8), 239, 243

Pressburg (Bratislava), 125, 168

printing, Jewish, in vernacular languages, 20–1, 83

Prossnitz (Prostejov), Moravia, 167, 186

prostitutes, Christian, and the Jews, 64, 200–1; Jewish, 201, 209

Provence, expulsion of Jews from (1498), 7, 32

rabbis, and rabbinic courts, 44, 187, 189, 191–2, 194, 254

Radziwiłł family, and the Jews, 28, 78, 118

Ragusa (Dubrovnik), 33–4, 49, 173

Ramires, Lopo (David Curiel), Amsterdam Sephardi merchant and banker, 108–9, 156

Ravenna, 8, 21

Reformation, the, and the Jews, 10–16, 35, 75, 81–2, 228

Reggio, duchy of Modena, Jews in, 79, 157

Reuchlin, Johannes (1455–1522), German Christian Hebraist, 14–15, 36

Richelieu, Cardinal, chief minister of Louis XIII of France, and the Jews, 116–17, 160

Rodrigues Lamego, Portuguese Marrano family settled at Rouen, 117

Rodriguez, Daniel, Sephardi spokesman and mercantilist writer at Venice and Split (late sixteenth century) 48–9

Romania, Jews in, 29, 45, 153, 238

Rome, Jews of, 17–19, 72, 74, 164, 170, 213, 220, 248; papal oppression of Jewish life in, 18, 22, 176, 181, 259; economic activity of Jews in, 170, 176, 181; poverty of, 176, 181; Jewish community constitutions at, 195–6, 197; Spanish Jews at, 17, 196; decline of Jewish community in, 181, 238; *aliyah* from to the Holy Land (1665–66), 212

Rossi, Azariah de' (*c*.1511–*c*.1578), Italian Jewish humanist, 18, 71

Rossi, Salomone de' (early seventeenth century), Mantuan Jewish musician, 76–7

Rotterdam, Sephardi settlement in, 50, 63–4, 198; Ashkenazi settlement in, 105, 154, 241

Rouen, Portuguese Marrano community at, 52, 83, 116; *see also* Pinto Delgado and Rodrigues Lamego

Rovigo, ghetto at, 73

Rudolph II, Holy Roman Emperor (1576–1612), and the Jews, 39–41, 87

Russo, Baruchiah (d. 1720), and the radical Dönme, 214

Safed (Galilee), 12, 26, 29, 33, 72, 78–9, 206, 258

Salomon, Gumpert (early seventeenth century), founder of the Gomperz family, 101–2, 108

Salonika, Jews of, 26, 29, 33–4, 48–9, 113, 170, 209; Jewish population of, 29, 238

Sanches, Francisco (1552–1623), Portuguese New Christian philosopher, 36

Sancta Clara, Abraham a (b. 1644), Austrian court preacher, 234

Sanuto, Alvise (early seventeenth century), Venetian senator, 61

Sarajevo, 48

Sardinia, 7, 17

Sasportas, Jacob (c.1610–98), Hamburg Sephardi rabbi and controversialist, 221

Savoy, duchy of, Jews in, 46–7, 57, 157–8, 161, 176, 180

Saxony, electorate of, expulsion of Jews from (1537), 11–12; readmission of the Jews to (early eighteenth century), 173, 242–3

Scaliger, Joseph Justus (1540–1609), Huguenot professor at Leiden, 54–5, 258

scepticism, 36–7, 53–4, 199, 216–18, 221, 258

Schaumburg-Lippe, Jews in, 97

Schmalkaldic League, War of (1546–47), role of German Jews in, 16

Schnaittach (Nuremberg), Jewish community at, 44, 187

Schoonenbergh, François van (alias Jacob Abraham Belmonte; late seventeenth century), Dutch Sephardi diplomatic envoy in Spain and Portugal, 137

Senigallia, Jews of, 114, 175

Septuagint, the, and the controversy over the Hebrew Bible, 218

servants, Christian, in Jewish homes, 142, 201–2

Seville, 59, 108

sexual relations, between Jews and Christians, church ban on, 64, 200–1, 245–6

Shabbatean movement, 215–16, 221, 254

Shirley, Thomas, English mercantilist writer, 56–7, 61

shop-keeping, restrictions on Jewish involvement in, 63–4, 65

Sicily, expulsion of Jews from (1492), 7, 17, 24–5, 114, 134, 179

Silesia, Jews of, 13, 89, 99–100, 167, 247; Jewish population of, 148, 169

silk industry, Jewish involvement in, 27, 179–80, 248

silver bullion, and the Jews, 137, 139, 172, 178, 242, 245, 256–7

Simon, Richard (1638–1721), French Bible scholar, and the Jews, 232–3, 258

slave trade, to the Caribbean, 137, 139

Slutsk, Grand Duchy of Lithuania, 119, 154, 186, 190

soap-manufacture, Jewish involvement in, 180, 182–3

Sobieski family, and the Jews, 29, 153

Socinians, 216, 221, 228, 258

Sofia, 29

Spain, 5–7, 24–5, 31, 33, 58–60, 70, 83, 204; expulsion of Jews from (1492), 3, 7, 9, 23–6, 27, 31, 207; exodus of Marranos from (1645–65), 154, 156–7, 158; Dutch, English and Hanseatic trade with, 91–3, 107–8, 151, 176–8, 247

Spanish Netherlands, debate over Jewish readmission to (1653–4), 155–6

Späth, Johann Pieter (Moses Germanus; 1644–1701), Christian convert to Judaism and anti-Christian polemicist, 227–8, 234–5

Speyer, bishopric of, Jews in, 42, 65, 96, 98, 240

spice trade, 52, 126, 173, 178

Spinoza, Benedict de (Baruch; 1632–77), 25, 199, 216–19, 221, 222, 232, 258

Spinozists, 217–19, 228–9, 235

Split (Spalato), Sephardi settlement in, 48–9, 113, 173

Stade (Elbe estuary), 44

state-finance, Jewish involvement in, 88–90, 132–6

Strasbourg, 12–13, 42, 65

strazzaria, see pedlars

Stuttgart, Jewish settlement in, 242, 245

sugar, refining, 65–6, 106, 179, 183; trade in, 62, 177, 206, 247; *see also* Brazil, Barbados, Martinique, and Surinam

Sullam, Sarah Coppio (c.1592–1641), Venetian Jewish poetess, 76–7

Sulzbach (Nuremberg), admission of Jews to (1666), 151, 230

sumptuary laws, 199–201

Surinam, Sephardi settlement in, 161, 177, 198, 203; Sephardi population of, 177; sugar plantations of, 177

Sweden, 118, 243; upsurge of Hebrew studies in (late seventeenth century), 229; *see also* Gustavus Adolphus, Christina of Sweden and Kempe

Switzerland, Jews in, 8, 37, 105–6

synagogue architecture, 220, 241

synods, Jewish, 186–7; at Augsburg (1530), 11; at Ferrara (1554), 20; at Frankfurt am Main (1603), 187

tailoring, 181–2

Tarnogród (Lublin), 122, 166

Tarnopol (Lvov), 121

taxation, 187–8, 191, 198

Teixeira, Diogo (Abraham Senior; 1581–1666), Hamburg Sephardi financier, 92, 138

Teixeira, Manoel (Isaac Haim Senior; c.1630–1705), Hamburg Sephardi financier, 136, 138–9, 142, 147, 152, 227, 246, 256

Tiberias (Galilee), 26, 206

tobacco, trade in, 126, 140, 161, 173–4, 178, 182–3, 247; spinning of, 179–81

Toland, John (1670–1722), Anglo-Irish deist and controversialist, 232, 249

Trebitsch (Trebic), Moravia, 167

Trent, persecution of Jews at (1475–6), 8

Trier, electorate of, 16; *Landjudenschaft* of, 192–3

Trieste, ghetto of, 148, 170, 223; Jewish population of, 238

Troki, Isaac of (c.1533–c.1594), Karaite anti-Christian polemicist, 84, 235–6

Turin, Jews of, 47, 73, 176; Jewish population of, 170; *see also* Savoy

Tuscany, Grand Duchy of, 9, 45–6, 49, 61, 157–8, 180, 238

Ukraine, the, *see* Volhynia, Podolia, Lvov etc.

Ungarisch Brod (Uhersky Brod), Moravia, 167–8

Urbino, duchy of, Jews in, 19–20, 46, 73; Jewish population of, 114

Usque, Abraham (Duarte Pinhel; mid-sixteenth century), Sephardi printer at Ferrara, 21

Usque, Samuel (mid-sixteenth century), Sephardi chronicler, 21, 70, 83

Usque, Selomoh (c.1530–c.1596), Sephardi poet, 76

Utrecht, 155, 212

vagrancy, among Jews, 171–2, 188, 203, 247

Valona (Albania), 48, 113

Venaissin, Comtat, Jews of, 22–3

Venezuela, Sephardi trade with, 177, 179

Venice, Jewish settlement in, 9, 19, 20, 45, 47–9, 60–2, 63, 73, 113, 115, 220; Jewish population of, 113, 164, 170, 239; Jewish emigration from, 63, 66, 181 n., 203; as Jewish cultural centre, 76–7; ghetto institutions at, 197–8; Shabbatean movement at, 212–13; Jewish crafts at, 180–1; and remittances to the Holy Land, 205–6; decline of Jewish community of, 113–14, 170, 238

Vercelli (Piedmont), Jewish community of, 47, 176

Verga, Selomoh ibn (early sixteenth century), Sephardi chronicler, 74

Verona, Jews of, 68, 73, 115, 180, 202, 239; *aliyah* from to the Holy Land (1665–6), 212

Vieira, António (1608–97), Portuguese Jesuit statesman, mystic, and mercantilist writer, and the Jews, 83, 110, 112 n., 225–6, 227

Vienna, first expulsion of Jews from (1421), 6; resettlement of Jews in (1570–1669), 39–40, 88, 96, 106, 194; second expulsion of Jews from (1669–70), 146–8, 149; resettlement of Jews in (late seventeenth century) 148, 164; Jewish population of, 89, 106; formation of *Judenstadt* in (1624), 89; anti-semitic preaching at, 233–4

Vilna (Grand Duchy of Lithuania), Jews of, 78, 119, 122, 149, 154, 186, 190, 211; Jewish population of, 241; Jewish crafts at, 154

Vitebsk, 119, 122

Volhynia, expansion of Jewish life in, 120–2, 165–6, 185, 190; *see also* Ostrog, Lutsk, Dubno, Chmielnicki, etc.

Voltaire, and the Jews, 232, 249, 254

Vorarlberg, 100

Vulgate, the, 21, 55

Wachter, Johann Georg (1663–1757),

Lutheran divine and controversialist, 228, 235

Wagenseil, Johann Christoph (1633–1705), German Yiddishist and Hebraist, 230–1, 235–6

Wallerstein (Nördlingen), Jewish community of, 44, 187

Wallich family, of Koblenz, 193

Wandsbek (Hamburg), 44, 92, 96, 146, 151, 254

Warendorf (Münster), Jewish community of, 74, 102, 193

Warsaw, exclusion of Jews from, 29, 153

Weikersheim 98, 193

Weisenau (Mainz) 9, 74

welfare, Jewish communal, *see* poor relief, education, hospitals

Wendel of Deutz (mid-sixteenth century), German Jewish money-lender, 23

Wertheimer, Samson (1658–1724), Court Jew at Vienna, 126, 132–3, 136, 138, 143, 194, 205, 235–6, 244, 256

Wesel (Cleves), 101–2

West India Company (Dutch), 106, 155, 161

Whitehall Conference (1655), 158–60

William the Silent, Prince of Orange, 23, 38, 50

William III, Prince of Orange, Dutch Stadholder (1672–1702), king of England (1688–1702), and the Jews, 127–9, 131, 137, 143, 163, 229

Wolf, Johann Christoph (1638–1739), German Hebraist and bibliographer, 229–30

wool trade (Balkan), 34; (Polish) 173, 247; (Spanish) 108, 177–8

Worms, Jews of, 6, 44, 69, 93–4, 96, 103, 143, 187, 240

Württemberg, 8, 239, 245–6, 247; *see also* Stuttgart

Würzburg, bishopric of, Jews in, 16, 65, 93

yeshivot, 79, 205, 208, 230–1

Yiddish language, 31–3, 205, 231

Yllan, García de (early seventeenth century), Antwerp Portuguese New Christian banker, 123–4, 227

Yllan, João de (mid-seventeenth century), Dutch Sephardi colonizer and messianist, 212, 227

Zamojski, Jan (late sixteenth century), Polish Chancellor, 29

Zamość, 29, 122, 154, 167

Zante, 114, 175

Zevi, Shabbatai (1626–76), Turkish Sephardi mystic and false messiah, 189, 209–14, 254

Zholkva (Galicia), 166, 189

Zionism, 212, 215, 224, 227, 255

Zoref, Heschel (1633–1700), Vilna mystic and Shabbatean, 214–15